MEXICO IN TRANSITION

by Philip Russell

Colorado River Press
Box 8004
Austin, Texas 78712

Copyright 1977 by Philip Russell

By the same author and illustrator: *Cuba in Transition*

SUPPLEMENTS:
Beginning in November 1977 *MEXICO IN TRANSITION* will be supplemented each November and April. For supplements send $1.00. Please specify date and country of supplement desired.

COLORADO RIVER PRESS
Box 8004
Austin, Texas 78712

COVER: *Jude Binder*
FRONTISPIECE: *Hector García*
CARTOONS: *Rius*
PROOFREADER: *Martha Helen McKenzie*
LAYOUT: *David Thurman*
TYPESETTING: *Ibid, Inc.*
PRODUCTION: *Austin Sun Graphics*
PRINTING: *Futura Press*

EDITORIAL ADVISORS

Bill Calvert
Nancy Folbre
Arnold Kendall
Leonore Russell
William H. Russell
William L. Russell
Ray Reese

To my parents

TABLE OF CONTENTS

I. HISTORY

1. The Conquest — 1
2. The Colony — 5
3. Independence — 12
4. Nationhood — 15
5. Juarez and Diaz — 19
6. The Revolution — 24
7. Institutionalization — 37

II. POLITICS

8. The State — 45
9. The PRI — 48
10. Echeverria — 55

III. THE ECONOMY

11. Development, Past — 59
12. Development, Present — 65
13. Agrarian Reform — 73
14. Foreign Debt — 82

IV. MEXICAN SOCIETY

15. Social Structure — 89
16. Workers — 94
17. Peasants — 101
18. Indians — 108
19. Women — 113
20. Unemployment — 119

V. SOCIAL SERVICES

21. Health — 121
22. Housing — 125
23. Education — 126

VI. OPPOSITION

24. Recognized Political Parties — 128
25. Mass Opposition — 132
26. Armed Opposition — 137

PART VII:

27. Media — 139
28. The Gringos, Past — 143
29. The Gringos, Present — 150
30. Environment — 156
21. The Future — 158

Glossary — 160
References — 161
Bibliography — 171
Map — 176

Year	Event	Page
1820	Independence 1821	p. 12
1840		
	Mexican-American War 1846-48	p. 144
	Liberal Constitution 1857	p. 19
1860		
	Maximilian and French Intervention 1862-67	p. 20
1880		
	Porfirio Díaz Presidency 1876-1911	p. 23
1900		
1910		
	Mexican Revolution 1911-17	p. 24
1920	Carranza Presidency 1917-20	p. 38
	Obregón Presidency 1920-24	p. 39
1930	Calles Presidency 1924-28	p. 41
	Cárdenas Presidency 1934-40	p. 43
1940	Oil Nationalization 1938	p. 43
	Avila Camacho Presidency 1940-46	p. 45
1950	Alemán Presidency 1946-52	p. 45
	Ruiz Cortines Presidency 1952-58	p. 45
1960	López Mateos Presidency 1958-64	p. 45
	Díaz Ordaz Presidency 1964-70	p. 45
1970	Student Movement 1968	p. 133
	Echeverría Presidency 1970-76	p. 55
1980	López Portillo Presidency 1976-[82]	p. 58

PART I: HISTORY
CHAPTER 1: THE CONQUEST

In 1325 the Aztecs founded Tenochtitlán on the present site of Mexico City. For the next two centuries they extended their empire from there, conquering vast areas. Aztec confidence, based on divine sanction and generations of military triumphs, was supreme. However early in the 1500's this confidence was shaken by a number of signs. A pyramidical light was seen in the eastern sky; a turret on one of the temples burst into flames; and then three comets were sighted. Finally the lake surrounding Tenochtitlán became turbulent. These signs were read by the royal sage as indicators of the imminent downfall of the empire.[1]

Soon afterward reports arrived of strange men in the Gulf of Mexico. In 1517 the Aztecs learned of the arrival in Yucatán of Francisco Hernández de Córdoba, the first Spanish explorer to visit Mexico. The next year news came of another expedition to Yucatán, and in 1519 word came of the arrival of Hernán Cortés's fateful expedition in "towers or small mountains floating on the waves of the sea."[2]

Cortés's expedition, which consisted of 10 ships, 608 men and 16 horses, followed the route of previous expeditions, sailing from Cuba to Yucatán. Upon arriving in Yucatán, Cortés found two Spaniards who had been shipwrecked there in 1511. Cortés picked up one, Jerónimo de Aguilar, who became the expedition's interpreter; the other said he preferred the life of an Indian and stayed behind.

After leaving Yucatán, Cortés's fleet sailed up the Mexican coast, trying to subdue and Christianize the Indians they met. The Indians were amazed that outsiders would come and immediately try to force a new religion and a new master on them.[3] While Cortés was sailing up the coast, a chief presented him with a woman as a gift. This woman, Malinche, who spoke both the Aztec language and the Mayan spoken in Yucatán, formed a translation team with Aguilar, and in addition became Cortés's lover.*

On April 21, 1519, the fleet arrived at the site of Veracruz. Soon after their arrival some members of the expedition decided they should forego further exploration and return to Cuba. However Cortés persuaded them to remain, using his strong personality and payments of "gold which is such a pacifier!"[4] Upon hearing of Cortés's arrival, Montezuma, the Aztec emperor, sent emissaries with a rich assortment of gifts, including a gold ornament as big as a cartwheel, gold nuggets, silver and ornate featherwork. The emissaries stated the gifts reflected the good will

---

*Malinche is seen as the first Mexican to sell out to foreigners and she is now used as a symbol of placing foreign interests or tastes ahead of Mexican ones.

1

of the Aztec emperor, but that the expedition members were not welcome in Aztec territory and should leave. The Aztecs offered gifts to their visitors should they prove to be human. Then they performed human sacrifices on shore to render homage to them in case they were of divine origin.[5]

This display of wealth only whetted the Spaniards' appetites. Cortés renounced his ties to the Spanish governor of Cuba (who had ordered Cortés to only engage in trade, not conquest) and declared himself under the direct command of the Spanish king. Cortés then began to explore the surrounding country and soon made contact with the Totonac Indians, one of the many groups dominated by the Aztecs. The Spaniards soon discovered that the Aztec empire was a highly centralized regime which extracted tribute from what is now central and southern Mexico. Most of those paying tribute had been conquered militarily, had distinct cultures, and often spoke a different language. The Spaniards seized upon this and promised the Totonacs protection in exchange for their allegiance.

On August 16, 1519, after having destroyed his ships to prevent any faint-hearted Spaniards from returning to Cuba, Cortés began to march inland along with several thousand of his new Totonac allies. As the expedition began to wend its way inland the Spaniards marveled at the strange people and the magnificent scenery. While passing Indian villages, the Spaniards would try to win their loyalty and Christianize their inhabitants. The Spaniards were quite successful at this since, as Cortés noted in a letter to the Spanish king, the Indians "would rather be Your Highness's vassals than see their houses destroyed and their women and children killed."[6]

After thirty days of marching the Spaniards reached Tlaxcala, a small nation unconquered by the Aztecs. The Tlaxcalans maintained their independence through tenacious defense of their homeland and the convenience an "enemy" provided for the Aztecs. Montezuma spoke of the prospect of conquering Tlaxcala saying:

> *We could easily do so, but then there would be nowhere for the young men to exercise themselves without going a long way off, and besides we always like to have people to sacrifice to our Gods.*[7]

Cortés immediately noted how he might benefit from the hostility between the Tlaxcalans and the Aztecs:

> *When I saw the discord and animosity between these two peoples I was not a little pleased, for it seemed to further my purpose considerably; consequently I might have the opportunity of subduing them more quickly, for, as the saying goes, "divided they fall."*[8]

The Tlaxcalans, thinking the strange intruders were secretly allied with the Aztecs, came out to attack the Spaniards. Cortés's notary demanded, in Spanish, the Indians' immediate surrender and the Indians responded with a shower of arrows and rocks. Having carried out the legal formality of asking for surrender, the Spaniards began to slaughter the Indians with a clean conscience.[9]*

A series of battles followed in which the Spaniards took advantage of their cavalry (the horse and rider were thought to be one animal by the Tlaxcalans) and their firearms. Despite the Tlaxcalans' overwhelming numerical superiority, they had no infantry tactics to combat the Spanish horsemen.[10] The Tlaxcalans even assumed the Spanish to be immortal, and to perpetuate this idea, the Spaniards buried their dead secretly. Finally after heavy losses on both sides, the Tlaxcalans surrendered and promised to help the Spaniards conquer their perennial enemies, the Aztecs.

The Spaniards next marched to Cholula, a city under Aztec control. When the Spaniards arrived the inhabitants were preparing to attack them and had "the pots ready to eat them in tomato sauce"[12] after the planned capture and sacrifice. However through an informer the Spaniards learned of the plot to kill them. Using this as an excuse, the Spaniards attacked first and slaughtered thousands of Cholulans with the aid of the Tlaxcalans. The Spanish historian and defender of Indian rights, Fray Bartolomé de las Casas, later commented on this massacre:

> *One of their various massacres was in a large city of over 30,000 called Cholula... where the Spaniards decided on a massacre or punishment (as they called it) to demonstrate their bravery and sow fear in the far corners of those lands.*[13]

Quetzalcóatl

*This was characteristic of the charge read to Indians which directed them to lay down their arms and accept the Spanish king and Christianity, or suffer the consequences. This charge, known as the requerimiento, was frequently read to Indians at such a distance that they could not hear it and in Spanish so they could not understand it. It concluded by saying that if they did not follow the instructions contained in requerimiento, the resulting havoc that would be wreaked on them would be their own fault, not the king's, the reader of the requerimiento's, or the Spanish soldiers'.[11]

The Spaniards then began to march to the nearby Aztec capital; and a final sign, a comet, was again read as a signal of the ruin of the Aztec empire.[14] As the Spaniards approached, the Aztecs had one last war council to decide whether to fight or welcome the Spaniards. Montezuma "preferred a half-way course, -as usual, the most impolitic."[15]

In a final futile attempt to stem the Spanish advance Montezuma sent more treasure. Despite Montezuma's repeating his order to leave Mexico, the sight of more gold only encouraged the Spaniards, who, as an Indian of the time noted, "hungered like pigs for that gold."[16] Ignoring the order, the Spanish arrived in Tenochtitlán after crossing the long causeway which bridged the lake surrounding the city.* When they entered the city the Spaniards were greeted by Montezuma and lodged in one of the royal palaces. To the amazement of the Aztecs, who had never seen firearms, Cortés had some of his cannons fired, adding to the impact of his arrival. An Indian commentator said the effect of the cannon fire was like tripping on magic mushrooms.[17]

After spending seven days as royal guests in Tenochtitlán,‡ the Spaniards not only saw they weren't conquering the Aztecs, but that they were in a shaky military position, surrounded by hundreds of thousands of Aztec warriors. Thus they formed a plan: kidnap Montezuma and use him to gain control of the empire. A group of armed Spaniards went to Montezuma's palace and forced him to return to the palace where the Spaniards were staying, threatening him with death if he resisted. Rather than risking death at the hands of the Spaniards, Montezuma permitted himself to be taken by them, claiming he was their "guest."

Montezuma continued to rule the Aztec empire, even though he was under the control of the Spaniards. He announced that he was ruling in the name of the Spanish king and even turned over the royal treasure to the Spaniards. In addition to his desire to save his life, several reasons have been offered for Montezuma's submission. Aztec tradition told of a fair skinned Mexican, Quetzalcóatl, who would return from the east to rule Mexico. Perhaps Montezuma had this prophecy in mind when he said to the Spanish:

> So because of the place from which you claim to come, namely, from where the sun rises, and the things you tell us of the great lord or king who sent you here, we believe and are certain that he is our natural lord, especially as you say that he has known of us for some time.[19]

The readings of fortune tellers may have prevailed upon him, since no other nation has ever felt as helpless as the Aztecs did at the appearance of omens and prophecies announcing its fall.[20] Montezuma's apparent submission

*This lake, Lake Texcoco, was divided into fresh and salt parts by a dike. Incoming streams were channeled into the fresh part, which was used for fishing. Water then passed into the salt section, where it evaporated as does water flowing into the Great Salt Lake in Utah, leaving salt to be collected.

‡At this time the Aztec capital was larger than any European city.[18]

might have been a ruse to get the Spanish out of the city.[21] In any case the Spaniards managed to gain control of the Aztec empire without firing a shot, although it seems unlikely that they could have maintained control without facing revolt.

Just as Cortés was seeing his ambitions fulfilled he received word that the governor of Cuba had sent a 400-man force to arrest him for not having returned to Cuba. Cortés immediately placed Mexico City under the command of one of his officers, Pedro de Alvarado, and made a forced march to Veracruz where the rival force was camped. Before he arrived in Veracruz Cortés sent runners ahead to make contact with the men of the other force. Then through a combination of bribes, tales of riches forthcoming, and playing officers off against their unpopular commander, Cortés undermined the will of the opposing force. When Cortés finally attacked, resistance was minimal. Thus Cortés managed to nearly double his force, since the newly arrived Spaniards were eager to join him and share in the expected Aztec riches.

Soon after this victory, Cortés was notified that the Aztecs in Mexico City were in revolt. After first asking permission of the Spaniards remaining in Mexico City, the Aztecs had staged a religious festival. In the middle of the festival Alvarado ordered his men to fire into the crowd; he claimed the festival was the prelude to an attack. After the Spaniards opened fire, the Aztec nation rose in arms and attacked the Spaniards' palace. Montezuma, still a captive, ordered the attacks to cease. The attacks then ended, but the Spaniards were still surrounded by the Aztec army.

At this point, Cortés returned, broke through the Aztec lines, and joined the Spaniards in the palace. Montezuma again tried to quiet the Aztecs from the roof of the palace, but was met by jeers and rocks from the enraged attackers below. One of the rocks struck him and he died shortly afterward, still a captive. The cause of Montezuma's death is unknown. Some claim the rock wound was fatal; others claim the Spaniards murdered him.[22] In any case, Montezuma's death only heightened the fury of the besiegers.

After withstanding the siege for 37 days the Spaniards decided to flee. They built a portable bridge to span the gaps the Aztecs had dug in the causeways to prevent their flight. The Spanish broke out of the siege on the night of June 30, 1520. However the portable bridge stuck in the first gap, forcing the Spaniards to ford the other gaps. Meanwhile the Aztecs fell upon the Spaniards and killed many of them, especially those so laden with stolen treasure that they couldn't defend themselves. This Spanish defeat is known in Mexican history as La Noche Triste (the Sad Night).

As remnants of the Spanish forces headed for the protection of Tlaxcala, the Aztecs attacked again. In the second battle though the tide turned; the Spaniards were able to use their firearms and cavalry effectively, and exploit the weakness produced by Aztec military customs. Combat to the Aztecs demanded specific rituals,[23] and the practice of carrying dead and wounded off the battlefield during combat tied up many Aztecs. On the other hand, the Spanish conceived of war as a means to power, which might require mass slaughter.

The Spanish were victorious and marched on to Tlaxcala without further combat. Once they were safely in

Tlaxcala, preparations were begun for the military conquest of the Aztecs. Cortés ordered a fleet built on Lake Texcoco and at the same time his Indian allies, especially the Tlaxcalans, raised large armies for the siege. The Spaniards were further reinforced by new arrivals from Spain and Cuba.

While the Spanish were gathering strength, the Aztecs were weakened by another contribution of the Spanish: smallpox. As the Aztecs had no natural immunity to the disease, epidemics swept the country, killing much of the population and demoralizing those who survived.[24] Among those who died was Montezuma's brother, who had succeeded him as Aztec emperor. The nephew of Montezuma, Cuauhtémoc, was then selected as the last emperor of the Aztecs.

After eleven months of preparation the Spaniards began their assault. First they marched around Lake Texcoco, subduing villages along the shore and cutting off aqueducts and food supplies to Tenochtitlán. Then they launched offensives down the causeways with the support of the newly-constructed boats which had been armed with cannons. The siege lasted for 85 days and met with stubborn resistance by the Aztecs, who forced the Spaniards to fight for every inch of ground. In order to deny the Aztecs cover as well as to provide for the effective use of horses and cannons, the Spanish and their 150,000 Indian allies began to destroy all the houses and fill all the canals they captured.[25]*

During the siege the Aztecs refused surrender offers, despite their high casualties, disease and near starvation. They taunted the Spanish saying, "Do you think there is now another Mutezuma‡ to do whatever you wish?"[26] Also they pointed out the plight of Cortés's Indian allies by yelling at them:

> Go on, the more you destroy, the more you will have to build up again hereafter. If we conquer, you shall build for us; and if your white friends conquer, they will make you do as much for them.[27]

To the horror of the Spanish, the Aztecs would sacrifice captured Spaniards in full view of the besieging force.

Finally on August 13, 1521, Cuauhtémoc saw the Spanish were closing in on the last Aztec-held section of the city. He tried to flee by canoe, but was soon spotted by the Spaniards, overtaken and brought to Cortés as a prisoner.

As soon as Cuauhtémoc was captured, Aztec resistance ended. "The less important survivors who emerged from the ruins were allowed to file out across the causeways, leaving behind them, instead of the fair city Cortés and his companions had first beheld, a mass of rubble and fetid corpses."[28] Cuauhtémoc wasn't as fortunate as his former subjects; he was imprisoned and tortured in an unsuccessful attempt to make him reveal the location of the Aztec treasure.

*Had the Aztecs resorted to guerrilla warfare, they would have undoubtedly fared better. Instead they chose to defend one fixed location, which was highly vulnerable to Spanish cannons and cavalry.

‡As is the case with many Aztec names, there are various spellings of "Montezuma."

Thus the conquest was completed, led by Spaniards, but carried out in large part by Aztec subjects who fought for the conquerors.[29] The Spaniards justified their conquest on the legal grounds that land controlled by heathens was theirs for the taking[30] and their sacred duty required them to convert those living there to Christianity. However the history that Father Bartolomé de las Casas presented to the King in 1542 stated:

> The cause of the Christians having killed and destroyed such an infinite number of souls has been simply that their whole end was the acquiring of gold and riches in the shortest time so that they might rise to lofty positions out of all proportion to their worth ...[31]

When he first came to the New World Cortés rejected an offer of land stating, "I came to get gold, not till the soil like a peasant."[32] It was his longing for gold and his audacity which determined that Cortés should be the conqueror of Mexico. However Cortés's defeat would only have put a stop to his own career. The conquest, part of the expansion of the Spanish empire, would have occurred anyway.[33]

Seen from the side of the Indians, the conquest was a double tragedy: military defeat and the end of the Aztec empire. The feelings of the Aztecs were recorded by an Aztec poet of the conquest period:

> *Broken spears lie in the roads;*
> *we have torn our hair in our grief.*
> *The houses are roofless now, and their walls*
> *are red with blood.*
>
> *Worms are swarming in the streets and plazas,*
> *and the walls are spattered with gore.*
> *The water has turned red, as if it were dyed,*
> *and when we drink of it,*
> *it has the taste of brine.*
>
> *We have pounded our hands in despair*
> *against the adobe walls,*
> *for our inheritance, our city, is lost and dead.*
> *The shields of our warriors were its defense,*
> *but they could not save it.*
>
> *We have chewed dry twigs and salt grasses;*
> *we have filled our mouths with dust and bits of adobe;*
> *we have eaten lizards, rats and worms...*[34]

In Mexico the conquest is now seen in much the same way as it was seen by the Indian poet of four centuries ago. Cortés, instead of being a national hero, is regarded as a ruthless invader. This feeling is shown by the conspicuous lack of his name on Mexican streets and monuments and by Diego Rivera's portrayal of him as a brutal killer in a mural in the National Palace. On the other hand, Montezuma and Cuauhtémoc are national heroes, and streets, monuments, and two of Mexico's most popular brands of beer bear their names. Perhaps the best summary of the conquest is on a plaque at the Plaza of Three Cultures in Mexico City. Here the final battle of the conquest is commemorated with an inscription which concludes:

IT WAS NEITHER A VICTORY NOR A DEFEAT, IT WAS THE PAINFUL BIRTH OF THE MESTIZO PEOPLE OF TODAY'S MEXICO.

CHAPTER 2: THE COLONY

Once the conquest was completed, the Spanish began the four-year-long process of rebuilding the city. As Aztec defenders of Tenochtitlán had prophesied, the reconstruction was done by forced Indian labor. At the same time expeditions extended Spanish control from Yucatán to Guatemala and Michoacán.

An expedition under Olid, one of Cortés's lieutenants, founded a settlement in what is now Honduras. Once there Olid declared his independence from Cortés and began to deal directly with the Spanish king.*Cortés set out on foot to arrest Olid in what proved to be almost as difficult an undertaking as the conquest itself. For nineteen months the expedition was faced with hostile Indians, starvation, wilderness and natural obstacles. Cortés brought Cuauh-témoc along as a hostage and in route had him executed, claiming he was planning an Indian revolt. No evidence has ever been found to support his claim.

Upon his arrival in Honduras, Cortés found Olid had already been overthrown and decapitated by members of his own settlement, so he returned to Mexico City. Shortly after his return Cortés was relieved of his command by the Spanish king, since Cortés's enemies had accused him of misconduct and the king feared his power. Because of this persisting jealousy Cortés was never appointed viceroy (the king's administrator) even after he was cleared of the misconduct charges. However he was rewarded with 25,000 square miles of land south of Mexico City which included many villages and tens of thousands of Indians. Later Cortés undertook further exploration and finally died in 1547 while on a return trip to Spain seeking additional reward.

The arrival of the first viceroy in 1535, fourteen years after the fall of Tenochtitlán, began three centuries of colonial administration. During this period, which one

---

*Ironically this declaration of independence is just what Cortés himself had done with respect to Velázquez, the governor of Cuba, and what Velázquez before him had done with respect to Diego Columbus, Christopher's son and governor of Hispaniola.

must remember is half again as long as the entire history of the United States, there was constant political, social and economic evolution. During the 16th century the colonial administration was instituted and a booming mining industry developed. The next century saw a general economic depression, brought about in large part by a sharp decline in Indian population and thus a decline in labor available for mines and agriculture. Finally in the 18th century there was a resurgence of economic activity resulting from increasing population and the more efficient administrative techniques of the new Bourbon dynasty.

The colonial period saw the imposition of an economic and social organization designed to favor Spain and produce materials for sale in Europe[1] in complete disregard and often direct opposition to the needs of New Spain (as colonial Mexico was called). Initially the Indian economic structure was left intact, since it was the only system capable of supplying Mexico's needs after the conquest. Then gradually Indians were integrated into Spanish economic organizations, and eventually into a growing world market.

Shortly after the conquest the Spaniards experienced a pressing need for labor; the land and mineral wealth couldn't be fully exploited by the very limited number of Spaniards. To harness Indian labor, a grant called the encomienda was copied from the Spanish colonies in the Caribbean. Cortés made these grants to reward his followers for their financing of and participation in the conquest.* Each grant gave a Spaniard the right to collect tribute in the form of clothing, food and other products from the Indians living in a certain area. In theory the Spaniard did not own the land or have the right to control the Indians or sell them. This enabled the conquistadores to be supplied through the existing Indian production system and meet the needs which they were neither willing nor able to meet themselves.

Supposedly the recipient of such a grant, the encomendero, had the obligation to Christianize and protect the Indians in exchange for tribute. However the first encomenderos consistently used Spanish authority to further their personal interests.[2] This resulted in an inhuman exploitation of the work force[3] and a general de facto control over the Indians' lives.[4]

Quite early the king displayed the same jealousy toward the power of the encomenderos as he did toward Cortés and tried to limit their power by techniques such as limiting the inheritability of the encomienda. However what finally produced the decline of this means of exploiting Indian labor was the Spaniards' need for labor in mines, fields and construction, combined with a sharp drop in Indian population.

To adjust to these changes, the repartimiento, or coatequil, was adopted. This system obligated Indians to work directly for Spaniards for a certain number of days a year for a fixed wage, rather than paying tribute. Each village would have to supply a certain number of workers, who would assemble in the village and march off for a week or two of work. After one group's labor obligation was fulfilled, the workers would return to their village and other workers would replace them. This institution, which took about 6% of each individual Indian's labor during the course of the year,[5] was especially significant in that it exposed Indians to European production techniques for the first time.

Economic and demographic change put an end to the repartimiento just as it did to the encomienda. By the beginning of the 1600's the demand for labor was still rising and the Indian population was still declining. In addition the Spanish were not satisfied with the sporadic nature of repartimiento labor, since it didn't provide a stable labor force or permit an individual worker to be trained for a specific job. Thus a third institution developed, debt peonage. This involved making loans or advances to Indians and then having them work as full-time laborers until the debt was paid off. However due to low wages, new loans, crooked bookkeeping, and payment in kind (not cash), the repayment of the loans was not a frequent occurrence.[6] Once the debt was contracted, the Indian and his children who inherited the debt found themselves obligated to a lifetime of labor. The Indian was forced by law to remain at work as long as the debt remained. Debt peonage had become the chief source of agricultural labor by the middle of the 17th century and so the repartimiento was abolished in 1663, except for labor in mines and public works.[7] In these two activities the repartimiento was continued until almost the end of the colonial period and its harsh nature was emphasized by a royal decree *limiting* repartimiento labor to work from sunrise to sunset.

The first Spanish estates began when individuals were given the right to use certain areas for grazing. These initial grants did not permit the owner of the herd to keep others off the land. The Spaniards' herds soon began to play havoc with unfenced Indian crops. Slowly the old view of pasture as a common resource changed and individuals began to deny use of pastures to others. This was a basic shift from the pre-Conquest view on land use.[8] Early estates relied on workers coming from nearby villages. As estates evolved, boundaries were fixed, and heavy investments were made in buildings, machinery and often irrigation works. A labor force living on the estate began to replace those coming in from Indian villages. During the 17th century these large estates, called haciendas, became the main source of income, replacing the declining mine.[9] The hacienda also began to take Indian lands to farm and to deprive Indians of land so they would have to work on the hacienda. This method of forcing Indians to work for wages was important since workers were in shorter supply than land.[10] Hacienda owners, or hacendados, appropriated Indian grazing land, took land left ownerless when the Indian population declined in the 17th century, bought lands from debt-ridden Indian nobles, and resorted to brute force if necessary. Despite the sincere efforts made by some viceroys to preserve a viable agricultural base for the Indian community, by the end of the colonial period only 15% of the land area was still controlled by Indians.[11]

The hacienda was "Half 'feudal', half 'capitalist', caught between past and future, it exhibited characteristics of both ways of life, as well as their inherent contradiction."[12] This dual nature was constantly manifest. The hacienda sold goods on the world market, yet often hacienda ownership was seen more as a source of prestige than profit.

*Rather than being financed by the king, most of the conquest of Spanish America was undertaken by private individuals in anticipation of being rewarded with booty and land.

Rather than trying to lower prices to increase volume of sales and win new markets, hacendados tried to control all available land, thus eliminating the possibility of competition and home-grown food. Often the hacienda would only break even in good years (when others could grow crops too), but then would make a fortune when it could sell its accumulated stocks at inflated prices in bad years. Finally the hacienda had a chameleon-like nature which enabled it to survive the vicissitudes of colonial life. In times of economic prosperity it would supply the world market, and when depressions hit it would become virtually self-sufficient and weather the bad times.[13]

Despite the resurgence of mining in the 18th century, the value of cattle and agricultural production still surpassed that of mining in 1800.[14] Even with the growth of international markets, most of the hacienda's production was marketed locally. Taxes on the shipment of goods within the colony (the alcabala) and the lack of good roads hindered sales in a larger market. Further limiting agricultural development were restrictions on growing crops, such as grapes (for wine), mulberry (for silkworms) and olives, which would compete with Spanish production.

The hacienda was the final form of mass exploitation of Indian labor, concluding the chain started by the encomienda and the repartimiento. As the Indians' lands were taken, they came to work on the haciendas, first through the encomienda, then through the repartimiento, and finally through individual arrangements, but it was always the same people doing the same things.[15]

The mine initially spurred the growth of the hacienda by providing a market for agricultural goods. Its chief products, gold and silver, kept New Spain's wealthy supplied with luxury imports and paid for the huge colonial bureaucracy. The mine also helped finance the Spanish monarchy, which took a fifth, and later a tenth of what was mined. It was through these shipments of precious metals that Spain hoped to maintain its international position and make up for its trade deficit.*

Mining activity increased rapidly after the conquest, and reached a high point between 1591 and 1600.[16] Then it began to decline due to the lack of Indian labor and the exhaustion of surface deposits. During most of the 17th century there was a depression in the mining industry. Subsequently it recovered so that by 1800, two thirds of the world's silver was being shipped from Veracruz.[17] Since mine labor was so arduous, the repartimiento was kept in existance to supplement wage labor in the mines even after it was abandoned in agriculture.

Like mining, commerce in New Spain was structured to benefit Spain, not the colony. Trade with other colonies,

*These shipments of precious metals were of special significance due to the prevailing mercantilist philosophy of the time (before the days of paper money and easy credit) which held that the amount of money circulating placed a limit on economic activity. Thus, unless there was hard cash (made of silver and gold) available for payment, economic activity simply wouldn't be undertaken and growth would be limited.

not to mention other countries, was banned. For most of the colonial period only the port of Veracruz could receive shipments from Spain, and only one Spanish port was permitted to export to Mexico. The number of convoys coming from Spain was limited, thus reducing the supply of imported goods and driving up prices and profits. High duties tended to limit imports to luxury goods. Additional price increases were forced by the trading monopolies in both Spain and Mexico City.‡ Commerce was further limited by thieves on the highways and the Spanish government's requirement that all cargos be shipped in Spanish-built ships with Spanish crews.

These constraints tended to inflate prices and made commerce an attractive investment, especially after the decline of mining in the 17th century. The markup on retail goods far exceeded the manufacturers' costs, so available capital in both Spain and Mexico was channeled into commerce. Manufacturing was generally left to others, increasingly the British. As with land ownership and mining, commerce was seen not only as a source of wealth, but of social standing.

Restrictions similar to those affecting commerce also limited manufacturing. Industries which might compete with Spain were prohibited; credit was lacking, as were roads to haul goods. Furthermore production was controlled by monopolistic guilds which accepted only full blooded, literate Spaniards as workers. These guilds placed restrictions on both the type of technology and quantity produced so as to benefit the Spanish craftsman. Industry carried no prestige with it, so those with capital invested their money elsewhere. As a result the production that did exist was largely in the hands of artisans, and involved textile-making and leather, gold and silver-working.[19] This production took place under the worst of conditions in factories which were often described as being jail-like, where workers were denied permission to leave the building and often were tied to the job by debts. What manufacturing did occur did not resemble the capitalism emerging in Europe since guild limitations on both individual initiative and production levels prevented new investments.[20]

One of the few institutions which tied the colonial society together was the church, which, like the rest of New Spain, underwent tremendous change during the colonial period. The church provided the rationale for the conquest and then became one of the main instruments of social control. In many instances priests would enter areas which Spanish armies had been unable to pacify and persuade Indians to cease resistance. Once active resistance to Spanish domination had stopped, churches were one of the main elements incorporating Indians into European life, teaching Spanish, crafts and farming techniques.[21] Economic considerations often determined the location of church missions, or as a Franciscan of the time put it, "Where there's no silver, there's no religion."[22]

Nevertheless many churchmen were sincere and suffered extreme hardship in the ministry. They recorded information on Aztec culture which otherwise would have been lost. Bishop Vasco de Quiroga founded "hospitals,"

‡This commercial monopoly, along with the colonial and church bureaucracy, made Mexico City the largest city in the Americas by 1650.[18]

which despite their name were socialistic communities for Indians inspired by Thomas More's *Utopia*.[23] The church provided some check on the rapacity of the early conquistadores. Foremost among the churchmen defending the Indian was Bartolomé de las Casas, who led a vigorous campaign against forced labor and mass slaughter of Indians. He pleaded that the Spaniards should recognize the Indian as a rational being who had the right to freely choose both his religion and job. Given Spanish prejudices, this was no simple task. Many of Las Casas's ideas found their way into law, although often such laws had little effect on actual practice.

A century after the conquest this missionary zeal and desire to protect the Indians began to wane. Increasingly ecclesiastics abused parishioners, kept mistresses, and used their confessionals and position in the church to profit in their personal business ventures.[24]

The Inquisition was another example of the shifting role of the church. Originally the Inquisition attacked religious unorthodoxy, but soon it came to be used for such overtly political ends as declaring it a heresy to sell horses and ammunition to Spain's rival France.[25] For a long period the Inquisition was a major means of social control in Mexico, as is indicated by its execution of 109 persons in Mexico City in 1649.[26] The rationale for such suppression was that dissenters of any kind were social revolutionaries trying to subvert political and religious stability.[27]

A more significant shift in the role of the church resulted from its acquisition of land. The church often received bequests of land which would never leave its hands. Much of the income from these properties was lent to hacendados. Then if the hacendados' crops failed, the mortgaged land was foreclosed on, adding to church holdings. Ownership of this land, as well as tithes and other direct payments by Indians, provided the church with enough wealth to become the main source of credit in New Spain. Much of the church land was simply left idle, while other lands were well-managed businesses, sometimes worked with black slaves. Church wealth became so great that the king, fearing its power, expelled the wealthy Jesuit order from New Spain in 1767 and confiscated its lands.[28] Finally the church retarded economic development by channeling a large part of the economic surplus toward non-economic ends.[29]

We can see two simultaneous trends within the church. One was the shift away from its early interest in the Indian, so that by the end of the colonial period there were only 120 clergy in Indian communities while there were 8,000 in Mexico City alone.[30] The other trend was the steady increase in the church's land and buildings, many of which can still be seen in Mexico. The main plaza in Mexico City is dominated by a colonial cathedral, as are the central plazas in many Mexican cities, the result of wealth extracted from the countryside.[31] Many churches and monasteries were constructed with the forced labor of the very Indians the church was protecting from the hacendado and the encomendero.[32] Even today in many small towns the major accumulation of wealth is a church built in colonial times.

....

Throughout the colonial period the highest status was held by officials of the colonial government, which had reproduced the splendor of the most magnificent medieval courts by 1538.[33] High colonial officials not only profited from office, but held significant power as well. They ceased to be household servants of the Crown and began to act as a semi-autonomous body which was jealous of its prerogatives. These officials formed an interest group comparable to the territorial aristocracy, the church and the urban elites.[34]

Not far behind the government officials were the mine owners, who were described by a contemporary observer.

Most of the competition for wealth took place between native-born Spaniards and creoles, Mexican-born persons of European ancestry. This split between the two groups and the granting of most high government and church posts to Spaniards resulted in antagonism and eventually rebellion by the creoles.

At the other end of the social ladder from the creole and the Spaniard were the Indians. Their communities were consistently forced to defend their land and their very existence from encroaching haciendas. They were obligated to pay tribute to the government and as early as the 1530's Indian leaders were being jailed due to the

The luxury and munificence of the mine-owners is something wondrous to see. As a rule the wife of a mining man goes to church escorted by a hundred servants and twenty ladies and maids in waiting.[35]

Also near the top of colonial society were the hacendados and merchants, whose lavish life style rapidly exhausted fortunes and gave rise to the saying, "Father merchant, son gentleman, grandson beggar."

inability of their communities to raise the tribute demanded.[36]

Early in the colonial period the king protected the Indian communities because he preferred to collect tribute from them himself, rather than letting the encomenderos increase their own power by taking them over and exacting tribute.[37] Later as the Indian population and productive capacity went down, the more productive hacienda began to be favored over the Indian community. The percentage

9

of the colonial budget coming from the tribute reflects the decline of the Indian community. In the 16th century tribute was the main source of income, while by the mid-18th century tribute provided less than 5% of the income, with the majority coming from the alcabala, the tobacco monopoly and mining taxes.[38]

The Spanish exacted greater tribute than the Aztecs had before the conquest.[39] In response to the burden of tribute and to Spanish oppression in general, Indian uprisings were common during the colonial period. Such uprisings were hampered by the Indians' division along ethnic and linguistic lines and their being prevented by law from owning horses or firearms. Examples of such uprisings include a two-year revolt in Durango 1616-8, continual warfare in Nuevo León in the 1610's and a rebellion in Santa Fe from 1680 to 1692 which resulted in the death of hundreds of Spaniards.[40]

Although a few Indians did acquire some wealth, especially those of the Aztec nobility, most lived in grinding poverty as a result of being left with the poorest land and having to pay tribute. Indians were further hampered by an inferior legal status, which was like being a perpetual minor, and in a court of law it took the testimony of six Indians to equal that of one Spaniard.[41] This, along with general cultural disintegration, produced the excessive, prolonged drunkenness which still characterizes much Indian life. Before the conquest consistent popular drunkenness had been unknown.[42] The resulting hostility of the Indians toward the Spanish was described by an encomendero who wrote the king saying, "They wish us all dead and cut into pieces and they let us know it."[43]

However all this pales in comparison with the inevitable result of the Indians' poverty, overwork, and exposure to European diseases: the rapid reduction of Mexico's Indian population by 1650. The 1576 epidemic alone killed two million Indians.[44] Modern estimates put the population *loss* at 95% of the 25 million pre-conquest population of central Mexico.[45]

Initially many Indians were enslaved and estimates of the number of such slaves run into the millions.[46] However due to the high death rate, high initial purchase costs, and the availability of Indian labor through the repartimiento and the encomienda, Indian slavery soon diminished in importance. In addition to legal slavery, the encomendero often exceeded his legal grant and treated Indians living on his encomienda in a manner which differed little if at all from actual slavery.[47] Black slaves were also brought from Africa. The total number of slaves brought to Mexico during the colonial period was about 250,000, a figure roughly equal the number of Spaniards who immigrated to Mexico during the same time.[48] However due to the high death rate and the lack of women to bear children, the maximum number of blacks never passed 35,000, and declined to 10,000 by the end of the colonial period.[49] Black slaves, free blacks and their children of mixed parentage were often in a worse position socially than the Indian who at least belonged to a community. Given their potential for revolt, blacks and mulattos were forbidden to own horses or assemble in groups of more than three.[50] Since the end of the colonial period the black population has largely been absorbed, although some blacks can still be found in coastal areas where slaves once worked on plantations.

Higher up on the social ladder were the mixed bloods, who due to the lack of Spanish workers, often came to occupy positions such as peddler, foreman, and skilled worker. In the early colonial period as many as 16 racial terms were in use for various racial mixtures, including *pardo* (black and Indian) and *morisco* (Spanish and mulatto).[51] These mixed bloods were eventually lumped into one category, the mestizo, a group also forbidden to carry arms. The mestizo was free of the constraints of the relatively static Spanish and Indian cultures. He was more independent, more mobile, more innovative, and was largely responsible for forging the distinctive Mexican culture of today. Often mestizos lived in cities, and their poverty was a major factor in food riots, such as the ones in Mexico City in 1624 and 1692 in which the viceroy's palace was burned.

The early colonial administration reflected the then-important European split between the feudal lord and the monarchy, although in the Mexican case the position of feudal lord was occupied by the encomendero. Later, as the encomenderos lost power, the monarch had to face a colonial administration based on church, aristocracy, and bureaucracy. These institutions, instead of attracting productive workers from Spain, drew viceroys, courtesans, adventurers, priests, lawyers, and soldiers.[52]

Despite the size of the colonial government, the viceroy had trouble exercising control in matters which threatened the interests of the hacendado or the church. For instance the king issued royal decrees banning the sale of Indians in 1588, 1609, 1618, 1631, 1662, 1663 and 1679 but couldn't enforce them since they conflicted with landowners' interests.[53] This inability to confront vested interests often resulted from the viceroy's desire to share the profits to be had in Mexico and particularly in matters involving Indians repeatedly made a mockery of protective legislation.[54]

The colonial administration was further limited by the frequent sale of office to the highest bidder, which resulted in both incompetent office holders and the idea that office was a source of personal wealth rather than a chance for public service. The immensity of Spain's New World empire sharply limited government control, and administration tended to follow economic events rather than determine them.[55]

Despite its weakness and inefficiency, the colonial government did appropriate vast sums. Colonial administrators squandered some of this wealth in their ostentatious living. However most of the wealth was sent to Spain, and by the end of the colonial period Mexico was furnishing Spain with ten times as much wealth per person as India was supplying to Britain.[56]

This flow of wealth to Spain had an effect quite different than one might imagine. The massive flow of wealth which began in the 1500's tended to stifle incipient Spanish industry by creating tremendous inflation. This inflation priced Spanish-made goods out of the market and resulted in Spain relying on other European countries for manufactured goods. As the flow of precious metals increased, Spain simply began to exchange these metals for manufactured goods and its own industrialization ended. By 1740 less than 5% of the goods consumed in

Spanish America were of Spanish origin.[57]

The tendency to neglect manufacturing was emphasized by other factors. Spanish society, dominated by clergy, monarchy and aristocracy, had little interest in financing industrialization.* There was also resistance to industrialization by merchants who reaped fortunes shipping Northern European goods to Spanish America. As a result the wealth of the New World caused Spanish power to decline, not increase. By 1600 Spain had slipped from its position as first world power, falling behind France and Great Britain, and was increasingly being pressured to make trade concessions to the British. Spain soon found itself in the position of being a trans-shipment point for New World bullion and northern European manufactured goods, with little internal development or even benefit for the majority of the people. This situation was summed up by the saying, "Spain held the cow, but Europe drank the milk." By 1700 it was abundantly clear that the Iberian monarchies had been subordinated to the French, and especially, the British.[59] Well before the end of the colonial period Britain had virtually eliminated Spain from world capitalist development.[60]

*The forces of the Spanish clergy, monarchy and aristocracy defeated the popular and bourgeois forces in the Battle of Villalar in 1521, thus cutting off the growth of the class which developed industry elsewhere in Europe.[58]

During the latter part of the 18th century a series of reforms was undertaken by Spain's new Bourbon dynasty in a futile attempt to adjust to a changing world. Trade limitations were eased, permitting more development, and stemming the flow of British contraband. Several Spanish ports were permitted to trade with Mexico, trade was permitted between Spanish colonies for the first time, and ships were allowed to sail individually rather than in convoys.

The government was made more efficient and centralized, thus increasing tensions when those accustomed to relative autonomy were placed under more effective Spanish control.[61] These reforms had a pronounced effect on the colony and spurred economic growth. By 1802 the number of ships calling at Veracruz was ten times the number 80 years earlier.[62] These efforts were too late however; reforms only accelerated economic development in Mexico, making the colony increasingly less dependent on and more hostile toward Spain.

When independence did come, precious metals began to flow directly from the New World to England, and manufactured goods were no longer shipped through Seville. As a result after three centuries as the leading colonial power of the world, Spain had little to show for its efforts and became just another underdeveloped country, dependent on northern Europe.

Miguel Hidalgo y Costilla

CHAPTER 3: INDEPENDENCE

By the beginning of the 19th century the Spanish empire in America was doomed. England's economic growth and its burgeoning trade with the New World were making the empire an empty shell. Each year more English goods were shipped to Spanish America, and the contraband which was completely removed from Spanish control likewise increased. Then in 1805 Nelson's naval victory over Spain ended her role as a major naval power.

From 1793 to 1808 Spain further weakened herself with almost constant warfare, much of which was financed by Mexico. Each of these wars interrupted the trade with Spain upon which Mexico was forced to rely. During this same period a flood of new ideas inundated Mexico. American independence set an example for Mexico; then came the French Revolution with its ideas of civil rights, individualism and equality. These ideas began to circulate widely, despite attempts by the viceroy and the Inquisition to ban books which dealt with them.

Finally the exploitative nature of the colonial administration alienated almost everyone. Spaniards exploited Mexicans and rich Mexicans exploited poor ones, while Mexico City exploited the rest of the country—a phenomenon still present. Thus we find the major uprisings of the independence period to the west and south of Mexico City rather than in the capital where many profited from colonial rule.[1]

In 1810 there was little to unite the Mexican population economically, culturally or politically. At the top of the social scale was the rich Spaniard, with his high church or administrative position, or commercial monopoly. He was quite aware that he owed his position to one fact: continued Spanish rule, and thus he would support the Spanish to the bitter end.

In the next group down was the wealthy creole who had prospered, especially by owning haciendas. He had three complaints: restricted access to top jobs, inefficient government administration which hurt him economically, and the monopolistic commercial position of the Spaniard which probably did more to push the creole toward independence than did any other single royal policy.[2] When the wealthy creoles did lend their support to independence, they were careful that the result would only be independence, not a violent social upheaval which would threaten their own position of privilege.

Further down was the creole of modest means who had to fight for second-rate jobs which corresponded neither to his aspirations nor his abilities.[3] This group wavered in its support for independence and its members became leaders in both the rebel and royalist forces. A parish priest, Miguel Hidalgo y Costilla, known today as the Father of Mexico, was a typical member of this group.

The most exploited members of New Spanish society were the Indians and mestizos who together made up more than 80% of the population.[4] They were almost universally illiterate and seldom acted as a unified mass due to their long-standing separation by law, tradition, language and self-image. To them the distinction between creole and Spaniard was unimportant; both were white exploiters who would eventually be the target of their efforts for social justice. However in 1810 Indians and mestizos were not involved politically.

• • • • • • • • • • • • • • • • •

The events which pushed the situation to the breaking point came in the first decade of the 19th century. In 1804 Spain ordered that all capital of the Mexican church be loaned to the Spanish government and that all church land be sold to finance its current war (this time with England). This not only angered the clergy[5] but cut off the major source of credit and thus alienated the hacendados, 95% of whom operated on borrowed money.[6]

Then in March 1808 Napoleon invaded Spain, forced the Bourbon dynasty out, and installed his brother Joseph on the Spanish throne. Pro-Spanish elements in Mexico demanded recognition of Joseph, feeling that any refusal to recognize a ruling monarch would inevitably loosen ties with Spain. However others in the Mexico City government declared the viceroy Iturrigaray free from Spanish control until the deposed Bourbon dynasty was returned to the throne. The viceroy then stopped sending money to Spain and began to make discreet contacts with independence-minded Mexicans.[7]

Finally in Spain there was a revolt against French-imposed rule and the rebels there began to demand loyalty from the American colonies. To further add to the confusion, different groups in Spain competed with each other so that by August 1808 both Asturias and Seville were demanding Mexico's loyalty.

At this point a group of rich Spaniards in Mexico, seeing what Iturrigaray's relative independence would inevitably lead to, staged a coup d'etat, arresting Iturrigaray and sending him off to Spain in irons. The Spanish rebels responded by demanding another 20 million peso loan to finance the costs of the war.

Thus it is hardly surprising that in 1810 a rebellion against Spain was being planned northwest of Mexico City. One of the leaders of this plot was Miguel Hidalgo, the village priest of Dolores, who served as a one-man community action project. He was promoting the development of agriculture and production by artisans, as well as producing theater, often his own translations of French works.

One of the people approached about the uprising reported the plot to Spanish authorities. When word reached the viceroy in Mexico City he sent a group of officials to arrest the plotters. This group arrived in Querétaro and informed a local official, the corregidor, of their mission. The corregidor's wife, doña Josefa Ortiz de Domínguez, or simply La Corregidora, was already involved in the plot along with her husband. After she learned of the arrest mission she was confined to her house to prevent information leaks. However she managed to get word to a sympathetic jailor on the ground floor who rode off Paul Revere-style to warn Hidalgo and Ignacio Allende, a fellow plotter, in the village of Dolores.

Upon hearing that "the Spanish were coming," Hidalgo uttered his immortal words, "Caballeros, somos perdidos, no hay más remedio que ir a matar guachupines."* He then set the church bells ringing in the early morning hours of September 16, 1810 (Mexican Independence Day) and informed a groggy populace that the rebellion had begun. The people of Dolores immediately supported Hidalgo, who freed the prisoners in the town jail to increase his forces.[8] The insurgents, 1600 strong, then marched to the town of San Miguel, beginning the liberation of Mexico. Many people working in the fields joined them as they went and when they arrived they occupied San Miguel without firing a shot. There the contradictions within the movement became apparent. Indians and mestizos began looting the town despite the efforts of Hidalgo and other leaders to stop them. "The Spanish-hating mob, feeling free from bondage, found no other way to avenge three centuries of wrongs."[9]

On September 28 the insurgents, now 25,000 strong, arrived at Guanajuato, which was the second most important city in Mexico due to its mines. Four hundred convicts were freed and joined the rebellion, as did many miners. Again there was looting despite the efforts of the more affluent officers to prevent it. The insurgents then began the siege of La Alhóndiga, the royal granary where the Spanish had gathered their families and fortunes. Finally the insurgents broke into the granary and "the crowd, full of passion and hate, thirsting for vengeance, entered the building, killing men, women and children alike, stripping the bodies of jewels and clothing, and sacking the riches the Spaniards had hoarded there."[10]

The next target was Valladolid (today Morelia), which was taken without a shot and then looted. The disorderly crowd which formed Hidalgo's army filed through the streets shouting "Long live the Virgin of Guadalupe," and "Death to the Spaniards." The force was composed of some 70,000 men, with four cannons, two of bronze and two of wood. The officers, many of whom had defected from the royal army, commanded poorly armed and poorly dressed workers and peasants.[11]

By this time the struggle had changed. Hidalgo did not want a caste war, but the Indians and mestizos soon converted it into that with their constant pillaging.[12] Until this point the independence movement was in the hands of creoles, who only wanted to replace the Spaniard with the creole, leaving the social and economic structure unchanged. However Indians and mestizos had other ideas.[13]

While advancing on Mexico City, Hidalgo issued several decrees which set the social content of the struggle, at least from his creole position. He decreed the end of Indian tribute, slavery (the first emancipation proclamation in the Americas), and the pulque tax (which fell mainly on the Indian).

While marching east Hidalgo passed through a town where one of his former students, José María Morelos y Pavón, was parish priest. Morelos joined the insurgents and was ordered south to take Acapulco. Further along the insurgents took Toluca without a shot and then as they approached Mexico City they met their first major resistance from royalist forces in the Battle of Monte de las Cruces. After heavy losses on both sides the insurgents finally triumphed over the royalist forces.

Instead of proceeding on to take Mexico City, Hidalgo ordered his army back to the west. This decision is one of the most controversial of Mexican history, and was probably based on the insurgents' lack of ammunition, the strength of Mexico City's royalist garrison, the approach of royalist reinforcements, and the weakness of Hidalgo's own poorly trained army.[14] Hidalgo may also have feared that his army would have looted Mexico City.

Soon after the insurgents turned west, they suffered a serious defeat at the hands of the disciplined, well-armed Spanish forces. Hidalgo and his supporters then withdrew to Guadalajara, after suffering massive desertions, and set up their headquarters. In January 1811 they were routed by the royalists after a lucky cannon shot landed in the insurgents' ammunition dump.

Hidalgo and Allende then retreated north through Aguascalientes and Saltillo. North of Saltillo the remnants of the insurgent army were captured by the Spanish just as its leaders were making a break for the United States in search of sanctuary and support. Hidalgo and Allende were tried by the Spaniards and shot in June 1811.

Jose Maria Morelos y Pavón

Hidalgo never had time to formulate a clear plan for government nor the opportunity to carry out one if he had. His progressive nature is shown by his abolition of slavery and the many measures taken to benefit the Indian, including the return of lands supposedly rented to

---

*Translation: Gentlemen, we are lost, our only recourse is to go kill Spaniards.

haciendas, but actually taken from Indian control. What never became clear though is what positive programs he would have carried out, since his acts generally consisted of abolishing unpopular institutions which benefited only the colonial government.

The death of Hidalgo and Allende shifted the focus of the insurgency to southern Mexico where Morelos was still fighting. Morelos was of poor origins and mixed race, and had worked for years as a mule skinner before entering the priesthood. Militarily he was a brilliant guerrilla leader who managed to liberate most of the area south of Mexico City and unite with insurgent groups to the west of it. His social programs went beyond Hidalgo's and included not only the abolition of slavery, but other major social reforms. He ordered the goods of the wealthy confiscated with half going to the poor and half going to finance the insurgent army. His 1813 plan called for racial equality and land distribution, and contained anti-clerical measures.[15] His position on land reform was especially important since the church and the Spaniards together held most of the land. Morelos said agriculture should be "based on many working small plots separately, with their own industry and labor, with no one individual having large expanses of unused land and enslaving thousands to work that land which was cultivated ..."[16] Morelos's programs not only foresaw the establishment of national independence, but also reflected the aspirations of the exploited lower classes of New Spain.

At this stage the rebellion reached its high point, with insurgents operating over most of Mexico. Both sides followed a scorched-earth policy which destroyed much of the productive capacity of central Mexico. The royalists burned villages and crops in areas supporting the insurgents. The insurgents in turn burned haciendas, looted towns, and drove cattle off in areas supporting the crown.[17]

The insurgents' major victory came when Morelos and his men held Cuautla for 77 days while it was under siege, demoralizing the Spaniards and giving other insurgents free reign to attack royalists. Finally the insurgents broke through the siege lines and escaped. The Spanish commander paid the insurgents this unwitting tribute:

> *If the perseverance and liveliness of the defenders of Cuautla had been moral and had been on behalf of a just cause, some day it would deserve a place of honor in history; confined by our troops and despite their need, they are constantly happy; they bury their dead with chimes celebrating the glorious death and they celebrate the return of their frequent forays with applause, dancing and drunken revelry... .[18]*

The struggle continued on until November 1815, when Morelos was captured by the royalists, tried and executed. With Morelos's death the independence movement began to decline. The royalist forces not only had arms and support from Spain, but the resources of Mexican landowners, creole and Spanish alike. Without Morelos, various insurgents began to struggle among themselves for leadership, and finally most were reduced to defensive holding actions, with some becoming little more than bandits. To further weaken the rebels, the viceroy offered pardons which were accepted by many insurgent leaders.

Agustín de Iturbide

This prolonged struggle saw the beginning of what became a characteristic of Mexico for more than a century: an enormous army. The army absorbed most of the national budget, had its own interests, and alienated wealthy creoles by denying them choice commands while taxing them to support it.

In 1821 events in Spain precipitated a crisis in Mexico. By this time the insurgents were left with only one significant fighting force, commanded by Vicente Guerrero, one of Morelos's lieutenants. The political situation suddenly reversed itself when the Spanish army in Cadiz revolted in favor of a liberal French-style constitution. This terrified the creole aristocracy, which feared social change more than independence.[19] In addition the success of other independence movements in the Americas made it clear that independence was inevitable, so the creoles began to act.

A creole officer named Iturbide, who had been retired from the royalist forces for being too bloodthirsty even for the Spanish,[20] was maneuvered into a command which would supposedly enable him to finish off Guerrero in Oaxaca and thus virtually end the rebellion. However neither Iturbide nor his creole supporters had any such intention. Instead Iturbide contacted Guerrero and got his support for a new independence movement. He then announced his Plan de Iguala which called for the independence of Mexico, and at the same time guaranteed the interests of landowners, including Spaniards, and even invited a Bourbon to the throne in Mexico.

The wealthy creoles immediately flocked to Iturbide's side, realizing that if they didn't get independence Iturbide-style, they might well have to face a major social revolution. From the beginning of the independence struggle until the preparation for Iturbide's coup, Spaniards and creoles acted in close alliance.[21] However the Plan de Iguala shattered this alliance and left only the Spaniard favoring continued colonial status. By October 1821 all resistance to Iturbide had been suppressed and the last viceroy sent over from Spain signed a treaty recognizing Mexican independence.

The independence struggle left some 400-600,000 dead [22] and reduced agricultural production by half and mining by more than half.[23] Politically it set the stage for the next century of Mexican history, leaving the interests of the hacendado and church intact and creating a large standing army which wouldn't disband.

Thus the consummation of independence by Iturbide, a representative of the Hispano-Creole aristocracy, had nothing to do with the ideals of social liberty and economic reform proclaimed by Hidalgo, Morelos, Guerrero and the other representatives of insurgent democracy. IT WAS NOT the same cry which resounded in Dolores.[24]

CHAPTER 4: NATIONHOOD

Once independence was achieved, there remained the gigantic task of social and economic reform, an undertaking more difficult than simple political emancipation.[1]

Mexico's independence, as we have noted, didn't resolve the basic social problems which had existed for centuries. These problems were to keep the country in turmoil for half a century and in many respects are still unresolved. Given this precarious foundation it is hardly surprising that in the first fifty years as an independent nation Mexico had over thirty presidents, more than fifty governments, two or even three governments claiming jurisdiction simultaneously, and one man, Santa Anna, as president nine times,[2] not to mention one empire, five constitutions and two foreign wars.[3]

The basic problem was that Mexico was still not really a nation, but merely a geographic area whose people were divided by class, language and race. The Indian population, half the total, was divided into many language groups and in most instances didn't speak Spanish. Most Indians lived at a subsistence level and thus had limited economic contact with non-Indians.

In contrast to the position of the Indian, there were various interest groups which kept privileges inherited from colonial times and which competed among themselves for power, ignoring the majority of the population. The two strongest special interest groups were the church, whose financial power had not decreased since colonial times, and the military. The military, which greatly expanded during the independence struggle, became a permanent institution and in 1825 received over 90% of the federal budget even though it wasn't fighting a war.[4] Both the church and the army moved in to fill the power vacuum left by the Spanish crown.[5]

The national government served as a weak link between various groups, but commanded the loyalty of none. Those interested in government were those who hoped to profit from it. The number of government employees rose rapidly, swollen by those seeking easy jobs and plentiful graft.[6] Various groups vied for political power and its spoils, submitting the country to

civil wars, coups, dictatorships, and revolts which took place without regard to the people's will. Political proclamations, uprisings by ambitious strongmen, takeovers, and reforms which offered nothing, used rural populations as cannon fodder, but failed to remember them in the hour of triumph.[7]

....

This course of history differs sharply from that of the United States which became independent less than half a century earlier. In New Spain the entire government had been built on a top-down basis, with power coming from the king. When this single legitimizing institution disappeared in 1821 there was nothing to bind Mexicans together.[8] Not only was it necessary to create new institutions, but it was necessary for them to win the respect of the population. In contrast, the British had allowed a significant degree of self-government in the American colonies. The institutions they created, such as JP courts, county courts, houses of burgesses, and town meetings in New England, remained intact after independence and provided a stable framework for the new government. Also the American colonies, with their economic diversity — shipbuilding, farming, and some manufacturing — had developed strong internal trade which held them together, while such trade was lacking in Mexico.

. . . .

Since no one group emerged from the independence struggle with political dominance,[9] struggles between interest groups dominated the first fifty years of Mexican independence. Two of these groups became known as federalists and centralists. The federalists represented the emerging manufacturing and commercial interests (bourgeoisie), intellectuals, anti-feudalists, and in general the upwardly mobile who wanted to loosen up the old system so that they might advance more rapidly. On the other hand, the centralists were anti-democratic and anti-reformist. They wanted a strong central government with Mexico City in control of foreign trade as in colonial times. This control of trade, to the advantage of Mexico City merchants, but to the disadvantage of outlying consumers, was one of the major issues of the time.[10] The centralists were supported by militarists who could count on receiving a large part of the taxes levied by centralist governments.[11] Also supporting the centralists were high clergymen, landlords, Spanish merchants, and monarchists.

By the middle of the century the federalists and centralists had evolved into groups known respectively as liberals and conservatives. The liberals were supporters of civil liberties and individualism, and saw the United States as a model for Mexico to follow in its development, ignoring the basic differences between the two countries.[12] The liberals constantly attacked the economic position of the Catholic church — attacks which if successful would open up economic opportunities for those very entrepreneurial liberals. The conservatives changed less; they represented more of a continuation of the centralist tradition with its backing of hacendados, militarists, monarchists, and high clergy. Interestingly enough, the proponents of industrial development in the early history of the republic, farsighted men in economic terms, were largely conservatives.[13]

Nevertheless these interest groups, be they liberal, federalist, centralist or conservative, agreed on more than they disagreed. The fundamental point of agreement was respect for the privately-owned hacienda, which the conservative owned, and which the liberal respected out of reverence for the institution of private property. This failure to attack the hacienda doomed efforts at development and social justice.

Both groups were also in essential agreement on another matter: the Indian was to stay at the bottom of the social ladder. In 1846 an observer commented on the lot of the Indian:

> *Certainly no visible improvement has taken place in their condition since independence. They are quite as poor and quite as ignorant and quite as degraded as they were in 1808....*[14]

Conservative hacendados continued to steal Indian communal lands while liberals proposed schemes for putting such lands on the "free market," another method for whites to increase their holdings. Neither group protested the slaughter of Indians which went on in the north in the style of the American west. Plans for incorporating Indians into the development process or improving their living conditions were never even put forth. The basic attitude toward Indians was expressed by José Luis Mora, a well-known liberal, who stated that when the Mexican-American War was over "the most urgent necessity is to repress the colored classes."[15] Given both abject poverty and attitudes such as this, Indian rebellions continued as they had in colonial times. A rebellion in Yucatán in 1848 took on the aspect of a full scale war, and indeed is called the War of the Castes. In the same year another major revolt broke out in the Huasteca area northeast of Mexico City. Liberals characterized the Huasteca uprisings as "riots lacking political objectives, aimed only at pillage and crime."[16] The Indian leading the uprising was called a communist, reflecting the radical political position of some peasant leaders.[17]

Finally there was general agreement among these elite groups that the key to developing Mexico lay in the hands of those of European ancestry. Acting upon this assumption, attempts were made to stimulate colonization by Europeans, feeling that this would hold back both the Indian and the US, which was beginning its expansion in the north.[18]

These splits along the lines of federalist-centralist and liberal-conservative were by no means the only splits among the ruling elite. Another basic issue was determining the absolute size of the country, or in other words, would Mexico stay one country or fragment into several. Originally Mexico included Central America, and in 1822 troops were sent there to keep it as part of Mexico, on the pretext of "protecting the population."[19] Then in 1823 troops were sent to El Salvador to suppress an anti-Mexican revolt there. Finally it became clear to the ruling groups in Central America that they would receive no advantage from being part of Mexico, so in 1823 they successfully declared themselves independent. Central America was then faced with the problem of whether it would remain one nation or divide further, an event which occurred in 1839 when it fragmented into the five republics of present-day Central America.

The same problem arose in 1834, when in response to a change from a relatively loose federalist government to a centralist government, both Yucatán and Texas broke away from the Mexican government. The Yucatán rebellion was suppressed by Mexican troops. Texas's rebellion was successful, although this success was based upon the interests of the US and the Anglo-Saxon settlers.[20] However the negative reaction of the Mexicans in Texas to the centralists was important, and indeed some Mexicans followed the Texas independence movement because they felt oppressed by the far-away government in Mexico City.

Further complicating the picture were a variety of conflicting economic interests which included free traders, artisans, and domestic industrialists, who shifted alliances to suit their convenience. Various interest groups tried to influence tariffs and trade protection policies. Consumers and traders wanted no tariffs, the former so they could get cheap goods and the latter so they could profit from trade. Artisans and industrialists wanted tariffs to protect them from cheap imports, but the artisans opposed industry because they were afraid of cheap factory production. None of these groups however was strong enough to bargain effectively with any of the major world trading powers.[21]

The revolts of the period were often stirred up by trade interests. In 1841 and 1851 governments favoring free trade were brought down by those wanting higher tariffs.[22] Customs house garrisons wanting tariff increases engaged in these revolts to further their own interests, and finally Great Britain, the leading power of the time, lent its support to the free-traders.

Each shift in government brought in a new constellation of interest groups. The first government, formed by Iturbide, let in European and US goods freely, ruining local industry[23] and producing a thirteen-fold increase in British imports from 1819 to 1823.[24] With his fall other interest groups took over and tariffs went back up again.

Still another part of the picture were the local and regional interest groups which formed

a multiplicity of local powers whose autonomy was the conspicuous sign of the weakness of the central power. Thus rather than there being a political power, there were political powers, the powers of those with property: landowners, Church, corporate bodies and estates of the possessors.[25]

These local interests filled the power vacuum left by the Spaniards[26] and often had more loyalty and power than the national government. They enforced their own tariffs which kept out competing goods from other states. At the same time these local interests began to trade directly with foreign countries, bypassing Mexico City[27] and reducing the power of the national government to control trade.

Tied closely to the regional interests was the hacienda, which came through the independence struggle unchanged as an institution. The hacienda, which served as a local power base, was the major economic unit of the country. It not only prevented progress, but was the major stumbling block to social justice, since agricultural workers kept in debt servitude and degradation made up more than half the population.[28]

Another element contributing to the confusion were those who rejected even the form of democracy. Many hoped for a return to Spanish rule, hopes which were kept alive by Spain's occupation of an island fort at Veracruz for four years and by an unsuccessful invasion attempt in 1829.

Ambitious militarists formed another important group since:

The Independence Revolution produced many military heroes who were idle after 1821 and who felt the obligation

to save the country. Many saviours lived a life of constant insurrections, barracks revolts and mutinies. Each saviour, after conning troops with promises of promotions, jobs and loot, put forth his revolutionary decree, which was no more than the substitution of an undoubtedly bad government or president, by himself, which would doubtless be no better.[29]

In addition monarchists pushed conflicts in directions which they felt would favor the establishment of a monarchy. Seeing their own weakness, they began to conspire with European powers in the 1840's and 1850's for the imposition of an emperor from Europe,[30] efforts which as we shall see in the next chapter were to bring war to Mexico in the 1860's.

Throughout this period there was a relative lack of power in the central government. Most of the economy functioned locally and much of what went on at the national level was in fact controlled by foreigners. Thus the nation was only a hollow shell, with limited power to influence events locally, nationally or internationally.

The tensions in the new government began to show early. In November 1821 Guadalupe Victoria and other insurgents were arrested for plotting a republic to replace the autocratic system favored by Iturbide. Then in May 1822 a conservative-backed army uprising put Iturbide into power as emperor. However he did not last long; in March 1823 there was an uprising against him in Veracruz. As the rebels approached Mexico City, Iturbide abdicated and went into exile. He returned in 1824, thinking the climate was again ripe for a monarchy. However his intelligence was faulty, and he was imprisoned and executed. Despite having consummated independence, Iturbide is now regarded as something of a political disgrace and his name, like Cortés's, is marked by its conspicuous absence on monuments and streets.

In 1824 the first constitution, a federalist-centralist compromise, was drawn up.[31] An election was held and Guadalupe Victoria was elected to become the first president of Mexico. The most significant aspect of his term was that he finished it, an event which did not occur again for some 50 years.

At the end of Victoria's term, the insurgent Vicente Guerrero lost the presidency by one electoral vote, but ousted the winner and took power anyway. Guerrero, the first dark skinned ruler of Mexico, represented the interests of the south, as opposed to those of Mexico City. He only lasted four months before he was ousted by his vice-president, who in turn was ousted by one of his fellow plotters, Antonio de Santa Anna. This was typical of the entire period until 1857.

Santa Anna had the distinction of betraying everyone, first the Spanish by helping Iturbide, then Iturbide by participating in the 1823 rebellion against him, then the vice-president who helped oust Guerrero, and later both the liberals and conservatives.[32] He was "a consummate master of the art of political intrigue, serving all parties and converting parties and men into instruments of his own ambition ..." .[33]

The most significant events of this period, other than the coming and going of governments, were foreign wars. In 1838 the French blockaded Veracruz and then occupied it in an attempt to get a favorable treaty from Mexico. Fortunately for Mexico, England pressured

Antonio López de Santa Anna

France into a settlement, since the occupation was interrupting British trade.[34]

Of far more significance was the Mexican-American War, which will be discussed in more detail later. The war came after a four-year dictatorship of Santa Anna (1841-45). The basic weakness of the nation was shown by President Gómez Farías's desperate attempt to raise money for Mexico's defense during the war. He asked the church for a fifteen million peso loan, a request which was denied by church officials[35] since they were more interested in church finances than in the territorial integrity of the "nation."

Even as American troops were approaching Mexico City, we find Santa Anna (at that time a general, not a president) pulling back the troops which he was commanding so he could engage in presidential politics in Mexico City.[36]

In the aftermath of the war, which resulted in Mexico's losing half its territory, Mexico went into a state of political shock. The only person capable of holding the country together was Santa Anna, who was called to head still another government. Once in power he set up another dictatorship which lasted until the Revolt of Ayutla in 1854, which pushed Santa Anna from power for the last time and ushered in the liberal era.

CHAPTER 5: JUAREZ & DIAZ

If our Independence movement cut the ties that bound us to Spain, the Reform movement denied that the Mexican nation as a historical project should perpetuate the colonial tradition.[1]

In 1853 Santa Anna became president for the last time, assumed the title "Supreme Highness", and set up a short-lived military dictatorship. His overthrow in 1855 ended the liberal-conservative power plays that dominated the first years of Mexico's independence. The conservatives, still looking back to the Spanish colonial model, were confronted with a liberal opposition whose economic base was the growing export business.* As their power grew, the liberals sought to dismantle the old economic structure and establish civil liberties, build railroads, break down barriers to internal commerce, and put the immense land holdings of the church and Indian communities on the market.[2]

In 1854 the liberals issued the Plan de Ayutla, calling for the overthrow of Santa Anna and the writing of a liberal constitution. The liberals, backed by artisans, small merchants and intellectuals[3] who resented the closed nature of Mexican society, then rose in arms against Santa Anna. In August 1855 after a little more than a year of civil war Santa Anna was forced from office and fled the country.

The first target of the liberals was the church lands which comprised about a fourth or a fifth of the national wealth.[4] In June 1856 the Law Lerdo, named for the Minister of the Treasury who drafted it, prohibited corporate ownership of land. According to the new law, church land was to be sold to farmers renting it or to the highest bidder, with the proceeds going to the church. The law not only undercut the power base of the conservative church, but gave new land for development, a new tax base, and a chance to tax the sale of the land.[5] However, rather than benefiting the small farmer whom the liberals held to be the basis of the ideal society, the sales mainly benefited the generals and liberal government officials who could acquire the large tracts which were auctioned

*Throughout Latin America the growth of liberalism during the 19th century was tied to the increase of exports.[7]

off.[6] Thus the Law Lerdo merely increased the holdings of the hacienda. As an observer noted in 1858,

> *The number of real landowners did not increase, some speculators engaged in unethical practices, some of the rich increased their fortunes and none of the poor ceased being poor.*[8]

Communally-owned village holdings were also broken up, often with little regard for legal technicalities. In 1868 a writer suggested suspending the division of Indian communal lands since "the variety of methods..., bribing judges and scheming with high authorities,.. used to usurp Indian lands is so amazing."[9]

On February 5, 1857 the liberals adopted a new constitution with great fanfare. This constitution is now regarded as a spiritual guide for the Mexican government and its proclamation date is still a holiday in Mexico. Ironically its high-sounding ideals and its provision for the separation of powers have never had much to do with the reality of Mexican government. Despite its positive provisions, such as civil liberties and the opening of voting to males without regard to land ownership or wealth, it totally failed to deal with the single greatest problem of Mexico, the grossly inequitable distribution of land.[10]

The conservatives' response was not long in coming. In December 1857 they launched a counter-revolt, took the capital, and kept Mexico in civil war until the end of 1860. The conservatives were initially led by a general who obtained a one and a half million peso loan from the church before joining the fight. The liberal president, Comonfort, made some unsuccessful conciliatory gestures toward the conservatives and ended up having the confidence of neither side, so he resigned the presidency and went to the US. This left the next in line of presidential succession, the president of the supreme court, to take the presidency.

The new president, Benito Juárez, was a full-blooded

Indian who in his early years spoke only the Zapotec language. Juárez, who at one time was an impoverished sheep herder, became a lawyer who was jailed for his defense of Indian rights. Later he served as governor of his native state, Oaxaca.

President Juárez set up his liberal government in Veracruz and pursued his fight against the conservative government in Mexico City. The US recognized the conservative government as did most European countries. Juárez had the support of most of the states of Mexico and of most of the population, and in addition, the Veracruz customs receipts, the major source of government revenue. In July 1859 Juárez nationalized all remaining church lands without compensation, since as long as land was held by the church it continued to generate revenues for the conservative opposition.* The nationalized property was hurriedly sold to finance the war, often at prices far below its real value. Such sales had the advantage of winning allies for the liberals, since if conservatives were to win the war, these sales would be invalid and the church would reoccupy the properties.

The conservatives were finally defeated in December 1860 and the War of the Reform, as the 1857-60 civil war is known, came to an end. The country was again ruined by war; the potentially profitable sales from church land had produced little income; and conservatives were still conducting guerrilla attacks against the government. To make matters worse, three-fourths of the customs revenues were already pledged to pay off foreign debts. As an emergency measure Congress suspended payment on the foreign debt — a not overly radical measure since Mexico had no money to make payments with.

This apparently innocuous act, coming as it did during the American Civil War (which prevented the US from enforcing its Monroe Doctrine and keeping others out of Latin America), gave Europe the pretext for massive intervention in Mexico. An alliance between Spain, England and France was soon formed to collect the debt and, as the British expressed it, to put an end to the terrible disorder.[11] Spain came hoping to reassert its old position, and England was afraid of what France might do alone and also wanted to be in a position to support the American South in the Civil War. The French however had the most far-reaching plans. Napoleon III was planning to impose a monarchy which would open the doors of Mexico for him and stop the spread of American influence into Latin America.[12] This would enable him to convert Mexico into an economic colony similar to the British colony in India.[13]

With the threat of imminent intervention based on the pretext of collecting foreign debts, the Mexican congress in November 1861 agreed to begin debt payments again. However, once set into motion the European powers were not easily stopped; in December 1861 and January 1862 French, British and Spanish troops landed and occupied Veracruz. The British and Spanish soon withdrew, with assurances that their claims would be met. The Spanish saw they were too weak to regain influence in the face of more powerful partners[14] and England decided, its debt claims met, to let France overextend and weaken itself, which is what happened.[15]

The remaining all-French force began to march inland, fighting its first major battle at Puebla, where it was soundly defeated by the entrenched Mexicans on May 5, 1862. This is the outstanding military victory in Mexican history and each year the "Cinco de Mayo" is celebrated as a major national holiday, a sort of second independence day.

The French retreated, got reinforcements, advanced and besieged Puebla from March to May 1863. Finally Puebla fell to the French, but its defenders showed Mexican determination to defend national sovereignty and gave others time to organize the defense of the country. The French then marched on into Mexico City, which had been abandoned by Juárez, who headed north, eventually taking refuge in Paso del Norte (today, in his honor, Ciudad Juárez). The French set up an administration backed by 34,000 troops. They tried to extend their control into the countryside, but were never very successful; as soon as their troops withdrew, popular uprisings and guerrilla forces made their control at best tenuous. To head the French-installed government, Maximilian, the brother of the Austrian emperor, was chosen by Napoleon III as emperor of Mexico. Even before leaving Europe, Maximilian signed a treaty with France making Mexico virtually a French colony. He agreed to pay not only the inflated debt claims of the French, but the cost of French troops then occupying Mexico.[16] Maximilian departed from Europe with the personal blessing of Pope Pius IX and arrived to head a conservative government. The Mexican reaction to this intervention was recorded by a French army officer who wrote that the Mexicans "flee when we approach and their attitude couldn't be more hostile. I don't know what we are going to do if this situation lasts another month."[17]

Maximilian had a small base of support: staunch conservatives, church hierarchy and hacendados. However his moderately progressive ideas acquired in Europe tended to alienate even this minimal power base. The real source of Maximilian's support lay in the French who exercised almost total control. All Mexican officers in Maximilian's army were subject to orders from any French officer, even a lieutenant.[18] Maximilian's private secretary noted

> many Mexicans in high positions are indignant at having to give their complete submission to the French not only in matters relating to war, but in questions relating to running the government.[19]

Slowly Maximilian's conservative government began to lose ground to the liberal forces led by Juárez, leaving Maximilian with only the territory within range of French artillery.[20] As Maximilian tried to broaden his appeals to liberals with such measures as not returning lands to the church, he only succeeded in further alienating his few supporters.

In 1866 seeing that collapse was imminent, the French began to withdraw, pressured by their commitments in the Austro-Prussian War. Early in 1867 the French were

---

*This nationalization, along with the Ley Lerdo and the changes embodied in the 1857 Constitution are known as the "Reforma," for which Mexico City's Paseo de la Reforma is named.

Benito Juárez

trying to make deals with the liberals as they were departing; they got nothing. With the French gone, Maximilian's empire began to disintegrate more rapidly. Juárez came from the north, defeated the Emperor's forces at Querétaro and captured Maximilian on May 15, 1867. Shortly afterward an ambitious general, Porfirio Díaz, came from the south and retook Mexico City for the liberals. In June Maximilian was executed by firing squad; Juárez resisted pressures to pardon him, knowing that a live Maximilian would only serve to promote other uprisings and prolong internal strife.

Thus the war ended, concluding not only a struggle by Mexico for its independence against French intervention, but between the old privileged classes and the new emerging middle classes, between those wanting separation of church and state and those opposing it, of federalist against centralists, and on down the line on all the issues of the liberal-conservative split.[21]

Despite having won the war, Juárez, like Churchill after World War II, did not immediately receive the thanks of his countrymen. He was re-elected president in 1871 only after Congress voted to break a tied election. The years after the end of the war were characterized by rebellions, men being pressed into military service, civil discord, and the opposition of almost all the press to Juárez and his associates.[22] In 1872 Juárez died in office.

During his presidency Juárez greatly strengthened the power of the federal government, as he confronted not only foreign invasions and civil wars, but also the task of unifying his fragmented nation. Although his liberal principles called for a weak central government, the reality of many interest groups and small markets demanded a strong national government if the country was to be integrated.[23] In order to obtain badly needed revenue, Juárez instituted high tariffs. The Juárez presidency began a trend toward a strong executive with little regard for the written constitutional model.[24] His administration was one in which men with high ideals and personal dedication tried to apply principles which were not in keeping with the times.[25]

Since his death Juárez has been regarded in much the same way as Lincoln in the United States. In fact his humble life style and scrupulous honesty remind one of Lincoln and contrast sharply with most Mexican leaders, before or since. However in keeping with his liberal respect for private property, he consistently broke up Indian communal land, even though this often meant the brutal suppression of Indians trying to defend their holdings. Juárez never presented a concrete program for dealing with social inequality, rather he merely declared all men to be equal before the law. Such abstract equality, with no relation to social and economic reality, was an empty concept.[26]

Following Juárez into the presidency was Lerdo de Tejada, whose presidency is noteworthy mainly for continuing the trend toward a strong executive and for being the bridge between Juárez and Porfirio Díaz.

Lerdo's term was cut short by Porfirio Díaz, a general who had commanded liberal Mexican forces in Juárez's home state of Oaxaca. Díaz, who was to rule Mexico for over a third of a century, made his first bid for power in the 1867 elections, and got a third of the vote. Failing to win by election, he staged an unsuccessful coup, to be followed six weeks later by another unsuccessful takeover attempt. In the 1872 election he ran again, getting only 20% of the vote. Then, with the support of the military which disliked Lerdo's anti-military policies, he staged a successful coup.

Díaz served as president for four years, relinquished the presidency to one of his cronies for the 1876-1880 term, and then returned to impose his autocratic rule over Mexico until 1911. During this period Díaz created a political machine over which he kept tight personal control. In form however there was a constitutional government which went through the motions of "re-electing" the dictator every four years.

Díaz, with the backing of generals, clergy, hacendados and merchants,[27] assumed all powers of government. Congress was only a showcase which Díaz referred to as "my herd of horses."[28] Those with the strength to threaten his power were bought off with government contracts, a governorship, or an army command — all means for great personal profit. The few who would continue to challenge Díaz were crushed.

Surrounding Díaz was a small group of advisors called "científicos," who helped formulate and carry out Díaz's policies. During the Porfiriato, as Díaz's administration is called, "... by fair means or foul, many científicos became notoriously rich."[29] These científicos, along with Díaz, formed a tight group which set government policy for decades, while rationalizing their actions with positivist philosophy.* The masses were held to be incapable of working efficiently, and in most cases were thought to be dirty, vicious, lazy and drunk. Furthermore their meagre wages were felt to be more than their productivity merited. From this it was concluded that the only salvation for Mexico lay in attracting European Catholic immigrants whose industry and intelligence could develop the country.[30]

Given this outlook, it is not surprising that the Díaz administration opened its doors to foreign investment, and in fact did what it could to encourage it. Those in power felt that Mexico had neither the resources nor the skills to develop itself. Mexico's minerals were soon being mined by Morgan-Guggenheim interests, its oil pumped by Standard Oil, and so on. Foreign investment came to control the most rapidly developing sectors of the economy: mining, railroads, utilities, banking and commerce. The generous terms awarded to these investors was no accident. Many high government officials owned shares in these foreign ventures. Thus little nationalistic legislation was forthcoming.[31]

---

*The positivists held that the most gifted would triumph over the weak, and that the talented were indeed the wealthy. Wealth was thus felt to be a measure of capacity and social responsibility. The poor, whose poverty indicated their lack of worth, were considered a rabble which would frequently necessitate violent suppression.[32] Not only would the upper classes promote development, but such development would provide economic opportunities. Without the efforts of the rich and their freedom to carry out development as they saw fit, equality was an impossibility and the country was doomed to dissolution and death.[33]

This foreign control became one of the main causes of discontent during the Porfiriato, especially for Mexicans employed by foreign firms. Generally Mexicans working in these firms were paid half what foreigners received and were denied middle and upper level positions. This resentment of foreign control was felt by everyone from the railway worker who could not advance in the American-owned railroad to the rich hacendado who wanted to go into business but saw the lucrative concessions already held by foreigners. Mexican businessmen who began to appear in large numbers during the Porfiriato were similarly alienated by the number of choice positions held by foreigners. Thus many Mexicans came to share the opinion that "The single most influential economic group was neither a rural aristocracy nor an urban bourgeoisie, but rather a *foreign* bourgeoisie."[34]

The sector of the economy which remained largely under Mexican control was the hacienda. The owners of these haciendas, beneficiaries of the recently expropriated lands of the church and Indians, formed the backbone of Díaz's support. Few of these hacendados adopted modern agricultural techniques and often land would be left idle while it was being held for speculation. The major change in the hacienda was the increasing amount of exports, such as henequen and sugar.

With the disappearance of church land holdings and the appropriation of most Indian communal land, the hacienda came to almost completely monopolize Mexican agriculture; 96.6% of rural families were landless in 1910.[35] Many supposedly free farm laborers soon fell hopelessly into debt to the hacendado and therefore were not permitted to leave. Those who tried to escape were returned by the authorities and charged with "robbery." These debts were inherited from father to son, so often those working off a hopeless debt never saw the first peso that started it. The extremely low wage scale for agricultural workers prevented debts from ever being paid off. These low wages in turn resulted from the over-abundance of agricultural workers who had been forced to compete for wages when they were driven off the Indian communal lands.

Much has been written of the conditions of agricultural workers during the Porfiriato. Thanks to científico economic planning, their living standard was below that of agricultural workers during the colonial period.[36] A US Senate report concluded that contract laborers "were slaves to all intents and purposes."[37]

To the peon, justice meant the unquestioned word of the **hacendado**, *administrator, jailor, and priest. And if the overlord needed assistance in keeping his peons in line, he simply called upon Díaz's rural shock-troopers. The poverty-stricken peasant had no hope of a better tomorrow, no promise of somehow raising himself from his deplorable status.*[38]

Throughout the Porfiriato the pressure on Indian lands increased, constantly pushing Indians into the labor market. The main land grabbers were the surveying companies which were rationalized as a means of making an accurate record of unclaimed land which could then be opened up for colonization by European homesteaders. In fact these companies served to enrich Díaz's cronies and foreign investors. The burden of proof of title was on those who occupied land — proof made difficult by the bribing of officials. One individual got 17 million acres in the state of Chihuahua (larger than the state of West Virginia), and one seventh of the entire country was divided up by 29 individuals and companies.[39]

Though both Indians and non-Indians lost land, the great burden fell on the Indian, who had no understanding of Díaz's "legal" system. Hardest hit of all the Indians were the Yaqui, whose fertile lands in Sonora were attractive to commercial farmers. When they began

Porfirio Díaz

to defend their lands, the Mexican army began a genocidal war which lasted for decades. Those Yaqui who survived capture were sent to Yucatán as forced laborers on the henequen plantations, where two-thirds would die within the first year.[40] Don Juan, himself a Yaqui, tells how his people fared upon capture:

The Mexican soldiers came upon us unexpectedly while my mother was cooking some food. She was a helpless woman. They killed her for no reason at all... the soldiers picked me up and beat me. When I grabbed onto my mother's body they hit my fingers with a horsewhip and broke them... I thought they had killed my father too, but they hadn't. He was wounded. Later they put us in a train like cattle and closed the door. For days they kept us there in the dark, like animals. They kept us alive with bits of food they threw into the wagon from time to time. My father died of his wounds in that wagon.[41]

Only slightly above the peon was Mexico's industrial labor force, some 400,000 strong in 1910.[42] Workers put in a 12-14 hour day and were often paid in chits only redeemable at the company store. Strikes were illegal; there was no workmen's compensation or retirement. Despite economic growth, workers' buying power was less in 1910 than it had been in 1877.[43] An example of the widespread child labor was the 1908 firing of María Díaz for union organizing in the textile mills after having worked there for four years. She was twelve years old.[44]

Those who dissented with Díaz were dealt with harshly, being imprisoned, drafted into the army, or simply killed. During the Porfiriato a Mexican wrote

The press is silent, newsmen have been imprisoned or murdered in the shadows of the jail; those persons who have shown opposition to the government are dragged from their beds at night to be killed in some secluded spot; the courts are in the hands of government lackeys; the peace that reigns is the peace of death.[45]

Organized opposition to the Díaz regime only began about 1900. The opponents were mainly middle and upper class Mexicans who resented the lack of opportunity for advancement. Their main complaints were Díaz's betrayal of the 1857 Constitution, the lack of democracy, renewed strength of the church, and foreign control which made it impossible for them to go into business. It was their own lack of advancement which motivated them, not the deplorable conditions of the peasant and the worker. In 1905 opposition members founded the Partido Liberal Mexicano. However even before the Revolution, this party was weakened by ideological splits — one part remained liberal reformers and another faction, many of whose members were forced into exile, turned to anarchism. The party ceased to exist before the Revolution of 1910-17 began.

All in all the lot of the average Mexican failed to improve and in many cases worsened during the Porfiriato. The Porfirian government not only opened up business opportunities for the wealthy, but forced the rest of society to serve them, by force if necessary.[46] Efforts of the elite to increase their wealth were more successful than ever before, since they were united for the first time since independence.[47] Thus they could shift their energy from internal power struggles to increasing their wealth and control over the rest of society. While foreign investors and a few Mexicans prospered, between 1895 and 1910 the mortality rate rose and life expectancy dropped.[48] By the end of the Porfiriato 16% of Mexico City's residents were sleeping on the streets[49] and the vast majority of the population was eating less of basic agricultural products than it had in 1877.[50]

CHAPTER 6: THE REVOLUTION

... more than thirty years of discontent among the peasant masses and the evident atrophy of the productive apparatus should be cited (and scholars have done so) as the main cause and motive force of the Mexican Revolution.[1]

The first decade of this century saw the decline of the Porfiriato. Up until then there had been economic growth, and repression had managed to divide potential opponents and prevent nation-wide opposition to the dictatorship. Finally divisions among the wealthy, which none of the factions wanted, opened up the way for mass participation in the revolution.[2]

The splits in the Porfirian elite resulted from changing economic conditions. Foreign mining interests and hacendados engaged in export agriculture hired employees away from the traditional hacendados, depriving them of their labor force. With the world depression of 1907 dissatisfaction became widespread as prices of henequen and minerals fell on the world market. As a result of this depression, the cheap credit hacendados had come to rely on suddenly dried up[3] and the científicos were held to blame.[4]

Foreign domination and enormous profits resulted in violence and strikes. In 1906 workers at the US-owned coppermines in Cananea, Sonora, went out on strike demanding, among other things, equal pay with Americans and access to American-held jobs. The governor of Sonora called in 275 armed American volunteers from Arizona to bloodily suppress the strike, killing 23 Mexican workers. The following year at Río Blanco, Veracruz, workers at one of the largest textile mills in the country struck to get the 14-hour day lowered to twelve. Díaz, a major shareholder in the mill, ordered the workers to return to the mills and had his troops fire on the strikers, killing and wounding hundreds of them and their families.[5] Neither strike was successful; the resulting violence however shook the country.

As Díaz, who was in his seventies, began to prepare for the 1910 elections, he found his traditional supporters

Río Blanco

divided. To further weaken his position in 1908 Díaz made the great tactical mistake of telling Creelman, an American newspaperman, that he would not run in the 1910 elections. Despite his later reversing himself, Díaz was never able to totally dominate the political scene again. Moving into the political vacuum around Díaz was Francisco Madero, a northern land owner representing the progressive hacendados who wanted to go into business, but felt blocked by the foreign domination of the economy. Madero, from one of the wealthiest families in the country, first ran for the vice-presidency, a spot normally reserved for a Díaz appointee. He later challenged Díaz and began campaigning for the presidency. His campaign drew tremendous crowds and had a broad base of disenchanted workers, intellectuals, members of the middle class and even hacendados.

Liberal landowners and businessmen feared revolution, and thus they were ready to make reforms and even replace the dictator with a more flexible form of government. When the revolution came it was as much a conflict between successive generations for power as an attempt to right injustice and create new social and political institutions.[6]

Madero's campaign successes were his temporary undoing; he was jailed in San Luis Potosí before the election. He was still in jail on election day when by official count he got exactly 196 votes nationwide.

While Madero was challenging Díaz in the north, opposition developed to the south of Mexico City in the state of Morelos. There land-grabbing from villages had been the most violent and peasant demands for the return of stolen lands were most threatening.[7] The massive land-grabbing responded to the pressure of the world market; Morelos, with 99.5% of its population landless,[8] was by itself the world's third greatest producer of sugar, after Hawaii and Puerto Rico.[9]

Resistance erupted in the village of Anenecuilco, where Emiliano Zapata was born. Zapata had inherited a small plot of land, so that although far from being wealthy, he escaped the grinding poverty of most of the population of Morelos. By 1910 the lands of his village, in an area where traditionally land was communally owned, were all gone. A neighboring hacienda was taking over parts of the village and had begun to plant sugar cane where homes once stood. In that year Zapata was chosen as chief of village defense, a job he undertook by going out with 80 armed men and distributing land stolen by the hacienda. Previously challenging land-grabs in or out of the courts had only gotten one sent to forced labor in Yucatán.[10] However at this time the political climate had changed and with Díaz preoccupied by Madero in the north, Zapata's land distribution not only went unchallenged,[11] but his example spread to other parts of the state.

While Zapata's land reform was spreading, Madero was released from jail on bail and fled to San Antonio, Texas. There he issued his Plan de San Luis Potosí, calling for a revolt against Díaz, free elections and legal review of previous land thefts. Nothing very radical. In fact for this reason Madero was supported by many wealthy Mexicans as a safe way to solve the problem of replacing Díaz without having a social and economic revolution. Madero even had Zapata's support at this time since Zapata felt that the mere mention of the agrarian problem in the Plan de San Luis offered at least some hope.

Events then began to move rapidly; there were uprisings in Chihuahua by Madero supporters, including Pancho Villa, and spontaneous land seizures continued to spread in the Morelos area. Then Villa and another rebel took Ciudad Juárez in May 1911. The same month Zapatistas took the cities of Cuautla and Cuernavaca in Morelos.

At this point Díaz lost the backing of the wealthy since they felt the army, staffed by aged generals commanding unwilling conscripts, couldn't stop Madero.[12] They opted for getting rid of Díaz in hopes of preventing conflict and social change. As a result the Pacto de Ciudad Juárez was drawn up and signed by Madero and the Díaz government. It called for Díaz to resign and go into exile and for his minister of foreign affairs to be interim president until elections could be held. Included in the pact was a provision that Díaz's federal army would remain intact, while the rebel forces which had supported Madero would be disbanded. This agreement which sought to end the revolution, disarm the peasants and establish the social system upheld by the federal army, said not a word about land reform. Díaz kept his word, resigned, and went into exile.

Upon Díaz's resignation, Madero started for Mexico City. He made a triumphal march to the capital, cheered along the way by enthusiastic crowds.

In August of 1911 presidential candidate Madero went to Morelos to negotiate with Zapata. There Zapata agreed to have the Zapatistas turn in their arms in exchange for Madero's promise to implement an agrarian reform. However when the Zapatistas began turning in their arms they were attacked by a reactionary general, Victoriano Huerta, and the caretaker government left by Díaz announced it wouldn't negotiate with "bandits."[13] After this, despite further negotiations with Madero, Zapata said no more guns would be turned in until agrarian reform was a reality. Although Zapata made no pacts with presidential candidate Madero, he did resist his brother's wanting to kill Madero on the spot, saying, "When he takes office and then fails, there'll be plenty of limbs to hang him from."[14]

In October, 1911 Madero and Pino Suárez were elected president and vice-president, respectively, in the most honest elections there have ever been in Mexico.

Once he was elected president, rather than dismantling the old Porfirian bureaucracy, Madero merely changed the personnel at the top. His positive contribution was to initiate one of the most democratic (politically) regimes Mexico has yet to see.[15] At the same time, "As always, millions of peasants continued stooping over on the haciendas of the Terrazas, the Creels and the other hacendados, as if there had been no revolution."[16] To his credit Madero did arrange an honorable settlement of the Yaqui Indian dispute. Madero no longer abetted the theft of lands; he was merely lax in redressing past thefts.

Madero felt that Mexico's greatest problem had been political and that he himself had resolved it by overthrowing Díaz. However he never dealt with the fact that his slogans "Effective suffrage" and "No re-election" meant little to the majority of the population which was impoverished and illiterate.[17] On the vital question of land reform he stalled, saying land reform could "only take place after a series of studies and actions that the government had not been able to carry out, since impatient individuals... violently prevented these studies."[18]

Zapata soon became antagonistic to Madero due to this unwillingness to implement land reform. Thus in November 1911 Zapata issued his Plan de Ayala, the definitive break with Madero, in which he charged Madero with abandoning the revolution and siding with the hacendados. The basic provision of the plan was that peasants had to use their own initiative to take back lands stolen from them. In addition they were charged with the armed defense of their reclaimed lands; dispossessed hacendados could take the matter to court *after the revolution* if they wished. Furthermore one third of each legally owned hacienda was to be purchased for landless peasants and lands of the revolution's enemies were to be seized. As was to be the case with future peasant participation in the revolution, there was no coherent ideology proclaimed by the peasants.[19] Furthermore they made the fatal mistake of concentrating on land reform and not struggling for political power.[20]

With the Plan de Ayala as its standard, by early 1912 the Zapatista rebellion spread to nearby states, despite a constant shortage of money, guns and ammunition. The liberal Francisco Madero responded with a program of strategic hamlets in Morelos.[21] While the Zapatista rebellion was spreading, other uprisings occurred and were crushed, including one by Porfirio Díaz's conservative nephew Félix Díaz.

Despite the opposition from both the left and right, Madero continued to cling to the political center. He postponed land reform, saying that there would be no seizure of land without payment, and that there was no money for payment.[22] Within a year of taking office Madero himself was caught between the conservatives wanting to smash Zapata and the middle class wanting concessions to be made to the Zapatistas for the sake of peace.[23]

Since Madero failed to pacify the Zapatistas, the conservatives made their move. There was a coup in February 1913 which started when conspirators released Félix Díaz from jail. When a call for Madero to resign failed, Félix Díaz and his backers took refuge in a Mexico City fortress called the Ciudadela. Madero appointed Victoriano Huerta to oust the rebels. However Huerta secretly favored the coup, and limited his military actions to sending troops loyal to Madero on suicide missions against the Ciudadela to get rid of them.

The rebels held out for ten days. During these ten days the two forces engaged in artillery duels in downtown Mexico City, carefully avoiding the "enemy's" cannons and creating a climate in which the population would welcome any settlement.[24] Then with US Ambassador Henry Lane Wilson as go-between, Huerta and Félix Díaz agreed to join forces, with Huerta to be interim president until elections could be held to elect the younger Díaz as president. Madero and his vice-president were taken prisoner and killed to prevent their leading resistance to the coup.[25]

Rebels in Ciudad Juárez, 1911

Madero's positive contribution was the freedom to organize political and labor organizations. However he didn't solve any of Mexico's problems due to his conciliatory approach to the old Porfirians, nor did he realize that the masses could be used as a power base.[26] This left him completely isolated and easy prey for the reactionaries. Furthermore his short regime was marred by nepotism and his placing his associates in office, as was the case of his vice-president. His economic policies were doomed from the start since his old fashioned ideas on economic liberalism ignored the reality of world colonial powers, trade protection and monopolies.[27] "Some individuals in history have succeeded in overcoming their class background; Madero was unable to do so."[28]

Huerta soon set up a dictatorship with the backing of conservative hacendados, bankers, rich merchants, high clergy and the federal army.[29] He put his men in governorships all over the country and dispelled the old adage of honesty among thieves by failing to call the election which was to give Félix Díaz the presidency.

Response to the coup was not long in coming. In the northern state of Coahuila, Venustiano Carranza, a well-to-do landowner and former Porfirian senator, declared Huerta's government to be illegal. His distance from Mexico City afforded protection which permitted his survival while opponents closer to the capital were immediately crushed.[30] After asking another general to head the opposition and being turned down,[31] Carranza began to organize his own opposition to the coup.

He issued the Plan de Guadalupe in March 1913 calling for resistance to Huerta but deliberately avoiding all social issues in order to build the broadest possible coalition against the dictator. The plan provided for the formation of a Constitutionalist* army with Carranza at its head. The army soon attracted a wide range of workers, peasants, intellectuals and dedicated young reformers.

For the first time members of the middle classes raised armies and acquired national prestige. These middle class figures differed from Madero in that they were backed by force of arms, a force which Madero either had not known how or had not wanted to use. Also they began a style of mass politics which Madero never imagined.[32] This populism began with the offering of concessions and reforms to the masses, in exchange for mass support in achieving political and military aims. This set a pattern for Mexico up to the present, the catch being that despite the mass support so freely given, the promises and concessions rarely saw the light of day.

The coup also brought the peasant leader into the forefront, removing him from the obscurity to which years of Díaz oppression and Madero co-optation had condemned him. In the south Zapata continued to defend his revolution and in the north a poverty stricken Villa returned from exile. He began his operations by gaining the confidence of a stable owner, renting two horses a day for a week. At the end of the week he rented eight horses with no questions being asked, and instead of returning the horses he launched on the conquest of much of northern Mexico.

*Carranza's army and political followers were subsequently referred to as "Constitutionalists."

Villa quickly built up a following among peasants, share-croppers, mule skinners and peddlers, all from the highly mobile, recently developed north which had a different social make-up than the villages of Morelos where the population had its roots in the same spot since before the Spanish conquest. Villa was ideally suited to his role since he was from Chihuahua and was of the same origins as his followers. As the son of a poor farmer he was forced to flee the law after shooting the landowner in a quarrel involving Villa's sister. While in hiding Villa developed a reputation for being a first class thief and rustler. Several times he tried to seek legal employment, but each time the police pursued him and forced him to flee.

At the same time Carranza's and Villa's armies began to march south, in Sonora another general, Alvaro Obregón, launched his career. Obregón, an upwardly mobile small farmer who had previously done odd jobs and worked on an hacienda, went from being small town mayor to being a general almost overnight. These three armies from the north began to close in on Huerta in Mexico City. The northern armies, except for Villa's, were generally led by middle class officers who commanded peasant masses.[33] As the armies moved south there were spontaneous uprisings and land seizures throughout the country.

Huerta meanwhile continued his brutal dictatorship, gaining "recruits" by picking the poor up off the streets and drafting them into the army. His regime was kept in power through systematic assassination of dissenters.[34]

Late in 1913 Villa began a rapid advance which gave him and his army, the División del Norte, fame as the strike force of the revolution. Typical of his style was his taking of Ciudad Juárez by capturing one of Huerta's troop trains which was headed south from Ciudad Juárez and then telegraphing back pretending he was its commander. He first requested and received a new locomotive and then said the tracks to the south were blocked. In response he received an order to bring the train back to Ciudad Juárez, which he did after filling it up with soldiers of the División del Norte. Upon arriving Villa easily took Ciudad Juárez, providing a great psychological boost to the anti-Huerta forces and opening up the way for trading cattle to the US for arms. As soon as he took the city Villa ordered that the stable owner who had rented him the eight horses be paid double the value of the horses.

By March 1914 all of Chihuahua was in the hands of the Villistas, and as governor Villa had an opportunity to carry out reforms. He ordered the confiscation of land and other properties of the wealthiest families. The revenues from these lands were then used for the public treasury, mainly to provide for the army, war widows and orphans. Income from the undivided estates was used to benefit the entire population of Chihuahua, the majority of whom were not peasants. Subdividing the haciendas would have had little effect on the non-peasant majority. After the revolution land was to be divided up among revolutionary veterans, war widows, and those who had had land stolen by hacendados.[35] In contrast to the communal tradition of Morelos, Villa had planned to break the hacienda up into small private plots and create agrarian communities.

During the period in which Villa controlled Chihuahua, there was relatively little change in the life style of the peasants, and only one spontaneous land seizure was recorded.[36] The major piece of legislation limited payments by sharecroppers to 50% of their crop. Instead of implementing an agrarian reform, the Villa government used revenues from confiscated estates to finance the División del Norte. It was in large part due to this income that the División del Norte became the strongest and best equipped of the armies defeating Huerta.[37]

The social content of the Villa administration can be gleaned from some reports of Villa's activities which appeared in the EL PASO TIMES. It was reported that he "... gave each poor person in Chihuahua clothing, shoes and other apparel from el Nuevo Mundo, the large department store which he confiscated from Spaniards."[38] At that time he reduced the price of beef from one peso to 15 centavos a kilo. Those who had lost their jobs due to the revolution could pick up free food at army commissaries.[39] Villa personally ordered free supplies for day care centers and when food prices went up, wheat and corn from confiscated estates were sold by the Villistas at reduced prices.[40] However Villa waited to start a land reform, since breaking up the haciendas would have cut off the flow of money from cattle sales which was used to buy arms. Also Villa wanted to delay the distribution of land until his own troops had returned.[41]

An example of Villa's honesty was supplied by the American war correspondent John Reed. He reported that Villa, who was commanding a huge army which controlled several states, wanted to send his son for education in the United States but was unable to do so since he didn't have the tuition for a half year's schooling.[42]

Once Chihuahua was under control, Villa and the División del Norte began to move south.

> ... the División del Norte was a peasant army. It was led by a peasant caudillo. Most of the officers were peasants. Its trains were loaded with armed peasant men and women, taking over Mexico. Wherever they passed the hopes of the peasantry soared, support was massed, and their mere passage produced uprisings and the sowing of haciendas from which the owners had fled.[43]

As the offensive got underway, antagonisms began to show between Carranza, a landowner and proponent of development, and Villa, the peasant leader. First Car-

Rebels with Cannon, 1911

ranza ordered Villa north to take Saltillo, diverting the División del Norte from its course toward Mexico City. Villa reluctantly obeyed the order and took Saltillo in May 1914, and then ignored an order to wait and marched south to take Zacatecas. From then on, Carranza and Villa were openly at odds, even though both were supposedly in alliance against Huerta. Carranza refused to even contact Zapata, calling him a "bandit."[44] Later in the "race" to the capital between Villa, Carranza and Obregón, Carranza cut off supplies of ammunition and coal for Villa's locomotives.

Despite their differences, the armies closing in on Mexico City did force Huerta into resigning and fleeing the country, leaving the way open for Obregón to triumphantly march into Mexico City in August 1914. At this time Obregón was sympathetic to Carranza and shared his animosities toward Villa. Once in the capital Obregón immediately moved to prevent Villa and Zapata from strengthening their positions. As had been previously arranged with Huerta's forces, positions facing Morelos were turned over to Obregón's men, thus preventing the Zapatistas from advancing into Mexico City. At this point Mexico was again rid of a reactionary dictatorship, but instead of being united, there were a variety of forces, ranging left to right politically from Zapata, to Villa, to Obregón, and to Carranza and his Army of the Northeast.[45]

With the Zapatistas bottled up in the south, and Villa stalled in the north, Carranza easily moved his armies south and took over the capital. At the same time the generally middle class leaders who had taken over state governments were carrying out reforms, giving an idea of what the future government would be like. Minimum wages were set and ranch-owned stores which had mercilessly exploited peasants were outlawed, but conspicuously absent was any ratification of the land seizures which had already taken place.[46]

In an attempt to assume undisputed control over the factions which had toppled Huerta, Carranza called for a political convention at Aguascalientes, mid-way between Mexico City and Villa's Chihuahua bastion. The convention opened with representatives from the armies of Obregón, Villa and Carranza declaring the convention to be sovereign and beholden to none of the generals whose armies had sent representatives. The convention then extended an invitation to the Zapatistas who arrived, not in limousines as the Carrancistas did, but bumming rides and sleeping where they could find shelter.

However the Zapatistas did bring what the convention was looking for, a political plan. Their Plan de Ayala, as weak as it was, was at least a plan and the convention soon accepted the provision for taking one third of each hacienda for the peasants. Eulalio Gutiérrez was chosen as president and both Villa and Carranza were asked to resign, in hopes of avoiding a clash between the two generals. During the convention the most revolutionary, popular and democratic debates of Mexican history took place.[47]

Seeing the convention turn to a position much closer to the peasants' than his own, Carranza withdrew and said he wouldn't resign while Villa was still commanding the División del Norte. Given Carranza's refusal to resign, Villa was named to command the convention army, which was really little more than the División del Norte, and was ordered to deal with Carranza, for whom the convention had little sympathy. To avoid Villa's forces Carranza withdrew from Mexico City and headed toward Veracruz, leaving a political vacuum. Despite having driven the oligarchy from power, the peasant leaders failed to take power for themselves. They just bided their time and finally turned power over to the middle class leaders of the convention.[48]

Following Carranza's withdrawal, Mexico City was occupied by the peasant armies of Villa and Zapata, in the legal role of representatives of the convention government. In many ways the occupying armies repeated the mistakes of Madero; they had eliminated the political power of the old rural hacendado, but did not dismantle the administrative apparatus inherited from the Porfiriato nor deal with urban business interests.[49] To make matters worse, when the convention government assumed control of the capital they found themselves without the slightest idea of what to do in terms of national policy, or how to deal with the problems of industry and city dwellers. They were peasants already longing for their own regions.

Zapata and Villa held a meeting at Xochimilco on the outskirts of Mexico City and could only agree to leave the convention in power. The result of the meeting was that Villa and Zapata agreed to abandon the center of the country and each return to his own region, whose limited horizons they had never been able to overcome. Thus Villa said, "This ranch is too big for us, it's better back home ... ." What they did do was establish a new government, without program, to oppose Carranza.[50]

Villa's and Zapata's decision not to advance on Carranza at this point is crucial to the history of the revolution. Instead of forming a unified command and attacking the Constitutionalists isolated in Veracruz, they decided to withdraw their armies to their own turf and carry on the struggle from there. Villa withdrew to the north and took Saltillo and Monterrey from the Constitutionalists. Villa was still interested in controlling land, especially land in northern Mexico, without regard for political priorities.

At this stage the urban masses, especially those in Mexico City, were still largely uninvolved in the revolution. Their experience with the revolution had been to witness the indecision of the convention government in Mexico City. They saw the conventionists carry the tactics of guerrilla warfare to national government. For example when the Villista General Urbina needed finances, he began kidnapping the rich and holding them for ransom, rather than simply expropriating or taxing them.[51] Similarly Villa dealt with his political critics by having them assassinated.[52]

Meanwhile Carranza, and Obregón who had followed him, were on the Gulf Coast without a political base, but with a world view which was both national and international in scope. During the respite provided by the failure of the convention army to pursue them, Carranza began to reorganize and take advantage of income from Yucatán henequen and Gulf Coast oil sales, revenue sources which would not run short as did the cattle Villa sold to the US. Carranza's first big move was a political one. In a complete reversal of his non-ideological stand taken for the anti-Huerta campaign, Carranza announced his own agrarian reform. The insincerity of this move was shown by his having recently ordered his generals to return lands they had distributed on their own, and by his subsequent lack of interest in implementing agrarian reform once he was president. In addition to its being political demagoguery, Carranza's agrarian reform differed from Zapata's Plan de Ayala in that it called for the reform to be implemented by military authorities, not the people themselves, a difference which proved to be fundamental.

This was the start of the trend toward populist government* and the announcing of policy in order to get mass support rather than to carry out the policy. In conjunction with the Constitutionalists' populist offensive, a military offensive began with Obregón moving west and capturing Puebla and Mexico City, left practically defenseless by Villa's withdrawal to the north.

In February 1915, shortly after Mexico City was retaken, Carranza made still another step toward attaining exclusive power by signing an alliance with the Casa del Obrero Mundial, the only significant workers' organization in Mexico. This was in sharp contrast to the attitude

*Populism has been defined as the mobilization and manipulation of the "available" masses so that one faction of the ruling class can use them to challenge another.[54]

of Villa and Zapata, who had shown no interest in the Casa while they were in Mexico City — after all, Casa members weren't peasants. The pact which Carranza signed with the Casa provided for the Casa to fight with Carranza, in exchange for which Carranza would guarantee basic reforms for the working class, such as food, money, equipment, meeting halls, printing presses and freedom to act.[53] Obregón also upstaged Villa and Zapata by passing out food to the urban poor, a problem which Villa and Zapata had ignored.

With this alliance consummated, Obregón set out to do battle with Villa, abandoning Mexico City once again to the Zapatistas. By this time Carranza had established an appreciable following. In addition to his formal alliance with the organized working class, he was supported by some members of the middle class who had felt stymied during the Porfiriato and who saw Carranza as the one who would promote economic development. Similarly the urban propertied classes, having no other alternative, lent support to the Constitutionalists. Also Carranza drew peasant support in many areas where Villa and Zapata were seen as removed from local affairs and lacking an agrarian reform such as Carranza's, the "legality" of which was constantly emphasized. ("Legality" meaning it was written on a piece of paper, not implemented by peasants themselves.)

With this backing Obregón marched north and met Villa at Celaya in the decisive battle of the revolution in

Emilio Zapata and Pancho Villa

Villa's troops, 1914

April 1915. Initially Villa suffered severe losses when he attacked Obregón's army in trenches defended by the then-novel machine gun. Later Obregón routed Villa with a surprise counter-charge and returned his army to the trenches. Villa once again employed the one tactic which had served him so well in the past, the cavalry charge. After inflicting further losses on Villa, Obregón again counter-attacked and routed the Villistas. In the lull between the two encounters, Obregón, in keeping with his populist style, announced a minimum wage program, a provision which has not been enforced to this day. Total casualties from the Battle of Celaya have been estimated at 10,000 of the 40,000 involved.

From this point on Villa's army began a sharp decline. Against the advice of many of his military advisors, Villa didn't concentrate all his forces for a final effort to stop Obregón, fearing Constitutionalists would take reprisals against his peasant followers in surrounding areas if his forces were withdrawn.[55] There followed a series of battles in which Obregón would dig in and then let Villa attack. Despite Villa's failure to concentrate his forces, he was near victory since Obregón became overextended, low on ammunition and supplies, and cut off from his rail link to Mexico City. At Aguascalientes for once Villa dug in and waited for Obregón's attack. However Obregón attacked from Villa's rear, forcing the Villistas out of their trenches, and eventually capturing Aguascalientes along with four million badly needed cartridges. This was the end of the División del Norte as a fighting force; its remnants straggled back to Chihuahua and dispersed. With Villa's army out of the picture, Obregón turned to occupying territory and by October 1915 he controlled most of northern Mexico.

After Villa's defeat Mexico City was permanently occupied by the Constitutionalists, who then turned toward Morelos, where events had gone on almost unaffected by the Carranza-Obregón-Villa struggle. After Madero was overthrown by Huerta the faltering Zapatistas had reunited and fought the dictator's forces. Huerta responded by continuing the suppression of Morelos and by creating "free fire zones" and removing "recruits" for his army by the box-car load, a practice which "resembled ... the calculated genocide that the government had practiced in racial wars against rebellious Indians in Sonora and Yucatán."[56]

After Huerta's fall the Zapatistas had linked up with the Villistas in the Aguascalientes Convention. Subsequently however they were driven back to the south as Obregón passed through Mexico City in pursuit of Villa, whom he judged to be the greater of his enemies. After Obregón marched off to the battle of Celaya, the Zapatistas reoccupied Mexico City. They

filtered quietly, almost embarrassedly, into the capital. Uncertain of their role there, they did not sack or plunder but like lost children wandered through the streets knocking on doors and asking for food. One night they heard a great clanging and clattering in the street — a fire engine and its crew. To them the strange apparatus looked like enemy artillery, and they shot at it, killing twelve firemen.[57]

While the Constitutionalists were fighting the Villistas, the Zapatistas turned inward and began to create the society they had long envisioned. Reforms went far beyond the Plan de Ayala and entire haciendas were expropriated without compensation. Officially the convention government still ruled in Morelos. However after Eulalio Gutiérrez became isolated from the peasant masses and defected to Carranza, with whom he had more in common politically, the convention for all practical purposes ceased to function in Morelos — the Zapatistas were in command. As soon as the remnants of the old governments upheld by Díaz, Madero and Huerta were out of the way, each village in Morelos began to carry out land reform on its own. An agronomist who went to help the Zapatistas describes how it was carried out:

> *We got to the place where the representatives of the two towns had been called together. Zapata called the elders to his side and listened to don Pedro Valero respectfully, in deference to his age and his past record defending the lands of Yautepec against the hacienda of Atlihuayán.. Later he turned to me and an engineer named Rubio and said, "The townspeople say this stone fence is the boundary, and the boundary will follow it. I know you engineers like straight lines, but the dividing line will follow the fence, even if it takes six months to measure all the zigzags."*[58]

By March 1915 Zapata could report, "The land reform question has been definitively resolved, since the towns in the state, in accord with their property titles, have taken possession of those lands."[59] The provision in the Plan de Ayala leaving two-thirds of each hacienda to the hacendado was ignored. While Mexico City was on the verge of starvation, people in Morelos were evidently eating more food than in 1910— and paying less for it.[60]

The situation in Morelos, not prior ideological positions, led to a form of home-made socialism. Much of the main industry, alcohol and sugar milling, had been abandoned by terrified hacendados. To the extent that resources permitted, these industries were put into operation by Zapatistas with the profits going to pay the army and support war widows. The Zapatistas left most of the sugar mills in private hands however, since they lacked the capital to reopen and operate them all.[61]

Peace in Morelos was only an illusion, reflecting the isolation of Morelos from the rest of the national scene. Even when news came of Villa's defeat at Celaya, no attempt was made to form a common front, when such an alliance was still feasible. The Zapatistas merely continued to attack the hacendado, and stated they welcomed "with pleasure the manufacturer, the merchant, the mine-owner, the businessman, all the active and enterprising elements which open new paths for industry and provide work to great groups of workers ... ."[62] The Zapatistas didn't realize that Carranza was no front for the old landed families, but rather for the clever, ruthless young army commanders from the north. Danger for Morelos lay in these agents of alien progress, not in reactionary hacendados.[63]

By 1916 the contrast between Morelos and the rest of Mexico was too glaring for the Constitutionalists to ignore. With Villa defeated and his forces scattered, Carranza turned his armies on Morelos, with the support of the Casa del Obrero Mundial, the United States, industrialists, the middle class, and the old Morelos hacendados who wanted their land back.[64] In April 1916 the Constitutionalist advance began. The advancing army appeared to differ little from Díaz's army of the previous decade. Its troops came not to liberate, but to conquer the local population, which at best was treated as prisoners of war.[65] By July 1916 all towns in Morelos were occupied and the commander of the Constitutionalists reported the campaign concluded. Once they had assumed control, the Constitutionalist officers began to systematically loot Morelos. Everything they could possibly move was taken to be sold in the black market in Mexico City.[66]

The agrarian reform was annulled, and due to their unpreparedness, the Zapatistas could offer little resistance during the first half of 1916. However by the latter half of the year they had regrouped and could once again effectively wage guerrilla warfare. The Zapatistas fought with the aid of the entire population, which served as observers, informers, suppliers of food and protection, as well as combatants who would take up arms for a battle and then return to their farms. By September 1916, except for towns and main communication lines, the whole state was again under Zapata's control.[67]

The government's response to this resistance was mass assassination. Guerrillas in turn stepped up attacks on railroads, sugar mills, factories and the southern limits of Mexico City itself. By December the 30,000 man Constitutionalist army which had occupied Morelos in May was demoralized and disintegrating.[68] At the end of 1916 the Zapatistas had not only regained control of the state and forced Carranza's armies to evacuate, but had progressed politically. A decree had been issued calling for the confiscation of both rural and urban properties of enemies of the revolution. Its practical effect was the expropriation without compensation of all the property of landowners and businessmen.[69] Also in the latter part of 1916 Zapata called for the organization of a political party to provide structure for his movement.[70] Local officials were elected at public meetings and schools were set up. It was an invaluable experience for country people to hear the teacher say that the Zapatistas were national heroes and that resistance was on behalf of their homeland and the poor.[71] Despite having created popular government and ridded itself of Constitutionalist troops, Morelos found itself isolated and devastated. Furthermore the enemy of the Zapatistas had merely been driven out of Morelos, it had not been defeated.

....

Once Villa had been defeated and Zapata contained in Morelos, the Constitutionalists felt strong enough to betray their recently acquired allies of the Casa del Obrero Mundial, which was the first group to feel the effect of the Constitutionalists dealing from a position of strength, not weakness. By early 1916 the Red Battalions, as the Casa units were called, had been disbanded, and the workers had been unceremoniously evicted from the elegant quarters they had been given in the Jockey Club (today the downtown Sanborn's in Mexico City). Similarly workers' reforms promised the previous year in exchange for the Casa's allegiance were abandoned.

By June 1916 the plight of Mexico City's workers had become desperate due to their being paid in near worthless paper money. At one time 90,000 workers went out on strike. This strike was settled by a small wage increase, but soon other wildcat strikes began, such as one by trolley car operators. This time Carranza arrested a delegation sent to bargain with him, had the army attack a workers' assembly, and decreed the death penalty for striking workers, those supporting the strike, and those attending strike meetings.

Carranza was now free of major opponents and without political commitments. Thus he could begin to fulfill *his* dream of creating a state uncommitted to any sector of the society.[72] Carranza managed to consolidate effective political control, something which had eluded Madero. He differed from Madero in that he felt that the society would never progress unless it overcame its backwardness. This was a major step beyond Madero's mere calls for suffrage and "No re-election."* In order to overcome backwardness Carranza sought to eliminate those opposing change, and then educate the population. Despite his being ambitious, there is no doubt that he sincerely felt his government would lead to progress for Mexico and a better life for its people.[73]

The year 1916 saw the end of major combat and the implementation of a coherent national policy by the triumphant Constitutionalists. Only Morelos remained outside their control. Carranza called for the holding of a constitutional convention to provide the legal basis for his government, and presidential elections to make his power "legitimate." The convention met and promulgated a new constitution on February 5, 1917, and in March 1917 elections were held to select Carranza as president.

Before examining the Constitutional Convention and the resulting constitution, it is worth considering why the armed stage of the revolution concluded as it did. The Constitutionalists benefited from planning on a national level and using populist tactics to broaden their support. Their most powerful weapon was their understanding of social problems, an understanding which they used to attract the masses.[74]

There were many opposing the Constitutionalists who were willing to die for a better Mexico, but these opponents lacked leadership, ideology and the sophistication to play national and international politics. Urban workers were few in number, unpoliticized,[75] and were led by opportunists. The early events of the revolution caught these workers by surprise and until 1915 they were largely spectators. Then in 1916 they decided to cast their lot with the most powerful leader, Carranza.[76]

Neither Villa's nor Zapata's hate of the hacienda was transformed into a coherent program against capitalism. They were anti-hacienda, not anti-capitalist. Their localism prevented them from forming a united front to combat Carranza. They never sought to obtain political power, and even when it was in reach, they did not take it.[77]

The Zapatistas failed to achieve victory largely because they were unable to attract support from non-peasants or even unify the peasantry on a national basis.[78] Peasants tended to be extremely naive politically; the American correspondent John Reed notes that a peasant he was talking to after Madero's assassination stated that he was fighting to put him back in office.[79] Often peasants had

---

*"No re-election" was the slogan anti-Díaz forces used to oppose his re-election. Ironically Díaz used this same slogan when he took power in 1872.

more allegiance to a local general, fighting for his own interests, than to their logical allies, Villa and Zapata, fighting in some distant state. Despite their willingness to fight, there was often a lack of clarity concerning just what they were fighting for, as this incident from the biography of a Chiapas Indian illustrates:

> We returned to Pachuca again and went to another village, where the Villistas attacked us. They asked us why we'd become Carrancistas, and I said: "The Huertistas made us go with them, and when Carranza started winning we had to change sides..." An old man with a big moustache said, "Well, what do you want to do now?" I said, "I just want to be on your side..." They signed us up and gave us weapons and five pesos each, and that made us Villistas.[80]

The essential difference between the Mexican Revolution and those in Russia, China and Cuba, which were to produce rapid re-distribution of wealth, was that the Mexican revolutionaries accepted the continued existence of private property. The major groups, with the partial exception of the Zapatistas after Villa's defeat at Celaya, were only dealing with the question of who should control private property.

The one revolutionary who attacked the institution of private property was Ricardo Flores Magón. He began his political career with the anti-Díaz movement and then became an anarchist and was forced to flee to the US. In the Mexican Revolution Flores Magón best represented the interests of the masses in that he was the only one to coherently propose a classless society. His political isolation from the masses, both locally and nationally, prevented him from influencing the course of the revolution.[81] In 1911 Flores Magón commented on the upcoming struggle saying that if the radical content was taken out of the revolution in order to achieve an easy victory, it would only postpone the real revolution for social justice.[82]

Instead of heeding the words of Florés Magón, workers and peasants, exposed to the grandiloquence of the Constitutionalists, thought they had found in the state a protector against the ravages of the hacendado and the industrialist. They were told, and are still told, that the Revolution was made for workers and peasants.[83] The million plus dead of the revolution was a high price to pay for these empty promises.

AULTMAN COLLECTION

Venustiano Carranza

CHAPTER 7: INSTITUTIONALIZATION

... there finally emerged, in 1917, the first clearly recognizable results of the Mexican Revolution. Those results were: a defeated peasantry, a crippled and dependent labor movement, a wounded but victorious bourgeoisie, and, for a divided Mexican people, a paper triumph—the 1917 constitution.[1]

No revolution has ever succeeded in putting the ideals which inspired it into effect after its triumph by trusting the government to do what the people should have done during the Revolution.
—Ricardo Flores Magón[2]

As soon as he had defeated Villa's peasant armies, Venustiano Carranza, hacendado and former Porfirian senator, began the long process of institutionalizing a government which would permit modern capitalist development in Mexico. First he undertook to legitimize his government by calling an election and writing a new constitution; then he proceeded to eliminate the remaining peasant resistance in Morelos. For the next thirty years Carranza and his successors continued to create the institutions necessary to maintain political control and promote economic development. The weakness of Mexican capitalism and the degree to which the state was destroyed in 1914 is indicated by the 25-year period (1915-1940) it took to restore the state.[3]

The first step in this process of institutionalization was the writing of a new constitution which would give the Carranza government added legitimacy and undermine resistance, especially of the Zapatistas. Thus a constitutional convention was convened. Only those persons identified as Carranza supporters were permitted to be delegates. No one represented Morelos and the areas which had been controlled by Villa. The result was a convention which was composed mostly of middle class professionals[4] in a country which was overwhelmingly illiterate and impoverished. However even this hand-picked group proved difficult for Carranza to handle. Despite Carranza's wanting only a rewriting of the 1857 Constitution, the spirit of reform in the group resulted in the production of a very different document. Despite Carranza's objections, a variety of progressive measures were included in the new constitution.

Article 27 made the control of land use a government power to be used for "public utility", thus providing the legal basis for Mexico's far-reaching agrarian reform. This article also gave the government power to control mining and petroleum exploration. Article 28 gave the government power to control monopolies and Article 123 contained a rich lode of labor rights. Included were minimum wages, the right to unionize and strike, maximum hours, and equal pay by sex and nationality to prevent American firms from underpaying Mexicans. Finally the new constitution provided for a strong executive, since it was felt that Díaz's extra-legal dictatorship resulted from the 1857 Constitution's having created a presidency too weak to function legally. In the future control would be no more democratic, but at least it would be legal.

In March 1917 elections were held to make Carranza's presidency legitimate. Less than 18% of the qualified voters turned out to elect him president.[5]

Once the constitutional convention and elections were over, the modern Mexican government began to emerge. The articles on regulating monopoly, land use, and labor made the government much stronger than it had ever been before and gave it a key role in shaping economic policy. Laissez-faire economics, even as official doctrine, had been replaced by a state which was to become the real motor of social development. All the elements of society, willingly or unwillingly, would have to submit to it.[6]

The government soon began utilizing reform as a political tactic. Carranza, who had originally opposed the inclusion of reforms in the new constitution, when confronted with them in the finished document, largely chose to ignore them. When he did carry out reforms, it was only when it suited his political purposes. In the future one of the main ways of quieting dissidents would be to make just enough concessions to pacify them, but not enough to alter the balance of power.

The immediate result of the new constitution was a government promoting class harmony and capitalist development.[7] This government abolished the old regime of private privilege, but in no way questioned the institution of private property. Even the veneer of established government was a thin one, since there were still no political parties and peaceful means for transfer of power would not exist for another twenty years. Finally the military caudillos adopted a political style which would last through the 1930's. They would manipulate the masses, without ever committing themselves to change. The hopes of the poor were constantly being raised, only to fall again with the political defeat of the caudillo who had raised them.

Having consolidated and legitimized his government, Carranza turned to eliminating the one remaining challenge to his power: Zapatismo. While the electoral and constitutional processes were going on, the Zapatistas were surrounded militarily, without any real political program, and under constant pressure from the outside:

The federal government, whether under Madero or Huerta or Carranza, was equally bitter against Zapata, and spread ruin among his followers. It became a war of extermination. The federal army, realizing that it was fighting a whole population, began to destroy that population. Villages were systematically burned. Fruit trees and crops were uprooted, women and children were concentrated in camps; it was war without quarter. In those nine years it is estimated that one third of the population of the state of Morelos was destroyed.[8]

By 1919 Zapata's dream had vanished. All the cities and haciendas had been reoccupied by the Carrancistas and the lands returned to the old Porfirian landowners. The remaining Zapatistas were forced into the mountains. In addition the Zapatistas no longer articulated a clear position; some made overtures to Carranza while Zapata spoke highly of the Russian revolution. However Zapata did present a clear picture of the government which had emerged from the revolution. In an open letter addressed to Carranza in March 1919 he stated:

> *Since you first had the idea of rebelling, ... since you first conceived the project of making yourself Chief and director of the misnamed "constitutionalist" cause, you... have tried to convert the revolution into a movement for your own gain and that of your little group of friends... who helped you to get on top and are now helping you to enjoy the spoils of war: riches, honors, business, banquets, luxurious fiestas, Bacchanalian pleasures, orgies of satiation, of ambition, of power and of blood.*
>
> *It has never crossed your mind that the Revolution was for the benefit of the masses, for that great legion of the oppressed which you aroused with your preachings... .*
>
> *In the agrarian reform [you have betrayed your trust]; haciendas have been given or rented to [your] favorite generals; the old landlords have been replaced in not a few cases by modern landholders dressed in **charro** costumes, military hats, and with pistols in their belts; the people have been mocked in their hopes.*[9]

Less than a month after writing this letter Zapata, desperate for supplies and men, contacted Jesús Guajardo, a Carrancista colonel whom Zapata had heard was at odds with his commander. Zapata suggested Guajardo defect and Guajardo pretended he was deserting along with badly needed men and supplies. Guajardo met with Zapata and to complete the picture he even had a Zapatista deserter shot for having deserted Guajardo's new "commander." After meeting with Zapata, Guajardo invited him to the hacienda of Chinameca in Morelos. Upon entering the hacienda on April 10, 1919, Zapata was cut down by gunfire in an ambush which Guajardo had laid for him. For his part in the ambush Guajardo was given 50,000 pesos in gold and a generalship. Once Zapata was dead the Zapatista movement ceased to be a major political force, although remnants of it existed in the hills until 1920 when the political climate became less harsh.

Once he had dealt with the Zapatistas, Carranza began to perfect instruments of political control which are similar to those still used. Carranza had a national labor organization created in 1918 to establish control over the increasingly active trade union movement. The new organization, called the Regional Confederation of Mexican Workers (CROM), was led by Luis Morones, who would become exceedingly wealthy through his position. Once this organization was established it was brought under increasing government control and used as a way for government to regulate activity within the labor sector. Independent labor action, within or without the CROM, was violently suppressed.

As has been the case ever since, organized peasants and organized labor were kept separated so that they could never form a united front and challenge the government. This separation was carefully cultivated by creating bureaucracies whose power would be threatened if "rival reformers" appeared. In his biography the peasant Pedro Martínez tells how members of the agrarian movement who came to his town were assassinated by officials of the CROM[10] who feared the undercutting of their power.

Not only were peasants kept separated from workers, but they were neglected during Carranza's presidency in terms of the major demand of the revolution: land reform. Only 0.1% of the land area of Mexico was distributed during the Carranza administration,[11] and much of that went to Carranza's cronies. The only solace was that these meager benefits were greater than the working class received.[12]

As Carranza began to abandon reform, he increasingly sought alliances with the old Porfirian landowners. The crucial flaw in this strategy was that, though their economic power was largely intact, the revolution had stripped landowners of political power. Political power had shifted to the recently-formed revolutionary army. Progressive elements were purged from the government and replaced by unprincipled politicians and militarists.[13] Carranza's appointees began a trend toward personal enrichment through public office on a scale previously unmatched. This enrichment served not only to satisfy the desires of those holding power, but to buy off challengers. The tone of the government changed so radically that by 1920 it was difficult to see any relation between the government's actions and the 1917 Constitution.[14] Except for Carranza's attempts to keep Mexico relatively free from US economic domination (something few of his successors have done), there is little of a progressive nature which can be found in his administration. After 18 years as a Porfirian senator, Carranza was unable to adapt to the new reality of Mexico.[15]

However if Carranza failed to understand and use social reform to consolidate power, there was someone who was a master at it: Carranza's old comrade in arms, Alvaro Obregón.[16] From his "retirement" in Sonora Obregón had kept in touch politically and had associated himself with reformist tendencies. By 1920 Obregón had allied himself with middle class military men who were dissatisfied with the course of the Revolution. His new allies resented the unfulfilled promises of the revolution and increasing power of hacendados. The enrichment of Carranza officials, repression of the masses and the assassination of Zapata only served to increase their dissatisfaction.[17]

The loose coalition around Obregón provided the basis for Mexico's last successful coup. In 1920 Carranza named as his hand-picked successor to the presidency a civilian candidate whom he thought he could control. He knew he couldn't control the other outstanding general of the revolution, Obregón. Carranza then summoned Obregón to Mexico City. Obregón, fearing betrayal, fled to Guerrero where he made an alliance with remnants of the Zapatista movement. From there he initiated his coup

Pancho Villa and wife, Luz Corral

against Carranza. Obregón had the backing of reform-seeking military men, peasants and workers, and thus Carranza fled the capital. He took the traditional path of Mexico's fallen leaders, down from the highlands to Veracruz to leave by sea with the traditional share of the national treasury. Carranza's career came to a halt when he was assassinated before reaching the coast.

Following Carranza's death a provisional president was installed and elections were held to choose Obregón as president. Once in office Obregón replaced Carranza's conservative allies with middle class reformers. Another result of the coup was Obregón's making peace with the remaining Zapatistas. A former Zapatista general was made military commander of Morelos, land reform was implemented (though only in Morelos) and another Zapatista was appointed as state governor.

What happened in Morelos though was not characteristic of what went on elsewhere. Obregón's government, as Carranza's had been, was based on the revolutionary army, not democratic institutions, and still had no institutionalized means of presidential succession. In this context reform was used as a method of political control, a tactic at which Obregón was a master. He didn't need to contain the masses through repression as Huerta attempted. Obregón formed a strong state independent of the need to rely on the support of any one sector. Porfirian hacendados were played off against peasants, workers and the still-weak industrialists, all of whom were overshadowed by foreign interests and the state. Again the real popular demand of the revolution, agrarian reform, was virtually ignored. Only 0.6% of the land area was distributed during the Obregón adminstration,[18] and as late as 1925 some 32 million hectares of land were foreign-owned.[19]

This failure to produce reform resulted in continued unrest. Military caudillos who challenged Obregón were executed by firing squad. Progressives not purged by Carranza were often dealt with by land owners. Carrillo Puerto, governor of Yucatán, who instituted land reform on his own was assassinated by land owners in 1924.[20] Agrarian leaders who formed peasant leagues to push for their rights under the agrarian reform laws were assassinated by the government[21] and referred to as "bandidos." Locally-based generals cooperated with landlords and state governors to run off those few who had received land in the agrarian reform.[22]

Meanwhile labor was asked to sacrifice and suffer deprivation (while generals and hacendados prospered) in order to free enough resources for economic development. The co-opted labor bureaucracy kept workers in line, and the official national labor organization, the CROM, became an appendage of the government.

Despite the widespread assassination of Obregón's rivals,[23] there was significant political activity at the local and regional level. The Socialist Party of Yucatán was founded in 1918, to be followed by the Socialist Party of the State of Mexico, the Socialist Workers Party of Veracruz, the Socialist Party of Michoacán and the Border Socialist Party in the north.[24] These socialist parties and other less progressive ones began to nominate and elect officials independently of the national caudillo.

In 1920 Villa, who was still undefeated although without real military power, decided to surrender. At this time he commented on Obregón saying, "I think that the Obregonistas have definitely broken with the Carrancistas, but I'm not sure they're any more in favor of the people's real interests."[25] Despite such comments, Villa was given a hacienda and the right to maintain a fifty-man escort at government expense. However in 1923, after boasting of his ability to muster a large force in support of the impending anti-Obregón uprising, Villa was assassinated, presumably on orders from Obregón.[26]

While Obregón suppressed all political and military challengers, he did open up mobility for the middle class. Members of the middle class enriched themselves quite rapidly, taking advantage of the power the government gave them. During the twenties they became virtually indistinguishable from those whom they had fought in the revolution. Often their wealth was based on public works contracts or simply on the pillaging of the public treasury.[27]

Progressive accomplishments by Obregón were few. Most notable was his emphasis on education under the guidance of the nationalist philosopher José Vasconcelos. Other than that, Obregón's main feat was re-establishing domestic order, thus permitting the economy to function smoothly after so many years of disruptions. Obregón also recognized the Soviet Union in 1924, the first Latin American government to do so. Ever since Mexico has maintained a progressive foreign policy to enhance its political image.

Other than that, little changed. The old property structure inherited from the Porfiriato was still virtually intact at the end of Obregón's term in 1924 and industrial production, though functioning smoothly again, was only slightly above the level of the late Porfiriato.[28] Since production did not increase, sacrifices had to be made by workers and peasants to permit the amassing of new fortunes and the respecting of old ones. In 1924 most Mexicans ate less, had fewer jobs and schools, and no greater political rights than they did before the revolution.[29]

However one can hardly call Obregón a failure since "the revolutionaries took power with the specific aim of abolishing the system of privilege which prevented the development of free enterprise and competition, but not to abolish private property."[30] Thus, although the Obregonistas took power under the mantle of reform, the reforms they dedicated themselves to were the destruction of Porfirian privilege and the opening of opportunity for themselves. These reforms were not addressed to the masses. In any case Obregón was the first Mexican president in generations to complete his term peacefully and leave office. His departure from the presidency began another Mexican political tradition, the outgoing administration's selecting its successor without popular control or even popular involvement.

The person to whom Obregón left power was Plutarco Calles, a school teacher turned revolutionary general. At the time Calles's nomination was announced the last significant coup attempt occurred, led by those who had hoped to gain power and had seen their hopes dashed by Obregón's announcement of the new president. Despite widespread military backing for the coup, Obregón's alliances with peasants and workers, a product of his populist style, served him well, and he was able to stay in office until his nomination of Calles was ratified by an "election."

Calles opened the door to US investment and created the concept of the "revolutionary capitalist," one who invests money productively rather than squandering it on lavish living. Meanwhile it was apparent to all that corruption was rampant and that many were becoming rich through the revolution. These new interests which emerged from the revolution formed a political group of which Calles was the arbiter for many years.[31]

In an effort to divert attention from the revolution's lack of progress, as well as to confront the reactionary challenge posed by the church, Calles began to enforce the religious provisions of the 1917 Constitution. The application of these previously unenforced articles weakened the base of the conservative church and divided Calles's opposition.[32] His attacks included limiting the number of priests and prohibiting foreign priests, and led to a nation-wide strike by priests which closed all the Catholic churches.

One result of this attack on the church was the Cristero Rebellion in the area west of Mexico City, which was encouraged and often led by priests. Most of the rebels were illiterate, conservative peasants reacting to the modernization being thrust on them by government leaders from the north. The Cristero movement, which resulted in some 70,000 deaths,[33] produced little change. Good relations with the church were only re-established when Lázaro Cárdenas took power in 1934 and wanted peasants and workers united so they could be mobilized as a class undivided by religious issues.

What the Calles government did do was to establish the principle that government was to be the supreme arbiter of political matters, dominating interest groups such as workers, industrialists, hacendados and peasants.[34] It also emphasized that the rich were necessary to develop the country economically. One institution which Calles didn't directly co-opt was the Socialist Party of Yucatán, which had become the most politically advanced of the independent parties. It would have joined the Third International* if its party convention hadn't been packed by

*In 1919 the Third, or Communist, International was founded in Moscow to coordinate revolutionary parties throughout the world.

Calles with CROM flunkies.[35]

Given the increasingly conservative nature of the Calles government, Obregón decided to make a comeback and challenge Calles's hand-picked candidate for the presidency. With a broad coalition ranging from campesinos to Mexican businessmen who resented Calles's favoring US investment, Obregón defeated Calles's candidate for president. This was the last successful challenge to the incumbent regime's designation of its presidential successor.

During the presidential campaign, CROM and its boss Morones launched a virulent anti-Obregón campaign. The labor federation saw Obregón as a challenge to its entrenched bureaucracy. In this atmosphere just after the election by 1928, president-elect Obregón was assassinated by a person generally described as a "Catholic fanatic." Calles, fearing confrontation with Obregonistas and blamed by many for having created the hate-Obregón climate which had resulted in his death, decided it would be best to resign. He did so but did not abandon power.

Calles continued to govern as the power behind the throne, making and breaking presidents. First Calles put in Portes Gil to finish his term. Then Ortiz Rubio was put into office for the term beginning in 1930. Calles later ousted his own choice as president when he disagreed with Calles on policy and choice of cabinet members. To finish the term ending in 1934 Calles selected Abelardo Rodríguez, "a typical, 'revolutionary' millionaire general."[36]

Shortly after his resignation from the presidency Calles created a national political party. This party largely completed the mechanism of political control begun with the 1917 Constitution. The party, initially called the National Revolutionary Party (PNR), cut out the sometimes radical independent parties such as the Socialist Party of Yucatán, and provided a way to mediate between various ambitious caudillos, each striving for national power. By eliminating such power clashes the new party not only prevented bloodshed between rivals, but prevented caudillos from mobilizing mass backing in their attempts to seize power. Such attempts were seen as endangering the political structure which had emerged from the revolution.

Most of the revolutionary caudillos, now aging and quite wealthy, were more than ready to accept the mediation of the official party, since they had too much personal wealth to risk losing it in an unsuccessful coup attempt. The new party provided a forum for choosing presidential candidates without popular participation. This feature has continued up to the present.

Calles remained the central figure with final word on party matters. The agrarian reform, which had slowed to a trickle during Calles's term, was brought to a halt. Agricultural workers ate less in 1936 than in 1896 and the low wage paid them in 1910 would have looked mag-

Cristeros attack train

nificent in 1934.[37]

Given this situation it was hardly surprising that as the 1934 elections approached, the political situation in Mexico was threatening to get out of Calles's control. Strikes were increasing in number and foreign observers spoke of the likelihood of new peasant wars. In response to this situation a faction opposing Calles was formed inside the official party. Its members were of middle class origin, felt dispossessed, and were in disagreement with the ruling faction. Weak in itself, this faction had to find support in workers' and peasants' movements, meeting their needs and fanning their revolutionary aspirations.[38]

The leader of this faction was a general of humble origins named Lázaro Cárdenas. Despite having had little formal education, he rose fast in the revolution and became governor of his native state of Michoacán, where he carried out extensive land reform on his own initiative. At the national level he exhibited sobriety and a commitment to reform generally lacking in the Calles administration.

As the 1934 presidential elections approached, Cárdenas began to campaign for the PNR's presidential nomination. Widespread support was forthcoming, especially from within the PNR, and from the army, workers and peasants. Finally Calles was put into the position of being virtually forced to nominate Cárdenas, despite his personal preference for another more conservative candidate. To nominate his favorite would not only have alienated important sectors of the ruling coalition, but would have risked rebellion by peasants and workers whose salaries were decreasing. Calles felt he could control Cárdenas as president and that power would inevitably make him more conservative.

Cárdenas faced little opposition in the 1934 election, and once elected he made the customary courtesy call to Calles, the "Jefe Máximo," on Calles's hacienda in Sonora. When he arrived Calles was playing poker with some other generals. Upon hearing that the president of Mexico was waiting to see him, Calles replied to an aide, "Entertain him till I'm finished."[39]

This state of affairs didn't last long though. Cárdenas immediately began to build a broad coalition to challenge Calles's position. Cárdenas already had substantial support from peasants, largely due to his 13,000-mile campaign tour which served, not to get votes (his election was assured), but to build a power base. On this campaign he did the unheard of, traveling to remote villages and listening to people's complaints. This set the popular style which was to characterize Cárdenas's entire term. His rapport with the common citizen raised the presidency to a legitimacy it hadn't had previously.

Once he assumed office Cárdenas began to support strikers and replace conservative Calles supporters with more progressive cabinet ministers, congressmen and senators. There followed verbal exchanges between Calles and Cárdenas, with Calles attacking Cárdenas for his "radicalism" and Cárdenas replying by publicly denouncing Calles's cronies who had enriched themselves at public expense. When Calles saw that he could no longer control Cárdenas, he tried to mobilize the forces of reaction to topple him. Cárdenas, however, with the backing of the military, workers, peasants and some churchmen, turned the tables on Calles and packed him, Morones, and 19 others into a plane and sent them into exile in the United States.

Once having deposed Calles, Cárdenas began to use the party and peasants' and workers' organizations to centralize power on a scale previously unmatched. At the same time he began the most far-reaching reforms any government since the revolution has carried out. It is no accident that changes took place, not immediately after the revolution, but in the 1930's and 1940's when the depression and World War II had weakened economic ties with the US.[40]

These reforms, in contrast to the "revolutionary" rhetoric of previous regimes, had a significant effect throughout the country. Their basis was state intervention in labor, agrarian reform, and education. And not only did the state intervene in these areas, but it began a massive public works program and pushed industrialization, feeling that only an industrialized Mexico could be independent and initiate real social reform. The most far-reaching change and the one which Cárdenas is still associated with was the agrarian reform. Once he had dealt with Calles, Cárdenas began the rapid transfer of former hacienda land to the peasants. The 45-million-plus acres distributed were more than three times the amount the previous revolutionary presidents had distributed.

The hacendados' violent response to land distribution produced a veritable civil war. Landlords resisted the agrarian reform with their private armies.[41] In a three-month period in 1936 more than 500 were killed in land disputes; in the first years of Cárdenas's administration 2,000 were killed in Veracruz alone.[42] However rather than backing down to the show of force by landlords, Cárdenas armed some 60,000 peasants. The land reform was carried out, thus opening up the country for economic development by breaking up the inefficient haciendas, freeing capital and peasant labor for industry, providing markets among agricultural workers, and in addition, creating a power base loyal to Cárdenas.

To maintain control over the peasants, Cárdenas created the National Peasant Confederation (CNC). The formation of this group was one of the final steps in the institutionalizing of political power. Although Cárdenas used the CNC to further legitimate demands of peasants, subsequent presidents have used this run-from-the-top-down organization to dominate peasant movements and head off protest.

Cárdenas also launched far-reaching reform within the working class. Workers were not only allowed to unionize, but gains were made in wages and workers began to feel that the government genuinely supported their aspirations. Workers were organized in a new national organization to replace the old CROM, which had no loyalty to Cárdenas. The new group, the Mexican Workers Confederation (CTM), however was run from the top down just as the peasants' confederation was. These two groups were kept apart to prevent any combined action which might threaten the established powers. When business rebelled at Cárdenas's support of the workers, Cárdenas told them, "Either accept the reforms demanded by the workers, or surely violent revolution will explode."[43]

Still another reform of the Cárdenas administration was the nationalization of the oil industry, which was made possible by the relative weakness of the US at the time. Prior to Cárdenas's presidency oil production was overwhelmingly controlled by British and American investors who often made fabulous profits. One company, El Aguila, made 45% profits in 1919 and 60% in 1920.[44] Oil production in Mexico reached its high point in 1921 when Mexico was the world's third largest producer.[45] By the mid-1930's the focus of the oil industry in Latin America had shifted to Venezuela. However oil operations in Mexico were still highly profitable in the thirties, and thoroughly disliked. Gasoline refined from Mexican oil sold in Mexico at a price 193% higher than outside the country, and kerosene at 341%.[46] In addition the oil companies obtained their leases at ridiculously low prices, deceiving land owners, falsifying titles, assassinating the uncooperative, inventing fake wills, and the like.[47]

Even though Cárdenas hadn't planned in advance for a confrontation, the climate was generally ripe for one when oil workers asked for salary increases during the Cárdenas administration. When the workers' salary demand was turned down, the government appointed a commission to study the salary question. The commission found Mexican workers got one fourth the salary of US oil workers but had twelve times the productivity.* The companies claimed they couldn't afford to pay more. When the Mexican Supreme Court ordered the companies to accept binding arbitration, the companies refused. Cárdenas was forced into one of two choices, either admit Mexican sovereignty was a joke or nationalize the oil companies. He chose the latter course in March 1938 and in the process brought forth great mass support. Demonstrations throughout the country supported the nationalization. People contributed their personal wealth to help finance the cost of reimbursing oil companies. Oil workers volunteered for overtime, repaired sabotaged equipment and learned how to operate machinery abandoned by foreign technicians.

The response to the nationalization wasn't long in coming. Oil equipment was no longer sold to Mexico and oil companies which owned the vast majority of the world's tankers would no longer ship Mexican oil. The oil that did reach Europe was often confiscated as being stolen.

*The high productivity was due to the large, shallow fields in Mexico.

just as Chilean copper was to be seized some thirty years later. The United States even began to implement other economic sanctions, but found this hard since US businesses wouldn't maintain a united front. Companies such as those engaged in mining operations were loath to see their profits end. However it was the international situation which finally led the United States to recognize the nationalization of the oil. With the approach of World War II the US needed all the oil it could get and it didn't want disputes with its neighbors.

Cárdenas promoted national development and relative economic independence from the United States. This was achieved in part through a decline in foreign investment resulting from the depression and the fear of Cárdenas's nationalism. The oil nationalization added to Mexico's relative economic independence. Thus Cárdenas not only kept the United States at some distance, but created the social and economic conditions necessary to permit subsequent rapid industrialization.

Cárdenas wanted to provide opportunity for indigenous groups to prosper and rise to the top. Given the economic domination of the United States prior to Cárdenas, the persistence of local monopolies and the continued existence of the old Porfirian haciendas, there had been little room for upward mobility on the part of Cárdenas's middle class supporters. Cárdenas did not propose the abolition of capitalism, but wanted to promote it on a more "just" or "humane" basis, by eliminating the worst forms of exploitation and increasing the internal market.[48]

Cardenas's presidency was dominated by his philosophy which "saw capitalism as a transitionary stage toward a form of social organization in which the capitalists were simply one other force among many which would struggle in the field of political and economic conflict."[49] In keeping with this philosophy foreign investors were forced to obey government decisions and change the treatment they had imposed on Latin American governments.[50] What Cárdenas didn't see though was that his style of managing all reform from the top down would enable subsequent presidents to totally dominate the Mexican scene. This domination would permit them to block further reform and in large part nullify those reforms Cárdenas did make.

The legacy of Cárdenas is a mixed one. While he did provide real benefits to peasants and workers, his authoritarianism was hardly distinguishable from that of Carranza, Obregón, Calles, or even Díaz. Everything was done for the people, but nothing was done by them. Cárdenas himself was above rampant corruption, but his supporters were among the most corrupt in Mexican history.[51] Despite these flaws he had a touch with the common people that no president before or since has had. Once in a blinding rainstorm

> The President saw an Indian with a straw cloak walking barefoot along a road. He stopped the car, ordered his aide to call the sopping-wet Indian, who got in the car and soaked it, and then he took the Indian where he wanted to go. The surprised Indian didn't even know whose car it was.[52]

At the end of his term Cárdenas was faced with two choices: pick a candidate who would push for further reform, or stick with the existing situation. Given the increasing wealth of Cárdenas's backers, there was little possibility for further change without risking what they had already gained. Even if Cárdenas and his backers had desired more reform, they had little maneuvering room since the right wing was launching a strong electoral challenge and was threatening revolt. In addition the international scene was most discouraging, with Republican Spain defeated, fascism spreading, and World War II on the horizon.

Cárdenas chose as his successor one of his officials, Avila Camacho, a middle-of-the-roader who stood for nothing more than maintaining intact the reforms which Cárdenas had instituted. The other possible candidate was Francisco Mújica, a dedicated reformer who had relatively little support. Mújica was opposed by organized labor bureaucrats who were afraid of losing their positions and by professional politicians who "mistrusted him, more for his sharp character and his reputation for honesty than for his ideological radicalism."[53] After seeing that he had little support Mújica quit seeking the nomination.

Even with his choice of the middle-of-the-road candidate Avila Camacho, the Cárdenas administration still faced a stiff electoral fight against the conservatives whose candidate had widespread backing of anti-reform interests. In order to get Cárdenas's man elected, the government used pistol-toting goons and broke up opposition rallies with clubs. Cárdenas's candidate did win the election, although it's hard to say by what margin since the government counted the votes and Cárdenas had decided before hand to rig the election[54] rather than risk seeing his reforms swept away by a loss to the right-wing candidate.

After the 1940 elections, although Cárdenas remained a public figure, he in no way attempted to maintain political power. This leaving of both the presidency and power completed the institutionalizing of the revolution.

Once Cárdenas was out of office his reforms, except for the oil nationalization, began to slip by the wayside. Cooperation with the US often proved to be more profitable than economic nationalism, and the increasingly wealthy strata holding high government office no longer held the same reformist ideas on workers' and peasants' demands. The 1940-46 government, opposed workers' movements, stimulated private investment, encouraged foreign capital to come in, and tried to improve relations with the US. In addition Avila Camacho reduced the amount of land distributed to peasants to a third that of the Cárdenas administration and permitted real salaries to go down while production and profits skyrocketed.[55]

During World War II rather than make demands, labor leaders, including independents and Communists, counseled labor peace and a united front against fascism. Once the war was over conservatives were so thoroughly entrenched and workers' and peasants' unions were so tightly controlled from the top down that there was little room for maneuvering.

The next president, again chosen by the out-going administration, was Miguel Alemán (1946-52). Alemán is remembered for his almost unlimited corruption, gross personal profiteering (even by Mexican standards), and the removal of obstacles to American investment. During his administration the army was used to crush strikes, and wage increases were not permitted even though the inflation rate was 10% a year. Radical peasants and opposition labor leaders were jailed and opposition labor unions had their recognition withdrawn.[56] Meanwhile government officials continued to found their own private companies and then give these companies lucrative government contracts. They bought land and irrigated it at government expense. They were able to profiteer from the agrarian reform by threatening to cut credit and retake already-distributed land if their graft was not tolerated.[57]

The next president was Ruiz Cortines (1952-8) who tried to compensate for the glaring faults of the previous administration. He tried to slow inflation and prevent workers' salaries from shrinking further. Mexican business's response was to send large quantities of money out of the country, thus emphasizing the limits of the Mexican government to make meaningful economic changes.[58]

From 1958 to 1964 López Mateos served as president. He, again in keeping with Mexico's tradition of progressive foreign policy, maintained diplomatic relations with Cuba and defended its revolution. In addition he bucked the pervasive cold war mentality by opening up trade with China. However his presidency saw the foreign debt increase $2.4 billion, four times the debt increase of the previous administration. Also during his administration rail workers were brutally suppressed, more foreign capital was let in, and the oligarchy increased its share of national income.[59]

The last two Mexican presidents to complete their terms, Gustavo Díaz Ordaz (1964-70) and Luis Echeverría (1970-6), represent the post-institutional phase. Their energies, as we shall see, were directed not at institutionalizing the government, but at coping with the problems inherited from their predecessors.

Part II: POLITICS

CHAPTER 8: THE STATE

The Mexican government has evolved from the structure which began to develop during the presidency of Juárez. Despite claims to the contrary by the current Mexican political establishment, the pre-revolutionary and the post-revolutionary state have many features in common. Prior to the Juárez administration the government never exercised effective control over the economy. Then in the latter part of the 19th century the state became the main promoter of development.[1] At this time investment was increasingly left to the state due to the size of the investments which were needed to modernize the country. The degree to which the state's power increased is shown by the 900% rise in government spending during the Porfiriato.

The role of the state in development, which began before the Revolution of 1910-17, was greatly expanded by the 1917 Constitution. Instead of using Díaz's personal power to promote development, post-1917 governments have used the powers granted by the reformist articles of the 1917 Constitution, especially articles 27 (agrarian reform) and 123 (labor legislation). These two articles, along with article 28 (regulating monopolies), have served to institutionalize the economy and to impose the goal of national development which arose from the Revolution.[2]

Reforms were not only carried out slowly, but became political weapons to defuse any opposition which might threaten the power of the state.[3] The clearest example of this occurred at the beginning of the Cárdenas administration when reforms were used to pacify both workers and peasants who were threatening to bring down the government.

In no case though have these reforms been revolutionary in nature. Instead what they did was to change the pattern of rural property-holding and break the almost automatic tie between owning land and holding political power. This pushing of the rural oligarchy from power was a phenomenon which occurred throughout Latin America since the oligarchic regimes were an obstacle to capitalist development.[4]

At the same time the state was removing the stumbling block posed by the old oligarchies, it began promoting economic development on a scale previously unmatched. The private entrepreneur had neither the will nor the resources to rebuild the transport system, restore the cities, and relocate those displaced by the revolution.[5] Once the state began actively promoting development, it never quit, since both politicians and Mexican businessmen have developed interests in the state's continuing to play a major role in the economy.

This role of the state in economic development expanded still further during the Cárdenas administration. During this six-year period government control was extended not only to the oil industry, but was increased in railroads, credit, and public works, all in an attempt to overcome the effects of the depression.[6] The government increased its role in agriculture and oil at this time by forming an alliance with workers, peasants, and the business interests which profited from the revolution. This alliance permitted the government to challenge the interests of the old landed oligarchy and of foreign investors.[7]

However, even though the state used these groups to challenge the old oligarchy, it never let them assume leadership.

At this time the revolution was directed by members of the rural and urban middle classes (mainly enterprising small property owners in the country and poor and middle class intellectuals in the cities).[8] These members of the middle class knew that they would have to initiate reform themselves if the Revolution was to be carried out.[9] Their leadership of these mass movements prevented any challenges to capitalism itself.[10]

The state underwent further evolution between 1940 and 1946. During this time the capitalists increased their power over the state, principally at the expense of the peasants, as political power followed on the heels of the capitalists' rapidly increasing economic power.[11]

....

The ousting of the old rural oligarchy, the increased role in economic development, and the use of reform to prevent mass movements from taking a revolutionary course have served the government well. Given the effectiveness of these policies, the government has continued with such programs as the agrarian reform for more than fifty years. (The Cuban agrarian reform took two years.) Also the state often supports demands of workers, as in the case of the salary demands made in 1973 and 1974, so as to prevent workers from openly defying the system. These benefits to both worker and peasant have been applied in an authoritarian, paternalistic manner and have been frequently used to defuse potentially violent situations.

While continuing to contain the masses with largely token reforms, the government has proceeded with the promotion of capitalist development, with little regard for social justice. Given its degree of dependency, the government has tried to maximize the opportunity for profits rather than making a clean break from economic dependency on the US.[12]

In promoting development and co-opting worker and peasant movements, the government has abandoned its 19th century model of relating to citizens as individuals. Rather it has adopted the form of a modern state where various sectors of the society have been organized into corporate groups. Each of these groups functions on its own, despite having its actions closely watched over by the state.[13] The organized groups which the state uses to further its ends include the organized peasantry (CNC), organized labor (CTM), and a general catch-all middle class organization (CNOP). The final group with which the government deals is the business community which both implements and profits from development.

As we have seen, little was done before the Cárdenas administration to benefit either workers or peasants. The real beneficiaries during the first twenty years of the revolution were those who owned businesses with government contracts. These supposed revolutionaries were forced into a political system in which groups and conflicts were institutionalized.[14] Certain public posts, legislative seats, land and credit were granted to peasants and workers in exchange for their loyalty to the state.[15] The state thus served as the imposed arbitrator between each of the organized sectors of society, an arbitrator which each sector had no choice but to submit to.

This pattern has continued, with each of the organized groups vigorously defending its own interests. Competition between each of these groups has become the key to the Mexican political system. To complete the picture, this competition is presided over by a president who exercises extreme, though legal, personal power.

Despite the state-imposed alliance between these groups, they have never been treated equally. Rather the state threw its power to the development of one group, the capitalists. This decision resulted not only from the personal advantage revolutionary leaders could reap from their own business ventures, but from the generalized feeling that only after industrialization could the government think in terms of social reform and relative economic autonomy from the US. As part of its support for business, the government has continually claimed capitalist development to be the key to meaningful social reform in Mexico.[16]

This favoring of business and channeling of government resources to increase private wealth has upset the very alliance between entrepreneurs and workers which the government forced on Mexican society. Increasingly entrepreneurs are the ones who are establishing control over activities of the state, at least in those areas which directly affect their interests.[17]

Much of what goes on in the Mexican political scene today is a struggle to define to what extent the state can continue as arbitrator of affairs and impose its will. For instance early in the Echeverría administration attempts to relieve the social pressures which exploded in 1968 were greeted with threats of a coup. Similarly when Echeverría expropriated large tracts of land in the closing days of his administration, many owners closed their shops and factories in protest. Such events indicate a weakening of the state in relation to business.

Ironically, as the state's autonomy appears to be waning, its role in the economy is becoming more important. Since the private sector is increasingly unable to generate financing or produce sufficient growth and jobs to maintain the status quo, the government has taken on these roles. This led to greater growth in the size of the government under Echeverría than under any other president in Mexican history.[18]

CHAPTER 9: THE PRI*

For over a hundred years we have suffered from regimes that have been at the service of feudal oligarchies but have utilized the language of freedom. This situation has continued to our own day.[1]

1. History

For almost half a century Mexico has been under the control of a political party which has been compared to the Communist Party in Russia and the political machine of the late Mayor Daley in Chicago. This party is similar to both in that it is run from the top down, has tried to prevent effective opposition from working outside its structure, and in rewarding some people quite well and in pacifying enough of the others to stay in power.

This political apparatus was established in 1929 by General Calles, shortly after the assassination of Obregón. The Partido Nacional Revolucionario (PNR), as it was known then, was created by Calles without popular participation. The PNR not only enabled Calles to maintain personal power by creating the facade of institutional rule, but served to prevent the often violent infighting between the powerful figures who emerged from the revolution. The previous decade had seen the 1920 coup which resulted in the death of Carranza, an attempted coup in 1924 which led to a destructive civil war, and the 1928 faction fight which ended in the deaths of three important generals.[2]

The creation of the new party also served to channel political activity into organizations under the control of the revolutionary caudillos, rather than giving such potentially threatening groups as the Socialist Party of Yucatán a chance to move into the existing political vacuum.[3] The PNR would serve as an umbrella organization through which the caudillos would mediate their political demands. The power of the Mexican state would insure, through armed force if necessary, that no power struggles took place outside the party.

Originally the PNR functioned as a coalition of regional groups. During the 1930's the PNR began to shift from mediating disputes between these groups to exercising power in its own right.[4] As the power of the Mexican state increased, the ability of the PNR to control party members also increased. This control was further strengthened by the central government's assassination of uncooperative regional strongmen.[5]

It's impossible to imagine a political group able to satisfy all aspirations, and the PNR was no exception. In the year after the party was founded, 1930, there was a strong political movement headed by the nationalistic philosopher José Vasconcelos. To stop this group's bid for power the government arrested and summarily executed 20 Vasconceios supporters in the village of Topilejo just south of Mexico City.[6] Some observers even claim that the 1929 elections were stolen by the newly-created PNR.[7]

In the 1934 elections, with no significant opposition outside the party, the major power struggle was between Calles and Cárdenas within the party. Once in office Cárdenas began to build his power base among mass organizations, a process which was formalized by reorganizing the PNR. Since the PNR had served its original function of controlling caudillos, it was given a new name, the Partido Revolucionario Mexicano (PRM), and a new role, controlling the peasants' and workers' organizations, the military, and the CNOP.‡ Each of these groups was organized and controlled from above, and prevented from forming alliances with other groups within the party. The newly-organized party resolved disputes between these

---

*The initials of the dominant, official political party, the Revolutionary Institutional Party.

‡CNOP stands for National Congress of Popular Organizations, a group which includes various organizations of professionals, small businessmen, and medium size farmers.

organizations and coordinated their activities, especially at election time.[8]

These changes had little effect on the everyday workings of the government since they only formalized the organizing style Cárdenas had been using for years. What it did do was provide an effective mechanism for mobilizing peasants and workers against the entrenched interests of landlords and foreign monopolies. As with the PNR, the newly-created PRM was swaddled in revolutionary rhetoric, and created without any popular control or participation. Its power continued to be a private internal matter maintained by violence, for its own ends, not those of society.[9]

At the end of Cárdenas's term in 1940 the newly-created party faced its greatest political challenge. As has been noted, not only were goons with pistols and clubs used against the opposition,[10] but Cárdenas agreed beforehand to rig the results of the election.[11] Violence against the opposition continued through election day, when some 30 assassinations took place in Mexico City alone.[12]

The official party was reorganized again in 1946 when it received its present name, the Partido Revolucionario Institucional, or PRI. The reorganization of the party reflected the success the party had, first in ridding itself of the regionally-based caudillos, and then in using the mass organizations to displace the landlords and foreign monopolies. World War II then helped the new entrepreneur-politicians by providing fabulous profits to those with political connections.

The reorganized party shifted power away from the mass organizations, which had already fulfilled their purpose, and toward the businessmen-politicians and the political apparatus they had built. The power of regional politicians was entrenched, the unity of organized labor was broken, distribution of land to peasants was slowed, and the mass organizations were left with little control over their own affairs.[13] At the same time the wielding of political power and decision-making was further removed from public scrutiny, "making them mysteries just less than impenetrable."[14] As was the case with the PNR and the PRM, the PRI was born without popular participation or consultation. "The 5.7 million Mexicans who went to sleep as members of the PRM, woke up as PRI members."[15]

The presidential elections in 1952 produced the last major split in the party. Miguel Henríquez, an ambitious general, when denied the presidential nomination, withdrew from the party and set up his own political group, the FPP (Popular Political Front). Henríquez's platform called for a true agrarian reform, freeing political prisoners, and the opportunity for political opposition. He quickly drew support from those who had followed Zapata and Cárdenas, as well as from members of the Communist Party and the Popular Party (now Popular Socialist Party).

After the election a large number of Henríquez supporters gathered in the Alameda Park in downtown Mexico City for what was called a victory party, actually a protest over what they felt was a stolen election.* The group was fired on by government forces and at least seven were killed. The government hoped this would end the radicalization which was taking place among Henríquez's urban organizers.[19]

2. FORMAL ORGANIZATION

On paper the political structure within which the PRI functions is a republic with state and municipal governments, and with the traditional division into legislative, executive and judicial branches. However in fact the federal government's executive branch completely dominates the political scene, so that one never wonders what the outcome of a supreme court case will be or how the legislature will vote. These are merely limp appendages of the executive branch.

The legislature is effectively controlled having legislators serve only one term and then leave office. Those who have followed the official party line and performed well can expect an appropriate government job or higher "elective" office. The legislature's contribution to the political process is reflected by its work load; it only meets 4 months a year, mornings only, two days a week. Rather than legislating, Congress legitimates the actions of the executive by providing the facade of legislative checks.[20] It also is a conduit for grievances, a training ground for politicians on their way up the political ladder, and a place for these politicians to make contacts.[21]

The supreme court, even though its judges are appointed for life, serves for little else than rewarding the faithful. Major decisions such as the US Supreme Court rulings on abortion, one man-one vote, and school desegregation are never handed down.

The executive branch not only dominates the entire federal level of government, but also the state and municipal levels. The president has the power to nominate all state governors and congressmen, and those nominated need not even be residents of the areas they represent. The 1972 appointment of Pedro Zorrilla Martínez as governor of Nuevo León violated the state constitutional requirement that the governor live in the state for the five years immediately preceding the nomination. During the previous five years Zorrilla Martínez had served as provisional governor of another state, Tamaulipas.[22] Once I met a congressman-designate from Veracruz. When I met him he had been told that he would be appointed as congressman from his native state of Veracruz, but he hadn't been told which district he would represent. At the time he lived in Mexico City, as he continued to do after his election.

The president also has the power to fire governors who perform poorly or who are in disagreement with him. President Echeverría fired the governor of Nuevo León

---

*Various factors contributed to the inability of Henríquez's supporters to create a stronger opposition; certainly it wasn't the lack of issues. Henríquez's supporters ranged from communists to disgruntled politicians, which made unified action difficult. Furthermore opposition to the PRI was divided by former labor leader Lombardo Toledano's running as another opposition candidate. Finally the candidate, himself a revolutionary general, was considered by some to be fickle and corrupt.[16] Despite all this, the FPP was officially credited with 579,745 votes.[17] Police broke up another FPP rally after the Alameda massacre and the party ceased to exist when the government ordered its offices closed.[18]

when he used a student movement in the state university to try to consolidate the power of Monterrey interests at the expense of the central government. Later he fired the reactionary governor of Guerrero, accusing him of embezzlement. In the process Echeverría strengthened his political position for the end-of-term jockeying for presidential succession. Finally in 1975 he fired the governor of Hidalgo who couldn't quell protests over his dishonesty and close ties with conservative landlords. Sometimes the firing stops short of outright dismissal, as was the case in Puebla in 1973 when the state governor was allowed to resign when he proved unable to control student demonstrations with anything less subtle than gunfire. Similarly Governor Zárate of Oaxaca resigned in favor of an army general in March 1977. This followed the government's firing on several demonstrations demanding the resignation of the governor and the head of the state university he had appointed.

The federal government not only controls the state politically, but takes 87% of all tax revenue. The state in turn has political power over the municipal level of government, and takes 10% of tax revenue, leaving the municipalities with only 3%.[23] This situation was neatly summed up by a state governor who said "The federal government screws me, and I screw the municipality."[24]

Finally, the PRI, in addition to being the key to office at all levels of government, exercises control over the national peasant and worker organizations. In addition there are many other mass organizations under PRI control, so that often the official party controls two, three or more organizations affecting a single individual. The power of these groups enables the PRI to put pressure on any political dissidents. Examples of such organizations include sporting clubs, medical care programs, and trade and professional organizations. Generally members of any of these PRI-sponsored organizations are automatically made members of the PRI, a status which mainly serves to inflate the PRI's membership statistics. Such "members" are subject to no party discipline, nor are they bound to follow the party's ideology, since it is so fuzzy as to be impossible to follow even if one tried.

Much of the political patronage of the PRI is dispensed through its three formal sectors, the peasant (CNC), worker (CTM), and mass (CNOP) sectors. Each sector is allocated various patronage jobs, including congressional seats, which are attractive for their salary (especially if one is a peasant), graft, and future advancement opportunities. The relative influence of each sector depends on its economic clout. Thus the peasants, despite being most numerous, have the least power, and the relatively few middle class CNOPers are the most influential.[25]

In order to carry out its political tasks, such as staging electoral campaigns, recruiting talented persons, co-opting dissenters, etc., the PRI relies directly on money from the federal government. Exact figures on federal government subsidies are not made public. Further funding comes from state and municipal governments, as well as from candidates themselves, who see meeting their own campaign costs as an investment which will pay handsome dividends.[26]

The PRI serves as a channel for the middle and lower classes to make demands on the political system, since they do not have the direct access to leaders that the wealthy enjoy.[27] Generally members of the elite are not even members of the PRI, but are above it. The PRI serves to maintain their power and forms a political conduit between them and the masses. Various interest groups, often organized by geographic region or industry, also exert political pressure. Such interest groups are thought to be subordinate to the inner circle of the ruling party. This inner circle weighs the demands of interest groups and makes decisions in terms of the long-term goals of the ruling elite.[28]

3. THE PRESIDENCY

The president dominates the entire Mexican political apparatus and appoints all important officials. His discretional power is much greater than that of other elected heads of state in that he has no legislative or judicial restraint. His great limitation is that he cannot be re-elected; no re-election being one of the basic premises the PRI adopted as a result of the Porfirio Díaz experience. He sets national priorities, mediates conflicts, allocates men and money, selects major office holders without interference from the legislative or judicial branches and with few constraints by PRI members.[29]

The role of the president as the arbitrator of disputed claims is clear. The powerful generally feel trying to influence him is a better course of action than openly challenging him. However over the last thirty years the president has ceased to be the undisputed master of the political scene he once was. Now he is just the most powerful member of the political elite, vying with businessmen, financiers, and the trade union bureaucracy. With these groups the president no longer deals only in terms of conciliatory consultation, but also frequently and publicly in terms of challenge and confrontation.[30]

The area in which presidential power is most dramatic is in choosing his successor. Each president, in addition to nominating his cabinet, state governors and the like, decides who will succeed him. The exact mechanism by which this choice occurs is simply unknown. Presumably the president discusses the possible candidates with the major interest groups with which he must deal. Then he inevitably chooses a cabinet minister of lower-middle class background[31] to be the PRI's candidate and Mexico's next president.

The process is similar, at least to the outside observer, to Nixon's designation of Ford as vice-president, and Ford's subsequent designation of Rockefeller. Presumably in each case the president selected a list of viable candidates, conferred with the interests he felt must be consulted, and then announced the name selected, but not the process used in the selection.

4. ELECTIONS

The one area in which the PRI functions as a traditional party is in carrying out elections. Generally the elections themselves are fair, but only because between each election the PRI has engaged in a wide variety of manipulations of unions, peasant organizations, and the press, which put them in such a strong position that it is not actually necessary for them to cheat on election day.

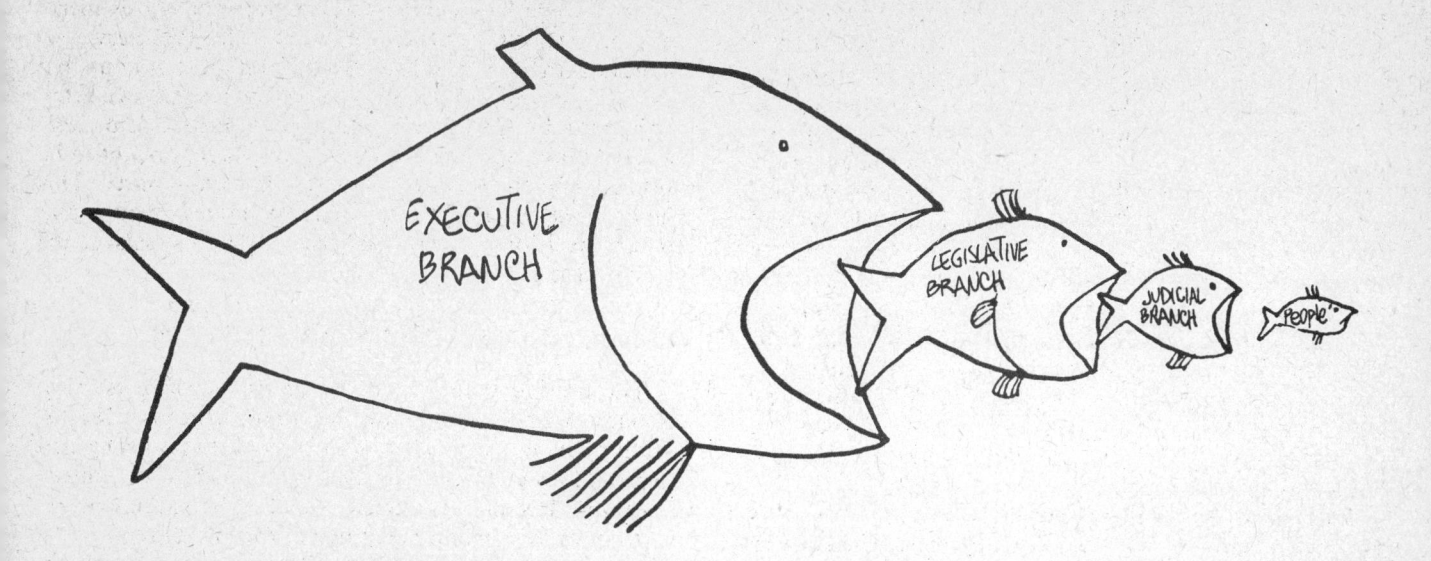

By far the most important election is that of president. Despite the use of the word election, what happens is that the president's designated successor begins one of the most intensive public relations campaigns in the world. Vast sums are spent on promoting the candidate who is already assured of a win. The candidate travels around the country amidst great fanfare, giving speeches, attending rallies, reviewing parades, etc. This ritual serves to convert a relatively obscure cabinet member into a familiar figure. Echeverría's campaign was estimated to cost $40 million.[32]

The efforts used in these campaigns are monumental. Peasants are trucked into rallies in exchange for free beers and a few pesos. The media is carefully orchestrated to sell the candidate. Organizations and individuals, realizing who will be running the country for the next six years, bend over backwards to lend their support. Often the results of these campaigns are visible for years, since buildings and mountainsides are plastered with slogans along the lines of "Nuevo León with López Portillo." Similar rituals occur for those appointed as candidates for other "elected" offices, though as the importance of the job lessens, so does the effort spent to sell the candidate.

At all levels the PRI nomination virtually assures one of office, despite the formality of elections. Since the founding of the official party in 1929 it has never lost a race for president, senator or governor. The congressional and local elections it has lost are usually the result of the nomination of some particularly unpopular figure as candidate, or the extreme incompetency of the incumbent PRI official. Even when the PRI machine cannot bring in the votes, there are other ways to keep office. "Those in power count the ballots, and they win all the elections save those they decide to lose."[33]

5. POLITICAL RHETORIC

One of the strongest weapons the PRI has to maintain its power over Mexican society, while failing to provide promised social justice, is its political rhetoric. The PRI tries to make people feel that in Mexico there is a third ideology and that there are no social classes and that the institution of private property has the characteristics of the good Samaritan.[34] Each presidential candidate is presented as if he has no class allegiances.

This rhetoric perpetuates a variety of political myths which attempt to convince the population that the PRI is serving them and that their best hope for current tranquility and future advancement clearly lies with the PRI. An example of this rhetoric was contained in the PRI's 47th Anniversary Statement:

> *The objectives which inspired our party's founders have not been forgotten. They are: assuring the country's stability and liberty; providing new leaders and continuity in government; incorporating the majority of the population into the political process; regaining the basic natural resources of the country for Mexicans; extending ever more broadly the benefits of education and redistributive justice; maintaining the order necessary for peaceful structural change; and the preservation of our essential national unity, in order to increase our independence and exercise national sovereignty.*[35]

The PRI also devotes much of its rhetoric to keeping alive the notion that the present government is the complete negation of the regime which existed under Porfirio Díaz, that it is the product of an authentic social revolution, and that the people gained political power in this process of overturning the Porfiriato. To enhance this image of being a revolutionary regime the PRI circulated a poster in Zapata's home state of Morelos which had pictures of Zapata and Carranza along with Zapata's slogan of "Land and Liberty." It is conveniently ignored that it was Carranza who had Zapata killed. This is typical of the PRI presentation of the 1910-1917 struggle as one happily united revolutionary family wrenching power from the forces of feudalism and then turning political power over to the people, who are now represented by the PRI.

The president is also portrayed as being above such

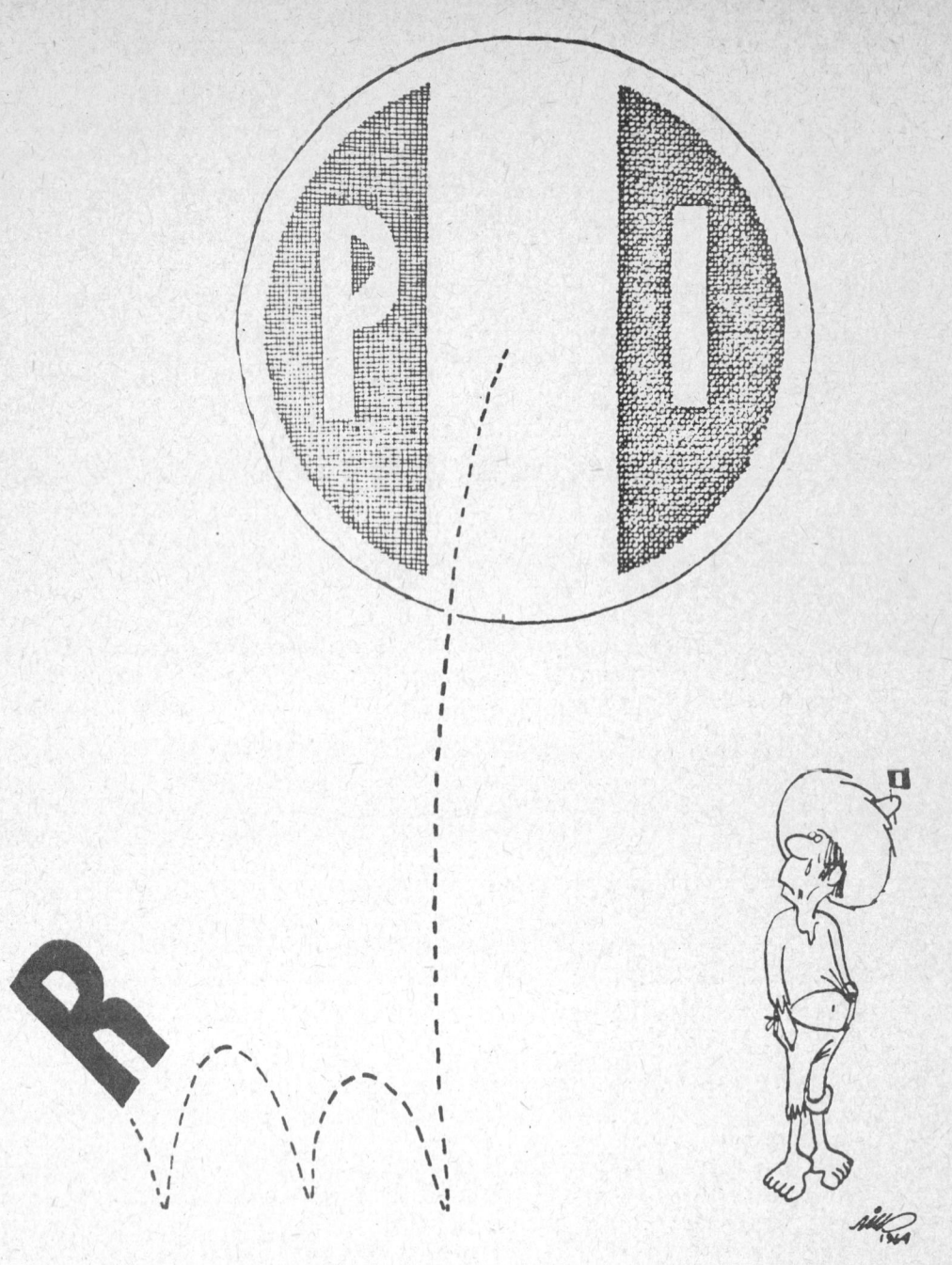

mundane problems as incompetence, making mistakes, or maintaining an unjust system. Political commentators blame problems on high taxes, American exploitation, or some cabinet minister, but not the president.

Industrialization is also held to be the answer to the social problems of Mexico. The masses are called to sacrifice themselves today (accepting low wages) for tomorrow's rewards and industrial progress.[36] This of course favors the businessmen who continue to amass fortunes rather than implementing the reforms which industrialization was supposed to make possible.

This political rhetoric has been so effective that violent repression has generally been unnecessary. A result of this unreality in speech is the withdrawal from politics by many citizens, leaving the elite with few restraints.[37] In addition anyone advocating change sounds exactly like a spokesman for the PRI, and tends to be dismissed as just another politician. The final result is:

> *All political language becomes a shared fiction; the meaning of words is inverted; there is a perpetual discrepancy between what is said and what is done, between social reality and the universe of speech.*[38]

6. CONTROL

In addition to its political rhetoric, the PRI has a number of ways of controlling the population, short of its instruments of last resort, the army and police. The multitude of PRI-controlled organizations all require that an individual be in good standing for participation. One who was on record as opposing the PRI would likely find himself in trouble with his trade union or one of the professional associations involving such groups as merchants, bank workers, engineers, lawyers, and teachers. For example within a trade union organized by the PRI, members are checked off as they vote in national elections, roll is taken at political demonstrations in favor of the PRI, and those opposing the PRI are frequently harassed, fired or transferred to undesirable job locations.[39] One May Day in Monterrey I marched by the governor's reviewing stand with the telephone workers' union. A union bureaucrat was greatly surprised when he found that not only was I not a telephone worker, but I didn't *have* to march.

The business community is kept in line by the import licenses which must be issued on some 80% of all imports. Since these imports must be approved on an individual basis by a PRI-appointed cabinet official, businessmen have little political leeway.[40]

In contrast the PRI rewards political cooperation with an almost endless list of appointive and "elective" positions, government contracts, etc. In fact one of the ways the PRI stays in power is the conscious recruiting of talented young people so that they will not end up in the opposition. One result of this recruitment is that many of the activists of the 1968 student movement are now teaching in the National University and its affiliated high schools. Once they are recruited, young people can move up the ladder quickly since no one can be re-elected to the same position. This contrasts markedly with the Porfirian government which in 1910 had an 80-year-old man at its head, and 25 of 27 governors over sixty.[41]

7. EVOLUTION

The 1968 student movement shook the entire political establishment and in many ways shaped President Echeverría's administration. However it had surprisingly little effect on the strength of the PRI. The PRI still has overwhelming political strength, so that in the 1973 congressional elections it got almost 80% of the vote. Generally the PRI's strength is greatest in rural areas, where it gets 95% of the vote, and weakest in large cities where it gets less than 60% at times. In urban areas middle class voters are better informed as to the nature of the political process and less vulnerable to political reprisals than are peasants.

The PRI specifically cultivates a political opposition to give the illusion of democratic process. In fact the PRI has been losing ground to both its right wing opposition (called the National Action Party— PAN) and to a left-of-center party (the Popular Socialist Party—PPS) and to those who either abstain from voting or fill the ballot with obscenities. The evolution of the PRI's strength can be seen by the percent of the vote which it claimed in presidential elections:

1929	Ortiz Rubio	99%
1934	Cárdenas	98%
1940	Avila Camacho	94%
1946	Alemán	78%
1952	Ruiz Cortines	74%
1958	López Mateos	90%
1964	Díaz Ordaz	89%
1970	Echeverría	79.8%

While these figures might seem to indicate a real erosion of power, given the PRI's ability to manipulate the election process both to keep alive the illusion of opposition or to repress it if threatened, they mean little. "What really matters, of course, is not how the PAN fares during elections, but how the balance of power shifts inside the PRI."[42]

One of the problems the PRI has in keeping alive the facade of democracy is the high rate of absenteeism, or non-voting, which tends to shatter the idea of broad popular support. In the 1970 presidential election, of 25.5 million people of voting age, 21.6 million registered, and only 14 million voted.[43] In the 1975 elections in the State of Mexico only 31% of the 1.6 million registered voters bothered to vote. In order to preserve the democratic image, great effort is spent to get people to register and go through the motions of voting.

Another problem the PRI has is internal splits. These have occurred in the past, as with the Henríquez candidacy, and still occur. Such a split came into public view in Veracruz in 1974. There local strong man López Arias pushed Carbonell, a state government official, as candidate for governor. Since Veracruz is a rich state, such a nomination would come under close scrutiny of the president. Rather than waiting for the presidential designation, local party officials announced Carbonell as candidate, hoping that Echeverría would accept him. However rather than trying to maintain the facade of party unity and accepting Carbonell as candidate, Echeverría publicly announced his own candidate, who became the official candidate and later governor.

The PRI has been losing an increasing number of local elections, and refusing to accept the fact. Often, rather than accepting a minor defeat, the PRI will impose its own candidate. For example in January 1973 in Tulancingo, Hidalgo, 23 ballot boxes were stolen by election officials, municipal employees and police. The opposition PAN party won the 9 remaining boxes by 241 votes. Nevertheless the PRI candidate for mayor was installed. A crowd of angry townspeople gathered at city hall and stoned it, breaking out all the windows. The response of the government was to call the police and army to occupy the town and hunt down members of the opposition.* When asked about the events there the PRI governor of the state commented, "The opposition lost by one vote, mine."[44]

Later in 1973 local elections were annulled in Jáltipan, Veracruz. The PRI had lost and PRI-appointed election judges decided to invent a technicality to avoid defeat. When members of the local PPS opposition protested, they were fired on by police and ten were killed.[45]

There was a similar occurrence in November 1974 when police had to be called in to quell demonstrations in the State of Puebla after 88 ballot boxes were stolen in municipal elections. To justify the ballot boxes being taken to PRI headquarters before the votes were counted, local officials said they were just taking care of them. Such actions were common after that election. As a result when the mayors "elected" at that time were installed, 13 had to

---

*The PRI's policy in Tulancingo was described by one commentator as the policy of the three double R's, "encierro, entierro y destierro" (jail, burial, and exile).

be protected by police and army units.[46] These are merely examples. Reports of such stolen elections, with or without violent protest, are common in the Mexican press. These losses by the PRI seem to be increasing. In any case though, the PRI is dealing from overwhelming strength and can decide to accept defeat or forcibly impose its candidate.

. . . .

Despite the various changes which have occurred in the last thirty-five years, the goals of the PRI have remained remarkably constant, and the PRI has generally done quite well at fulfilling its first two goals. These goals have been described as, in decreasing order of importance: 1. political stability, 2. economic growth, 3. public welfare, and 4. Mexicanization of the economy.[47] The last two goals have clearly been sacrificed for the first two.

Sporadic violence notwithstanding, the primary goal of political stability has been achieved remarkably well. The record of having each president since 1934 serve out his term and only his term is hard to match in any part of the world. The price for this stability though in human terms has been high, as we shall see in succeeding chapters.

Likewise there are few countries in the underdeveloped world which can match Mexico's success at reaching the second goal, economic development. Thirty years of rapid economic growth have greatly contributed to the stability of the PRI regime. It remains to be seen how the 1976 devaluation and the subsequent economic crisis will affect the PRI.

According to the PRI, goal No. 1, political stability, should lead to goal No. 2, economic growth, and that in turn should lead to goal No. 3, public welfare. What in fact happened is that the model of development imposed on Mexico by those who set PRI policy has precluded the fulfillment of the public welfare goal. The profits private businessmen have been allowed to accumulate have taken precedence over public welfare.

As to goal No. 4, Mexicanization, there has been little progress, since the policy-makers themselves represent interests which have chosen to work closely with foreign investors to increase the rate of economic growth. There is increasing pressure though to accelerate Mexicanization as more and more Mexicans feel squeezed by the multinational corporations and foreign indebtedness.

Despite the relative success in maintaining its principal goals of political stability and economic development, there have been significant failures. Often these failures can be attributed to more reactionary elements who fail to shift with the times. For example in the case of municipal elections mentioned above, the problems could easily have been avoided by some sort of primary elections. This way to eliminate the imposition of unpopular candidates was suggested in 1965 by Carlos Madrazo, then president of the PRI. Conservative elements in the party, fearing the loss of their local fiefdoms, bitterly opposed the measure and Madrazo was removed as head of the PRI.

A second and more severe criticism can be directed at the way the current structure of the PRI hinders the realization of its own goal of economic development. With constant rotation in office there is less incentive toward long-term projects which can only be finished during the term of later office-holders. Rather there is a tendency toward showy projects which can be finished in one term and thus add to the initiator's prestige. President Alemán's construction of the University City outside Mexico City and Lake Alemán in Veracruz are classical examples of such projects.

Similarly the constant rotation of office, while insuring that would-be dissidents will have a chance for jobs, limits expertise acquired for a certain job, and creates a tendency not to take risks. This is further emphasized by personal advancement being often more dependent on cultivating the good will of higher party officials than in serving the public interest.[48]

Finally the lack of political competition needed to make an official responsible to the electorate has fueled the centuries-long tradition of graft in Mexico. This graft functions at all levels, and often the amount siphoned off into politicians' pockets seriously limits the reach of government programs. Those who rise to high political posts rarely need more than six years to accumulate enough capital to retire for life.[49]

As long as it can keep up economic development, it appears that the PRI will continue to dominate the political scene. None of the non-electoral groups have sufficient strength to challenge the PRI, and in the electoral arena the opposition is more dependent on the PRI's admission of defeat than on the will of the voter.

CHAPTER 10: ECHEVERRIA

In October 1969 it was announced that Luis Echeverría, then Minister of Interior (Gobernación), had been selected as the next president of Mexico. Then on November 15, 1969, the PRI officially nominated him as its presidential candidate. Even though his election was assured, Echeverría campaigned extensively, visiting remote areas which had not seen a president since Lázaro Cárdenas. And the motive was the same as Cárdenas's, winning mass backing for his upcoming administration. Unlike most PRI presidential candidates, Echeverría began to attack the policies of the incumbent regime even before taking office. In addition he proposed far-reaching reforms for Mexico, claiming his presidency would initiate a serious attempt to renovate the political and economic structure. However the specific content of these reforms was never made clear; his campaign speeches were "a torrent of statements and improvisations, many of which were vague, incomplete, and even contradictory."[1]

In July 1970 Echeverría was elected to the presidency, getting 79.8% of the vote. The man who was elected to the presidency for the 1970-6 term had never before held elective office. He began his career in 1946 with a three-month journalistic stint with the Mexico City paper EL NACIONAL. An article he wrote at that time commented that "malintentioned provocateurs agitating in the universities were causing problems for the revolutionary government."[2] That same year he began to climb the bureaucratic ladder of the PRI by becoming an aide to the party's president.

During the Ruiz Cortines administration (1952-58) he served as number three man in the education ministry. During his tenure there the army occupied the Politechnic Institute to quell a student movement that demanded new buildings and a greater student-faculty voice in university administration. The result was one wounded, 75 beaten, 300 tear-gassed and three arrested.[3]

The next twelve years, from 1958 to 1970, Echeverría spent in the Interior Ministry, the department in charge of domestic affairs and internal security. In 1958 while he served as Undersecretary of Interior, the army was used to smash a rail workers strike and some of its leaders were jailed for over a decade. In the Díaz Ordaz administration (1964-70) Echeverría moved up to Secretary of Interior, a post which put him in command of the national security apparatus when several hundred participants in the 1968 student movement were killed.

In the aftermath of these events, Echeverría took office, hoping to alleviate some of the injustices which had produced the movement. He had two choices given the level of discontent: either institute a Brazilian-type military government or implement meaningful reforms. He attempted the latter.

Echeverría called for fairer distribution of income, attacking "the excessive concentration of income and the neglect of much of the population which threaten the harmonious continuation of development."[4] Other reforms which Echeverría advocated included decentralization of industry, reducing the foreign debt and the balance of payments deficit, and controlling foreign investment.

A new slogan was coined to describe his political reformism, the "apertura democrática," or "democratic opening." The premise of the "apertura" was increased opportunity for certain types of opposition, such as that of students and other middle class groups, which would not endanger the stability of the regime.[5] To make this reform meaningful, Echeverría removed many restraints from the media, freed political prisoners still in jail from the 1968 student movement, and generally tried to give the image of encouraging ideological diversity and criticism. Again following the lead of Cárdenas, he proposed that reforms be carried out by bureaucratic organizations, without permitting the participation of independent mass groups.

Echeverría's administration differed from that of Cárdenas in that Echeverría did not have the support of business. Cárdenas's reforms were supported by the emerging Mexican business sector which wanted to move into the area occupied by hacendados and foreign monopolies. Echeverría on the other hand had to confront established business interests, which have more influence over government than business did during the Cárdenas administration. Today much of the government is under the direct control of moneyed interests, and representatives of these interests occupy important positions. For example Echeverría's first foreign minister was Emilio Rabasa, grandson of the Porfirian foreign minister of the same name. Head of the mining development commission was Lorenzo Ramos y Zabal, grandson of the Porfirian governor of Sonora who called in American volunteers from Arizona to break up the strike by Mexican miners at Cananea. Finally Echeverría's last appointment as finance minister was Mario Ramón Beteta, nephew of President Alemán's pro-business finance minister. While these individuals were not representative of Echeverría's appointees, they do indicate the degree to which members of the old elite influence government.

Echeverría began to push his reforms, presenting himself as a liberal challenging those with antiquated social values. Rather than expressing the problems in class terms, he presented the problems as matters to be resolved with technology. He felt Mexican business understood that the reforms he proposed would not upset the class structure, but rather preserve it. On this basis he expected business support.[6] To further his reformist image, a great effort was made to appeal to young people. The voting age was lowered, young technocrats were recruited for government jobs, and Echeverría frequently stopped in at universities around the country for informal discussions with students.*

The image of the "apertura democrática" was irreparably damaged on June 10, 1971, when a group of students on a peaceful protest march through the streets of Mexico City was attacked. Government-organized goons attacked the students with staves and guns, leaving several dead and many more wounded and beaten. Echeverría's response was to attribute the attack to reactionaries within the government, not to his appointees. The only official action taken was to fire the Díaz Ordaz-appointed holdovers serving as mayor of the Federal District and Chief of Police. However no one was ever punished for the attack nor was the government-organized unit which carried out the attack ever disbanded.[7]

In September 1971 Echeverría gave his first state of the union address, and hardly mentioned the incident of June 10. Rather he stressed the technical problems facing Mexico's economy and announced that the government would try to slow down the rate of economic development slightly so resources could be diverted to carry out reforms. In other words, government spending would shift from promoting economic development to promoting social welfare.

By this time the split between the business elite and the Echeverría administration was obvious. Businessmen had formed a power block which clearly was in no mood to compromise with the government on reform.[8] Rather than trusting government to make decisions about concession or repression, the Mexican business sector was directly pressuring and publicly critizing the government for not taking a more repressive stance toward popular movements. To make matters worse, those at the bottom of the social ladder were becoming increasingly restive.

In response the government decided to build a mass base in order to deal with recalcitrant businessmen. This attempt at base-building continued through the September 1972 state of the union address, which presented nothing of novelty. At this time the government was finding its rhetoric a little shop-worn and was having trouble mobilizing popular support. Powerful, ultra-conservative, rural landowners effectively prevented any mobilization of peasants, fearing that such a mobilization would inevitably threaten their interests. Efforts to organize the working class were no more successful, since the principal demand of the workers, union democracy, would undermine the entrenched union bureaucracy.

Echeverría's reformist policies came into conflict with the conservatives in the city of Puebla in May 1973. There police under Governor Bautista O'Farril, a representative of the conservative Puebla business community, fired on student May Day demonstrators, killing five of them. Echeverría, realizing that this was no way to build a broad base for his reformist policies, forced the resignation of the governor.

As the possibility of securing peasant and worker support began to wane, Echeverría realized that there was little possibility of meaningful reform within the existing system. His attention therefore shifted to international relations and Third World problems. In 1972 Echeverría began his foreign travels, which included a speech at the UN General Assembly, and trips to Japan, Peru, Chile, Canada, the US, Great Britain, Belgium, France, the USSR, and China. These trips gave Echeverría the opportunity to launch himself as a champion of the oppressed Third World. In addition Echeverría sought to establish economic ties with the nations visited in order to lessen dependence on the US.

The elections at the middle of the presidential term on July 1, 1973, showed the extent to which Echeverría had failed to muster popular support for the regime. In the Federal District, where voters are best informed and best able to choose between parties, the PRI only won a majority in 12 of 25 electoral districts. If one adds annulled* votes and votes for unregistered candidates, the PRI only got a majority in two districts for a total of 30.1% of the registered vote.[9]

The failure of the "apertura" was again made apparent by the August 1973 occupation of the National University by troops, a move to prevent it from functioning as a center for the student left, which had frequently leafleted and held rallies there.

The 1973 state of the union address was notable in containing an endorsement of family planning and in stating that Mexican peasants had paid for much of the industrial development of Mexico by receiving such meager wages that profits could be invested elsewhere.

Later in September 1973 the bitterest outbreaks of government-business hostility occurred. The coup in Chile on September 11 was violently criticized by Echeverría and this criticism alienated businessmen over-

---

*In the spring of 1975 Echeverría made the first appearance of a Mexican president at the National University since the 1968 student movement. He was driven from the stage by boos and a variety of missiles hurled by the students.

*Annulled votes can signify a blank ballot, or as is often the case, one filled with obscenities.

joyed by the coup. Then on September 17 the patriarch of one of the largest, most conservative interest groups in Mexico, Eugenio Garza Sada of Monterrey, was killed in a kidnap attempt by leftist guerrillas. This unleashed a virulent anti-communist campaign which culminated in the burial of Garza Sada. His funeral oration contained threats to the president, who, according to the Monterrey business interests, had failed to maintain public order while doing his best to further Marxism.[10]

This crisis soon passed and overt clashes between the government and business were replaced by an increasing interest in the presidential nomination for the 1976-1982 term. The degree of relaxation of tension between business and government was shown by the November 23, 1973 statement of a representative of CANACINTRA (the association representing industrialists) who announced "support without reserve for Echeverría."

The fourth state of the union address in September 1974 took place in an atmosphere of crisis: unprecedented inflation, union demands for a 35% wage increase, the kidnapping of Echeverría's father-in-law by urban guerrillas, and the kidnapping of the governor-designate of Guerrero. At this time Echeverría was under pressure to give in to the business elite's demand not to increase salaries. This would have implied an end to the state's role as mediator, and its substitution by a repressive regime, converting the government into a mere appendage of the business community.[11]

Echeverría's speech stressed the importance of the state arbitrating disputes between economic groups. He noted that even business benefited from reduced labor violence and unrest, and that "slowing necessary reforms for fear of inflation would be to leave the future of the country in the hands of those few who have benefited from inflation."[12] In addition to attacking those who were trying to deprive the government of its mediating role, he tried to woo organized labor with a wage increase. Since he could mobilize mass labor support for a wage increase, he was successful at bucking business interests. Such increases were backed by labor bureaucrats since wage hikes didn't threaten their entrenched positions. This attempt to offset earning power lost through inflation was of limited effectiveness since even before the salary increases went into effect on September 13, 1974, many manufacturers had already increased their prices.

In September 1975 Echeverría gave his next to last state of the union message, stressing how the state should continue to play a major role in the economy and in solving Mexico's problems. This statement turned out to be a prelude to the nomination of his successor later that month. His choice for Mexico's next president was Finance Minister José López Portillo. López Portillo graduated from the National University law school in 1947 and taught there in the Faculty of Law and Political Science for the next eleven years. In 1958 he joined the PRI planning commission dealing with finance and elections. Later that year he went to work in the education ministry under Echeverría. He left there in 1959 and spent five years as the director of planning for the Ministry of Natural Resources, planning port and border city expansion. López Portillo next served as president of the Commission of Administrative Reform, where he studied electricity production. This led to a three-year appointment by President Echeverría as head of the Federal Electricity Commission, the government-owned monopoly which produces electricity. Finally in 1973 Echeverría appointed him Secretary of the Treasury.

When Echeverría chose him to be the PRI candidate, López Portilla, like Echeverría before him, had never held elective office. His appointment was interpreted as the triumph of the liberal, reformist elements over the more conservative elements favoring the supposed front runner, Interior Minister Moya Palencia.

On several occasions López Portillo's campaign appearances sparked student demonstrations. In Monterrey for example PRI signs were burned, trucks turned over, and several people injured when an appearance of López Portillo turned into an anti-government demonstration.[13] Nevertheless the candidate continued his "campaign," despite the lack of the usual token opposition from the PAN party. This left López Portillo as the only one on the ballot.

On July 4, 1976 the elections took place and López Portillo was credited with 16,703,801 of the total 17,695,043 ballots cast.[14] Independent sources claimed the abstention rate was over 50%, far higher than the officially declared 28%.[15]

Echeverría's last state of the union address was a list of the accomplishments of his administration. The education budget at the end of his term reached 40 billion pesos, five times the rate in 1970. Public school enrollment was up three times, reaching 16.6 million. During Echeverría's term 130,000 kilometers of roads were built, nearly double the 70,000 kilometers in existence in 1970.

In addition iron and steel production capacity reached 10 million tons, double the rate six years earlier. Likewise electricity production doubled, reaching 12 million kilowatts. What Echeverría didn't state in his address was that he had failed to resolve the problems which produced the 1968 student movement and that as his administration ended Mexico was much more dependent on the US than when it began.

López Portillo's inaugural address on December 1, 1976 stressed the theme of austerity. Absent were Echeverría's reformist rhetoric and appeals for Third World Unity. Rather López Portillo's remarks were aimed at winning the confidence of the business community. The president of the US Chamber of Commerce in Mexico said the inaugural address reflected "the kind of philosophy that businessmen can understand."[16]

López Portillo's first major acts were to announce his cabinet, including six ex-governors and six ex-senators,[17] and his budget. His 1977 budget called for a 38% increase in spending. If inflation is considered and the usual budget overruns do not occur, government spending for 1977 will be only slightly above the 1976 level. A sixth of the budget was to be spent on agriculture, while industrial development rose from 24% to 33.3% of the budget, including a 96% rise in spending for energy development.[18] There was little to offer the dispossessed, or to stop the decline in real income which occurred in 1976.[19] These initial moves were not out of character for a nephew of the prominent Porfirian senator, José López Portillo y Rojas.

José López Portillo

PART III: THE ECONOMY

CHAPTER 11: DEVELOPMENT, PAST

Despite the unequal distribution of goods in pre-colonial Mexico, production was for the benefit of the Aztecs and the nation was not dominated by foreigners. This situation changed rapidly with the arrival of the Spaniards. During the colonial period the economy increasingly benefited foreigners and the wealthy few in Mexico who catered to their needs. Economic growth was limited by commercial restrictions, especially the requirement that trade only be with Spain. Mexico was forced to rely on Spain for many products since such activities as wine making, silk production, and most manufacturing were prohibited. Finally rather than trying to develop Mexico's tremendous agricultural potential, men and resources were channeled into mining.

The Totonac Indians of the Gulf Coast provide a concrete example of the effect of the conquest. Prior to the arrival of the Spaniards these Indians tilled their fertile, irrigated land and led a relatively easy life. Soon after arriving the Spanish appropriated their farm land and began to grow sugar cane for export. The Totonacs were forced to produce their food on unirrigated hillsides nearby. Since these hillsides didn't provide sufficient food for the population, many Totonacs were forced to work on the plantations in order to get money to buy food. Others had to leave the region due to the lack of sufficient jobs.[1]

By the end of the colonial period we find much of the economy based on gold and silver export and the import of luxury goods for the elite. Communication lines were built mainly to serve mineral export, leaving the nation with many isolated markets which slowed the development of large-scale agriculture and manufacturing.

The precious metals mined in Mexico and lost to the country forever were instrumental in the economic development of Europe.[2] This gave the North Atlantic area a competitive edge in marketing and manufacturing technology and permitted the underselling of Mexican producers. Once the North Atlantic powers began producing cheap goods for the world market, subsequent Mexican industrialization became extremely difficult.

The export trade supported a small group of wealthy merchants who fought any attempt to make Mexico self-sufficient since that would deprive them of trading profits. Their lavish life style used resources which might otherwise have been invested in such economically beneficial projects as roads. The high incomes of these merchants could have been used to give modest incomes to many individuals, thus providing a large market for locally produced goods, rather than a small one for foreign luxuries.

INDEPENDENCE:

The war for independence, rather than leading to economic independence,* merely destroyed much of the existing productive capacity and left the economy even more dependent on foreigners. Worst hit were the mines which fell into hopeless disrepair. Beams rotted and tunnels filled with water, while the Spaniards with mining knowledge and capital fled the country. Similarly many of the most productive haciendas were destroyed.

Roughly half of the capital in the country was destroyed by the war for independence.[3] This destruction prevented the redistribution of profits which had formerly been taken by Spain. Rather the loss in production equaled roughly what Spain had been taking.[4]

NATIONHOOD (1821-1857)

Once the Spanish had been defeated, the country came under the economic influence of Britain. In exchange for diplomatic recognition by the British, a necessity at that time for a country expecting to take an active part in world trade, Mexico had to make commercial concessions and accept loans on unfavorable terms.[6] Once these loans had been made, more loans were necessary to repay the first ones. In order to get the new loans, Mexico had to agree to further trade concessions and accept more British investment. The English were well aware of the possibilities for expansion that Latin American independence provided. Lord Canning, the British foreign minister, stated in 1824, "The deed is done, the nail is driven, Spanish America is free; and if we do not mismanage our affairs sadly, she is *English*."[7]

The British promoted the idea of free trade (an advantage to their already established industry) and opposed tariff protection for the industry which was beginning in Latin America.[8] This was especially damaging to the Mexican textile industry, one of the few industries which had developed during the colonial period.[9]

Rather than opposing foreign trade, the dominant groups in Mexico often supported increased trade with Britain. This dependence suited both the British and Mexican elites since the British wanted to export manufactured goods and Mexicans wanted to profit from commerce.[10] These interests began what became a self-perpetuating system of underdevelopment and foreign domination. Once this trade pattern became established, the wealth transferred abroad prevented the accumulation of enough of a surplus for domestic development.[11]

The one significant attempt at independent development was the establishment of the Banco de Avío in 1830. This government-run bank was to make loans to new industry. Due to constant changes of government and the inability of any government to marshal a large amount of wealth, the bank accomplished little and was abandoned in 1842.

*Political independence did not coincide with the beginning of any particular stage in Mexican economic development.[5] The surge of mercantile trade which the Bourbons stimulated late in the 18th century continued until the middle of the 19th century. There were few significant changes in Mexican economic dependency until the last half of the 19th century. These changes will be discussed later in this chapter.

The most significant economic activities of the post-independence period were agriculture, mining and textile manufacturing. Agriculture, mainly for subsistence or local markets, produced 220 million pesos a year, while industry only produced 100 million.[12] After independence mining was largely carried out by the British, and was generally confined to precious metals. The only modern factories, replacing the artisan, were textile mills. However competition from already-booming British mills, coupled with the pressures for free trade, prevented Mexico from becoming self-sufficient even in textiles.

Commerce also changed little after independence, and the same goods were exported as during colonial times, mainly precious metals and a few agricultural products such as henequen, a fiber used in rope making. Imports were also the same: luxury goods for the wealthy, and mining and manufacturing equipment.[13]

As the Mexican historian Justo Sierra noted, the merchant and the landowner abandoned

> *their businesses, little by little, to the foreigner—the hacienda, the farm, the food store to the Spaniard (who had returned), the clothing and jewelery shops to the Frenchmen, mines to the Englishmen —they at last took refuge in the bureaucracy, that superb normal school for idleness and graft which has educated our country's middle class.*[14]

Before the Juárez administration, the government was unable to tax effectively and control economic matters. The church was still receiving five times the revenue of the national government.[15] There was no bank to make loans until 1864 (except for the Banco de Avío). The capital which was available, rather than going into industry, went into currency speculation and real estate, or was sent abroad.[16]

The dismal state of Mexican transportation also retarded development. Roads were in a terrible condition, and were often plagued by robbers. Most production was therefore for local markets. The transportation situation was so bad that the cost of a new textile machine manufactured in London was equal to the cost of moving that machine from Veracruz to Mexico City.[17]

> *It is highly probable that interregional trade and internal commerce in Mexico were more highly developed at the time of the Aztecs than they were in the mid-nineteenth century.*[18]

The attempts to remedy the transport problem by building railroads show how ineffective both government and private enterprise were. The first concession for a railroad from Veracruz to Mexico City was granted in 1837. This concession was cancelled in 1840 since nothing had been done. The second concession was given in 1842 and then cancelled in 1849 when only five kilometers had been built. By the time another decade had passed, the entire country only had 25 kilometers of railroad.[19]

LIBERALISM 1857-1911

The presidency of Juárez, which began in 1860, marked the beginning of a century of economic development. Church and Indian communal lands were taken from their owners and put on the market. This drove many, especially Indians, off the land and into the wage labor market. Finally the Juárez government, strengthened during the wars of the 1860's, had the power to implement the economic policies it chose, something earlier governments were unable to do.

Following the Juárez and Lerdo governments was the 39-year-long Porfiriato. Díaz promoted railroad building and welcomed foreign investment with open arms. In addition the Porfiriato created the social conditions for the Mexican Revolution, an event which accelerated the rate of economic development.

The Porfiriato saw Mexico leave a mercantile economy and enter modern capitalism. In so doing Mexico reflected the changes which were occurring throughout the world economy. This transformation involved:[20]

> *1. A shift from artisans and peasants owning their own tools and land to their becoming wage laborers.*
>
> *2. Vastly increased industrialization and mechanization.*
>
> *3. Foreign control over the Mexican economy being exercised through direct investment in Mexico, rather than through international trade.*
>
> *4. The old mercantilist industry, which was technologically primitive, small scale, largely independent, and not vertically integrated, was replaced by much larger monopolistic corporations which were international in scope.*
>
> *5. Free trade began to break down and was replaced by tariffs and trade monopolies.*

These changes resulted in a much greater international division of labor, a division which, as the economist Paul Baran noted, was like the division of labor between horse and rider.

The "científico" planners consciously pushed Mexico into the international market since they felt that tying the internal market to the world market would automatically produce economic, political and social progress. Actually these ties submitted the national economy to foreign control and impoverished increasing numbers of people.[21] These planners felt Mexican private interests were too weak to follow the British model of privately financed development. As a result Mexico was linked to international markets largely through government-financed projects.[22]

The government encouraged investment by suppressing workers' and peasants' movements which would have raised labor costs above the bare minimum. The strength of the government guaranteed a peaceful setting for business, free of the tumult of the first half century of independence. This welcoming of investment and encouraging of railroads was quite lucrative for high government officials who frequently formed business partnerships with foreigners or accepted large bribes for necessary permits.

The building of the rail network was the outstanding achievement of the Porfiriato. In 1875 there were only 578 km. of railroad, by 1910 there were 20,000 (compared to 23,000 today).[23] To encourage construction, the government paid private corporations 6,000 pesos per kilometer, forced those living near the right of way to work on construction, gave free right of way, and provided a twenty-year tax-free period for the railroad companies.[24] In order to provide such subsidies to the highly profitable (but tax free) railroads, the government increased its national debt by 355% from 1890 to 1911.

Massive railroad construction had far-reaching effects which included (1.) the development of large markets for agricultural goods, (2.) the increasing of the central government's military capacity, (3.) making the country more coherent politically and economically, and (4.) increasing mining activity.[25] Railroads also enabled large numbers of people to move from one area to another, permitting the development of northern Mexico.[26]

Railroads reflected the worst aspects of foreign domination. Most of the income of the railroads either went to pay for imported goods or was removed from Mexico in the form of profits and interest on loans.[27] There was little stimulus to Mexican industry from the railroads since rolling stock and even iron for bridge building was imported. The rail companies charged more if products were destined for a Mexican destination than if the same product was hauled the same distance for export.[28] Since export was the main function of the railroads, the routes chosen by foreign companies were determined largely by the shortest way from mine to the nearest port or US city, not by the needs of the Mexican economy. For example a shipment from Mazatlán to Durango, a distance of 150 kilometers, had to travel 1600 kilometers through Nogales, Arizona, and El Paso, Texas.[29] The railroad structure of modern Mexico is one of the lasting legacies of underdevelopment.

Despite the fortunes made by exporters and railroad magnates, rural populations received little benefit from rail construction and often suffered from it.[30] Since the railroads made it possible to use land for export crops, those who had previously occupied land were often forced out by those with greater economic and political power. The disruption of existing populations was so great that one can correlate agrarian uprisings during the Porfiriato with the location of railroad building.[31]

A final effect of the railroad was to establish the United States as the principal trading partner of Mexico. Before the completion of rail links to the US, 60% of Mexican trade was with Europe and 30% was with the US. After the rail lines were completed, the proportions were reversed, 60% of trade was with the US and 30% was with Europe.[32]

Despite the activity in railroad building and mineral export, 70% of the work force was still in agriculture.[33] Although these workers were supposedly free, the hacendado's private police force, as well as government police and the army suppressed agricultural workers. There was still debt peonage (though less), and often, as John Kenneth Turner described in his famous expose BARBAROUS MEXICO, people were dragged off city streets and forced into work on plantations where their lot was little better than that of a slave.

The buying power of agricultural workers went down substantially during the Porfiriato.[34] Hacendados appropriated lands they didn't need (much land they had was underutilized) since they wanted a cheap, permanent labor force. Such a labor force could not be obtained if people had access to their own lands. The poverty of Porfirian agricultural laborers was not due to their isolation and lack of integration to the developing economy, but was precisely due to their incorporation into this economy.[35]

Production of such staples as corn, beans and wheat decreased since resources were increasingly devoted to growing crops for export. German coffee growers dominated Chiapas, Spanish and Cuban tobacco growers were found in Valle Nacional, and the Tehuantepec rubber plantations were under the control of Americans.[36] In Yucatán Mexicans produced henequen for export. However the marketing of the fiber was controlled by the International Harvester Company which exported it for use in hay bailers.

The economic accomplishments of the Porfiriato were far from the universal progress the "científicos" had prophesied. A magnificent rail system had been built, but one which served foreigners, not Mexicans. Growth centered around meeting the world demand for raw materials.[37] Another strong area was industry, which grew 12% a year from 1878 to 1911.[38] The railroads, mines and factories though were only a small part of the generally sluggish, predominantly agrarian economy. Overall economic growth during the Porfiriato was a far from spectacular 2.7% a year, at a time when the population was increasing at 1.4% a year.[39]

Foreign control increased much faster than overall growth. At the end of the Porfiriato 77% of all capital invested in non-agricultural enterprises was in the hands of foreigners. Forty-four percent of foreign investment was US-owned, while Great Britain had 24% and France had 13%.[40] The economic activities foreigners invested in can be seen by the percentage of foreign control in various areas of the economy in 1911: [41]

Mining	98.2%	foreign controlled
Banks	76.5%	"
Industry	84.3%	"
Electricity	87.0%	"
Petroleum	100%	"
Railroads	61.8%*	"

The failure of the Porfirian planners was in thinking that they could achieve economic development without changing the political system which was based on the technologically backward hacienda.

*Including American interests in the government-run railway.

The Revolution of 1910-17 simultaneously helped and hurt development. Henequen and oil, both products in demand in the international market, sold well. In 1917 Mexico was producing 15 times as much oil as it had in 1910. The oil production emphasized Mexico's dependent position in the world economy; by 1917 Royal Dutch Shell had reportedly produced 40 million barrels of oil, paying only $50,000‡ in taxes.[42] Generally the areas isolated from combat, such as Mexico City, Yucatán, and the west coast, prospered economically. In contrast the mines, railroads, and haciendas of central Mexico suffered heavy damage. The combined positive and negative effects of the revolution led to Mexico's economic growth being comparable to that of Brazil and Argentina at the time.[43]

Mexican society, including the Villistas and Zapatistas, was united around the idea that the hacienda should be replaced by smaller, but still capitalistic, economic units. It was the victors, businessmen and hacendados in disagreement with the Porfirians, and a middle class radicalized in the process of the revolution, who determined the subsequent course of Mexican development.

It was not an anti-capitalist revolution as is often maintained, but a revolution to reform the political institutions and property holdings in order to make capitalist development viable, freeing it from privileges and making it politically and economically independent.[44]

Given the slow pace of reforming political institutions and property holdings, it took more than a decade to overcome the material destruction, loss of life, and emigration to the US which occurred during the Revolution. Furthermore the weakness of post-revolutionary governments permitted regional caudillos to re-establish the regional taxes and local tariffs which had been abolished during the Porfiriato. This tended to destroy the national market and led to confrontations between the caudillos and the central government.[45] Growth for the 1920-9 period was a disappointing 1.7% a year.[46]

The presidents of this period attempted to stimulate growth in various ways. Carranza tried to rebuild the state, seeing no other force capable of reconstructing the economy. Obregón achieved much needed political stability. Finally Calles understood that social reform could not only be used to maintain power, but to stimulate economic development.[47] During Calles's administration the Bank of Mexico was created as the first financial institution which could implement government economic planning and allocation of credit. In 1932 all banks were required to associate with the Bank of Mexico and it soon became a major force in development. Calles also initiated massive government investment in roads and irrigation works, facilitating the growth of agriculture.

By the mid-1920's production was only slightly above that of the Porfiriato. Then with the coming of the depression there was a sharp economic decline. The value of exports in 1932 was one third that of 1929, and imports

‡The dollar sign in this work indicates US dollars. Figures originally given in pesos have generally been converted into dollars at the then-current-rate of exchange. From 1954 to 1976 the peso was worth eight US cents.

were well below the 1900 level.[48] This decline greatly increased unemployment. In order to stimulate the economy the state increased its financing of industry, enabling public office holders to amass some of the largest fortunes in the country. This state spending increased even more rapidly after Cárdenas took office in 1934.

From 1926 to 1940 foreign investment declined from $1.75 billion to $411.2 million.[49] This resulted from the government taking over some foreign-owned enterprises such as mines, and from the general nationalistic climate which many foreigners perceived as hostile to foreign investment. Increasing this trend was the oil companies' shifting operations to the richer, more hospitable shores of Venezuela. In addition during the depression developed countries simply lacked investment capital.

When Cárdenas took office the economy was more like the colonial economy than Mexico's current economy. The nation's agriculture was dominated by the hacienda and most goods were still of foreign manufacture. Raw materials, especially oil, dominated the export scene. In 1926 foreign oil companies exported some 90 million barrels.

The sudden loss of raw material markets during the depression shook the country out of the notion that it could go on exporting minerals forever.[50] In response to this, and the feeling that social progress and economic independence were only possible through manufacturing, industry was encouraged. Tax breaks were given new industries and tariffs prevented ruinous competition from foreign products. Even the exporters backed this industrialization after their traditional markets were cut off. They felt their best hope was to invest their capital in industry.[51]

Cárdenas managed to form an alliance, not only of exporters and manufacturers, but of peasants and workers, all of whom wanted to challenge the hacendados and foreign monopolies. Allying with business interests was no contradiction since Cárdenas felt "the capitalist class was *necessary* for the progress of Mexico."[52] This new alliance was further strengthened by the large government contracts Mexican businessmen received.

Other institutional changes promoted economic development. Agrarian reform increased consumer demand in rural areas. As haciendas disappeared, many found themselves without ties and moved to the city, stimulating the housing industry. The government offered increased amounts of credit to stimulate new development. Only 15% of the credit was foreign, with 46% coming from private Mexican sources and 39% from public funds.[53] Also throughout the country improvement in income distribution increased the domestic market. Finally Cárdenas's increased public spending stimulated the economy.

Economic performance during the Cárdenas administration contrasted sharply with previous administrations. Industry, which grew 31% from 1934 to 1941,[54] overcame the depression and began its unprecedented expansion. When foreign investors did come in, Cárdenas made them come in on equal footing with Mexican businesmen, rather than holding themselves above Mexican law.

Cárdenas's own words illustrate the degree to which he based his hopes on Mexican business being able to solve the country's problems. In his 1939 confrontation with Monterrey businessmen, Cárdenas told the most conservative group in the country:

> *I cordially invite you to cooperate in the task of nation building. I consider your cooperation very desirable; I admire your knowledge, experience and spirit of enterprise. I see you as major promoters of progress and of the national culture. I am pleased to state that industrialists who willingly abide by the law, with understanding and patriotism, have hard and fast guarantees for their investments.*[55]

While he was taking power away from foreign investors, Cárdenas gave the state unprecedented control over labor relations. In 1938 he said the government should

> *determine what the country produces and how to organize commercial distribution. This will undoubtedly benefit the country enormously since state economic organization will fix the share capital should receive, the share workers should get, and the share which the state itself should receive.*[56]

At the end of the Cárdenas administration Mexico had perhaps the best opportunity in its history for autonomous development. The vicious cycle of low income, low investment, low growth, low income, etc., had been broken. Foreign investments in 1939-40 were only 13.0% of all investment, foreign loans were only 5.2% of borrowing.[57]

World War II brought more rapid change to the Mexican economy as the demand for Mexican-produced raw materials and manufactured goods rose. Manufacturing increased 54% from 1940 to 1946,[58] while earnings went up six times.[59] As Mexico's other trading partners were cut off by the war, the US increased its share of Mexican foreign trade from 63.4% in the 1935-9 period to 86% from 1940 to 1945.[60] Rather than leading Mexico to autonomy, the businessmen who fattened themselves on Mexican reform and World War II decided to seek increased personal profits through closer ties with the US. Their rapidly accumulating wealth gave them the political power to steer the country on this course. This gave rise to a period of what is called "stabilized development," which lasted through the 1960's. It was characterized by high foreign investment, constant economic expansion, low inflation, and increases in wages for some workers, but little for the majority of peasants, unskilled workers, and city dwellers without steady jobs.[61] The following figures show how Mexico grew after the depression:[62]

	GNP, % annual increase	Population, % annual increase	GNP per capita, % annual increase
1930-40	4.8	1.7	3.1
1941-50	7.2	2.7	4.5
1951-60	6.2	3.1	3.1
1961-5	6.5	3.4	3.1
1965-70	7.1	3.5	3.6

CHAPTER 12: DEVELOPMENT, PRESENT

The transnational corporations have taken millions of dollars to their country of origin, leaving millions of Mexicans in misery.[1]

RESULTS:

Since World War II the increase in Mexican personal income and gross national product have been spectacular. Per capita income rose from $150 a year in 1950 to the equivalent of $1310 before the 1976 peso devaluation.[2] Even after taking inflation into consideration, personal buying power has increased 150% since 1940.[3] From 1940 to 1950 the gross national product grew at 6.7% a year, from 1950 to 1960 it grew at 6.1%, and from 1960 to 1969 at 7.1%.[4]

This growth rate was well ahead of the rate for Latin America as a whole, which grew at 2.5% per person per year from the late 1930's to the early 1960's, while Mexico was growing at 3.6%. Brazil's growth rate during this period was 2.26% per person per year.[5] Even in the 1960's after Brazil began its rapid economic growth, Mexico grew at a rate of 3.3% per person per year, compared to Brazil's 2.6% and 2.2% for Latin America as a whole.[6] In fact Mexico's growth rate during the last decades surpassed the growth rate of England and the US during their highest periods of growth.[7]

These decades of economic expansion have radically transformed the Mexican economy. Industrial production now includes such technologically sophisticated products as color TV's, cars and air conditioners, and provides 36.6% of the national product, compared to 27% in 1936.[8] Mexico's exports, traditionally based on agriculture and raw materials, are now 52.6% industrial items.[9]

METHODS:

This prodigious growth is the result of many factors. Mexico is the 14th largest country in the world, both in population and area, and has rich mineral resources. In addition government policies have led to the introduction of foreign capital and technology, and have promoted low wages, land reform and public education on a massive scale. It is only the combination of these factors which has led to Mexico's growth; in isolation no one factor would have produced these results.

POLICY: The presidents of Mexico since Cárdenas have made their foremost objective economic growth. Monetary and banking policy was designed to get investment out of commerce and peasant agriculture and into industry,[10] and in addition large sums have been borrowed abroad to further growth. This economic policy reflects the personal interests of decision-makers. "Mexican economic development would be very different if the official party effectively represented workers' and peasants' interests."[11]

STATE: One of the key elements of Mexican development has been strong government participation in the economic process, not only in regulation, but in direct investment. The government owns some 585 corporations which employ over half a million workers[12] and which represent an investment of $21 billion.[13] These corporations engage in such activities as running railroads and air lines and producing oil, steel, fertilizer and electricity. However rather than resulting in a more egalitarian income distribution characteristic of socialist countries, the results of the government's role have been quite different.

State investment does not occur as part of a planned economy, but rather as a supplement to private industry in areas too big, too risky, or too unprofitable for private investors. There are no rigid rules as to the areas in which the government may or may not invest. An example of massive government investment is the new Lázaro Cárdenas-Las Truchas Steelworks, in which the government is investing $300 million, along with $124 million by international lending agencies, and $326 million by foreign suppliers.[14] Government investments, such as those in steel, have provided a wide variety of services, machinery, and raw materials to private businessmen who use them in manufacturing, construction and agriculture, and then keep for themselves the profits generated.

Rather than competing with privately-owned industries, these investments provide them with cheap goods and services. Thus although 46% of all investment is publicly owned, only 10% of the national product is produced by the government.[15] An example of cheap services by government is the low rates charged by the railroads, which are mainly used by industry. From 1966 to 1974 in supplying low-cost rail service, the nationally-owned railroad company subsidized the private sector to the tune of $902 million. In 1974 alone government subsidy to industry was $1.3584 billion dollars.[16] The principal means of transferring this subsidy was low electricity, petroleum, and rail rates.[17]

The political effect of this close association between government and private industry has been the strengthening of the political ties between government and capital.[18] These close ties have led to the de facto domination of the Mexican government by financial interests and foreign investors.[19] Government investment is now increasing faster than private investment. New government investments in industry alone increased from $100 million in 1974 to $214 million in 1975.[20]

This massive government intervention in the economy initially produced cries of protest from conservative businessmen, but this has died since "it is hard to imagine a set of policies designed to reward private enterprise more than those of the Mexican government since 1940."[21] If government investment, which increased at a rate of 30% a year from 1970 to 1975,[22] continues to expand more rapidly than private investment, conflict between the state and private sectors may again erupt. This is what has happened in Brazil when the state sector began to rival the private sector.[23]

IMPORT SUBSTITUTION: A key concept of Mexican development has been import substitution, which was initiated during the Cárdenas administration. This policy involved determining what consumer goods were being imported (stoves, cars, etc.) and then setting government policy to encourage production of these items in Mexico, and in theory eliminating the need for imports. For the last thirty years this policy has dominated Mexican economic planning. The government has encouraged the establishment of factories to make items being imported, and at the same time has made it harder and harder to import consumer goods. The government has promoted local manufacturing by (1.) requiring import permits for certain types of goods, (2.) placing tariffs on imports, (3.) tax exemptions for new industry, (4.) public institutions giving credits to private corporations, and (5.) government production of certain necessities for industry, such as cheap electricity.[24]

The major flaw in this policy of import substitution is that decisions as to what to manufacture in Mexico were left up to private businessmen, who were guided by profits. They decided to produce highly profitable consumer goods, usually for the wealthy, and neglected such areas as machine tools which would give Mexico the capacity to produce its own factories. Not only is it necessary to import manufacturing equipment, but once production begins, many of the raw materials and components going into the final product have to be imported. In automobile manufacturing for example 40% of the parts and components are imported.[25] During the 1960's at the height of import substitution, exports went up 7% a year, while imports went up 12% a year.[26] Then from 1970 to 1974 exports increased 22.1% a year while imports went up 27.0% a year.[27] Ironically import substitution, which was supposed to make Mexico more independent, has made it more dependent.

In any case there is now general agreement that import substitution of consumer items has been accomplished, and that solutions to Mexico's economic problems lie elsewhere. Evidence of this is the fact that 50% of Mexico's imports are now manufacturing equipment and 35% raw materials used in industry.[28]

FOREIGN INVESTMENT: In order to get the capital and technical know-how needed to produce consumer goods, foreign investors have been encouraged to set up factories in Mexico. This has produced a rapid increase in foreign investment, which went from $1.1 billion in 1960 to $2.8 billion in 1970.[29] In 1976 foreign investment amounted to $4.267 billion.[30]

In 1973 76.5% of foreign investment was American owned, while Germany had 4.2%, United Kingdom 4.1%, and Switzerland 3.8%, followed by Canada with 2.1%, Sweden with 1.7%, and Japan with 1.6%.[31] Some of the areas which are most strongly controlled by foreign investment are chemical production (67.2% foreign controlled), machinery (62%), electrical machinery production (79.3%), rubber (84.2%), tobacco (79.7%), and auto manufacturing (66.4%).[32] The areas into which foreign investment goes have changed radically during the course of the century.

The table below shows how foreign capital was distributed at different times:[33]

	1911	1940	1950	1960	1968
Agriculture	7.0%	1.9%	0.7%	1.8%	0.7%
Mining	28.0%	23.9%	19.8%	15.6%	6.0%
Oil	4.0%	0.3%	2.1%	2.0%	1.8%
Manufacturing	4.0%	7.0%	26.0%	55.8%	74.2%
Electricity	8.0%	31.5%	24.2%	1.4%	
Commerce	10.0%	3.5%	12.4%	18.1%	14.8%
Communication & Transport	39.0%	31.6%	13.3%	2.8%	

The table below shows how direct American investment in Mexico has increased since World War II:[34]

1929	$ 682 million
1943	286 million
1950	415 million
1960	795 million
1966	1248 million
1970	1786 million
1972	1993 million

Of the $1.993 billion of direct American investment in 1972, $1.385 billion was invested in manufacturing, $124 million in mining and smelting, and $32 million in petroleum.[35]

This new investment has been instrumental in increasing production. From 1950-67, 54.6% of the increase in production resulted from new investments (by both Mexicans and foreigners). Only 19.8% came from the increase in the size of the work force, and 25.6% from increases in the productivity of the individual worker.[36] These foreign corporations control a majority interest in 134 of the largest 500 corporations, and have partial interests in 40 others.

While foreign investment represents only 5% of total Mexican investment, its effect is far larger than one might imagine. Foreign investment has been concentrated in the most dynamic, fastest growing sectors. It is especially important in manufacturing, which is some 40% foreign-owned. Foreign control is extended when a foreign company is the sole buyer of the product of a Mexican firm. Thus for example, a Mexican battery maker might make batteries which only fit in American-built cars.

RESERVED FOR MEXICANS: The government has felt that some economic activities are so vital to the national interest they should be either controlled by the government, by Mexicans only, or predominantly by Mexicans. Thus the Mexican government is the exclusive producer of petroleum, basic petrochemicals, electricity, and runs the rail, telegraph, and telephone systems. Activities reserved exclusively for private Mexican citizens include radio, television, natural gas distribution and forestry. In other activities such as fishing, agriculture, soft drinks, transportation, steel, glass, cement, and fertilizer production, majority control must be by Mexican citizens.[37]

CREDIT: In order to implement its policy of rapid industrialization, the government has channeled funds into areas it considers of primary importance. Priority access to credit is given to what is known as "productive investment," that is, the production of items which will increase production, as opposed to non-productive luxuries. The first priority is given to the federal government itself, then to federally financed activities such as fertilizer production, and then to private "productive" investment, and finally to other private investment.[38] In his inaugural address López Portillo stated investment priorities, in decreasing order of importance, would be agriculture, energy, petrochemicals, iron and steel, capital goods, transportation, and basic consumer goods.[39]

A key institution in the providing of credit has been a government credit institution known as Nacional Financiera. This institution has been a major source of credit to both private and government-backed projects. Its purpose has been to (1.) foster industrialization, (2.) permit the import substitution program to be carried out, (3.) develop the infrastructure (roads, airports, electricity, etc.), (4.) develop Mexican business talent, (5.) reassure Mexican businessmen that the government is its friend, and (6.) reduce the role of foreign investment.[40]

Credit from Mexican savings channeled through both public institutions such as Nacional Financiera and private banks has provided about 90% of the investment in the last two decades,[41] with the rest coming from abroad. However recently there has been an increasing reliance on foreign borrowing to finance new public and private investments. This increase in foreign borrowing has resulted in a sky-rocketing national debt (see Chapter 14).

RATE OF INVESTMENT: Government policies aimed at stimulating development, especially tax incentives and credit, have resulted in a relatively large percentage of what is produced each year being re-invested to increase production still further. The percentage of production invested each year increased from 9.05% in 1939 to 30% in 1966.[42] From 1965 to 1971 the rate of investment averaged about 20%.[43]

POLITICAL STABILITY; A final key to Mexico's post-World War II growth has been its political stability. Mexico has not been racked by the violence and frequent changes of government which have plagued many other Latin American countries. Such upheavals not only produce material destruction but leave in their wake a jumble of constantly changing policies and scare potential investors.

CONSEQUENCES:

It has become obvious in the last decade that industrial development per se was not the solution to Mexico's economic and social problems that its proponents held it to be. This section will present some of the major drawbacks of Mexico's model of development. In addition, many of the following chapters deal with problems which are closely related to the way in which Mexico is developing.

LOSS OF CONTROL: Perhaps the most striking feature of current development is the degree to which Mexican business and government have lost the power to make vital decisions. In the 19th century foreign corporations largely confined themselves to deciding what to export from Mexico. However since the import substitution program began, foreigners now make many of the decisions regarding what is made in Mexico for use by Mexicans. Frequently these decisions are not made with regard to Mexican interests, but to maximize profits for multinational corporations. Such decisions take into account for the desire to hold on to markets, to use raw materials produced outside of Mexico by the multinational or its affiliates, and to use a standard product style and manufacturing technology, rather than adapting to Mexico's needs.

Attempts by the government to exercise effective control over multinationals have been hampered by the size of the companies, many of which have budgets larger than the budgets of the majority of the world's countries. In cases where the Mexican government stipulates that a majority of stock must be owned by Mexicans, it has been shown that control also can be acquired by financing, technology, technical assistance, and supply and marketing agreements.[44] Many corporations, though nominally owned by Mexicans, have de facto signed away management rights in exchange for skills and resources obtainable from the multinationals. Many contracts signed by Mexican companies stipulate that supplies will only be bought from the parent firm and that products made in Mexico will not be exported. The US Senate study on the multinationals found clauses prohibiting the export of goods produced in Mexico in half the cases it studied.[45] In addition agreements which provide for a foreign company to supply certain technology or certain management services frequently channel much (if not most) of the potential profits out of Mexico without their even being taxed.

Further compounding the problem of controlling foreign corporations is the phenomenon of "namelenders" (prestanombres), Mexican citizens who claim to own Mexican corporations which are actually owned by foreigners. These namelenders are particularly insidious since they enable foreign corporations, posing as Mexican corporations, to take advantage of government financial incentives designed specifically to stimulate Mexican-owned business.

The problem of controlling corporations is extremely difficult. Often those in charge of controlling them have a stake in the company to be controlled, or are offered bribes to look the other way. Payments to government officials such as Lockheed's $112,000 and Uniroyal's $420,000 are rarely made public.[46] Even in cases where there are no conflicts of interest, the sophistication and financial resources of the multinational corporation make it difficult for the overworked, less well-trained government inspectors to be in a position to determine exactly what companies are doing.

JOINT VENTURE: One of the ways the government has tried to reassert its control over the economy is through the promotion of joint ventures. These involve corporations, with some foreign investments, but with majority Mexican ownership. In theory this would provide the company with foreign technical skills, but permit the Mexican owners to exercise control.

In practice though this control has been non-existent due to maneuvers by the multinationals. Often the foreign partner will retain 49% of the stock, and then distribute the rest to many small investors who can never get together to outvote the 49% block. In other cases the stock is only given to those who can be trusted not to vote against the interests of the foreign corporation. Finally, since it is not explicitly prohibited, stock sold to Mexicans sometimes confers no voting rights.[47]

If a joint venture is formed by forcing a foreign-owned corporation to sell the majority of its stock to Mexicans, it is called "Mexicanization." This often provides an effective smokescreen for the foreign operator to hide behind.

Ironically, "Mexicanization," which seemed an extreme measure when it began in the nineteen-forties following the 1938 nationalization of the Mexican oil industry, is now seen as guaranteeing foreign investments against expropriation and providing access to essential raw materials.[48]

TYPE OF TECHNOLOGY: The type of technology used by most multinationals also creates problems. Most of the manufacturing by foreigners uses processes developed for the US, where labor is costly. These same manufacturing techniques have been brought down to Mexico unchanged. As a result multinationals have 2.5 times as much investment per worker as Mexican companies in the same industry.[49] Given the presence of the multinationals and their domination of the local market, there is little incentive to develop alternative technology, and there is little spending for research.[50]

The use of manufacturing techniques developed for use elsewhere has had several consequences. They are considerably more expensive than other alternatives and thus drain foreign currency reserves. Such production techniques are designed to save labor, which is exactly what Mexico, with its overwhelming unemployment, does not need. The use of these techniques throughout Latin America has resulted in a decrease of the manufacturing work force, despite the tremendous increase in manufacturing output.[51]

TRANSFER PRICING: The division of manufacturing into steps carried out in different countries and the great power of the multinationals have led to a practice known as transfer pricing. This involves the main office of a company, most often in the US, directing a branch in one country to sell products to another branch at well below or well above going world market prices. This enables any specific branch to run its costs up so high that it can truthfully declare that it made little or no profit in a given country, such as Mexico. Of course the other branch which sold high will then declare a whopping profit. Usually the branch that declared the profit will conveniently be located in an area where taxes are low.

This practice of transfer pricing is widespread in the Mexican pharmaceutical industry, which is foreign-controlled. In a study of this industry it was found that of 13 important ingredients, only one was bought from the parent company at prices below world market prices. Five of the other ingredients were bought from the parent firm at prices from one to two times the world market prices. Five others cost from two to ten times the international market price, and two others were bought at a price over ten times the international market price.[52] The Mexican pharmaceutical industry is estimated to make as much as $400 million a year using such pricing schemes.[53]

HECTOR GARCIA

This procedure is also useful for escaping US customs duties. Litton Industries was caught by the US government undervaluing goods produced in its Mexican plants and then shipping them into the US.[54] In this case, rather than trying to avoid what would appear to be excessive profits in Mexico, Litton was merely trying to hold down the import duties on goods shipped from Mexico to the U.S.

These transfer pricing schemes can become quite complicated, and are more difficult to control than a simple two-way transaction between branches of a corporation. Often transfer pricing involves a dummy office set up in some tax haven such as the Bahamas. In such cases goods are sold cheaply to the dummy corporation, then marked up tremendously and sold to another branch of the company by the dummy office. That way the original manufacturing branch has a low profit rate, as does the branch finally using the product. However the dummy office which only exists as a figment of corporate imagination, has huge tax-free profits. An example of such a dummy office is the Nassau branch of the Fidelity Bank of Philadelphia, which consists of a desk, a closet, a file cabinet and phone. This branch makes individual loans as high as $120 million.[55]

SHAPE MARKET: This relative lack of control by Mexicans has meant that decisions about what to produce are not planned in terms of national welfare or national development, but instead are left to individual companies, which decide to produce what will generate the highest profits. Investors have consistently decided that the highest profits are not to be found in areas which would serve best for self-sustained, independent development, but are found in such unproductive areas as cars, large shopping centers and luxury hotels.[56]

Not only are the areas chosen for investment often detrimental to the economy as a whole, but the design of individual products also fails to reflect Mexican needs. An example is the American-style farm tractor manufactured in Mexico. At 77 horsepower the smallest model is too large and too expensive for many Mexican needs. Due to the absence of any suitable model, the government has begun to manufacture a 26 horsepower Russian design which is much more suitable for small holdings.[57] American influence in product styles is widespread, from gas-guzzling Ford Galaxy station wagons to throw-away beer cans. Such production, and the advertising generated to stimulate its purchase, attempts to create a society of super-consumption modeled after the United States.[58]

STRUCTURE: The structure of industry which has grown up since the import substitution program began has a number of disadvantages. Since it is designed to produce only for the Mexican market (parent firms usually don't want competition for its branches elsewhere), it often produces in such small quantities there are no savings from mass production. Also such production, carried out within each nation's boundaries, does nothing to further Latin American regional integration.

Furthermore such operations often have neither the advantages of true competition, nor the economy of one single producer. Several companies usually build plants to produce the same product. For instance there are seven different automobile manufacturers in Mexico. The Mexican government never licenses a single company to make a specific product at a reasonable agreed-upon price, thus avoiding costly duplication of production facilities.

Another structural disadvantage of the system is the extreme size of the operations set up by multinationals. Increasingly markets are dominated by a few huge corporations, which makes it very difficult for new companies to compete. In industry, 15% of the firms have 80% of the investment.[59] Would-be entrants to the market are also deterred by the multinationals' ability to share costs worldwide on research and ad campaigns, and by their shifting obsolete equipment from branch to branch. Also the new domestic corporations can't have their initial losses covered by other branches of the same corporation.*

BUYING OUT: The impact of foreign manufacturing firms has been increased by the buying-out of Mexican-owned firms. Such purchases by foreigners have often been made with money borrowed from Mexican banks, rather than with money brought into the country. In the case of the individual banker it makes good business sense to lend money to a multinational with huge assets rather than to a local entrepreneur with limited assets. The result of this practice is that credit which might otherwise be used by Mexican industries has been used by foreigners who often invest nothing. Once such a take-over occurs, an endless drain of money in the form of royalties, profits and licensing fees begins.

---

*John Deere, for example, expects to have losses for ten years after it sets up a new operation. These losses are covered by the parent corporation, something which is impossible for a domestically-owned corporation.[60]

A study noted that of 412 foreign subsidiaries in Mexico, only 143 were established as new enterprises. Existing Mexican firms were purchased in 112 cases, while the others resulted from the division of already-established subsidiaries.[61] Another study showed that 6 of 7 firms owned by multinationals were formerly Mexican-owned and were bought out.[62] A more recent study however showed the effect of new legislation prohibiting such purchases. Only five Mexican firms were bought out by foreign companies in 1973 and only two were in 1974.[63]

HIGH PROFITS: Still another result of the import-substitution model is the extremely high profit rate. Producers are protected from foreign competition by tariffs, and from new domestic competition by their size. Generally there is no competition between already established firms. Profits on the Mexican stock exchange in 1973 were 48%.[64] Despite the recession, profits were up 45% in 1974 and 30% in 1975.[65] Much of the profits come from the high prices charged by competition-free manufacturers, whose prices average 80% higher than those in the developed world.[66] One study estimated that the overall profit rate for multinationals, counting royalties and technical agreements, was 19.0%.[67] The US Senate study of the multinational in Mexico estimated the 1972 profit rate at 16.2%.[68] This study however noted that these declared profits are nearly meaningless, since profits can easily be disguised as costs charged by the home office for "managerial services" or "technical aid." The manager of a US affiliate in Mexico admitted that the "use of payments for technology is the easiest legal way to transfer profits out of the country."[69]

SOCIAL EFFECTS: Although the social structure of Mexico will be considered in more detail later, it is worth pointing out that the "progress" generated by Mexico's industrialization has failed to benefit the majority of the population. Production is for middle and upper class consumers, while manufacturing techniques used have resulted in only a small part of the work force getting industrial jobs.

FINANCIAL DRAIN: In theory Mexico's development was to give it greater independence; however the opposite has been the result. Despite the rationalization that Mexico needs foreign capital to develop, the multinationals have consistently taken out more money than they have brought in. From 1966 to 1969, $465 million was brought in for direct investment, while $976.8 million was taken out in profits.[70] The amount of profits, royalties and other payments taken out of Mexico increased from $357.8 million in 1970 to $704.8 million in 1974 and $1.0528 billion in 1976.[71]

TRADE DEFICIT: Mexico has been burdened with a growing trade deficit, or in other words, it spends more abroad than it takes in each year. This deficit is largely a product of the import substitution model of development. Rather than spending the last decades building facilities to produce their own factories, Mexican industry has concentrated on more profitable consumer goods. In order to manufacture these consumer goods, manufacturing facilities (capital goods) have to be purchased abroad. In developed countries capital goods are from 20 to 40% of the gross national product, in Mexico they are less than 15%.[72] Given the increasingly sophisticated nature of technology, Mexico is becoming more dependent on imported capital goods. Capital goods were only 56.2% of imports in 1960, while they were 73.2% in 1965.[73]

UNDER ECHEVERRIA:

The Mexican economy under Echeverría reflected the negative aspects of both import substitution and the world economic crisis.

The worst problem was inflation. From 1957 to 1970 inflation was only about 2% a year.[74] However during the Echeverría administration inflation became a major problem due to the increasing cost of imports, high government spending to stimulate the economy, agricultural scarcity and speculation.[75] The result was 21.4% inflation in 1973, and then 20.7% in 1974 and 9.5% in 1975.[76]

Mexico's trade deficit soared during the Echeverría administration. The balance of payments deficits were (in millions of dollars):[77]

1971	$ 846
1972	$ 916
1973	$1415
1974	$2876
1975	$4056
1976	$2700

Finally there was a decline in the rate of economic growth. In 1976 the growth rate was 2%, the lowest in 25 years. Economic growth in previous years was:[78]

1972	7.3%
1973	7.6%
1974	5.9%
1975	4.2%

The government responded to the economic crisis by trying to force modernization on domestic industry and by legislating controls on multinationals designed to eliminate or temper some of the abuses mentioned earlier in this chapter.

> *What is at stake, basically, is how the benefits of multinationalism will be apportioned. And it is plain that the Latin American nations intend to claim a larger share through a variety of investment rules.*[79]

One such piece of legislation is the 1973 Law to Promote Mexican Investment and Regulate Foreign Investment. This law limits the areas in which foreigners can invest and what share of companies they can own. For example only 40% foreign ownership is permitted in secondary petrochemicals. These ownership limitations can be waived on an individual basis if the new investor is seen as one who will create exports and new jobs or will locate outside presently industrialized areas.

Another law is the 1972 Law on Transfer of Technology and Use and Exploitation of Patents and Trademarks.

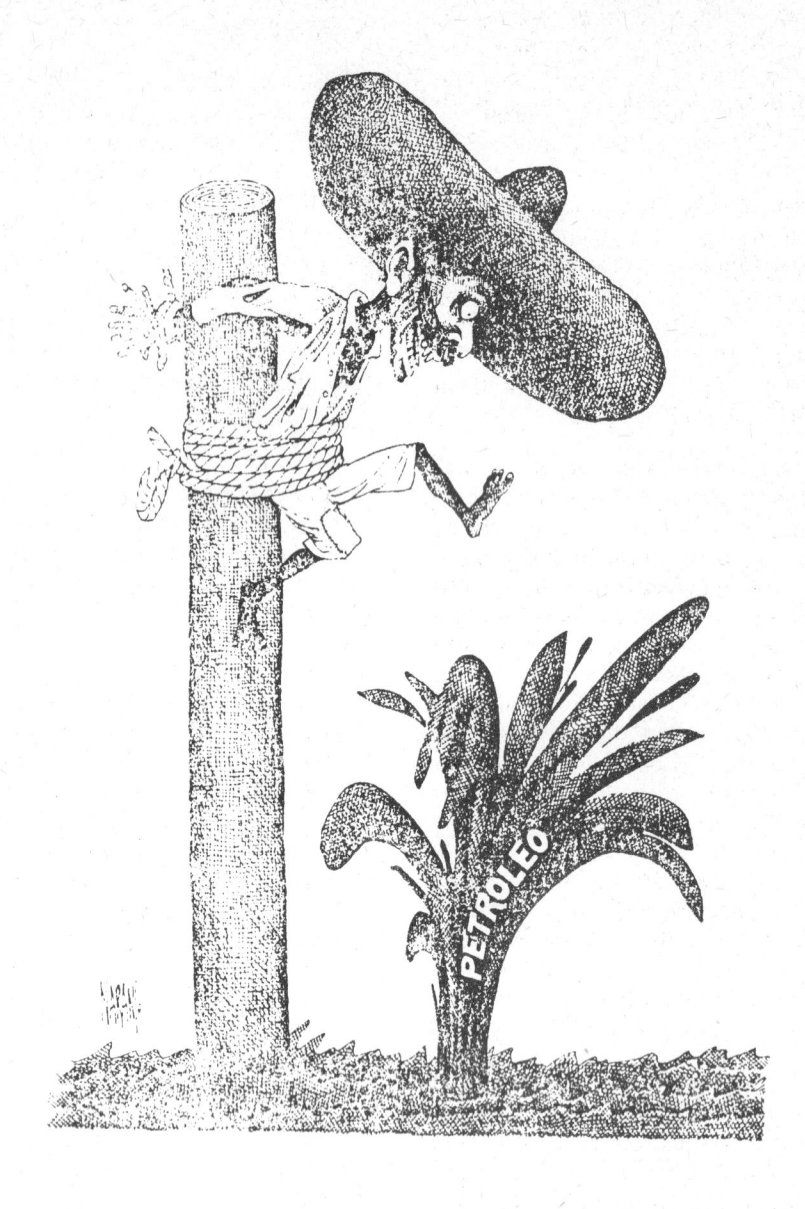

This law bans contracts which prohibit the export of goods manufactured with foreign patents. It also sets a limit on how much a Mexican firm can be charged for technology, especially if other sources for the same technology are available. Contracts which give managerial control over a Mexican firm to a foreign patent owner or supplier of technology are prohibited. Another 1976 law has a clause permitting the government to limit the amount paid for the use of foreign trademarks. This law reflects the feeling that it is not worth using up foreign exchange just to have the word CREST on a tube of Mexican toothpaste, and so on for the hundreds of foreign brand names sold in Mexico.

Eventually this law will require all firms to adopt Spanish (or Spanish sounding) brand names to replace the abundance of US brand names found on Mexican goods. The difficulty of legislating an end to dependence is shown by the fact that the new brand names required under the law are being developed in the US using high price American media and legal specialists. The costs of such development are charged to the Mexican subsidiary.[80]

The new laws, despite their appearance of providing meaningful control over multinationals, seem to be largely a matter of show, designed to convince the populace of the government's good intentions. A major weakness of the laws is the provision that restrictions on foreign investment can be waived in specific cases if the investment meets rather vague criteria of decentralization, employment or export. Another major stumbling block is simply the lack of will or political clout to implement such laws. In a discussion of these laws, the book GLOBAL REACH notes:

In an early-1973 internal memorandum, the staff economist of a large global bank gave his "preliminary feeling" that Mexico's new law on regulating foreign investment and controlling the transfer of technology "will NOT have a drastic impact on foreign investment in Mexico." Such laws he points out "are more visible to the public than a mere change in practice and thus help fill the quotient of nationalism necessary in public policy."[81]

If anyone were to doubt that the Mexican government was no longer welcoming foreign investment, an ad in BUSINESS WEEK dispelled that. In the October 20, 1975 issue the Mexican government bought a 20 page ad whose primary message was to tell businessmen how profitable Mexico was to invest in. Foreign investors seem less enthusiastic, and their new investments declined from $362 million in 1975 to $330 million in 1976.[82]

....

The negative results of multinational development and import substitution became apparent in August 1976. At that time the peso was devalued for the first time in 22 years. The devaluation had its roots in the inability of the economic system to keep growing. To pump some life into the economy, Echeverría resorted to massive foreign borrowing, rather than let the economy stagnate and worsen social problems. Tens of billions of borrowed dollars were converted into pesos and put into circulation, nearly tripling the amount of money in circulation during the Echeverría administration.[83] Much of the borrowed money was spent by the government, leading to a six-fold increase in government spending during Echeverría's administration.[84] The result of placing so much money into circulation would be obvious to anyone who had taken an elementary economics course: inflation. Just before the devaluation, both wealthy and middle class Mexicans began to exchange pesos for dollars, feeling a devaluation was inevitable. They converted an estimated $4 billion from pesos into dollars and forced the Mexican government to devalue the peso.

In theory devaluation should help the balance of payments by making exports cheaper. However Mexican industry, which has grown up behind trade barriers, is in many cases too inefficient to compete, even with the devaluation. Commodity exports, on the other hand, are sold at international prices, and therefore the only change with devaluation will be a windfall profit for exporters. It is also hard to cut down on imports, despite their higher price, since most imports are vital to production within Mexico.

....

Mexico's bargaining position in the world has significantly improved with its new oil discoveries, which might give Mexico the opportunity to become a major exporter of oil. The exact size of the deposits still hasn't been determined, but it is estimated that there are about 11 billion barrels.[85] These new finds enabled Mexico to go from importing oil early in 1974 to exporting it by the end of 1974. However the rate of domestic consumption has been rising nearly as fast as reserves. In 1970 the reserves would have lasted 20 years at the 1970 rate of consumption, the 1975 reserves were only good for 13.4 years. The 1976 estimates only extended reserves to 24.9 years.[86]

Other factors have shifted the balance of power somewhat toward underdeveloped nations such as Mexico. Citizens of the underdeveloped world are much more aware of the effects of foreign investment. Such incidents as ITT's involvement in the overthrow of Allende have driven home the necessity of controlling multinationals.[87]

The bargaining position of the multinationals is changing in that raw materials and cheap labor sources are in ever-increasing demand. Countries having these resources to offer can now play Japan, Europe, and the US off against each other, rather than having to take what the US has to offer.[88] In addition the increasing strength of the socialist economies provides still more options for foreign trade, as does the increasing availability of alternative sources of credit.[89] Socialist countries have also shown that it is possible to make a contract with a multinational which involves neither the multinational's deciding what will be produced nor the investor's perpetually taking unlimited profits from the host country.

Finally control of the multinational is becoming more feasible simply because more information is available. Only since 1970 has sufficient information been available to enable underdeveloped countries to develop information banks, discover who really owns corporations, and share information on contracts signed by various underdeveloped countries.[90]

CHAPTER 13: AGRARIAN REFORM

Medium and large landholders and agrarian entrepreneurs dominate commercial agriculture and are the backbone of the agricultural bourgeoisie. They are the real heirs of the revolution, not the peasants.[1]

1. HISTORY

As long ago as the 18th century viceroys said that agriculture and commerce were being blocked by huge estates which were often neglected by their absentee landlords. The dominance of the large estates was further increased in the 19th century when liberal reform laws resulted in the transfer of church estates and Indian communal lands to private hands.

During the Porfiriato (1872-1911) large estates formed the basis of Mexican agriculture and their owners were staunch backers of Díaz. When Díaz left office 1% of the population owned 70% of the workable land. In the state of Chihuahua one family owned 5 million hectares and in the state of Hidalgo three families owned over half the land.[2]

As the estates increased in size, their role changed. Originally the hacienda was more efficient than the Indian communal land in that it utilized ox carts, crop rotation, and fertilizer. However by the end of the 19th century it blocked economic development by tying up much of the land and paying such low salaries that a large market for industrial goods could not be created.[3] Furthermore the failure of the majority of the hacendados to adopt modern technology limited the ability of export agriculture to finance industrialization. Low levels of production limited the supply of agricultural goods for industry and city dwellers.[4] Finally the hacienda was generally undercapitalized due to the constant drain of capital from Mexico by foreign investors. This lack of money for investment resulted in low productivity, lower wages in agriculture, and a readiness for revolution on the part of the peasantry.[5]

Since peasants wanted revolution and entrepreneurs felt the hacienda blocked their progress, it is hardly surprising that virtually the only point of agreement among the various factions at the beginning of the revolution was that the hacienda should be abolished. Madero dealt with the problem gingerly in his Plan de San Luis Potosí, stating that stolen lands should be returned to villages. Zapata's 1911 Plan de Ayala called for stolen lands to be repossessed by the peasants themselves, not by some government body. In addition it provided for the expropriation of one third of each legally owned hacienda, with land taken going to landless peasants. In fact there was total expropriation of haciendas in Morelos while the Zapatistas were in control. Then in 1915, largely to win over Zapata's supporters, Carranza proclaimed his agrarian reform, in beautiful legal prose. Carranza's reform was to be executed by military authorities themselves, not the peasants, and it provided for peasants living outside the hacienda but not those living on hacienda land.

Article 27 of the 1917 Constitution was basically a reaffirmation of the 1915 law. Reform was to take place at the will of government officials, not peasants. This put tremendous power in the hands of generals who frequently abused it by giving lands to themselves or their cronies.

Once the agrarian reform was on the books little happened until the Cárdenas presidency. Carranza, lacking a major power base, allied himself with the hacendados, and only distributed 0.1% of the land area of the country. Obregón, with his more populist style, did little better, distributing 0.6% in his four-year term. The next president, Calles, distributed 1.5% and the following three presidents who governed until 1934 passed out 1.8%.[6] Most of the lands which were distributed to peasants before 1934 went to towns which could show they had lost land through fraud or violence.[7]

Even the distribution of small amounts of land met with bitter resistance from landowners. This resistance was heightened by the agrarian reform's prohibition against resale of land distributed, thus depriving the hacendado of the chance of recovering his land once it was taken by the agrarian reform. Since the agrarian reform law specified that land distributed had to be within 7 km. of the community requesting it, communities were often driven from their homes by gunfire and burning so they would no longer fulfill the residency requirement.[8] Hacendados could also appeal decisions in courts, where friendly judges abounded. By 1928 5,000 cases had been appealed, and of the 2,000 decided, 90% of the decisions were in favor of the landlords.[9] The Cristero Revolt, with its hacendado backing, also slowed the agrarian reform since government officials, including agronomists, were likely targets for attack.[10]

The agrarian reform also encountered opposition within the government itself. Carranza, Obregón and Calles, the principal figures up to the time of Cárdenas, all wanted to promote economic development. None of them thought that giving land to the peasants was a way of increasing agricultural production. Rather the agrarian reform was seen as a method of calming the peasant politically so that agriculture could be developed by large, modern farms. Plots measuring only four hectares were distributed, with the idea that they would supplement the income of the peasant, who would also have to work for wages. By the 1920's it was assumed that the land distributed to the peasants was less productive, and the distribution of land virtually ceased.

This "inefficiency" was the perfect example of the self-fulfilling prophecy. Initially it was assumed that land given to peasants wouldn't produce very much. Therefore in order not to take more land out of production than was necessary, only small plots were given to the peasants. And in order to conserve scarce capital, there was virtually no credit or technical assistance provided. Also following this line of reasoning the land distributed was generally of poor quality. When production indeed turned out to be low, this was used as justification for terminating the agrarian reform.[11]

The result was that by 1930 the 0.3% of farms which were over 10,000 hectares made up 55.8% of the land area.[12] Given the decline in agricultural jobs due to the loss of markets in the depression, it is hardly surprising that Cárdenas found the peasants ripe for revolt when he took office in 1934.

In order to defuse the potential for rural violence and stimulate economic development, Cárdenas greatly increased the amount of land distributed and changed the basic conception of the agrarian reform. He expected farms owned by individual peasants to cut the stranglehold on the economy exercised by the hacendado and to provide agricultural products for both export and domestic use. In order to make the peasant holding economically viable, he increased the size of the plot given to peasants, gave out fertile irrigated land, founded a credit bank, and provided technical aid. Peasants actually living on haciendas, as opposed to those living in independent communities, were made eligible for land. To protect peasants from retributions by former owners some 60,000 peasants were armed to protect their holdings.[13] Before this in a three month period during 1936 over 500 peasants were killed by landowners.[14]

Statistically the results of Cárdenas's land reform are impressive. Some 9.1% of the land area was distributed,* as compared with 3.9% of the land by the presidents from

---

*This was 9.1% of the total area of Mexico. It was a much higher percentage of the workable land.

Diego Rivera associating agrarian reform and Christ, used to combat clerical hostility to land distribution

Carranza to Cárdenas.[15] The 1930 census showed that the ejido, the community receiving land, owned 13.4% of the lands farmed without irrigation, and 13.1% of the irrigated land. By 1940 this total had risen to 47.4% of non-irrigated land, and 57.3% of irrigated land.[16] Furthermore to avoid the threat of expropriation owners often sold hacienda lands to peasants in advance of the agrarian reform. Many workers no longer tied down unproductively on the hacienda were freed for urban jobs. In addition production was diversified and land the hacendados hadn't bothered to use was put into cultivation.[17]

Despite this major transformation of rural Mexico, there were drawbacks. Former owners were allowed to keep water sources, buildings and 100 hectares of irrigated land or the equivalent in unirrigated land (many times more than the peasant was given to start his production). Often the hacendado used this nucleus to dominate the same peasants commercially, rather than through land ownership. Furthermore many of the large holdings remained untouched. The 1940 census shows some 300 properties which together occupied 30 million hectares. Nevertheless the hacendados as a class were displaced from power, in most cases without compensation, and ceased to be the backbone of Mexican agriculture.[18]

After Cárdenas left office in 1940, the land reform began to reflect the pressure of the right wingers and entrepreneurs wanting to exploit large scale holdings themselves. High quality lands were no longer distributed, and less credit and technical assistance were provided to the ejido. This began rather suddenly during World War II since it was felt that the agrarian reform was slowing production, and that the right wing would withdraw from the war effort if it was not placated by the termination of what it felt to be a communist plot to deprive owners of land.[19]

Given this initial impetus, it was easy for pro-business President Alemán (1948-52) to further slow the land reform. Alemán declared the agrarian problem to be solved, and further reduced the area of land distributed. He increased the maximum legal holding to 100 hectares of irrigated land (or its equivalent in other lands). The government also looked the other way when many landowners disguised the size of their holdings by registering sections of their lands in the names of relatives or name lenders (those who hold the land on the deed as a legal fiction to permit the old owner to keep using it). Those who had land expropriated usually lost their lands as a result of political maneuvering, not due to any concern for the peasant.[20] As was the case with the agrarian reform before Cárdenas, the best lands and those irrigated at government expense often fell into the hands of those who were close to the powerful.[21]

As a result of this shift private holdings increased. From 1940 to 1950 non-irrigated land held by the ejido declined from 47.1% to 44.1%, and irrigated land held by the ejido went from 57.3% to 49.8%.[22] The sharp decline in irrigated lands in the hands of the ejido was due to land newly irrigated at government expense coming under private control. This shift was even more dramatic in the State of Sonora, site of peasant unrest at the end of the Echeverría administration. In 1940 40% of the workable land in the state was ejido land, in 1950 only 17% was.[23]

The agrarian reform has continued to the present, although it is now more demagoguery than economic policy. Once Cárdenas had cooled tensions in the countryside by distributing some 20.1 million hectares of land, distribution was sharply reduced. The following figures indicate the amount of land distributed by subsequent presidents:[24]

Avila Camacho	5.97	million hectares
Alemán	5.43	"
Ruiz Cortines	5.77	"
Lopez Mateos	9.0	"
Díaz Ordaz	23.05	"
Echeverría (thru Nov. 1975)	10.55	"

The figures for the last two presidencies are misleading since they reflect the distribution of huge tracts of nearly worthless land. From 1965 to 1968, 91.3% of land distributed was suitable only for pasture, forestry, and gathering, while only 0.5% was irrigated.[25]

This half-century-long agrarian reform has been fundamental to the economic development of Mexico. A total of some 70 million hectares of land has been distributed to about 3 million peasant families.[26] In addition some four million hectares of land have been irrigated, although by no means all has gone to poor peasants. The three million families who received land were also converted from potential rebels into firm supporters of the government, and in addition the loyalty of millions more was obtained by keeping up their hopes of getting land. Finally the agrarian reform produced a major shift in power away from the hacendado, not to the peasant, but to various government officials in charge of administering the agrarian reform and allocating credit.

The breaking up of the old hacienda system permitted Mexican agricultural output to grow faster than that of any other Latin American country from 1934 to 1965.[27] From 1947 to 1955 agricultural production increased faster than either the manufacturing sector or the economy as a whole.[28] Gains in agriculture from 1935 to 1955 were 5.8% a year, mainly a result of increasing the area under cultivation, while from 1956 to 1966 production increased at 3.4% a year, mainly a result of increases in irrigation and productivity per unit area.[29]

However the agrarian reform has failed to redistribute rural wealth. Massive government investment in roads, irrigation, and credit did not benefit the peasantry as a whole, but served to channel funds to large landowners, to those who supply them with industrial products, and to those who market and process the crops.[30] Such investment has also greatly benefited the exporters who in 1975 exported $835 million worth of agricultural products, 29% of Mexico's exports.

2. THE EJIDO

The basic unit of the Mexican agrarian reform is the ejido. Ejido refers to either the community which has been granted lands under the agrarian reform, or to the lands which have been granted. In order for peasants to receive lands and thus constitute an ejido there must be at least 20 agricultural workers in one community who have little or no land or other assets. These twenty or more persons must then file a petition with the government stating that they would like to be granted a certain piece of land within 7 km. of their community. In order to be expropriated the land specified in the petition must be owned by a single person who has land in excess of the legal limit. The land ownership limit established by the agrarian reform is 100 hectares of irrigated land, or other units of land which are roughly equivalent and whose maximum size are determined by the quality of land, the presence of irrigation, and the type of crop grown.

Once the claim is processed the members of each community receive plots of land, officially ten hectares for each adult, although in many cases there is not enough land and they receive less. Then they elect a set of officers to administer the newly created ejido and begin farming. In the vast majority of cases each farmer is granted an individual piece of land which he farms himself, and whose crop he is free to consume or sell. The organization of the ejido serves mainly to obtain credit for the individual farmer and to tie him into national political and peasant organizations.

The farmer who has received land is called an ejidatario. In many ways he is just a small farmer, although there are significant differences. To prevent land from being sold and concentrated back into large estates, the ejidatario cannot sell his plot. As long as the ejidatario farms the land it is his, and if he dies the plot can be inherited. However if he abandons the land or leaves it fallow for more than two years the land is returned to the control of the ejido and is allocated to a landless member of the community. Along with the inability to sell land there is the inability to mortgage the plot, so the farmer cannot put up his land as collateral to secure a loan for his farming. In order to resolve this problem the government makes funds available through the Ejido Credit Bank.

In a few instances what has been called a collective ejido has been tried. In these ejidos, which were created during the Cárdenas administration, a variety of communal work and land ownership patterns were tried. Generally these collective ejidos were set up on the best irrigated land. In contrast to most ejidos, they were also given adequate technical aid and credit, and proved quite efficient. However after the Cárdenas administration communal ejidos were seen to be political threats by conservative rural landowners and were divided into individual plots. This division was carried out by such tactics as appointing administrators of the collective ejido who were known to favor breaking the ejido into individually-farmed units, despite the wishes of its members. Such farms were then subdivided without the consent of their members and subsequently credit and other imputs were only given to individuals, not the collective. In other cases individuals were given the opportunity to acquire ejido land for themselves or to illegally profit from ejido business if they helped de-collectivize the ejido.[31] These tactics destroyed most of the collective ejidos by the 1950's.

Most ejidos coexist with other landholding patterns. There are still some of the old pre-conquest communal landholdings left, especially in areas of high Indian population, such as Oaxaca. These lands occupy some 5% of the national area.[32] Generally these communal lands are controlled by the municipal government and are used for pasture and lumbering. Almost without exception lands suitable for large-scale farming has been taken over by outsiders during the course of Mexican history. With the spread of "modern" ideas and population increase, communal lands are being appropriated by individuals and converted into private property.

Despite the government's having committed itself to the agrarian reform and the ejido, the most economically significant form of landholding is the private farm. In 1960 the area harvested by ejidos was 4.9 million hectares, while private farms over 5 hectares had 5.05 million hectares, and private farms under 5 hectares had harvested 0.8 million hectares.[33] The area harvested is the best way to determine the relative importance of ejido and private holdings since much of the land given to ejidos is of such poor quality that it is not used for crops. In addition to the ejido land which is divided into individual plots, other lands of poor quality are kept undivided and are used by all ejido members. These lands, which comprise some 77% of all ejido area,[34] are often of little economic value and are used for pasturing and logging.

There is still much controversy about the ejido system and its efficiency, a controversy often clouded by imprecision in defining the term "efficiency." Rarely do the polemicists note whether they are speaking of efficiency in terms of crop value per hectare harvested, crop value produced by a given amount of human labor, or return on money invested. Discussion of efficiency is further complicated by the ejidos generally being located on poor land, growing different crops, and having less capital and modern technology than the large private farms to which they are compared.

In terms of return on investment the ejido returned 2.35 pesos for each one invested, while private holdings over 5 hectares returned 1.88, and those under five hectares returned 2.88.[35] This would make the ejido and the small farm seem quite efficient when compared to the large farm. However these figures only take into consideration money invested and not the value of the labor put into farming by the self-employed small farmer or ejidatario. If his work is figured in at the value of the minimum wage one finds that the units over five hectares return 1.8 pesos for each peso invested, private farms under five hectares return 0.7 pesos and the ejido 1.4.[36] In other words the small holdings are farmed by the self-employed who make up for their lack of machinery by putting in long hours which do not produce enough return to pay themselves the minimum wage.

In terms of return per agricultural worker there is an even sharper contrast, since the large farms have many workers achieving high output through the use of machinery. Workers on farms over five hectares produce 16,700 pesos per worker per year, workers on private farms under five hectares produce 1,850 and those on ejidos produce 2,950.[37]

In terms of value of produce per hectare, in 1960 farms over five hectares produced 25% more per hectare than the ejido and 40% more than the farm under five hecacres.[38] Production on large farms is increasing faster than on small ones due to the combination of good land, access to credit, modern technology, irrigation, and the ability to grow and market valuable cash crops such as cotton. Small farms and ejidos tend to grow more traditional crops such as corn which have lower market value, but which require less investment in fertilizers, pesticides, and the like.

This question of ejido efficiency again is largely a self-fulfilling prophecy, since most policy makers have not wanted even a remote threat to the capitalist, privately-owned farm, and thus have channeled credit and access to technology into the modern private sector, which then not surprisingly increases production faster than the ejido or small farm. In addition the ejido was conceived at a time when the individual farmer plowing with a mule was the norm. The shift in agricultural technology since then has favored the large farm.

An example of how resources have been concentrated outside the ejido sector is provided by tractor ownership. Some 80% of the farm tractors in Mexico are on private farms with an average of 43 hectares per tractor. Ejidos in contrast have 128 hectares per tractor.[39]

The ejido is no longer an effective means of checking peasant unrest since there is little land left to be distributed. While there are large estates which have successfully evaded the agrarian reform either through political influence, intimidation of peasants, or feigned subdivision of land, the basic problem is that there is simply not enough land left to distribute. If all possible lands were distributed, including desert lands suitable only for hunting and gathering, only some 181,581 peasants, or 5% of the 4 million peasants eligible, would benefit.[40] If the maximum legal limit for land holding were cut in half this still would not solve the problem, because even then only some 7% of landless peasants would receive land.[41]

3. PROBLEMS

The continued implementation of the agrarian reform over fifty years after its inception reflects its original purpose: pacifying the peasantry. In contrast to this piecemeal, drawnout approach was the action of Cárdenas in the Laguna Area in north central Mexico. Production in this area was vital since it produced cotton which could be sold for foreign exchange. Cárdenas was faced by intransigent land owners and widespread strikes by agricultural workers. In order to calm the situation and at the same time not interrupt production, Cárdenas ordered an agrarian reform in the area. It took 40 days from the time the order was given for agronomists to come in, measure the land, and distribute it to peasants.

In contrast to this one instance of efficiency, the time from filing to receiving land *averages* 14 years, rarely takes under five years, and may drag out for over thirty years.[42] During this time the solicitors, if they persevere, must expend considerable sums for travel to government offices (often in Mexico City), legal fees, and bribes to officials to get their claims expedited. In one extreme case lands near the town of Buenavista, Puebla were ordered distributed by Zapata in 1912 and were finally turned over to the peasants in April, 1975.[43]

In a few cases hacendados have been able to simply stall and threaten their way to a stalemate, permitting them to retain lands. In the hacienda of Obrajuela, located in the Bajio region northwest of Mexico City, 50 peasants requested lands in 1936. Immediately the hacendados and priests began to pressure the solicitants against taking the land. Thirty of the fifty were sold 10-12 hectare plots of poor land, which pushed them above the legal limit for solicitants. They were to pay for these lands with money made from selling their crops in the future. The remaining twenty solicitants were constantly harassed while the hacendados did a fake subdivision of their land by transferring interests to cousins and children and thus claiming their lands were below the legal limit. Today the wage laborers living on the hacienda have received no land, and in fact don't even own their own houses.[44]

A second failure of the agrarian reform has been the inability to create an economically viable farming unit. Despite the agrarian reform, highly-profitable, privately-owned land holdings perpetuate the social problems the agrarian reform should have solved. Old haciendas, such as Obrajuela, through political connections, subterfuge or violence simply have avoided the agrarian reform. However this type of holding is the exception and no longer is the main problem which must be dealt with. The main problem is a new type of landholding called the neo-latifundia. This may involve the nucleus of the the old hacienda which was subdivided and in which the hacendado kept the best 100 hectares of land, and the improvements. Also the neo-latifundia can be a newly-acquired piece of property which serves as the basis of capital accumulation. In both cases since the surrounding ejidatarios lack capital and marketing experience, the private owner simply begins exploiting them financially and commercially rather than as landowner. He makes usurious loans to them, and then buys crops from the generally illiterate peasants who lack means of transport, and resells the crop at a much higher price.

A second form of neo-latifundia has no fixed base at all. Rather an entrepreneur moves into an area and rents various ejido plots. He then farms them intensively with modern machinery, extracting the maximum profit in the shortest possible time. Generally these operations move from spot to spot, so little is invested, and there is no concern for the long-term productivity of the land. Given the high cost of capital, machinery, and chemicals used (as compared to prices in the developed world), payments made for labor and rent must be low. High rent and wages would drive the costs up so high crops could not be sold in the international market.

Alongside these modern units are the vast majority of ejidatarios who lack credit, and are forced to grow largely for their own consumption, or rent out their lands to the neo-latifundia and then work as wage laborers. Once this process gets started, the neo-latifundia accumulates capital, buys machinery, and puts the ejidatario at an even greater disadvantage, forcing more rental, and permitting even greater capital accumulation by the neo-latifundia. The continued existence of small farmers (or ejidatarios) however is crucial. Small farm-owners will work on the large estates to gain needed cash. However they are partially self-supporting, so wages paid them need not be high. Also their owning a small piece of land insures that they do not migrate to the city in search of a higher paying job.

It seems likely that this trend toward concentration of agricultural income will continue. Government spending for credit, public works, subsidies for fertilizer, etc., channels wealth into the hands of the modern commercial growers and leaves the small farmer and ejidatario behind. The least well-equipped 50% of farms have only 1.3% of all farm machinery, while 0.5% of the largest farms have 44% of farm machinery.[45] Furthermore productivity of agricultural workers is rising faster than salaries so that in 1950 salaries were 26.7% of the value of agricultural produce, while in 1967 they were 21%.[46] This channels still more wealth to growers. An example of the speed with which modern capitalist farming is taking over is provided by nitrogenous fertilizer consumption: in 1950 104,000 metric tons were used, in 1960 2,243,000 were used, and in 1970 3,780,000.[47] The result is that income in agriculture is distributed much as it was in the Porfiriato[48] and more unequally than in the society as a whole.[49]

Another failure of the agrarian reform is in land distribution. Lands are sometimes registered as unproductive or as cattle ranches, since both categories have large legal limits. Once it is so registered, the land is put to some other use, as when the government irrigates it at public expense, permitting it to be farmed. Holdings in the Yaqui Valley of Sonora where conflict broke out at the end of the Echeverría administration show how irrigated lands are often concentrated in the hands of a few. There some 85 individuals held 116,800 hectares of fertile, irri- land.[50] According to the 1970 census 50.7% of all farming units take up 13.1% of the land area and produce 32.3% of value. On the other hand 0.5% of the farming units take up 28.5% of the area and produce 32.2% of value.[51] Data show this concentration to be increasing with some 80% of the increase in production taking place in the top 4.5% of farming units.[52]

Even though only 0.7% of all investment in agriculture was foreign in 1968, there was still a high degree of foreign control. This is achieved through sale of supplies such as feed and fertilizers. In addition foreign investment in agriculture, 90% from the US, is growing faster in percentage terms than investment in industry. In 1960 foreign investment amounted to $63.34 million dollars and by 1970 it was $235.5 million.[53] Such direct investment in agriculture however is no longer the key to rural wealth. Rather credit, selling inputs (fertilizer, seeds, pesticides, etc.) and marketing a crop can be more profitable than mere land ownership.[54]

Firms such as United Brands and Heinz are buying an increasing share of Mexican produce and exporting it or processing it and selling it to Mexicans at 20 to 30 times the price of the natural food. Food-processing is a $2.73 billion-a-year industry which produces 25% of the total value of manufactured goods.[55] Foreign companies set the style of food packaging and force Mexican-owned firms to rely on the same type of packaging. Since the packaging techniques rely on foreign technology, they make even the Mexican-owned producer selling to Mexicans dependent on foreigners. Of the 53 largest firms engaged exclusively in food processing, 26 are under total or majority foreign control.[56] Together these foreign firms account for 75% of the food processing.[57] Three-fourths of the soft drinks are sold by Coke, Pepsi and Orange Crush. Three-fourth of the fruit and vegetables are canned by Heinz, Campbells and Del Monte. Gerber makes 80% of the baby food and Carnation 85% of the evaporated milk.[58]

Anderson Clayton, which purchases 60% of the Mexican cotton crop, provides an example of how a company can control agriculture without owning land. This firm offers package deals to those with no other source of credit. Included in their contracts in addition to credit is the supply of seeds, pesticides, fertilizers, and insecticides. It not only supplies these products but supervises their application. Finally the contracts include the sale of the cotton produced to Anderson Clayton at the price the company sets.[59] In addition Anderson Clayton also produces cooking oil, cotton seed, peanuts, safflower, sorghum, soy, insecticide, herbicide, fertilizer, bird food, cattle feed, lard, gelatine, margarine, flour, candy, chocolate, sauces and soups, coconut, and peanut products. This production takes place in 63 plants located in twelve states and the Federal District.[60]

Foreign agri-business has been subsidized by the Mexican government, just as foreign industry has. As in the case of industry, the agricultural multinationals decide what to produce, with what technology it will be produced, and where the produce goes.[61] Government subsidies often go for developing land to be used for export crops. Also the government has aided research in high-yield crops carried out by the Rockefeller and Ford foundations. These crops require a "package" of foreign inputs and are designed for export. Furthermore the cultivation of these crops requires land tenure, market and credit policies detrimental to the majority of peasants.[62] Owners of irrigated land pay the government so little for the water they receive that the charges don't even pay for the cost of maintaining the irrigation system, let alone paying off initial investment.[63] Just as was the case with industry, little consideration was taken of the social consequences of introducing agrarian technologies developed in a different social setting.

The frequent shifts in policy and the piecemeal method in which the agrarian reform was carried out over the last fifty years has produced a chaotic system of large and small private properties, ejidos and public properties. For example in the municipio of Río Grande, Zacatecas, the map in the agrarian reform administration office shows the landholding pattern, a hopeless jumble labeled fraccionamientos, colonies, small properties, enlargements, ranches, cattle land, private land, pasture, allotment, new population center, and tierra de labor.* In addition there were 89 different segments labeled ejidos, some representing separate ejidos and others representing non-contiguous ejidos. This of course did not include the various plots into which the ejidos have been divided. Such a jumble makes rational agricultural planning a near impossible task.

*Even the staff working the office was unable to explain many of the labels.

Another problem is the preference Mexican investors have shown for industry in recent years. In 1972 only 4% of private bank credit went into agriculture.[64] Government banks were doing little to take up the slack since only 3% of the small farmers and 20% of the ejidatarios were getting credit from them.[65] When government credit is available it often involves such a high degree of control by government officials that the ejidatario becomes a virtual employee of the government.

In the last 20 years some $300 million have been taken out of agricultural profits and invested elsewhere.[66] Further depleting the amount of money available to agriculture is the increase of industrial prices relative to agricultural prices. From 1950 to 1968 the amount of industrial goods which could be purchased by the sale of the same amount of agricultural produce declined by 16.8%.[67]

4. PRODUCTION CRISIS.

The variety of problems affecting Mexican agriculture, such as underutilization of workers, low rates of investment, and chaotic land tenure have led to the near stagnation of agricultural production. This is especially serious given Mexico's 3.5% annual population increase. Further agravating the problem of food supply is the export of much of what is grown and the inequitable distribution of that which is left. The top 15% of the population consumes some 50% of all agricultural products.[68]

This decline in agricultural production is a recent occurrence. From 1934 to 1965 Mexican agricultural production increased 3.25 times. However from 1965 to 1970 agricultural production only increased at 1.2% a year, and from 1970 to 1973 it was only 0.5% a year.[69] In 1974 production decreased 1.2%.[70] From 1965 to 1974 production went down 2.6% per year per capita.[71] In 1975 for the first time in a decade the 4% increase in agricultural production surpassed the population increase.[72]

There are several reasons for this failure. After 1955 the spectacular growth in the world market for agricultural goods fell off. Also by this time the easliy developed land and water resources had been tapped.[73] Much of the previous increases in production had come from increases in area. However from 1968 to 1972 the area cultivated decreased from 15.0 million hectares to 14.5 million.[74]‡ Large holdings that do exist are underutilized, a significant factor since 55% of the land is still in the hands of 13,000 people.[75] Furthermore the limited buying power of most of the population discourages investment to increase production.[76] Finally even research in agriculture has been neglected, with only 0.07% of the national product being spent on agricultural research.[78] Research that has occurred has been aimed at modern farms, leaving the typical peasant farm with low production.[79]

A result of this decline in production per capita has been massive food imports. The cost of food imports rose from $112 million in 1971 to $664 million in 1974,[80] making Mexico a net importer of food for the first time in its history in 1974.[81] These figures for grain imports and

‡While it is still possible to put more land under cultivation, Mexico is faced with the unpleasant reality that only about 6% of its land is arable. In fact the State of Illinois with its 8 million people has more arable land than Mexico.[77]

exports show the boom and bust of Mexican agriculture:[82]

    Avila Camacho presidency (1940-1946)   1.8 million tons of grain imports
    Miguel Alemán presidency (1946-52)   2.1 "
    Ruiz Cortines presidency (1952-58)   2.7 "

Then agriculture reached its peak and

    López Mateos presidency (1958-1964)   0.6 million tons of grain exports
    Díaz Ordaz presidency (1964-70)   5.6 "

Then production began to slow:

    First year of Echeverría presidency, 1971   almost zero
    Echeverría presidency, 1972-April 1975   5.8 million tons of imports

Echeverría's agricultural policy centered around raising agricultural production and controlling peasant unrest. The efforts at increasing production relied mainly on huge increases in investment and credit for agriculture. The agricultural budget went from 14 billion pesos, with 4 billion pesos for credit in 1970, to its 1975 level of 60 billion, with 20 billion going for credit. In addition to credit the agricultural budget was spent for irrigation, research, agricultural schools and price support programs.[83] Included in the educational efforts are 300 middle level training centers for agricultural technicians, with some 60,000 students. During the Echeverría administration an additional 1.5 billion pesos were channeled into fertilizer plants, and 1.8 billion into new sugar mills, roads, and rural electrification.[84]

An effect of this massive spending is to channel more capital into the hands of large-scale agricultural entrepreneurs, since they are by far the major recipients of government subsidies. Even the education given the technicians in agricultural schools mainly serves the large growers since the technicians are trained to work on large, well-managed, highly-capitalized farms.

A second major shift of the Echeverría administration was to try to make the ejido a more viable productive unit by re-creating the cooperative ejido. This would permit the use of modern equipment, better planning, and increase the ejidatarios' production and income. However given the government control which inevitably accompanies government credits, the cooperative ejidos would become in actual fact state enterprises, with the ejidatarios being de facto wage laborers in a government-administered enterprise.[85]

At first glance the collective ejido might appear to resemble the Chinese commune. However the results are quite different from those resulting from the Chinese model, since the collectivization stops with the ejido. Once the crop leaves the ejido it enters the market, and most of the profit is retained by subsequent processors, middlemen and retailers.

An example of how outside forces affect a collectivized ejido is provided by the ejido El Vergel, in Gómez Palacio, Durango. This ejido is a large, collectively organized dairy farm. While the members of the ejido share returns from milk sales, these returns are diminished by the fact that milk must be sold to the only major buyer, Leche Lala, at the prices which the buyer sets. Through Leche Lala the ejidatarios are forced to support a variety of other totally un-cooperative institutions. In addition to supporting the Lala Company itself, they finance the repayment of the loans which Lala received from Mexican banks, which in turn received loans through a variety of international lending agencies, many of which are ultimately financed by American banks. The Lala Company is tied to the US through the purchase of various packaging machinery and the payment of license fees to Ex-Cell-O Corporation for the license to produce milk cartons.[86]

Finally the cooperative ejido is limited by resistance from the right wing, which sees such institutions as part of the Red Menace setting up Soviets in the countryside. In large part due to this right wing pressure the original plans for a massive shift to the collective ejido have been shifted to a "pilot project."[87]

Still another factor to overcome is the ejidatario himself who, in addition to having the traditional peasants' respect for land ownership, has seen generations of corrupt ejido officials absconding with community funds. Thus in most cases the ejidatario's experience leads him to prefer to grow and market his own crops rather than trusting the dubious honesty of an ejido official. Echeverría commented on this feeling saying, "Yes, collectivization of the ejido is desirable, but we'll have to wait until the peasants ask for it."[88] Not surprisingly by 1975 only some 800 of the 22,000 ejidos had been collectivized.[89]

Echeverría responded to falling agricultural production by channeling massive resources to the countryside. Even if these resources do stimulate production, their transfer to the hands of the wealthy give little indication of a better future for the 40% of the population eking out a living from agriculture. He left López Portillo with one of his most critical problems. Cultivated area has been the same since 1950, but population has increased 150%.[90] The percentage of farm laborers owning land declined from 42% in 1940 to 33% in 1970.[91] Finally the 1976 crop, affected by bad weather, wheat rust and the unrest of November 1976,[92] *declined* 2.1% from the previous year.[93] López Portillo's approach to the agrarian problem is unclear. On the one hand he has stated that the solution to the problems of the countryside is collectivization,[94] while claiming that the problems "are no longer of justice but of efficiency."[95]

CHAPTER 14: FOREIGN DEBT

The enormous debt that the dictatorship has saddled the country with has served to enrich government officials. Justice demands that their assets be used to pay off that debt.
—*Program of Mexican Liberal Party, 1906.*[1]

For the first fifty years after Mexican independence the principal means of foreign domination was trade. Then under Porfirio Díaz investment became important, especially in railroads, mining and public utilities. After such investments became politically sensitive, investment was shifted to manufacturing. In the last twenty years foreign debt has far surpassed direct investment in value and has opened up a new channel for foreign control.

This foreign debt is the owing of money by Mexican individuals, companies, or the government, to some institution outside the country. Just as with the transfer pricing schemes set up by the multinationals, these debts can become quite complicated. A comparison of direct investment and foreign debt indicates the degree to which foreign investment is being supplemented by foreign loans (figures indicate millions of dollars):[2]

	New foreign investment	Foreign Credits
1970	200.7	280.4
1971	196.1	281.2
1972	189.8	546.0
1973	286.9	1370.7
1974	362.2	2499.2
1975	362.0	3028.0

1. FORMS OF DEBT

GOVERNMENT (OR PUBLIC) DEBT: Most of the foreign debt involves loans made to the Mexican government by foreign banks or international agencies. Once the loan has been received, the government spends it, usually on infrastructure: irrigation, highways, electrical power plants, etc. A specific example of such borrowing is a $214 million loan from the World Bank in 1974. Of this $77 million went for irrigation in Sinaloa, $47 million for irrigation on the Pánuco valley, and $90 million for highway construction. Altogether the Mexican government has received $1.8 billion in loans from the World Bank.[3]

Mexico received $3.775 billion from the Inter-American Development Bank, the World Bank, the Export-Import Bank, and the Agency for International Development (AID) from 1961 to 1974. Of these funds 31% were invested in agricultural development (especially irrigation), 24% in transport and communication, 21% in energy production (especially electricity), and 16% in industry and mining.[4]

Sometimes an individual lender will not want to take on all of a loan, so a group of lenders will put up the money. An example of this occurred in 1976 when 56 banks put up an $800 million loan to the Mexican government.[5] Also since the World Bank has limited resources, often another bank, such as Chase Manhatten, will lend money to the World Bank, which in turn lends it to Mexico. It is more politically acceptable for Mexico to be in debt to public agencies such as the World Bank than it is to be in debt to a private US bank.

Mexican businessmen frequently carry out the activities which the government borrows money for. In these cases the government turns borrowed money over to private industry to build new factories or carry out construction projects. The private firms are then expected to pay back the government, so it in turn can pay back the original lender.

The vast majority of bank loans come from American banks, although in many cases to escape American currency regulations, loans are made from US-owned branches located in Europe or the Carribean. Of the outstanding loans to Mexico by US banks in 1972, $1.308 billion were directly from US banks, and $3.692 billion were made from overseas branches.[6] The total amount owed by the government at the end of 1976 was $20 billion.[7]

PRIVATE DEBT: About half as much is owed by the private sector as is owed by the Mexican government Such debts can be owed by banks, Mexican corporations, multinational corporations operating in Mexico, or individuals. An example of such a private loan is the $150 million loan by 19 US banks to the Industria Minera Mexico.[8] These loans may enable foreign banks to control supposedly-Mexican corporations. For example the Mexican airline Mexicana de Aviación in its May 6, 1976 stock market report stated that it had $143 million assets, but debts of $77 million to Bank of America, Export-Import Bank, First National City Bank, Boeing, and Wells Fargo.

The total amount of the private debt is hard to compute since there is no way to monitor all the loans individuals, Mexican banks, and companies obtain.[9] Often borrowers may want to conceal loans, or lenders may want to hide the loans for tax purposes. To accommodate such persons there are Swiss-style secret accounts that pay from 10.4 to 14.1% interest. Before devaluation there was an estimated $1 billion in these accounts.[10]

Not only are these private transactions hard to trace, but the government does not control the use of the money. Often such loans are used for trips abroad, real estate speculation, lavish homes, etc., rather than for development.

2. AMOUNT OF DEBT

The amount of the foreign debt is several times the value of all direct foreign investment, although due to its complexity, its political sensitivity, and the number of individuals involved, exact figures are not available. Estimates are complicated by the number of ways the debt is reported, such as total debt, total foreign debt, debt for loans of a year or longer, private debt, loans by US banks, etc. These figures give an idea of how the debt has grown:[11] [12]

1950	$0.5062	billion
1959	$0.6486	"
1963	$1.315	"
1969	$2.910	"
1970	$7.246	"
1972	$13.519	"
1974	$17.387	"
1976	$30.000	"

This rapid growth began in the López Mateos administration (1958-64) when it was decided that neither Mexican nor US investment was pushing development as fast as the government would like.[13]

During the Díaz Ordaz administration (1964-70) the debt increase was five times the rate of new foreign investment, and 13.4 times the rate of debt increase of the three previous administrations. From the Avila Camacho administration (1940-6) through the Díaz Ordaz administration foreign investment increased 5.6 times and debt increased 70 times.[14]

In his first state of the union address Echeverría noted that Mexico's foreign debt was giving foreigners too much control over the economy. He proposed slowing the rate of debt increase; however just the opposite happened. During his administration public foreign debt increased at $1.3 billion a year, compared to $660 million a year during the Díaz Ordaz administration.[15] Six percent of this was invested in the phone system, 26% in electrical generation, 11% in oil, and 8% in road and bridge construction.[16] The increase in the government debt in the last 26 years has been 40,000%.[17] A 1976 estimate of both public and private debt is $30 billion.[18]

The following figures show who Mexico's creditors were in 1972:[19]

Owed to U.S. banks	$5.000 billion
Owed to Export-Import Bank, Inter-american Development Bank, and U.S. Government	$1.478 billion
Owed to bond holders	$0.583 "
Owed to European, Canadian and Japanese banks	$1.500 "
Owed to depositers in peso accounts in Mexican banks	$0.958 "
Foreign trade credit	$1.500 "
Total	$11.019 "

The rapid increase in the debt is due to (1.) the government's refusal to use Mexican resources to finance development (this would mean higher taxes to cut back on luxury consumption), (2.) the inability of inefficient tariff-protected industry to generate exports, (3.) the backwardness of agriculture which makes it necessary to buy food abroad, (4.) multinational investors who constantly send out profits and royalties, leaving the country without foreign exchange.[20]

This however is only part of the picture since Mexico reflects a world-wide trend toward increasing indebtedness. Private banks loaned a record $78 billion to foreign countries in 1976, up from $61 billion in 1975. This reflects the state of the world trade system in which underdeveloped countries simply cannot pay for what they use (especially oil). In addition there is a near-universal tendency for politicians to accept goods today and leave the problem of payment to their successors. Finally institutions such as the World Bank and the International Monetary Fund have pushed the notion that countries can most easily escape underdevelopment through loans and the imports loans bring from the developed world. In 1976 the indebtedness of the Third World was estimated at $200 billion.[21]

3. EFFECTS

The foreign debt makes it difficult to know just who is benefiting from the Mexican economy. Similarly it is hard to know just who is responsible for existing conditions when Chase Manhatten (David Rockefeller) makes a loan to the World Bank (Robert McNamara), which in turn makes a loan to the Mexican government (López Portillo), which in turn may pass the money on to a private contractor. Such loans make it possible to do things which would be politically impossible if done openly. For example Cárdenas's nationalization of the oil industry has been largely abandoned. This reversal has not occurred through direct ownership, but by mortgaging the oil industry. In 1974 57% of new investment the oil industry was financed by foreign loans.[22]

Responsibility is further diffused when loans are passed on to private Mexican corporations. Then individual businessmen are free to make profits, but if they go broke, the government has to repay the foreign lenders. In other words Mexican taxpayers pay if the loan isn't repaid by the businessmen, and the businessmen keep the profits if the venture makes money. Initially the costs of many of the loans are borne by American taxpayers who underwrite the costs of lending agencies such as the Export-Import Bank.[23]

FOREIGN CONTROL: The foreign debt is permitting foreigners to exercise increasing control over Mexico. Once in debt, more loans are needed to repay old ones, and to get these new loans, Mexico has to act in accordance wtih the desires of the lenders. If the lender doesn't like the project, no loan. Similarly reliance on such credit increases the use of foreign imports, since many loans only serve to disguise installment buying. Much of the $4.5 billion worth of imports from the US in 1975 were financed with foreign loans.[24]

The type of institution exercising control over Mexico is illustrated by the fact that 47.5% of the debt is owned to Bank of America, Chase Manhatten, Chemical Bank, First National City Bank of New York, and Morgan Guarantee Trust.[25]

A specific example of this control was provided when the Mexican government received a $21.5 million dollar loan from the Agency for International Development in 1965. In order to get the loan the Mexican government had to (1.) affirm that the country was not controlled by the international communist movement, (2.) say the Mexican government wanted to avoid such control, (3.) refuse to cooperate with or receive aid from communist countries, and (4.) agree with the economic sanctions on Cuba.[26]

Another instance of such control was the $1.2 billion loan made by the International Monetary Fund after the 1976 devaluation. A condition for the loan was free convertibility of the peso, a provision which would allow multinationals to continue to remove profits from Mexico.[27]

Along with foreign control comes interest paid on the loans. This interest could become a form of tribute, disguised as interest payments. Such tribute could consist of raw materials, food and manufactured goods shipped to the US to cover interest payments, without the principal of the original loans ever being repaid.

The average interest on the debt is about 10%.[28] If one uses the previously cited figure of $30 billion as the amount of debt, that comes out to $3.0 billion paid out each year in interest alone, approximately the value of Mexico's exports each year. The rate of interest paid has been going up since there has been a shift from the relatively easy terms of international agencies to the higher interest rates of commercial banks. Even this estimate of the annual interest rate fails to consider that often loans are for the purchase of US goods. This may mean that a more expensive US-made item is purchased, so the interest is actually higher than the stated rate.

These loans tend to convert government-owned companies into agencies of American banks. In 1973 the government oil company paid $30.6 million interest on its debt, up from $4 million in 1968. Its debt went from $990 million in 1970 to $2.56 billion in 1975.[29] The government electric company paid $851 million interest in 1972, up from $171 million in 1969.[30] As of December 31, 1974, its debt was $3.03 billion, 67% of the value of the company. This debt was up from $1.26 billion in 1970.[31] To the extent this interest and principal are actually paid back rather than just being refinanced, it means higher prices and lower consumption for the Mexican population.

INTERNATIONAL AGENCIES: Many loans come from international agencies, especially the World Bank. In order to receive such loans countries have to abide by certain rules. Since lending agencies reflect the views of major capitalist countries, nationalization of investments by borrowers is not tolerated. Furthermore recipients are pressured into certain monetary policies which favor foreign investment and do not interfere with taking profits out of the country where investments are located.

Foreign loans

International agencies prescribe fiscal remedies which often result in unemployment, recession and a lower standard of living, but which protect multinational interests.[32] Any policy which distorts the "free market," such as freezing the price of food, is likewise frowned upon.[33] These international agencies are not accountable to the taxpayers of any country, but rather to international financiers.[34]

REDUCED OPTIONS: The increase in the debt tends to lock Mexico into its current economic policy and make change harder. Foreign banks support the current government, since they rightfully fear any new government might not feel responsible for the fiscal irresponsibility of the present government. The debt also forces the country into maximizing the earnings of foreign currency so it can pay back loans. This seeking foreign currency is not always in keeping with Mexico's needs. For example much land is used for growing cotton desired for export rather than for growing food for domestic consumption. This debt is in large part nullifying the increased independence new oil reserves and control over multinationals would provide.

DELAYS REFORM: Rather than reducing consumption in order to accumulate wealth for industrialization as the USSR and Japan did,* Mexico is trying to have its cake and eat it too. While its wealthy are jetting off to Europe and driving luxury sedans, foreign loans are being used to pay for industrialization. The lack of tax reform has led to conspicuous consumption, which in itself uses

*These two countries industrialized well after industrialization of the North Atlantic area and thus serve as models for late development.

up large amounts of foreign exchange (money for foreign auto parts, travel, etc.).

TECHNOLOGY: The reliance on foreign debt produces development along much the same lines described in the chapter on development.‡ Bankers are much more willing to finance projects similar to those found in the US, rather than ones tailored to Mexico's needs. Often lenders make deliberate attempts to get underdeveloped countries hooked on US food and technology. In the 1950's aid for food and development was given away or sold on very generous terms. Once tastes for such products had been acquired and alternative suppliers (say of food and transportation) had been neglected, terms became increasingly steep.[35]

The imposition of foreign technology through loans has been particularly insidious in agriculture. To the extent that foreign loans have gone into agriculture, they have been used for such purchases as tractors, fertilizers, and herbicides, all of which are capital intensive. This lowers farm employment, and produces migration to the city, urban squalor, and the need for food imports for the urban masses who no longer produce their own food.[36] Nor is there an attempt to use loans for making Mexico self-sufficient in agriculture:

> *For the World Bank to finance such institutional reforms in developing countries as would lead toward self-sufficiency on food account would run counter to American interests.*[37]

4. WHO BENEFITS?

The Mexican government's main interest in increasing the debt is continued economic development. Since growth has slowed even with constant borrowing, the lack of such financing would slow development to unacceptable levels. This was expressed by the Mexican Secretary of the Treasury who stated, "The question isn't borrowing or not borrowing, but growth or stagnation."[39]

This increase in the debt enables Mexico to receive large quantities of goods without, for the present, offering anything in return. It also permits the government to continue its massive subsidies to private industry. Such subsidies have permitted rapid expansion without industry having had to pay the cost of growing food to feed its workers, building transport facilities, constructing generating plants, etc. In order to continue meeting industry's needs, imports by government agencies increased from 24% of all imports in 1970 to 38% in 1975.[40]

Private Mexican business has had little choice but to start relying on foreign credit. The extreme increase in government spending has dried up most domestic credit. Government domestic borrowing has increased faster than the amount of loans made by Mexican lending institutions, thus leaving the private sector with less credit in 1975 than in 1970. In 1970 the government took 13.2% of domestic savings; in 1975 it took 52.6%.[41] This has dried up credit for small and medium-sized business and

‡Perhaps the most eloquent testimony of the effect of relying on loans more than human resources comes from the French invasion in the 1860's. Maximilian, borrowing heavily abroad, spent 50 times as much as Juárez, and lost.[38]

forced large corporations into international money markets. Foreign borrowing by private corporations went from $19.4 million in 1970 to $128.6 million in 1974. In 1975 the Industria Minera Mexicana took out a single loan of $225 million. Similarly multinationals operating in Mexico increased their foreign borrowing from $41 million in 1970 to $349 million in 1975.[42]

US banks continue to make loans for a variety of reasons. Often US goods simply can't be sold if no credit is available. Also even though complete repayment of the loans is looking increasingly unlikely (see next section), bankers still see a variety of advantages in continuing to make loans.

These loans permit American banks to manage Mexican businesses and extract profits from them in the form of interest, Echeverría's investment laws notwithstanding. Many apparently Mexican corporations are in fact hollow shells mortgaged to American interests. For example the Compañía de la Fábrica de Papel de San Rafael y Anexas, S.A., as of December 31, 1974, had a $5.5 million debt to First National City Bank, a $10 million debt to Bank of America, and a $2.96 million debt to the Export-Import Bank. In order to keep the company afloat financially, new loans had to be taken out, and in order to get the new loans, certain concessions had to be made to lenders. As the company noted in its 1974/5 report to the Mexican stock exchange:

> *In the loan contracts with First National City Bank and the Bank of America National Trust and Savings Association, and with the Export-Import Bank of the United States, certain restrictions were established regarding maintaining working capital, and the relation of assets to short and long term liabilities. On December 31, 1974, the company failed to meet some of these obligations and the company management obtained a temporary exception as to their completion.*

Similarly the apparently Mexican company Aceros Ecatepec, S.A. owes $21.6 million and its 1974/5 report to the stock holders stated:

> *When the company's new loan offer was accepted, it assumed certain capital obligations including restrictions on declaring dividends and increasing capital, except under certain conditions and with the knowledge of the creditors.*

Finally US banks feel great pressure to make loans simply because if they don't some other bank will, and banks which don't make loans don't stay in business very long.

5. WHAT WILL HAPPEN?

The orthodox theory is that Mexico takes out loans, invests the money to increase production, which in turn generates additional income which can be used to pay back the loan. Then the country is left debt free with new factories, power plants, highways, and the like. According to this theory, if loans were not obtained, new investments and economic development would not only be slowed, but the countries which are already industrialized would increase the distance between themselves and underdeveloped countries like Mexico.

REPAYMENT: In order to be repaid not only do loans have to be used for productive investments, but they have to generate the foreign currency needed for repayment. However many of the loans go for projects with little prospect for earning foreign currency. For example the Export-Import Bank and Chase Manhatten each lent $1.25 million to Jets Ejecutivos to purchase executive jets for Mexican businessmen. The Comisión Federal de Electricidad has borrowed $667 million from the World Bank. Some of this loan has been used to buy generating equipment for factories producing goods for export. However much of the generating capacity resulting from these loans, rather than earning foreign exchange, is used to produce luxury items, light neon signs, etc. The 1976 devaluation makes repayment much harder since a company must take in twice as many pesos to pay back $1 of foreign debt.

Figures concerning the debt are pessimistic. Indebtedness grew at 34% from 1971 to 1976,[43] far faster than the economy as a whole or the ability to generate foreign currency to repay the loans. In order to repay these loans Mexico must rely on three major sources of foreign income: exports in excess of imports, tourism, and new foreign investment.

Exports have been far overshadowed by imports, so that from 1957 to 1972 there was a negative trade balance of $1.921 billion.[44] Then from 1973-5 there was a trade deficit of $8.348 billion.[45] There was an improvement in the balance of trade in 1976 due to the recovery of the US economy, more sales of oil, and less buying of foreign steel and food. As a result the 1975 deficit of $3.7 billion was reduced to $2.7 billion in 1976. It should be kept in mind though that not only would Mexico have to have a favorable trade balance to help pay the debt, but it would have to overcome the huge interest on the debt which in 1975 equaled 80% of the value of Mexican exports. In 1976 interest increased 83.7% over 1975.[46]

Foreign investment offers a possible source of foreign currency, but in fact profits, royalties and other fees have made foreign investment a liability which drained $1.526 billion from the country from 1957 to 1972.[47] As has already been noted, the annual drain had risen to over $1 billion a year by 1976.

The one consistent source of foreign currency has been tourism. However the amount of currency brought in has offset only a small part of trade deficits and multinational operations. To make matters worse, money spent abroad by Mexican tourists has been rapidly increasing, while there has been a decline in the amount of money spent in Mexico by foreign tourists. Mexican tourists spent $32 million outside the country in 1975, up 18.9% from 1974. In 1975 earnings from foreign tourists entering Mexico were $960 million, down 7% from 1974.[48] The long term trend was shown by the fact that in 1965 tourist earnings offset 62% of the trade deficit, while in 1975 only 20.1% was offset.[49] This trend was reversed by the 1976 devaluation. The surplus from tourism and border transactions in 1976 was $1.125 billion, up 14.3% from the 1975 surplus.[50] This was largely due to the sharp decline in Mexican tourists leaving the country.[51]

The loss from these *potential* sources of foreign currency was $5.1 billion from 1957 to 1972.[52] The losses since 1972 have been substantially higher.

A possible method of repayment is the sale of Mexico's newly found oil deposits on the international market. Oil exports will go from 153,000 barrels a day in 1977 to 500,000-700,000 by the 1980's.[53] However, based on the incomplete information available, the size of the deposits is not large enough to meet rapidly expanding domestic demand and liquidate Mexico's foreign debt.

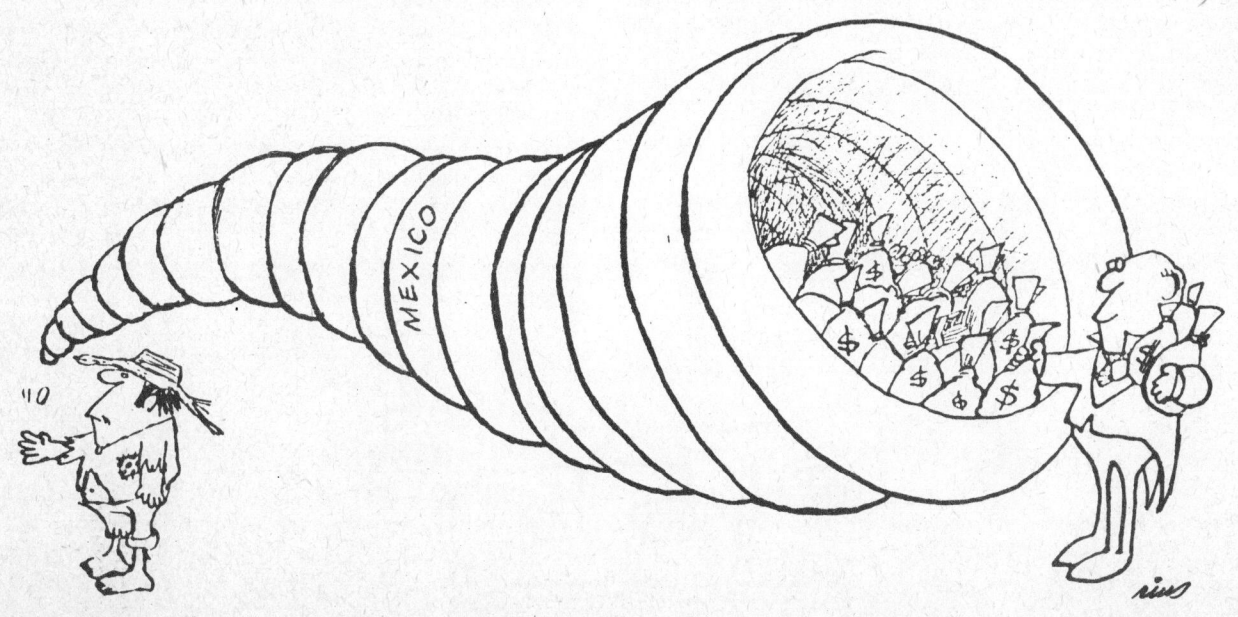

REPUDIATION: A possible course of action would be to tell the World Bank, Chase Manhatten, etc., that the debt simply won't be paid back. This happened with Czarist bonds when the Bolsheviks took power. A more recent example occurred in Ghana when a new government came to power following a coup in 1972 and decided that there was no reason why it should be tied to its predecessors' mistakes. Ghana's finance minister stated, "It is impossible to convince any Ghanian that public money would be better spent on paying such debts than in developing the country."[54] Seeing the problem as a political one, Ghana did not repudiate the whole debt, but only that owed to Britain, thus hoping to maintain friendship with its other trading partners.

The experience of the Allende government in Chile shows what effects a cut-off of international credit can have. Once Allende took power foreign credit quickly dried up, spare parts became scarce, and food imports normally purchased abroad on credit were no longer possible. Allende didn't even repudiate the Chilean debt, he just displeased international financiers.

In Mexico repudiation would be a serious matter since the Mexican economy is much more integrated into the American economy and dependent upon it for credit, technological know-how, spare parts, raw materials and food. The almost certain lack of imports after repudiation would produce severe shortages. These shortages would cut the current standard of living of the wealthy. Since they are the ones who make major decisions, it is unlikely they would advocate repudiation. Also the resulting shortages would affect the rest of the population and produce a volatile political situation. Unless the regime in power had mass support, something high-living PRI functionaries are unlikely to muster, resistance to the government would rise.

At a time when the country was less polarized, mass support for the government was a reality. For example President Cárdenas enjoyed mass support when he nationalized the oil industry in 1938. It was Cárdenas who commented on debt repayment in his 1936 state of the union address:

> *The Mexican government's attitude concerning the foreign debt problem hasn't changed. Its desire to meet its foreign obligations continues to be subordinated to the necessity of devoting most of the country's resources to its economic and cultural progress.*

DEFAULT: Default differs from repudiation in that it is the inability to repay, rather than the unwillingness to repay. It can be viewed as a political challenge and produce sanctions, or it can be viewed as a short-run problem, which will be overcome. In the latter case default would have little significance and probably would be handled by granting more loans to cover payments due.

Default occurred in 1928 when Mexico suspended debt payments without repudiating the debt. Repayment was only resumed in 1941.[55] A more recent example of default occurred in 1975 when Zaire couldn't repay its foreign loans because copper prices fell so low that it couldn't use anticipated receipts from copper sales for repayment. In the case of Zaire there was no major crisis and new loans were made to cover the payments due.[56] The initial loans by private banks were covered with loans made by multinational agencies, letting the private banks off the hook at public expense. The willingness to continue making loans to Zaire, which was vital to US operations in Angola, and the unwillingness to aid Chile when it *was* repaying loans only emphasizes the political nature of who gets loans and who doesn't.

In any case banks are now aware that default on a massive scale is a real possibility. Numerous articles have appeared discussing the repayment problem, and as an advisor to the Federal Reserve Bank of New York noted, "Everyone is talking about possible defaults."[57] The extent to which countries are behind in debt payments is a closely guarded secret.[58] A possible solution, which is advocated by the banks themselves, is to have new loans issued by some public agency such as the IMF to cover old ones.[59] This would shift the cost of any default from the banks to the taxpayers of IMF countries.

MORE OF SAME: There is no reason that the current system cannot continue into the forseeable future. In such a case Mexico would continue to receive new loans which would be used to pay back old ones, as well as to cover trade deficits, profits and royalties taken out of the country. To the extent new loans do not cover interest and principal due, goods and services can be demanded from Mexico to make up the difference.

In his posthumous testament former President Lázaro Cárdenas commented:

> *I feel that if the growth of the foreign debt continues as it has for the last two decades, it will provide a means for perpetuating dependency, and as to its effects, Mexican history is very eloquent.*[60]

Another reason for continued financing by banks is that holding the foreign debt is something like having a tiger by the tail; you can't let go. Various banks now have over $500 million invested in Mexico, and any refusal to make new loans could produce a financial crisis and result in massive loss to creditors. Thus to keep the climate of confidence, banks have little choice but to continue issuing new loans.

If Mexico were an individual, the obvious solution would be to declare bankruptcy. Something analogous to bankruptcy was proposed by the underdeveloped nations at the UNCTAD conference in Kenya in May 1976. They called for a moratorium on debt payments, which easily could have become de facto bankruptcy. Not surprisingly, this idea found little support among the developed nations, capitalist or socialist.[61] The outcome of debt repayment is far from certain, simply because there is no precedent for the massive foreign indebtedness of the underdeveloped world. In the 1970's the non-oil exporting underdeveloped nations have borrowed more than in their entire previous history.[62]

PART IV: MEXICAN SOCIETY

CHAPTER 15: SOCIAL STRUCTURE

The Mexican case deserves attention from those developmental economists who are still occupied with growth rates of national product. It is painfully apparent that rapid growth is not a sufficient condition for progress.[1]

Ties with multinational corporations and foreign lenders influence the type of technology Mexico uses, what it makes, and how it is integrated into the world financial structure. This influence can be seen when Mexico is compared with advanced nations, when rural Mexico is compared to urban Mexico, and when wealthy Mexicans are compared with poor ones. The differences observed result from differences in the political strength of these groups. Rich areas, both nationally and internationally, channel resources and capital to their benefit and to the detriment of poor areas. The same is true for wealthy Mexicans and urban Mexicans, who shape policies which benefit them at the expense of the poor and the rural Mexican.

Mexico and the rest of the underdeveloped world are clearly losing ground with respect to the developed world. In 1900 the underdeveloped world had a per capita income one half that of the developed countries. Now it has one twentieth the per capita income.[2] The degree to which this gap continues to widen is shown by the fact that per capita income in the developed nations went from $2381 in 1963 to $3561 in 1973 (Increase: $1180). In the same period the underdeveloped nations only increased their income from $185 to $252 (Increase: $77).[3]

Just as Mexico is losing ground with respect to the developed world, rural Mexico is losing ground with respect to urban Mexico. The formulation of policy by and for the benefit of urban Mexicans has given rise to what has been called "internal colonialism." This phrase refers to the manner in which urban areas deprive rural areas of wealth by paying low prices for agricultural products while charging high prices for manufactured goods, by investing agricultural profits in urban enterprises, and by the government spending taxes disproportionally in urban areas. In addition foreign currency from agricultural sales has been used to develop urban industrial centers.

In large part due to this relationship families living in urban areas got 233% more income than those living in rural areas.[4] Illiteracy in cities such as Mexico City is 10%, while in rural areas such as Chiapas, Oaxaca, and Guerrero it ranges from 42% to 45%.[5] Six times as many urban children finish primary school as rural children.[6] Similarly 60% of urban workers have social security, while only 11% of rural workers do.[7]

As a result of such disparities in income and social services, as well as the greater availability of city jobs, there has been a massive migration from the countryside to the city. From 1940 to 1950 400,000 left agricultural jobs, from 1950 to 1960 480,000 did, and from 1960 to 1970 800,000 did.[8] The following figures show how rapidly Mexico has become urbanized:[9]

    1910 28.7% of population urban
    1930 33.5%   "
    1950 42.6%   "
    1970 58.6%   "

Mexico's rate of urbanization has even been high by world standards. In 1950 Mexico City was the world's 13th largest city, in 1974 it was the sixth largest.[10] It's projected that by 2000 Mexico City will be the world's largest city, with a population of 32 million.[11]

The same mechanisms which create rural-urban disparities also create regional disparities. Oaxaca, in the impoverished south, has only 8% of the per capita income of the Federal District, which includes Mexico City.[12] The Federal District not only towers above poor regions economically, but in some cases overshadows the rest of the country as a whole. It receives 57.6% of the imports of the entire country, reflecting the concentration of both consumer spending and industry there.[13]

Mexico's economic development over the last fifty years has increased buying power for almost the entire population. This development has paralleled development in the world as a whole in that the gap between the rich and the poor has widened. This is especially significant since one's perception of well-being is determined much more by comparison with those nearby than by noting improvement over one's grandparents. In 1950 the top 5% of income earners made 22 times more than those in the bottom 40%. By 1969 they were making 34 times as much.[14]

The following figures show how the top and bottom of the population share total national income:*[15]

Percent of national income received by:	1950	1963	1969
bottom half of population	19.1%	15.7%	15.0%
top 20% of population	59.8	62.6	64

Even though those at the bottom are getting a smaller share, given the increase in total national income, the purchasing power of even the bottom increased up until the early 1970's. Recent inflation however has reversed this trend.[16] In terms of actual income the vast majority of the country remains poor. The 1970 census showed that 71.7% of income earners made less than $80 a month,[17] and only 2.7% received over $200 a month.[18]

Mexico, despite having had its revolution, is worse off in terms of income distribution than most of the rest of Latin America. The bottom half of the Brazilian population gets 19.8% of income, in Argentina 23.4%, compared to 15% in Mexico.[19] Apologists for Mexico's uneven income distribution still claim that ultimately economic development will eliminate the problem. In this regard it should be noted that income distribution in the US has not changed since 1950, despite significant economic development.[20]

There has been so much concentration of wealth in Mexico that the need for reform is obvious. Often the name of Lázaro Cárdenas is held out, and the would-be reformers long for another Cárdenas to come riding up on a white charger to institute reforms. What they fail to note is that there has been a fundamental change since the time of Cárdenas. In the 1930's Mexican business allied itself with Cárdenas to attack the large land holders and foreign capitalists. Now Mexican businessmen are the problem, and talk of a repetition of Cárdenas is just wishful thinking.[22]

There is a strong relationship between the increasing maldistribution of income and the type of technology being introduced in Mexico. The new machines being introduced require fewer and fewer workers, and increasingly more money is needed to finance the purchase of machines. As the part of workers in production decreases, so does their share of national income. Similarly as investments by the already wealthy become more important, their income rises.

Once income becomes concentrated, the nature of the products bought tends to further concentrate income. Wealthy persons tend to buy products, cars as opposed to brooms for example, which require fewer workers and more machines to make. This stimulates production in areas of the economy requiring capital and relatively few workers. To illustrate this process one can observe that $1000 added to the income of a rich person will generate fewer jobs than will $1000 added to the income of a poor person. The rich person will tend to spend his increased earnings, if he doesn't spend them abroad, on a second (or third) car, a color TV or the like, products which require relatively few workers to produce (ie, are capital intensive). The poor person however will tend to buy furniture, a broom or clothes which require more labor for each dollar of sales (ie., are labor intensive).

The failure of wages to rise as fast as productivity has led to a further worsening of income distribution. While output per worker went up 64% from 1940 to 1960, wages only went up 23%.[23] The difference went into the pockets of factory owners as manufacturing profits went up 817% from 1940 to 1950 alone.[24]

At the very top of the income ladder are the owners of large establishments, who number perhaps 0.5% of the population.[25] This sector is tightly organized into several formal institutions such as CONCANCO (Confederation of National Chambers of Commerce) which was organized by Carranza in 1917. For many years these formal organizations of businessmen have been influential bodies with easy access to the government.

In recent years there has been a shift in power from these business organizations to various financial-banking groups. Their power has grown at the expense of the government and especially the president.[26] Investment decisions made by these groups affect the entire population.[27] They have pushed industrialization at the expense of agriculture and have chosen capital-intensive production techniques. In decreasing order of importance these financial groups are the Banco Nacional de México, the Banco de Comercio, the Banco de Londrés y México,

---

*Developed countries not only have more income to distribute, but distribute it more equally. In the US the top 20% of the population gets 41.1% of income, the bottom gets 40% gets 17.2%.[21]

HECTOR GARCIA

the Banco Comercial Mexicano, the Banco Mexicano, the Banco Internacional, and the Banco del Atlántico. The directors of these banks often sit on the boards of government-owned banks and thus influence public as well as private investment. It has been estimated that these banking groups together control some 85% of Mexican capital.[28] Each of these groups form large financial-industrial conglomerates. The Banamex group for example, is made up of the Banco Nacional de México, the Financiera Banamex, the Financiera de Ventas, the Asociación Hipotecaria Mexicana, the Arrendadora Banamex, and controls 45 firms and owns an interest in 52.[29]

Private business has been the main beneficiary of the industrialization which began in the 1940's. As late as the 1950's however there was disagreement in the business community on whether industrialization should be carried out with foreign or domestic capital. Big business was already finding out that association with foreign investors could bring handsome profits. Their spokesman announced that "measures taken against foreign capital are measures taken against national capital."[30] Taking a different position were the middle and small businessmen who were unattractive partners for foreign investors, and whose size and outdated technology made competition with multinationals risky. The spokesman for this group was José Lavín, president of a business group, CONACINTRA (National Chamber of the Industries of Transformation), which at that time represented small and medium business.[31] He stated CONACINTRA's position was that Mexico "should impose its own form of national development"[32] and that those who let their names be used to hide actual ownership of foreign companies are "employees of the United States in Mexico."

At this time large industry developed a concern about the needy. Their spokesman stated, "Whether you want to or not, you have to accept foreign investment, because we can't let the constantly increasing population die of hunger."[33] As the stream of foreign investments turned into a flood in the 1960's and profits for those working with multinationals increased accordingly, the nationalism of the industries in the CONACINTRA suddenly disappeared.[34]

Since then businessmen have been remarkably united and the most obvious divisions in the business community have been geographical. The best-known of these groups are centered around Puebla, Guadalajara, and Monterrey. Of these the Monterrey group has consistently been the most conservative. This was the group which challenged Cárdenas's policy of labor reconciliation in 1936 by meeting workers' demands with a massive lockout. Cárdenas responded by coming to Monterrey in February 1936 and presenting his famous 14 points which were to form the basis for relations between government and business. The three salient points were that (1.) government is the supreme arbiter of disputes within the country, (2.) small groups of communists were to be tolerated, and (3.) businessmen shouldn't increase tensions and cause rebellion.

Despite Cárdenas's having reasserted government supremacy in 1936, disputes have continued to flare up between the Monterrey group and the central government. In 1971 a representative of the Monterrey group was governor of Nuevo León, the state in which Monterrey is located. When he attempted to put the state university in the hands of sympathizers of this group, Echeverría once again had to assert the authority of the central government by firing him. This same Monterrey group launched bitter attacks at Echeverría and his "left wing policies" after the patriarch of the group, Eugenio Garza Sada was killed in a kidnap attempt by urban guerrillas in 1973.

In contrast to the sometimes stormy relations between Mexican businessmen and the government, Mexican businessmen and multinational corporations have had much more cordial relations.

> *When top executives see their careers tied to the global fortunes of their company rather than to the national economy, they become remarkably tolerant of outside economic penetration and even foreign domination of their country. They see themselves as members of an international class, closer in what they eat, wear, read and think to company people in other countries than to their fellow countrymen outside the company gates, many of whom are likely to be poor, barely literate and hungry.*[35]

The relation between Mexican businessmen and the multinationals is a symbiotic one. Local business realizes it could not maintain its privileged position without the backing of foreign interests (witness Chile), and conversely the multinationals realize their presence would not be tolerated if local interests didn't keep the way open for them.

Wealthy Mexicans are notoriously undertaxed. Before the 1975 tax increases, taxation was estimated at 12.5% of the national product, one of the lowest in the world, and well below the U.S. rate of 30.1%.[36] Despite this low rate tax evasion was estimated at $4.5 billion in 1975.[37] Those who evade taxes are the wealthy who can hide them, something a worker receiving a pay check cannot easily do.

In 1975 a 40% tax increase was instituted in an attempt to control inflation. Significantly these new taxes were on consumption, rather than on corporations. An example of the new taxes is the 15% tax on restaurant meals. The rationale for not taxing companies directly was that it would lead to such a decrease in profits that the rate of investment would decline.[38] This tax rate is a still low 17.5% of the national product.[39]

The ability of the business community to effectively block fiscal and political policies by massive withdrawal of currency from the country has been repeatedly demonstrated. In 1973 when relations were tense between business and the government, there was a cash outflow of about a billion dollars. This tension resulted from Echeverría's progressive rhetoric, his trips to such third world countries as China, and urban guerrilla activity. An estimated $10 billion left the country before the 1976 devaluation,[40] with $4 billion leaving in the summer of 1976 alone.[41] Another $1.5 billion left the country during the crisis at the end of Echeverría's term.[42]

The twenty percent of the population which ranks below the top 10% and above the bottom 60% is considered the middle class. They got 22.64% of the income in 1963,[43] and are the group which has benefited most from Mexico's economic development. This group forms a major new consumer market, thus making possible the rapid growth of industry. Despite the dreams of many reformers that the middle class is the key to functioning democracy, throughout Latin America the middle class has consistently opposed agrarian reform and other progressive measures. They are quite intent on improving their standard of living, without doing anything for the groups below them.[44] Octavio Paz characterized the middle class as a group with high responsibility, mediocre income, and no political voice.[45]

....

The 1970 census showed that 27% of the population, or 12.9 million persons, worked. Of these, agricultural workers constitute the largest single group with 5.1 million workers, or 39.4% of the work force. The percentage of agricultural workers in the work force has steadily been declining, but the 1970 census showed the first decline in the absolute number of workers in agriculture. The rest of the work force is divided into industrial workers who make up 22.6% of the work force and service workers who make up 38%. The following figures show how the work force has grown (figures indicate millions of workers):[46]

	agricultural workers	industrial workers	service workers	total
1940	3.8	0.9	1.3	6.0
1950	4.8	1.3	2.1	8.2
1960	6.3	2.0	3.7	12.0
1970	5.1	3.1	4.8	13.0

Over 70% of income earners are now salaried, one of the highest rates in Latin America.[47]

....

At the bottom of society are those without political power, trade unions, adequate income or public services. It is difficult to make any generalizations about them since they include Indians living in remote mountain areas, migrant farm workers and shanty dwellers on the fringes of large cities.

Economically they were hardest hit by the recession which occurred in the latter half of the Echeverría administration. Since they start off with so little, any reduction in income hits them hard. Also they aren't unionized, so they don't get the wage increases which have kept organized labor more or less up with inflation.

HECTOR GARCIA

Finally they are hit harder by inflation than the average Mexican since they spend a higher percentage of their income on food and food prices have increased more rapidly than prices in general. In 1974 food prices went up more than twice as fast as the general price index.[48]

The poor are most obvious in the shanty towns surrounding the major cities, especially Mexico City. There the same system which produced agrarian problems and forced them out of rural areas has left them without adequate jobs or housing. In Ciudad Nezahualcóyotl, a large slum on the east edge of Mexico City, 50% of the children die before age four, and only 12% of those starting primary school finish.[49] There 90% of the population suffers from chronic hunger, malnutrition and acute parasite infection, 46% of the population is unemployed, and 34% is underemployed.[50] These shanty towns or "colonias proletarias" make up 35-50% of Mexico City's population and their population is growing from 10 to 15% a year.[51]

CHAPTER 16: WORKERS

Neither the government nor the workers knew just what the labor legislation provided for in the 1917 Constitution was to mean in actual practice. The mere statement that legislation was forthcoming and the expectation of a better standard of living were sufficient to guarantee worker support for the post-revolutionary government.[1] The government hoped to use its alliance with the working class to promote class conciliation, to aid industrial development by providing a docile labor force, and to use workers in the attack on privileged landowners and foreign investors.[2]

The early history of the national trade union organization, the CROM (Revolutionary Congress of Mexican Workers), organized in 1919, reflected government priorities. CROM leaders set policy in secret meetings without the participation or even the knowledge of the membership. One of these secret sessions committed the CROM to supporting Obregón in the impending showdown with Carranza. At this time the government provided 95% of the CROM's budget, although it did so secretly to maintain the facade of worker control. The timely support for Obregón's coup resulted in CROM leaders being rewarded with high posts in the Obregón administration.[3] In order to maintain tighter control over workers, membership in the CROM was increased from 100,000 in 1920 to one million in 1924.[4] Membership in the CROM became increasingly necessary for the organizing of strikes.

When Calles took office in 1924 he cemented the links between the state and organized labor by appointing CROM leader Morones to the cabinet. As soon as the CROM could count on solid government support, it began to attack, not business, but independent labor unions.[5] By 1925 the repression of labor dissidents was being carried out with tactics similar to those in use today. Labor organizations were controlled from the top down, strikes not officially sanctioned were declared illegal, strikebreakers were used, labor leaders were bribed, and the army was used to break strikes which could not be dealt with by other means.[6] All strikes had to be approved by the central committee of the CROM. Often the CROM would call strikes just to get kickbacks from the management to arrange a speedy settlement.[7]

As was the case with the agrarian reform, the implementation of labor legislation provided for in the 1917 Constitution was slow. Federal arbitration provided for in Article 123 was only instituted in 1927 and federal labor legislation was not passed until 1930. In order to keep tight government control over organized labor, Calles relied on those who thought the government would be an impartial friend of labor and on those who were willing to sell out to the government.[8]

After Obregón's assassination Calles saw that the CROM was a political liability since it was so closely identified with the climate of hate which had preceded the assassination. Calles no longer needed CROM support to bolster his position, so he withdrew his backing for it.[9] The CROM, having its power base in the government and not in the workers, then went into a rapid decline. Calles's successor Portes Gil was a long-time enemy of the CROM's leader, so the CROM suffered still further. Due to the weakness of the CROM and the corruption of its leadership, many workers bolted from the CROM and set up independent unions.[10] Then as the depression began it became apparent that the CROM would do little for its members. As a result still more members withdrew from the CROM, leaving the labor movement weak, dispersed, and divided into many organizations.[11]

When Cárdenas took office in 1934, Mexico was still in the depths of the depression and the labor movement was in disarray. One of Cárdenas's early moves was to court labor support, support which proved invaluable in his showdown with Calles. In order to solidify the labor movement once again and make it into a force which could be used by the government, he unified labor into one national group called the Mexican Workers Confederation (CTM). This group was formed in 1936 by uniting several existing groups. It is the only mass group which was formed with popular backing. Before the CTM's founding workers had been demonstrating for labor unity. Once it had united labor the CTM called for other sectors of the society to join with workers to struggle against international reaction and fascism, thus guaranteeing the development of the revolution.[12]

Cárdenas saw a unified working class as a necessary tool to force the submission of privileged groups, thus

JAVIER INIGUEZ

making economic development possible. He repeatedly sided with strikers, although he insured workers' demands were always economic, and did not deal with such questions as who was to control the factories.[13] He said that strikes were acceptable if their demands did not exceed the resources of the company being struck. Since most of the major strikes were against foreign companies, they had the additional effect of strengthening Mexican business. Strikes not under government control fared quite differently. The 1936 rail workers strike, one of the few out of government control, was declared illegal before it began.[14] [15]

Another key to Cárdenas's labor policy was the granting of congressional seats to union officials. Supposedly this would give them the chance to legislate in favor of workers. However beginning with the 1937 elections, labor officials have consistently tried to get congressional seats at any price, including the sacrifice of workers' interests. This handing out of congressional seats became an effective means of control, since the chance to occupy the seat was awarded to those who had served the interests of the CTM and the government.

Cárdenas felt that workers and owners were not necessarily enemies, and that workers' interests could be protected with adequate political and judicial safeguards.[16] Cárdenas attempted to provide such safeguards, but in the process created a government-controlled structure which his successors have used to control labor.[17] It was the CTM's lack of political and ideological independence which led to imposed leadership, organizational ties to the government, and subsequent entrapment of workers in the government apparatus.[18]

By 1940 the industrial labor force was smaller than in 1910, but produced three times as much.[19] This resulted from artisans coming to work in modern factories. These workers recently arriving from cottage industry or the fields provided a weak foundation for trade unions. In addition, union activity in the early 1940's was reduced since workers were convinced that they shouldn't disturb the war effort with strikes. Also the oversupply of job seekers made strikes difficult, as did government control of labor.[20] As a result from 1940 to 1944 there was a 37% decline in industrial salaries.[21] Salaries only surpassed their 1939 level in 1966.[22] These extremely low salaries permitted capital accumulation and rapid development well before the beginning of massive foreign investment. In fact, the CTM maintained national development as its major priority, and its slogan was changed from "for a society without classes" to "for the emancipation of Mexico." The feeling that workers were building a better homeland for all was used as a substitute for salary increases.[23]

At this time the government was subsidizing the CTM with cash, buildings and land. This permitted it to maintain its control of the CTM and use it to keep salaries low and maintain labor peace, thus attracting foreign capital. The possibility of labor organizing outside state control made President Alemán (1946-52) resort to even stronger control over labor. In 1947 the Federal Labor Law gave the Secretary of Labor the right to recognize or veto duly elected union officials. This provided the government with de facto power to impose union officials.[24]

Alemán's anti-union policies became obvious when he used the army and police to suppress an oil workers strike in 1947.[25] The next year, when leaders of the rail workers union violated government policy by not accepting the no-strike, no-wage-increase policy, Alemán imposed the unpopular Jésus Díaz de León as head of the rail workers union. In order to consolidate Díaz de León's control of the union, union locals were occupied and elected officials were ousted with the widespread participation of the secret police.[26] Such heavy-handed treatment was necessary to set an example for union militants who, in response to massive inflation, were making demands for higher salaries.[27]

Once Díaz de León was installed as head of the rail union, impositions followed in other unions. Such officials became known as "charros," after Díaz de León who fancied the ornate dress of the typical Mexican cowboy or "charro." Through the use of these charros during the Alemán administration, buying power of workers was lowered, rates of production were increased, as in some cases were working hours.[28] Rapid industrialization based on the over-exploitation of labor continued.[29] Alemán's legacy to trade unions included (1.) increased union control, (2.) goons to break strikes, (3.) systematic violation of labor laws and union regulations, (4.) total abandonment of union democracy, (5.) pillage of union funds, and (6.) collaboration behind workers' backs between union leaders, government and business.[30]

The major break in this imposed labor peace during the fifties was an attempt to re-establish independent leadership in the rail union. This movement began in June 1958 when union dissidents refused to accept their leaders' decision ratifying a contract which provided no wage increase, despite a rapidly developing economy. Their low wages, as workers pointed out, were made necessary by the low rail rates charged domestic and foreign industry. The demand for higher wages was backed up by a two-hour work stoppage. Pro-government union officials stated that the work stoppage was due to "the single and exclusive desire to cause trouble, since it had been organized by communist elements opposed to the Union Executive Committee."[31] By the second day the work stoppage had been extended to four hours and rail officials began to negotiate directly with dissident strike leaders, bypassing nominal union leaders. Finally President Ruiz Cortines offered a $17.20 a month increase. Since it was assumed violence would follow if the offer was not accepted, workers went back to work.

Rail workers then concentrated on electing honest union officials. On July 12 Demetrio Vallejo was elected Secretary General of the union. When incumbent union officials refused to recognize his election, insurgent workers called for another series of work stoppages. Police then began to occupy union locals, and so Vallejo telegraphed STOP ALL TRAINS. The government responded to the paralyzation of the rail system by sending out troops to protect strike breakers, arresting 200 workers, and by the management ordering the firing of all strikers. Finally government mediators said new elections could be held if the strike ended. The strike was called off and Vallejo was again elected Secretary General

59,759 to 9.[32]

The government still refused to recognize the new union officials. To force recognition another strike was called in March 1959. On March 29, 1959, to break the strike, 9,000 workers were fired, workers were driven from company-owned housing even before the strike began, and Vallejo and another strike leader, Valentín Campa, were jailed until 1970. They were charged with a legal catchall called "social dissolution," which in actual practice meant "trouble making." From the breaking of the rail workers' movement until the Echeverría administration there was no serious challenge to the charros.

2. UNION STRUCTURE

The government-run union structure established during the Cárdenas administration still persists. Corrupt union officials draw up and sign contracts, determine pay scales, promotions, and work rules all without discussion by or approval of workers, and support the government without question.[33] These leaders follow government policy to keep in the good graces of the PRI and thus maintain their personal position within the union. Their union position allows them to demand payoffs from companies to maintain labor peace, and at the same time collect salaries for the jobs at which they are nominally employed (but don't perform).[34]

Despite their being sold out to the government, these union leaders become entrenched powers in their own right, and must be dealt with as such by workers, business and even the government. The head of the CTM, Fidel Velázquez, has been in power since 1941 and has built up a personal fiefdom similar to that J. Edgar Hoover built up in the FBI. No government has yet been willing to risk ousting him. Velázquez, in order to maintain his power, often relies on the support of foreign corporations, the majority of whose workers are nominally led by him.

The political power of these leaders has become considerable, and they share only some interests with organized labor, and almost none at all with the majority of workers who are unorganized.[35] These union leaders, realizing their position is dependent on the incumbent government, have become strong supporters of both conservative Mexican policies and of international corporations.[36] They keep the anti-US issue out of the workers' movement and use cold war rhetoric to get rid of non-conformists.[37]

The formal structure of organized labor is quite complicated. In all there are some 16,489 unions[38] which are organized by craft, profession, company, group of companies, or national industry. The unions are then united into large federations similar to the AFL-CIO. The

Demetrio Vallejo, rail worker arrested in 1959

largest of these organizations is the CTM, which has dominated organized labor since Cárdenas. Another group is the CROC (Revolutionary Congress of Workers and Peasants), organized in 1953. About 3 million unionized workers are in PRI-dominated unions, and only 250,000 are in relatively independent unions.[39] Unionized workers are only a small part of the total work force. In the industrial sector about one million are unionized, and over 4 million are not.[40] Of the total work force, only about 25% or 3.25 million are unionized. The most highly unionized workers are in the public sector and in large, modern companies paying relatively high salaries.

Workers are kept subservient to their leaders, and ultimately to the PRI, in a variety of ways. Often unions are made up of former peasants who are satisfied with their meager earnings and have no experience with trade unions. Elections are often crooked, and can be nullified by labor officials if the "wrong" candidates get in.[41] Those who manage to get into office with their good intentions intact are subject to bribes, threats and violence.[42] The whole process is thoroughly corrupt, and often in labor tribunals litigants pay off court officials and union representatives.[43]

Union structure has many features designed to perpetuate the status quo. A provision known as the exclusion clause permits the union heirarchy to fire anyone making trouble. Failure to support the PRI is sufficient grounds for firing via the exclusion clause.[44] Even minor officials, once on the bureaucratic ladder, realize that their advancement is based on pleasing their superiors, not the rank and file.[45] Sometimes union officials have their own paramilitary groups to maintain union control, and in addition the police and military serve in that capacity from time to time. The oil workers union is estimated to have a 2000-man paramilitary force to back its leaders.[46]

The oil workers union is a classical example of corruption. Permanent jobs are sold for $5,000. Contractors doing work for PEMEX, the national oil company, have to pay bribes to union officials which amount to 2-3% of the contract. Workers are forced to do unpaid labor for officials, such as repairing their homes.[47] They are forced to buy in high priced stores whose profits are siphoned off by union officials. Violence often marks the competition for control of workers and sale of jobs. Workers are threatened at assemblies and some 30,000 permanent workers are classified as "temporary," giving them no job security and leaving them at the whim of union officials.[48]

Sold-out unions have provided an economic climate which has attracted foreign investment for decades, minimized inflation (up until the 1970's), and permitted high earnings for investors.[49] However despite their many drawbacks these unions do provide some benefits. They negotiate wage hikes which cover most if not all of the loss due to inflation; they provide a degree of job protection; and they provide social security benefits not available to the majority.[50]

3. WAGES

Organized labor in Mexico is extremely heterogeneous and generally is in a privileged position in relation to the rest of the society. There is cottage industry existing alongside modern factories, and there is an extremely wide range of pay. This makes any unified labor action very difficult, not to mention the problems of forming alliances between organized labor and other sectors.

Workers are often categorized by the size of the factory they work in. The following table shows the division of workers by large factory (over $1.6 million invested), medium factory, and small factory (under $240,000 invested):[51]

	% of total factories	% of total workers	avg. no. of workers per factory	average annual wage	% of total production
small industry	96.9	45.9	6	$ 889*	22.6
medium industry	2.3	23.9	137	$1835	25.8
large industry	0.8	30.2	485	$2599	51.6

The average annual wage for all industrial workers was $1631 in 1970. Despite the large number of unemployed workers who would potentially bring salaries down even further, imported capital-intensive equipment in large industry requires a small number of workers who can be relatively well paid to keep them docile.[52]

Workers in certain industries get much higher salaries than in others. Those in basic metal products, the highest paying, receive 54% more than the average of textile workers, 77% more than in the food industry, and 97% more than those working in the clothing and shoe industries.[53] Blunting the nationalism of workers is the fact that in foreign-owned industries workers get 40% higher salaries than in domestic industry.[55]

Salaries were 19.4% of the national product in 1974, while they were 31.2% in 1960 and 34% in 1950. This compares very poorly with advanced countries such as the US where salaries are 70% of the national product.[56] Of the 16 million people now working, only 42% earn more than $40 a month.[57] Only 30% of salaried workers get the legally established minimum wage or better.[58] The right to pay less than the minimum wage is used as a form of political control. If a factory owner gets out of line, he is forced to pay the minimum wage.[59] Given the low salary, the supposed right to an eight-hour day is often a fiction, and workers find themselves having to work more than one shift, or at more than one job.

*This figure only reflects the average in small factories, not the lowest. In 1973 a CTM official denounced the employment of 30,000 child laborers between the age of 8 and 12 in factories in the State of Mexico. Their pay was 40¢ a day.[54]

Despite these pessimistic figures, the unionized labor force is not an oppressed group when compared to the rest of Mexican society. Seventy-two percent of the workers in industry and construction, the most highly unionized areas, make more than the median income, and 17.2% are in the top five percent of income earners.[60]

4. ECHEVERRIA

In keeping with his reformist image Echeverría sided with dissident labor groups during the early part of his administration. The possibility of toppling the entrenched labor bureaucracy and installing more responsive officials was even left open. By 1974 dissidents such as the electrical workers and rail workers were operating with relative freedom, and a number of independent strikes had won significant labor victories.

One of these early victories was at the Mexican Nissan factory, near Cuernavaca, where Datsuns are made. The plant has 1237 employees organized into an independent union. Despite the union's independence, there were the standard Mexican labor complaints, including 30% of the work force being "temporary" workers, who got new "temporary" contracts each 28 days. On April 1, 1974 the workers went out on strike, demanding permanent contracts and a wage hike. As with other recent strikes, the movement drew widespread local support from students and other workers. Finally the Secretary of Labor stepped in and arranged a settlement granting workers a 22% raise, 15% more permanent employees, and the cost of transportation to work.[61]

Despite the success of the Nissan strike, many local labor organizers have been repressed. The most publicized case was that of Efraín Calderón Lara, a law student and labor organizer from Mérida, Yucatán. While attending law school Calderón helped form various unions outside the CTM. He organized city bus drivers in Mérida. Drivers had to hold 60 buses "hostage" in order to get the company to recognize their union, which they called Jacinto Canek after the 18th century Yucatán Indian rebel. Later Calderón organized some 600 shoe workers.

On February 13, 1974 he was going to meet with some workers he was organizing at a construction company. Before he got to the company he was kidnapped by police. Later his body was found, showing signs of torture before he was killed. In one of the rare cases of prosecution for such crimes, eight policemen were arrested and two policemen were given 25-year sentences. The ex-police chief involved was fined $3,200 and released. Calderón's independent union activity not only threatened the interests represented by the local government, but also the CTM. It was stated at a union meeting that if the government didn't eliminate Calderón, the CTM would.[62]

As the Echeverría administration drew to a close, even the relative tolerance for such independent activity as the Nissan strike was reduced. The splits within the administration made any concessions to workers difficult, since workers might use such splits to increase their power. Furthermore the economic crisis demanded that increased control be placed on workers. The changes within the union movement have served to strengthen, not weaken entrenched officials. The 1973 wage hike of 20% and the 1974 hike of 22% enhanced the power of the bureaucracy, since the wage increases were negotiated through established channels. These raises though were a meager reward for workers, since as the Secretary General of the CTM admitted, workers got less pay after the increases than they had previously due to inflation.[63] What they did get was at least partial compensation for inflationary losses, something lacking for the ten million non-unionized workers.

A strike at the Spicer plant, which manufactures most of the automobile axles in Mexico, shows how the labor climate changed during the last half of the Echeverría administration. The problems at the Spicer plant were typical. Forty percent of workers had no permanent contracts, and thus lacked benefits. Permanent contracts were sold. The union was led by charros. No one could account for union dues, and seven years had passed without a meeting.[64] The plant was 60% Mexican-owned, and American interests, including the Dana Corp., owned the other 40%. In its 1974/5 stock market report Spicer reported a profit of $5.44 million.

When workers began to organize an independent union, outsiders were brought in by management to pack meetings. Other company responses to organizing efforts were beatings, firing workers, changing of organizers' shifts, and threats of mass firings. Despite that on June 13, 1975 workers went on strike demanding permanent positions for "temporary" workers, the rehiring of those fired for union activity, the recognition of an independent union, and a pledge by the company to stay out of union affairs.[65]

On August 7, after 7,000 people had taken part in a solidarity march for Spicer workers, the company agreed to a partial settlement to end the strike. Temporary contracts were to be extended 4 to 6 months, the fired could return to their jobs, no reprisals would be taken, and $80 in back pay would be given to strikers. However when workers returned to the plant some were beaten, and police ringed the plant, refusing to let the workers' lawyer enter. Workers responded with meetings, marches, and slowdowns in the plant. The company fired 164 workers on August 18, at which time all workers again went out on strike.

The strike movement gained widespread support and on August 28 100,000 people turned out for a solidarity march which was stopped by police. In September 45 meetings at schools and universities in Mexico City were held in support of the workers. Later Echeverría issued what was in effect an ultimatum: 485 workers, including 35 of those fired, could return as non-union workers, free of the sold-out leadership, but without any right to elect their own leaders. Workers, seeing the government was solidly allied with management, had little other choice than to accept the offer, thus ending the strike.

Electrical workers have been challenging the charro leadership within the electrical workers union (the SUTERM). The progressive workers are led by Rafael Galván, head of a union originally founded for workers in the American Power and Light Company. After this company was taken over by the government in 1960, this relatively democratic union co-existed with another union established in the 1930's for workers in the government-owned electric company. Echeverría arranged for a merger between the union led by Galván and the old-line union. Typically, the merger took place in 1972 without members of either union voting for it.[66] Galván, the head of the democratic union, held the loyalty of most of his former members within the newly formed union, the SUTERM (Single Union of Electrical Workers of the Mexican Republic). He began to attack the undemocratic nature of the union, and so in March 1975 the SUTERM leadership, inherited from the old undemocratic union, expelled Galván and six of his supporters. Since then Galván has been an active organizer against entrenched union officials in the SUTERM and other unions.

The high point of the movement was a massive rally held in Mexico City on November 15, 1975 at which the insurgents demonstrated under the theme of "labor without Fidel," referring to long-time CTM head Fidel Velázquez. By the organizers' estimates some 150,000 turned out to demonstrate their dissatisfaction with the lack of union democracy.

The Democratic Tendency, as the dissident workers are called, continues to organize and hold rallies throughout the country, encouraging labor democracy and supporting independent union activity. The government and labor establishment continue to intimidate Galván supporters. Pistol-toting goons broke up a rally in San Luis Potosí in January 1976.[67] When a second Mexico City rally was called for February 27, 1976, the PRI staged a rally for the same time and place. The Democratic Tendency's rally was postponed to avoid violence. When the second mass rally was finally held it was greeted by 27,000 soldiers and police, backed up by 15 anti-riot tanks, 25 military tanks, and four helicopters.[68]

The inability of the dissident electrical workers to convert widespread support into concrete action was shown when they called a strike on July 16, 1976. Their demands were that electrical workers fired for their activities in the Democratic Tendency be rehired, that the company stay out of union affairs, and that elections for union officials be held with direct secret vote. On the day of the strike electrical installations were occupied by troops, and workers not in the Democratic Tendency kept working. Goons beat strikers and forced them to sign letters supporting the charro leadership of the union. In San Luis Potosí strikers were taken to a local military base and held.[69] In other locations strikers were fired. The strike was soon broken, and many strikers were forced to sign pledges of loyalty to the charros before being allowed to return to work. To further weaken the Democratic Tendency, nuclear energy workers were removed from the electrical workers union and assigned to another union.[70]

Regardless of the outcome of the Galván-led protests, they have succeeded in showing that the old union structure is thoroughly disliked, and that it is becoming harder to hold dissidents in line. With such mass backing, labor dissidents challenge not only union bureaucrats, but domestic and foreign business interests which rely on union officials to pacify workers. Galván seems to represent a relatively small threat to the system as a whole, given his background as an ex-senator and his publicly announced support for the candidacy of López Portillo. However his success does indicate that union structure is the weakest link in the PRI-government hegemony. While his demands are not radical, and may in fact increase acceptance of the present system, they do have the potential for starting movements which could get out of the control of the elite, just as the divisions at the end of the Porfiriato did.

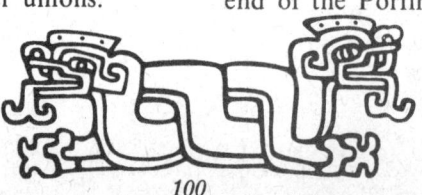

HECTOR GARCIA

CHAPTER 17: PEASANTS*

The peasant masses who formed the backbone of the Revolutionary armies continued their struggle for land into the 1920's. As we have seen in the chapter on agrarian reform, there was little willingness on the part of the government to support the peasants' cause. In most cases peasants were not well organized and they met with violence from landlords. However in Veracruz the peasants were organized under Usulo Gálvan into the Socialist League of Agrarian Communities.

This socialist league united the peasants and provided armed defense against the incursions of hacendados who resisted even the most timid agrarian reform measures of the 1920's. The League's perception of the half-way nature of the Revolution was stated in their Second Congress:

There is only one way: violence, the PROLETARIAN REVOLUTION. It must be said clearly. The Revolution will not take place in the cabarets where pro-hacendado congressmen squander our money.

*Peasant is used in its broadest sense here, meaning poor agricultural worker.

The Revolution will catch fire in the countryside where misery, pain and an absolute lack of justice will make the discontent of the outcasts explode.[1]

Despite the League's political perceptions, or perhaps because of them, it made little headway. Calles divided the population along religious lines with his persecution of the church, causing class interests to be forgotten. In addition his radical rhetoric, as contrasted to his deeds, misled peasants, and frequent assassinations of peasant leaders broke peasant organizations.[2]

With Calles's turn to the right, the peasant movement, lacking clear objectives, fragmented and ceased to play a major role.[3] Then the depression came and agricultural exports fell, cutting the number of jobs available to peasants. Rural unemployment was increased by the deportation of 500,000 Mexican agricultural workers from the US.[4]

101

Pro-hacendado attack on agrarian reform, directed to peasants:
Dear Farm Worker,
   Don't let yourself get caught up in the flattery and false promises that the agrarian reformers make, offering you land that was given to them by a government of bandits. Justice won't be long in coming and will see that these lands are returned to the power of the hacendados, because the agrarian reform has been a failure. Think for a moment, the agrarian reformers aren't the owners of the ejido, things will soon change. Don't take land that belongs to another private property owner, because its owner wants it. Show that you are an honorable man and that you don't take land belonging to someone else. It's not yours.[6]

Poem favoring agrarian reformers, by Concepción Michel

(They say) that us agrarian reformers are a bunch of thieves because we don't want to be the boss's oxen. But tell me, comrad, who gave them the land? They're the ones who are thieves. that's what I say. Let the rich and government officials start working. The nuns and priests. Let them come help.	(Dicen) que los agraristas somos una punta de ladrones porque no queremos ser los bueyes de los patrones. Pero dimi compañero, ¿La Tierra quién se las dió? Que los ladrones son ellos, eso es lo que digo, Que los ricos y gobiernos se pongan a trabajar. Las monjas y padrecitos Que se vengan a ayudar.[5]

Cárdenas confronted this stiuation of desperation and potential revolt by initiating an effective agrarian reform. He strengthened the peasant leagues and passed out 60,000 guns to enable peasants to protect themselves from hacendados. While Cárdenas did provide for defense of peasant interests, he also set up strict top-down control over the peasant movement.

In 1938 Cárdenas created the National Peasant Confederation (CNC) which initially had a radical tone and was supported by the Communist Party.[7] However as Mexico began its turn to the right in the 1940's, the situation began to change rapidly. In 1942 communists (small c) were forced out of the CNC on the grounds that it was necessary to maintain a united front for the war effort.[8] During the 1940's what has been called the counter-agrarian reform began. As land distribution slowed, the landless population grew 33% from 1940 to 1950 and the buying power of peasants went down 46% from 1939 to 1947.[9] This trend continued, with buying power decreasing another 6% from 1950 to 1960.[10]

Since the shift to the right, Mexican peasants have received little support from the government and have received few of the benefits of industrialization. The classic example of the treatment of Mexican peasants in the post-World War II period is provided by the life and death of Rubén Jaramillo. Jaramillo was from the state of Morelos and had been a Zapatista in his youth. In 1938 he was the president of the administrative council of the co-operative sugar mill in Zacatepec, Morelos. There he led an anti-alcoholism campaign, emphasizing that the sale of alcoholic drinks was one of the main ways merchants exploited peasants. When the beer distributor's gunmen came after him he was forced to flee. Four years later he led peasants demanding a look at the books of the supposedly co-operative mill, which was in fact a source of graft for political appointees. Again he was forced to flee for his life. He was forced to flee again when federal police tried to arrest him at a 1946 rally supporting an independent candidate for governor of Morelos.*

Jaramillo's last target was a 27,000 hectare estate in Morelos. This land had been given to peasants in presidential decrees of 1922 and 1929, decrees which had never been implemented, since the land belonged to a friend of the governor. The agrarian reform administration gave assurances the land would be given to peasants, then withdrew its pledge. It had become public knowledge that the lands would be irrigated at public expense and made quite valuable, too valuable for peasants. Jaramillo's response was to organize 5,000 landless peasants to occupy the lands.

On May 23, 1962, at 2:30 P.M. at No. 112 Calle de Mina, Tlaquiltenango, Morelos, 60 soldiers and police arrived at the Jaramillo's home with two army trucks and two jeeps. They picked up Jaramillo, his pregnant wife, three sons, took them to an isolated area nearby, and machine-gunned them.[11]

This is just an example of the frequent violence and the collaboration between police, the army, and landlords which has continued to the present day. This violence is

*Given the extremely high death rate for peasant organizers, such flight is merely the most rational approach to permit one to continue organizing.

necessary to maintain the status quo in rural Mexico. Despite three million peasants having received some 70 million hectares,[12] these peasants are still at the mercy of various commercial interests which keep them in dire poverty.

2. PEASANT LIFE

The lot of the Mexican peasant has largely been shaped by forces at the national and international level. The agrarian reform was implemented by the national government to eliminate the threat of rebellion. Today the peasant for whom the agrarian reform was supposedly instituted has become a source of cheap labor for agribusiness. The peasant's small plot insures that he will remain in the area and thus be available when needed for wage labor. Also the small plots provide some income, thus lessening the wages agribusiness must pay to ensure survival of its seasonal wage laborers.

MARKETING: One of the principal means of exploiting peasant labor is paying the peasant a very low price for his produce, then greatly increasing the price, leaving most of the profits with middlemen. Studies reflect the degree to which this exploitation occurs. Avocado growers in one study were found to get only 1.3% of the retail price of the avocados they grew.[13] In another case the producers got 17% of the retail price of tomatoes. These same tomato growers had to operate on credit which cost them from 5 to 10% per month.[14] The other 83% of the retail cost of the tomato was spread between the trucker who hauled the crop some 60 miles to Mexico City, the cops on the highway who had to be bribed to let the truck pass, the marketing cost at the farmers' market in Mexico City which included the paying of more bribes, and finally two middlemen between the market and the retailer.

Often the role of the middleman is played by the village store keeper, who may begin as just another small farmer or ejidatario. If he manages to accumulate a little capital, he will set up a store, then often buy a truck, which is used to haul crops out of the town on the way to buy goods for the store. Finally such store keepers accumulate enough capital to become the local loan sharks. In one town, Nuevo Ixcatlán, Veracruz, store keepers, 5% of the population, received 50% of the income.[15]

Most of the crop prices in Mexico reflect the presence of modern farming units, where each worker has a high output. Small farmers are obliged to sell at these prices, even though their output is far less.[16] Also the same forces which are driving the peasant population off the land are making the peasant who remains less self-sufficient. In 1940 50% of the peasant population lived mainly from their own produce, while in 1969 only 18% did.[17] The small amount paid peasants for their produce does not mean the urban worker can buy inexpensive foods. Given the extreme mark-up by middlemen, the prices paid to the producers could double with little effect on the final consumer.

CONASUPO: In order to provide at least some protection against commercial abuse of the peasant, a government buying agency has been set up to guarantee a fixed minimum price for food. In theory this agency, the CONASUPO, would always give the peasant the opportunity to sell to the government if the middlemen didn't offer at least as good a price. However in actual practice the benefits to the peasant have been quite limited. Along with the rest of the rural governmental apparatus, the CONASUPO is fraud-ridden, and peasants are often paid less than the stated prices with the administration pocketing the difference. Another way for CONASUPO to cheat the peasant is for the crop to be declared of a low grade, when in fact it is of a higher grade.[18]

The traveling middleman with his truck who comes to a farmer is often a more attractive buyer, since the crops must be brought to the CONASUPO warehouse before CONASUPO will purchase them. Private middlemen on the other hand come to the farm and pay in cash, immediately, with no paperwork. To sell to CONASUPO the grower must arrange for transporting his crop to the warehouse, and often wait for his sale to be processed. Finally CONASUPO has a limited number of purchase sites and limited storage capacity.[19]

LOSS OF CONTROL: Despite the prohibition against sale of ejido land, a provision designed to prevent the peasant from losing his land, the peasant is losing *control* over his land. Peasants who rent land to modern high technology planters can make more than they can by farming the same land themselves. Even those peasants farming their own land are losing control, since credit institutions only give loans for the growing of certain crops, forcing the peasant to grow what the creditor wants grown. Once the loan is made the creditor frequently reserves the right to supervise production at each stage to protect his investment. This supervision can include the administration of planting, fertilization, pest control, irrigation and harvesting, and converts the supposed owner into little more than a wage laborer on his own land.

Illiterate ejidatarios are often abused by government banks more interested in their own account books than the growers they supposedly serve. Often defective or unneeded products, such as last year's seeds or unsuitable fertilizer, are unloaded on the peasant, who has no choice but to accept the product and the debt accompanying it. In one ejido an observer noted "goods were simply delivered to the ejidatario's field, charges made in the books of the bank, and each client left to decide how to use his 'purchase' ".[20] This is typical of what happens agribusiness pushes the use of sophisticated products that peasants are not trained to use. In addition to forcing sales of questionable use to the grower, the ejido bankers, among the most corrupt officials in the country,[21] simply pocket much of the money allocated for loans.

USURY: Often no government source of credit is available and growers are forced to rely on private lenders. Interest on private loans to small growers runs in the neighborhood of 8% a month.[22] Closely tied to usury is the practice of buying a crop from the producer before it is harvested, at prices well below the anticipated market price. Such purchases are made from one to three months in advance of the harvest and have the effect of a loan bearing as much as 50% a month interest. An example of such advance buying in Oaxaca occurred when producers were paid one peso per kilo for sesame which 90 to 120 days later sold for two and a half pesos.[23]

The inability of the ejidatario to mortgage his land makes it difficult to obtain credit through normal channels. This legal provision against mortgaging serves the same function as the prohibition against outright sale: the prevention of large estates being formed from small ones. However the small land owner finds it almost as hard to get credit as the ejidatario, since banks prefer not to deal with small farmers. "One only has to imagine a modern bank in the process of foreclosing 3/4 hectare of land five hours by path from Chalchicomula, just to collect a debt of $64.00."[24]

RURAL BUREAUCRACY: Another factor contributing to rural poverty is the swollen federal bureaucracy which supposedly aids the farmer. In actual practice government officials see the peasant as a person who can be exploited and who cannot fight back due to his lack of political clout or knowledge of modern bureaucracies.[25] Ejido presidents are often imposed from above by outsiders.[26] Once in power they violate ejido rules and cling to power for years, taking a cut of loans going to the ejido and keeping the ejidatarios under control with the threat of violence, cutting off credit, or the illegal taking away of his ejido plot.

Above the ejido president is another layer of functionaries such as PRI officials, and representatives of the treasury, water resources and agrarian reform ministries of the federal government, all of whom tend to become wealthy in their modestly paid posts.[27] The PRI in rural areas generally is much more authoritarian than in urban areas, and is the sole acceptable channel for complaints. Repression follows quickly in rural areas when protests are made outside PRI channels.[28]

CACIQUES: A common figure in rural Mexico is a cacique, who can be considered as a one-man rural mafia. Caciques acquire political and economic power over a certain rural area, often an isolated locality less subject to public scrutiny. Usually their main power base is the personal control of an area's cash crop, such as coffee or cattle.[29] Along with control of the major cash crop they often appoint all local officials, and in turn guarantee the state government that the area under their control will be politically tranquil and that it will supply peasants for political rallies. Caciques make money from bribes, loan sharking, lumber concessions, and public works contracts they control.[30] Caciques with ties to an ejido may also come to control as many as 80% of all the supposedly individual plots in the ejido.[31]

Since the cacique has the support of state and regional government there is no appeal to higher authorities to control the cacique. In addition to relying on government support, caciques maintain their position by handing out jobs and favors to the sympathetic and by widespread use of violence to silence opposition.[32]

An unusual example of a cacique being overthrown occurred in a small town in Tlaxcala in 1973. There the cacique appointed the municipal president, owned the main local store, and took a part of the earnings of workers at nearby textile factories. However when he personally granted a quarrying concession that threatened the town's water source, there was a revolt. The cacique was driven from town, and his house (by far the largest in town) was burned, as was his store and car. When police arrived in a paddy wagon to "restore order," the truck was overturned and burned. When the police piled out, they were stoned by the women from the town, who knew it would hardly fit the policemen's macho image to shoot down unarmed women. Facing the prospect of shooting the women or being stoned, they were literally run out of town. After that a municipal president was chosen by the town.

WEALTH DISTRIBUTION: Wealth in rural Mexico comes not only from land ownership, but from monopolistic control of commercial and financial resources, and of the distribution of goods and services.[33] The concept of the free market is rarely applicable, and highly profitable commercial monopolies are often maintained by violence. A result of this violence can be seen on a trail leading out of Huautla, Oaxaca, where there is a monument to a murdered Indian. The Indian tried to organize a coffee producers' co-operative and was shot by local coffee merchants in order to preserve their monopoly.

The following table shows how land (including ejidos) is distributed and how landholders benefit.[34]

	Number of holders	% of irrigated land held	% of crops produced
Small	2 million	3.9%	21%
Medium	300,000	27%	24.4%
Large	79,000	70%	54.3%

The small farmers cannot support themselves from their plot, and are therefore forced to work as wage laborers. Half of them produce less than $40 of crops a year and they tend to eat their produce rather than sell it. The large landholders consume little of what they produce and rely almost entirely on hired labor. The 12,000 most wealthy landholders each produce at least $8,000 of crops a year and control 37.6% of irrigated land. They are closely tied to commercial, financial and industrial interests which profit from agriculture.

There are also some four million wage laborers known as jornaleros,[35] up from 1.5 million in 1950.[36] They get only a tenth of agricultural income, but form half the agricultural work force.[37] The typical jornalero earns from $34 to $56 a year and averages 65 days of work to support a family. They are virtually unaffected by social legislation and often are not supported by peasant organizations. The conditions of these workers vary greatly, since they are paid up to $5 a day on large northern estates, but are miserably paid in central and southern Mexico.[38]

Individuals in rural areas frequently get income from several sources, and often a single individual will be a merchant, a grower, a wage laborer, and an employer of wage labor all within a year. Some 300,000 ejidatarios own small private farms.[39] Many of those with small farms also work for wages, or have small stores and produce handicrafts. This diversity of income sources among the rural poor makes it hard to organize around any one issue. Also the mere ownership of even the smallest plot tends to create the consciousness of a landowner in its holder, and obscures the exploitation of both small holders and jornaleros by the same com-

HECTOR GARCIA

mercial and political institutions.

The following figures show the distribution of income for rural families in 1960:[40]

> 29% of rural families make less than $24 a month
> 35% of rural families make from $34 to $48 a month
> 17% of rural families make from $48 to $80 a month
> 19% of rural families make over $80 a month

This contrasts with the non-farm families where only 10% make less than $24 a month.[41]

The significant division in rural population is not between land owners (including ejidatarios) and non-landowners, but between those who live from their own labor and those who exploit the labor of others. The owners of family-sized plots and sub-family sized plots, and landless workers are in the former category. Large land owners and the many varieties of agribusinessmen and public officials fall into the latter group.[42]

Low income and its maldistribution has led to the flow of people from the countryside to the city. Not only does the city provide more income and services, but the buying up of rural land by agribusiness, population increase, and increased mechanization tend to push peasants off land.[43] The result of this migration is shown by the decline in the percent of workers in agriculture:[44]

> 1930 68.6% of workers in agriculture
> 1950 58.3% of workers in agriculture
> 1970 39.5% of workers in agriculture

4. PEASANT ORGANIZATIONS

The National Peasant Confederation (CNC) is the organized national group which was set up by Cárdenas to mobilize peasants and provide a means for controlling them politically. Officially the CNC is charged with (1.) defending peasant interests, (2.) pressuring the government into taking action on matters relating to peasants, and (3.) the education of peasants. The CNC serves mainly as a pressure group for ejidatarios, who are tied to the CNC through the ejido organizational structure. Owners of small farms rarely join, while owners of medium-sized farms are represented by the CNOP and large farm owners have direct access to policy makers.

Organizationally the president of each ejido is the link between the ejido and the regional, state and national divisions of the CNC. The national CNC in turn forms one of the three major sectors of the PRI and serves as a way to keep peasants in check. Peasants failing to follow the dictates of the PRI, as interpreted by the CNC, have credit and other government services cut off. Similarly ejido presidents expect their fellow ejidatarios to be politically passive and not endanger the incumbent's presidency. The CNC also serves to bolster the image of the local PRI by trucking in large numbers of peasants for "spontaneous" rallies. Attendance at these rallies is rewarded by a few pesos and free beer, while non-attendance can incur the displeasure of a cacique or ejido president.

The CNC lobbies for more land, higher agricultural prices, and more government aid to agriculture.[45] It is also an effective channel for complaints of a strictly local nature, such as the request of a town to have a road built to it.

The general orientation of the CNC is indicated by the slogan adopted at the 12th National Congress of the CNC in 1972, "Production increase will make the revolution."[46] Generally the CNC has been rather ineffectual even though it supposedly represents the largest constituency in the country. This results from the fact that peasants are no longer *the* political force in Mexico. The present sector now has less influence in the PRI than either workers or the middle class (CNOP).

UGOCM: The failure of the CNC to meet peasants' needs led to the formation of the General Union of Mexican Workers and Peasants (UGOCM) in 1949. This group was closely tied to the Popular Party (now the Popular Socialist Party) and at its peak had some 300,000 members, 70% of them peasants. By 1956 the UGOCM had lost most of its influence, except in certain locations in the north, where it continues to organize peasants to sieze land holdings. It was the principal group organizing peasants in northwestern Mexico during the crisis at the end of the Echeverría administration.

Originally the UGOCM was thought of as a group to unite workers and peasants. However the government refused to recognize it as a legal bargaining agent, so few workers joined. Before its decline it engaged in two major campaigns. In 1949 it backed the candidacy of Jacinto López, the Popular Party candidate for governor of Sonora. Despite lack of support for the PRI candidate, President Alemán had him installed and sent in troops to attack the ejidatarios who had supported the other candidate.[47]

The second major campaign involved dramatic occupations of American-owned cattle estates near Cananea, Sonora. These estates were in violation of the constitutional provision prohibiting foreigners from owning land near the national border and were above the land-holding limit set by the agrarian reform law. After many well-publicized marches and land occupations the UGOCM was able to force the government to nationalize the land and distribute it.

CCI: As a result of the ineffectiveness of the agrarian reform, another peasant league called the Independent Peasant Center (CCI) was formed in 1963. This group was most active in the Laguna area, Sonora, and Baja California, all in northern Mexico. One year after its founding it split into two factions, one under the moderate Alfonso Garzón and one under the more radical Danzós Palomino. The immediate cause of the split was that Garzón, himself a former CNC official, made overtures to the PRI and tried to purge communists from the CCI.[48] This led to the withdrawal of Danzós and those sympathetic to the Mexican Communist Party.

Both factions continue to call themselves the CCI. The Garzón faction drifted back toward the PRI and the CNC. On the other hand the Danzós-led faction has continued to engage in radical peasant organizing. His faction is still close to the Mexican Communist Party, and its effectiveness is indicated by the number of times Danzós has been in jail in the past decade.

Both the CCI and the UGOCM have been closely tied

to the faction fights and internal splits of the PPS and the Mexican Communist Party, matters which have had little meaning for the peasant. Being dragged into these fights has hurt both of these movements,[49] as has the repression, isolation and lack of issues common to all peasants.

5. ECHEVERRIA

The most frequent response by peasants to their desperate economic situation is what is called a land "invasion." Such invasions are occupations of large holdings by groups of peasants with little or no land. Frequently peasants have requested lands occupied in accordance with the agrarian reform. Then after fifteen or twenty years of dealing with the bureaucracy, they take matters into their own hands. These invasions occurred throughout the country during the Echeverría administration, and often were met by repression from land owners, the police and army.

The list of invasions is long. EL DIA listed 46 invasions in the state of Chihuahua alone.[50] Landowners themselves admitted 500 occupations in a three-year period,[51] while an article in EXCELSIOR claimed 600 invasions in the states of Tlaxcala, Guanajuato, and Michoacán.[52]

One of these invasions occurred in the state of Tlaxcala where peasants occupied the 13,800 hectare estate of San Miguel Mimiahuapan, near the city of Tlaxcala. The occupiers came from the adjoining village whose 3,500 people together had only 6,000 hectares. Despite having petitioned for the division of the hacienda in 1938 there had been no response from agrarian reform officials. After the occupation agrarian reform officials said that if the occupiers didn't leave they would be burned out. When that threat failed they offered credit and deeds to land, provided of course the occupiers would leave first. When that tactic failed, arrangements were finally made to purchase part of the hacienda land for the occupiers, thus in part meeting their demands.[53]

Not all invasions have such happy endings. In October 1975 an occupation took place near Río Muerto, Sonora. Peasants had requested the land occupied in 1945. They had not received land though, since the area had been divided among family members of the owner, making the size of the holdings below the limit set by the agrarian reform law. One of the owners was a 12-year-old boy. The response to the invasion was a police and army attack on the encampment which killed 7 and wounded 14 of the occupiers.[54] Enraged peasants from around the state marched 15,000 strong to the state capital and staged a massive demonstration. To appease demonstrators, the governor, who had already made the mistake of not supporting López Portillo's candidacy, was replaced.

In October 1975, near Tlapacoyan, Veracruz, peasants were attacked by 200 landowners and their hired gunmen, armed with pistols and automatic weapons. This time the situation was different though. On October 6, 1975, after 40 years of requests, residents of Tlapacoyan had received land in accordance with the agrarian reform. Twenty days later the cattlemen who had owned the land attacked, killing six of the new landowners, and wounding eight of them. After the attack the homes which had been built there were bulldozed.[55]

In early 1976 there was another wave of land invasions, with 50 occurring in the state of Sonora alone.[56] Such invasions have become a political hot potato. If the invaders are evicted, the government faces massive peasant discontent and appears to side with the rich landowners. However if peasants are allowed to remain, rural agribusiness protests, and begins to withhold investment, hurting agricultural production. In an effort to calm agribusiness interests, the Secretary of the Agrarian Reform stated that in the first half of 1976 there were only 327 invasions of the 1.5 million private land holdings.[57]

An attempt was made to stage a peaceful protest concerning rural conditions in Tlaxcala and Puebla. On April 12, 1972 groups left Tlaxcala and Puebla on a march to Mexico City to protest the lack of land and the systematic breaking of promises by agrarian reform officials. En route to the capital agrarian reform officials said that if the march was stopped all demands would be met, but on a one-by-one basis. When that tactic failed the route of the march was blocked by a sizable contingent of the army and the marchers were forced to turn back.

One of the chief organizers of the march was Ramón Danzós Palomino, a long-time peasant organizer affiliated with the left branch of the CCI. In response to his organizing both during and after the march to Mexico City, he was arrested in July 1973, driven to Atlixco, Puebla, and charged with theft and "inciting to commit crimes" in connection with his participation in land invasions. When bond was raised for his release on these charges, he was charged with trespassing in connection with another land invasion and no bond was set. To protest his jailing in February 1974 some 10,000 people marched from Puebla to Atlixco. Finally the government released him in July 1975, never admitting the real reason for his jailing was "having led groups of peasants with undeniable rights who were not permitted to acquire land due to the legal subterfuges of the affected owners."[58]

In Veracruz the conditions of sugar cane growers led to a massive strike. Growers there had received land under provisions of the agrarian reform. However growers in zones surrounding the mills are required by law to grow only sugar cane. In addition they have no choice but to sell the cane to the mill at the price the mill offers. With no control over their own production, and only $800 a year income,[59] the growers struck the mills, refusing to deliver the cane to the mills until they received more for their crops.

The government's response was not long in coming. On January 8, 1973 two army regiments backed up with armored vehicles broke through picket lines which had been set up at the San Cristóbal mill and ended the strike.

Attempts reminiscent of César Chávez have been made to organize migrant laborers in northwestern Mexico. These growers work closely with the leaders of peasant organizations to keep peasants in line. Many of the workers have already been organized under the CNC, UGOCM or sometimes the CTM. Leaders of these groups often argue against land takeovers. The CTM officials working with peasants are as corrupt as those in industry. They maintain a black list of strikers and organizers, don't enforce minimum wage standards or social security laws, and consistently yield to growers' contract demands. The growers have been adamant in refusing to yield to organizing efforts or in raising the workers' wages since they are afraid of being priced out of the vegetable market in the US.[60]

The Echeverría government did little to improve conditions for the rural population. There has been some extension of social security to agricultural workers. As late as 1969 only 1.9% of the workers in agriculture and cattle raising were covered by social security. The workers recently granted social security benefits are the better organized ones, such as cane workers, henequen workers in Yucatán, and workers in the Laguna area in northern Mexico.

The other major policy shift of the Echeverría administration was an attempt to limit the profits of middlemen who drive up prices for consumers and yet contribute nothing to production. Financial resources of agencies such as CONASUPO were increased, and a new government buying agency, TABAMEX, was established to purchase tobacco from growers.[61]

The Echeverría administration consolidated the various peasant groups to present the facade of a unified peasant movement working with the government. This consolidation, ratified with a document called the Ocampo Pact, united the CNC, UGOCM, and the right wing of the CCI, an act which took place in front of Zapata's house in Anenecuilco, Morelos. The speech given at the ceremony gave no indication of any substantive changes, and in fact totally ignored the existence of rich land owners and the systematic repression of peasant protest.[62]

Echeverría's parting shot was the expropriation of 240,000 acres in Sonora, of which 100,000 acres were irrigated. This was met with bitter attacks by business. In protest factories and stores, including 6,000 in Monterrey alone, closed from one to 24 hours.[63] Even though the lands taken were among the most valuable in Mexico, this did little to resolve the problem of landless peasants. Only 9,000 received land of the 4 million eligible. Shortly after López Portillo took office, the Supreme Court declared the expropriation unconstitutional and ordered the land returned to its former owners. However the return to former owners was delayed pending an appeal by peasant groups. Whatever Echeverría's motives were, this expropriation hit rural landowners, the group which most consistently opposed his reforms. It also granted land only to peasants belonging to pro-government organizations, leaving the clear message that radical groups could not deliver land.[64]

Once business confidence had been established López Portillo reversed the supreme court decision, declaring that returning lands to their original owners would be too likely to provoke violence. The consolation offered the former owners was 600 million pesos compensation.[65]

CHAPTER 18: INDIANS

The Indian is, in his own terms, not a problem, but he does have a mestizo problem.[1]

During the colonial period there was a reduction in Indian population, as well as widespread land loss and assimilation of many Indians. The Laws of the Reform gave a legal basis to the process of taking Indian lands. In keeping with the prevailing liberal beliefs of the time, all special legal status and land-holding laws for Indians were abolished. During the Porfiriato concern was frequently expressed for Indians, but coherent programs to benefit them were few and far between.[2] Porfirian decision-makers saw the Indian as a person unable to help develop the country, a task which was felt to require people of European descent.

In the post-revolutionary period national leaders praised Indians and declared them to be part of the Mexican nation. Meanwhile the Indian continued to be exploited at the local level by non-Indians.[3] Like other reforms emanating from the Revolution, programs benefiting the Indian were slow in coming. Lázaro Cárdenas instituted the first national program on behalf of the Indian in 1936 when he set up the Autonomous Department of Indian Affairs. This agency began the process of tying the Indian more closely to the national economy, a move which favored ascendent national business interests.[4] Finally in 1948 the National Indian Institute* (INI) was established. Rather than being a radical innovation, the INI was simply a combining of various previously existing programs.[5]

The basic idea of the INI was to provide a variety of services for the Indian which would largely be supplied by Coordinating Centers. These centers function as welfare agencies located in areas of high Indian population. The centers build roads and provide agricultural credit and health and educational services. In addition government agencies buy crops from Indians to limit commercial exploitation of Indian growers. This work has limited impact in that the programs are voluntary for both Indians and non-Indians. Indians are not forced to avail themselves of services, and in fact often reject them as being too alien. Conversely the government has no power to stop commercial exploitation by non-Indians. The INI's ability to affect local economies is limited by its own budget. In some areas such as Tehuacán and Orizaba profits of trading monopolies dealing with Indians have exceeded the entire national budget of INI.[6]

*In Spanish: Instituto Nacional Indigenista

HECTOR GARCIA

A key concept of the INI program is the "promotor," an Indian who is given special training, usually as a teacher or agricultural extension agent, and then sent back to his own community. Generally the "promotores" have more success in reaching Indians than outsiders since they share the culture of those they teach. The task facing "promotores" is indicated by the fact that of the one million Indian children, only 250,000 attend school.[7]

I visited one of the coordinating centers at Atlacomulco, State of Mexico, in the Mazahua Indian region. The center itself is a rather unimposing one-story building where few of the center's activities are carried out. Most of the work is done in outlying communities some distance from the center. For an area inhabited by 120,000 Indians the center has 17 non-Indian employees and 45 "promotores." The non-Indian employees include a veterinarian, a sanitation worker, an economist who studies corn marketing, and one doctor for the 120,000 people of the area. The weakness of the INI was illustrated after my visit when six Maxahua leaders were assassinated for opposing the logging of communal lands by caciques.[8] This was only the continuation of a long series of land-related murders in the area.[9]

The most persistent criticism of the INI is that the result of increasing contact with and dependence on the outside fostered by the INI will inevitably lead to the destruction of the Indian community. INI programs are "directed and planned by anthropologists who proclaim themselves to be for the Indian, but whose end is that he cease to be one."[10] The basic result of the INI programs is that the Indian is increasingly incorporated into the dominant economic system and that the Indian community plays a smaller role. The ways Indians are being exploited are becoming more and more like the ways non-Indians are exploited.[11]

This destruction of the Indian community as an economic unit results from the INI's failure to create structures which promote the political and economic independence of the Indian community. Rather its programs accelerate integration into the national economy. As long as changes induced into the Indian community do not come from the Indians themselves, they will do nothing to alter the system of outside dominance, and will not give the Indian community the chance to strengthen itself.[12]

In Mexico the concept "Indian" is more cultural than racial, and one finds individuals generally accepted as Indian who have light skin and blue eyes ("ojos claros").[13] The trait which most strongly characterizes an Indian is speaking one of the many Indian languages found in Mexico. Other traits associated with the status of Indian include certain occupations, such as cattle raising, distinctive patterns of dress, an Indian surname, and various customs such as going barefoot and living in a hut.[14] Indians are members of a community which is the individual's primary source of identity, giving an "us" vs. "them" mentality, "us" being the Indian community, and "them" being everyone else. The fact that dark-skinned people can be considered non-Indian and light-skinned individuals may be classed as "Indian" emphasizes that "Indian" refers more to social relations with the rest of society than one's genes.[15]

Much which is generally considered "Indian" is in fact Spanish in origin. Plowing with an ox and raising cattle are both associated with Indians, but are of Spanish origin.[16] Even many of the distinctive patterns of dress worn by Indians are adaptations of Spanish colonial styles. Finally the Indian community itself, the heart of Indian identity, in many cases resulted from the Spaniards locating Indians into "strategic hamlets" to facilitate control.[17]

The exact number of people classified as Indian is somewhat arbitrary in that there is no precise way to determine if a certain individual is indeed an Indian. In any case the following figures indicate the number of persons classified as Indian by the census:[18]

	Number of Indians (millions)	Percent of total population
1900	1.8	15.3
1910	1.7	12.9
1921	1.9	15.2
1930	2.3	16.0
1940	2.5	14.8
1950	2.4	11.2
1960	3.0	10.4
1970	3.5	7.3

The introduction of DDT and sanitation has greatly lowered the mortality rate for Indians and has led to a rapid increase in the Indian population. However a countervailing force is the tendency for Indians to migrate to the city for economic reasons, and then for their children to lose their Indian culture and identity. In addition many Indians who remain in the same spot become assimilated into the Mexican national culture and cease to show any traits that are distinctively Indian; they simply become peasants. In many cases where part of the community is undergoing assimilation, more traditional community members oppose the assimilation with social and magical sanctions, and even use physical force to prevent those being assimilated from adopting non-Indian ways.[19]

In the Indian community there is little division of labor and the family is the basic unit of production and consumption. The amount each worker produces is low due to the frequent use of pre-Hispanic and colonial technology and the lack of cheap credit. The traditional nature of the economy is emphasized by the fact 80% of Indians are agricultural workers, 43% of whom own no land.[20] Further limiting the amount produced is the theft of all but the worst lands from Indians over the centuries. Those lands retained by Indians are still subject to unlawful appropriation by non-Indians.

In the traditional Indian community there is relatively little economic stratification, and little exploitation of Indians by other Indians. Rather there is individual production, with all producers being at roughly the same economic level. Often there are sanctions against rising above the rest of the community economically. These sanctions are applied through community pressure and the threat of witchcraft. The most widespread method of leveling out an individual's economic gains is the holding

HECTOR GARCIA

of ceremonial offices in the Indian community. These offices require the spending of one's entire capital to stage elaborate fiestas. Often such conspicuous expenditure will not only use up one's accumulated wealth, but drive the office-holder into debt for years. The chief expenditures of the office-holder are for liquor, food and fireworks, all of which are consumed lavishly. Holding these offices, not possession of wealth, is the main form of social stratification. The disadvantage of such expenditure to the Indian community is that it prevents the accumulation of a surplus which might be invested in increasing productivity. In many cases though the ceremonies have lost their old significance and merely provide outsiders with an opportunity to sell goods to Indians. Beer companies have even revived such festivals to increase sales.[21]

Indian communities are subject to a variety of extra-legal forces. Caciques flourish in isolated Indian areas. Non-Indians often beat or kill Indians and go unpunished.[22] The PRI political machine provides few channels for grievances, and mainly relates to Indians by hauling them off in trucks to vote for the PRI.[23] Finally the third of the Indian population that does not speak Spanish, and the majority of Indians with limited knowledge of the national culture, have even less defense against extra-legal control.[24]

Along with extra-legal control comes a paternalistic, condescending attitude on the part of non-Indians. Non-Indians typically call Indians by their first name, regardless of their age. Few Indians ever rise to any national or even regional prominence, and the only Indian since the conquest with a prominent place in Mexican history is Benito Juárez. He is the Booker T. Washington-Ralph Bunch-Martin Luther King of Mexico in that he is inevitably mentioned when the question of Indian oppression comes up. As Don Juan noted, "I am an Indian and Indians are treated like dogs. There is nothing I could do to remedy that, so all that I was left with was my sorrow."[25]

A pervasive aspect of life in the Indian community is its economic exploitation by outsiders. Large-scale farmers in Indian areas and farmers hiring migrant workers both pay extremely low wages to Indians. Similarly merchants not only charge Indians prices higher than the going market price, but frequently cheat Indians and exercise trade monopolies which close off other lines of supply. A classic example of such a commercial monopoly is provided by the Pedrero family in San Cristóbal de las Casas, Chiapas. This family has grown quite wealthy by controlling the regional cane liquor supply. The monopoly has been enforced by the assassination of Indians, the destruction of stills operated by others, and the jailing of moonshiners, not for moonshining, but for competing with them, all with the cooperation of local authorities.[26]

The extreme exploitation of Indians is made possible by their inability to demand better prices, or to tap other sources of supply and distribution. In addition Indians are often tricked into debt so they can be made to perform wage labor to pay off the debt. Merchants, labor contractors and large landowners all provide usurious loans which Indians have no choice but to accept. Prices on manufactured goods are further inflated by the number of middlemen involved.[27]

Examples of economic exploitation abound. In the Sierra Mazateca in Oaxaca, an area perhaps 50 miles by 20 miles, Indians were paid $(US) 0.02 or 0.03 per kilo of coffee, and were provided with loans which carried interest rates of 10 to 20% per month. The area is served by four doctors.[28]

An Otomí village had only 30 of 80 school-age children in school. Wage laborers received $(US)0.16 a day, plus their noon meal and two liters of pulque, a drink made by fermenting maguey. Individuals in the town were expected to supply from $40 to $56 from their own funds to pay for the village fiestas. This money, which would plunge the individual deeply into debt, went for candles, incense, food, fireworks and pulque.[29]

The violent aspect of relations between Indians and non-Indians was driven home by the killing of six Indians in Huejutla, Hidalgo, in August 1975. The Indians, who didn't even speak Spanish, were killed by local property owners. The reason was that these non-Indian property owners thought the Indians *might* be planning to occupy their lands.[30] In another case 110 Indian homes were burned in Arroyo Jerusalén, Chiapas, to drive Indians away so they could not petition for land.[31]

One of the difficulties the INI has in dealing with these problems is that Indian problems are not seen as part of the larger problem of rural Mexico.[32] Rather than making broad-based attacks on problems common to all peasants, the Indian is singled out and dealt with in isolation.

The Echeverría administration has greatly increased the scope of the INI program. The number of coordinating centers has increased six times since 1970, and now total 67. The budget for INI has risen accordingly, with the authorized 1976 budget being $19,360,000.[33] This increased activity greatly accelerated road building, which for better or worse, has more closely linked the Indian with the rest of the economy. The inability of the INI to substantially affect the Indian is emphasized by the fact that even the increased INI budget only provides $6 per year per Indian. From that budget 51% is paid out as salaries,[34] mostly to non-Indians. In addition vehicles are purchased from non-Indians, administration buildings are built and maintained in Mexico City by non-Indians, etc.

During the Echeverría administration there were two major conferences where Indians from various areas could exchange information, publicly denounce their treatment, and lay the groundwork for change. In October 1974 such a conference was held in San Cristóbal de las Casas, Chiapas. An Indian there stated, "We see that our voice is ignored by authorities. We see that officials pay no attention to us, scold us, and give us the run around, but do not help us solve our problems."[35]

Indians there told of continued thefts of Indian land. A case cited was the invasion of San Francisco Colony, Chiapas, by the 46th Battalion of the Mexican army. Soldiers drove Indians off their land with the approval of local authorities, and in the process beat and robbed the Indians who had lived there and burned their houses. Then the land was turned over to non-Indians with political connections.[36]

Instances were cited of Indians working 13 hours a day and getting paid $0.16. These same Indians are forced to buy rotten meat, for which they are charged by the kilo, kilos which weigh from 500 to 800 grams. Children in the area begin work at the age of eight, and pay is often in tokens, merchandise, or alcoholic drink, rather than cash.[37]

The spirit of the conference was summed up by the statement, "Why do we have the worst lands, given that we have lived here from time immemorial and that the mestizo is a newcomer?"[38]

This conference in Chiapas was only a beginning, not a solution, as was emphasized by subsequent events in the Tzotzil Indian community in Venustiano Carranza, Chiapas. Indians there had suffered for years under Agusto Castellanos, a non-Indian cacique. Despite the murder of several Indians by the cacique's men, there was no response by authorities. However when the cacique was subsequently murdered, the army and police launched an attack on the Indian community, with shooting lasting for six hours. When the firing died down, two Indians had been killed, six wounded, a hundred arrested, and sixteen had simply disappeared.[39]

In 1975 the PRI organized an Indian conference. Representatives from over 70 Indian groups met in Pátzcuaro, Michoacán. The final document drafted by the Indians stated the basic problems of the Indian: lack of land, credit, and the slowness of the agrarian reform administration in processing claims. These problems were ones which Indians share with the entire peasant population, but which are heightened by the special cultural and ethnic aspects of their relations with the rest of society.

The unanimous theme of the conference was that, in addition to having the right to a decent standard of living, Indians had a right to their own cultural identity and to having teachers from their own linguistic community. At this conference Indians openly questioned the basic idea of Mexican Indian policy that Indian progress and well-being require the Indian's cultural death.[40]

Indians there protested the incorporation of Indian communities into "commercial systems which pillage our crafts and sell us alcohol and corrupt our children through radio and TV programs which have nothing to do with our customs and way of life." However rather than completely rejecting Mexican culture, they stated they wanted to learn Spanish "to establish contact with the most positive elements of the national and international culture and to obtain knowledge to improve our industrial and agricultural technology."[41]

CHAPTER 19: WOMEN

Women are half of society. If women are not free, society is not free.

HO CHI MINH

Nurse in Revolution

The now-repealed provisions of the 1917 Family Relations Law show what was formerly legally required of women and what is still to a large degree expected of them:

>—*Article 41: A husband is free to abandon his wife, but not visa versa.*
>—*Article 42: A woman is responsible for domestic duties, a husband for family support.*
>—*Article 44: A woman must have the husband's permission to obtain a job, and the husband can cancel the permission with two month's notice.*
>—*Article 479: Unmarried women from the age of 21 to 30 must have parents' permission to live away from home.*

The Epistle of Melchor Ocampo, which was formerly required at all civil marriage ceremonies, states:

> *The woman, whose principal sexual endowments are self-denial, beauty, comprehension, perspicacity, and tenderness, should and will obey the husband, and provide consolation and counsel.*

Recent changes in the law have ended legal discrimination against women in both marriage and divorce.[1]

The above articles which were put into law in 1917 are completely out of touch with the reality of women's participation in the 1910-17 Revolution. In that struggle there were women officers in the Constitutionalist army, and many women took a direct part in combat, especially in the Red Battalions of workers.[2] Also there was an entire combat unit of women in the Zapatista army under the command of an ex-tortilla maker named La China.[3]

The turbulence of the revolution led to a challenging of the traditional roles assigned to women. One manifestation of this was the first feminist congress held in Mexico, which took place in Yucatán in 1916. However rather than evolving into an on-going women's movement, such as the American suffragettes, progress toward women's rights was blocked by Carranza, Obregón and Calles.[4] Women were even excluded from the agrarian reform since it was felt women would have access to land through their husbands. Cárdenas introduced legislation to give women full legal rights. Despite the passage of this legislation, it was never implemented since it was felt that such a policy would offend the right wing in the critical period at the end of the Cárdenas administration. Also it was felt that giving women the right to vote in the 1940 elections would only add a large number of presumably conservative voters to the voting rolls.[5] It wasn't until 1953 that women were granted full voting rights in all state and national elections.

Despite the removal of these legal barriers for women, there are still legal provisions which discriminate against women. Women still have no voice at ejido assemblies.[6] Similarly the social security program provides pensions for sisters and disabled brothers of deceased workers, on the assumption that neither sisters nor disabled brothers will be able to care for themselves.

This pension provision reflects the widely held belief that women "should" be in a dependent position. One manifestation of this feeling is that men and even some women strongly resent having a woman as their boss.[7] There is a widespread feeling that even if single women do work, the woman should quit work after marrying. A study found that 74.7% of men and 57% of women felt that in any case it should be the husband who decided if the wife would work.[8]

Sex roles are established early in childhood. Girls are encouraged to help their mothers with housework and wait on brothers and fathers. Docility and timidity are encouraged, and marriage and child rearing are portrayed as their future. Boys are encouraged to engage in outdoor sports, and they are oriented toward education and careers. Schools rigidly define sex roles by the general practice of making boys wear uniforms with pants and girls uniforms with skirts.

MACHISMO: A major influence on Mexican women is the Mexican male's "machismo." Machismo involves males defining themselves as superior individuals who should wield authority. Also there is a blatant double standard, with the male assuming the perogative to come and go and philander to his heart's content. The woman in contrast is expected to remain faithful through all this, stay at home, do what the male demands, and submit to beatings. The woman's chief concern is held to be caring for home and children. Men are presumed to be aloof and are frequently absent from the home even when not working. The stereotype of this behavior is so widespread that women are conditioned to feel that leaving the husband is of no avail since all men will treat her alike.[9]

The image of machismo is surrounded by virility and exaggerated aggressiveness, and intransigence in interpersonal affairs.[10] Machismo

> *is described in different ways by different writers, however they almost invariably project the picture of the aggressive male protagonist, alone and withdrawn—constantly preoccupied with the image he is conveying, constantly concerned to create the impression of masculinity and courage, invulnerability and indifference to the attacks of others.*[11]

Women who don't passively accept such behavior are accused of being aggressive and castrating.[12] Such failures to accept a female sex role would probably not even be discussed in these terms. Except in intellectual circles that have had contact with feminists, sex roles are so institutionalized that they are rarely considered as sex roles.

While the concept of macho exists throughout Latin America, it is generally agreed that Mexican machismo is the most virulent form. The Mexican poet Octavio Paz[13] attributes this to the Spanish conquest. Prior to the conquest women were not degraded and fidelity was expected of both partners. The conquest then saw the force and violence of the conquistador exalted while the Indian was repeatedly violated and had little choice but to suffer stoically. The subsequent centuries of violent, aggressive male figures riding roughshod over society only institutionalized machismo.

ABORTION: Abortion is prohibited except in cases of rape or to save the mother's life. Despite the prohibition against abortion, an estimated one million abortions take place each year.[14] This prohibition is especially hard on women who cannot purchase the services of a qualified private doctor. The inability of the poor to obtain such services forces them to back-room practitioners. As a result of attempts to obtain such abortions, 13.4% of all admissions to gyno-obstetrical wards in hospitals result from botched abortions.[15]

Despite an awareness of the ill effects of the ban on abortions, there is little impetus toward legalizing them. The male Minister of Health and Welfare stated, "We will never be inclined to authorize abortions or legalize them even though we know there is a very large number of abortions occurring."[16]

STATUS: Many factors tend to perpetuate the woman's inferior position. Given the macho image, men feel threatened by any failure of women to accept a docile role. Similarly many women who have accepted, or resigned themselves to such a role, feel threatened by other women who fail to. Re-inforcing the present position of women is the Catholic Church. Not only is it firmly against the legalization of abortion, but it provides a model of a male-dominated institution which relegates women to supplemental roles, thus lending divine sanction to the domination of women.[17]

The government is also a major factor in the maintenance of the status quo. Despite having removed legal barriers to women exercising civil rights, there is little affirmative action to promote equality for women. Also the government follows the world-wide pattern of appointing men to most if not all important posts. Within the PRI women are compartmentalized into a National Feminine Grouping, a classification which presents the image of women not having interests in common with men, but instead only being concerned with feminine issues. The degree of women's participation in government can be seen by the list of appointees for the senate in 1976. Of the senators appointed, only one was a woman, the head of the Feminine Grouping of the PRI.[18]

EMPLOYMENT: Generally jobs obtained by women are an extension of the domestic role assigned to women at home. The majority of women employed work as domestics (cleaning and cooking), in food services (cooking), the garment industry (sewing), in hospitals (caring for sick), or in schools (caring for children). Often in keeping with the pervasive image of the woman as a sex object, sexual favors are expected by male superiors at the job.[19]

Laws which require employers to grant maternity leave and provide day care facilities result in discrimination against women since such laws raise the cost of hiring them.[20] Despite the legal requirement for day care facilities where large numbers of women work, at the beginning of 1974 there were only 115 such facilities with a capacity for 70,000 children.[21] Only 2.6% of working women are provided with day care.[22]

The percentage of women in the work force has been increasing as is characteristic of countries undergoing economic development. The participation of women in the work force has been as follows:[23]

1930   4.6% of workers
1940   7.4%   "
1950   13.6%   "
1960   18.9%   "
1970   19.0%   "
1974   19.1%   "

The 1970 census also showed that while 71.7% of men over 12 work, only 16.4% of women over 12 work.[24] The percentage of women who work varies greatly from region to region. In the more developed areas the figures are high, 29.7% in the Federal District, and 20.1% in Nuevo León. In contrast in the less developed areas the figures are much lower, such as 10.2% in Yucatán and 9.1% in Zacatecas.[25]

Little progress has been made at increasing the employment of women in traditionally male areas. In construction, oil and gas, and mining only 1.2% of the employees are women, and this figure includes women who cook and clean up after men.[26] Women are only 18% of the manufacturing work force. However in the garment industry where women can apply their "domestic skills," 63% of the employees are women.[27] Included in this number of women in the garment industry are women doing piece work at home where they are without legal protection and exceedingly difficult to organize.[28]

Of the 2.4 million working women recorded in the 1970 census, 69.6% work in the service sector. Most of these jobs, which have low status and income, require little or no training. Included in the service sector are some **488,433 domestics, one of every five working women,** and secretaries.[29]

Domestics, due to their lack of organization, are among the most exploited workers. They are usually totally dependent on the employer, and often must ask permission even to leave the house. Rather than having ties with other domestics, frequently they assume the values of the family for which they work.[30] Treatment of domestics is generally degrading. Their stereotype is that they are simple country women who never get sick, never tire or need entertainment, and have no other aspirations than domestic service.

The following figures show what portion of the female work force is employed in different areas of the economy:[31]

	% of all women workers
agriculture	10.8
mining, oil, gas	.5
manufacturing	18.1
construction	0.7
services	42.9
transport	0.7
government	2.8
unspecified	9.7

The 9.7% listed as unspecified reflect the large number of women on the economic fringe, who may sometimes work as a domestic, take in laundry, sell in the street from time to time, and do occasional piece work for a factory. Also presumably included in this category are prostitutes.

Pay for women is poor. They make up 19% of the work force, but 30% of workers making under $16 a month, and only 6.4% of workers making over $576 a month.[32] The average male income is $106 a month, while the average for women is $81. The lowest paid women are agricultural workers who average $37 a month.[33]

A woman's mere taking of a job is not necessarily an act of liberation, given the frequent lack of job training, sex discrimination, and the common practice of doing piece work at home.[34] Often it is felt that since the woman will only work until she is married or has a child, it's not worth the effort to train her.[35]

Regardless of whether a woman is working, it is assumed that she will be the one who will take care of the home. This presumption is given legal sanction by the Civil Code for the Federal District and Territories which specifies in Article 168 that women "shall be in charge of the administration and care of the home." Article 169 notes that women can accept employment provided that such employment does not damage the "mission" imposed in Article 168, nor injure family morale or family structure. Finally Article 170 states that the husband can prohibit the wife from accepting employment if the job conflicts with fulfilling the obligations set forth in Article 168, with disputes between spouses on the matter to be decided by a judge.

EDUCATION: Many in Mexico feel that since women will just get married there is less reason for them to study than men. This is quite significant since once the opportunity for study has been passed up, this feeling becomes a self-fulfilling prophecy. Since they are not prepared for a career, women do indeed tend to get married and stay at home. It is especially common for women not to receive education when a family's resources are scarce and a choice must be made between letting the male or the female child continue in school.

The drop-out rate from school is shown by the percentage of men and women studying at different levels:[36]

	% of males in schol	% of females in school
primary	80.9	86.8
secondary	16.3	12.5
higher education	2.8	0.7

The number of women attending college again illustrates the feeling that women need not have professional education. This feeling was summed up by the cliche: MUJER QUE SABE LATIN, NI TIENE MARIDO NI BUEN FIN (The women who knows Latin has neither a husband nor a good future).

Those women who do go on to college are still channeled by sex. These figures show the percentage of women enrolled in each area:[37]

	% of all women in higher education
Humanities	45.6
Science	5.4
Law & Social Science	27.4
Engineering	2.0
Medical Science	16.0
Agriculture	1.1

CLASS DIFFERENCES: The 5.7 million peasant women over the age of 12 were the largest social group in the 1970 census. This group has the most traditional values and has the lowest rate of employment (528,000 employed) of any social group. This figure however only reflects one thing: the way census takers gather data. In fact peasant women are the most economically active of all women since they still function where the family is a major productive unit. Given her low buying power and the absence of restaurants, laundries, and the like, the peasant woman is directly responsible for food preparation,

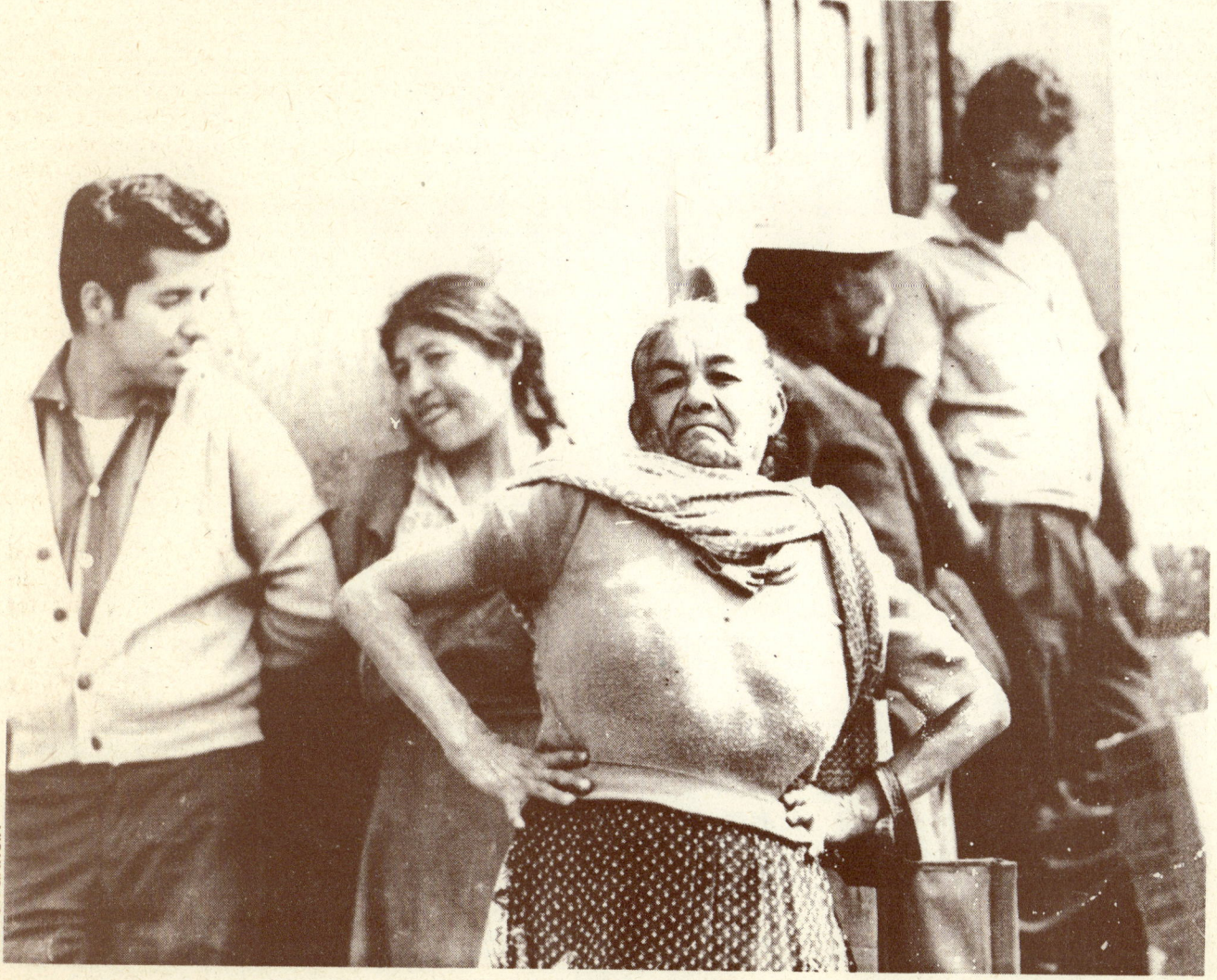

HECTOR GARCIA

clothing the family, washing, and child rearing. In addition at planting and harvest time she often works in the fields. She is also expected to bear a large number of children due to the past record of high infant mortality and the children serving as a supplementary source of labor. To the extent that the peasant household as a productive unit hasn't been destroyed by the development of capitalist agriculture, the typical pattern is for the man to produce raw material and for the woman to process it.

Despite the peasant woman's integral role in the economic process, the peasant male reserves decision-making power in both home and community. Traditionally, peasant women aren't even allowed to leave the home during the day if the male is gone, and in fact sometimes women will have others do shopping for them so they will not have to leave the home.[38] This traditionalism extends to a strong double standard. Given this traditionalism prevading the community, there are very strong sanctions against women who violate traditional norms.[39]

The lot of the Indian woman, though it varies from ethnic group to ethnic group, is generally similar to that of the non-Indian peasant woman in that the home is a basic economic unit. However the Indian male does not share the non-Indian's desire to dominate or exploit women, or other men for that matter.[40] Indian women generally have more say in running the household, at their job, and in spending family funds than most other women do. The Indian woman's relative freedom however, does not extend to the community as a whole. One Indian group, the Zapotecs, has developed quite a reputation for being good entrepreneurs and Zapotec women often travel great distances by themselves to buy and sell.[41] The Indian woman has virtually no impact on the national scene due to her lack of skills and education.

This relative freedom at the domestic level is offset by the extreme poverty which afflicts the Indian community. In the typical case of a Mazahua community, Indian girls begin to assume domestic duties at the age of five, and at seven are responsible for the care of younger children. By nine they are doing full-time domestic work, and by 13 at the latest they are expected to be doing all adult domestic and agricultural chores. Marriage generally occurs at age 14 or 15, and the average number of children per woman is ten, of which three or four survive to adulthood.[42]

Although progress has been made, women from more affluent homes are still not encouraged to enter professions as are men. The home for middle class women is more oriented toward consumption than production. In these households the decision on the number of children to have is based on how children will affect the quality of life of the parents.[43] Many middle class women adopt a media image of the American woman. They depend on their husbands for support and on servants for domestic work.

The middle class generally holds female parasitism to be a virtue. The most beautiful adornment for the home and husband is the wife, living testimony of his honor, wealth, and power. The idleness of the wife is an indispensable prerequisite for being well bred.[44]

Poor urban women often set up a store in the home, take in laundry, or engage in some other money-making activity due to the frequent unemployment, irresponsibility or absence of the husband. Given the lack of money to rent a separate house, there is often an extended family present. In such cases a woman's brothers will often serve as a better source of long-term support than the husband whose earning power and reliability may be suspect. The importance of the extended family, involving ties which need not include the husband, and the publicly accepted norm of male irresponsibility, put the woman in a central role in the family. This gives the woman a greater degree of economic and emotional independence. For these reasons poor women appear less alienated than the women of the middle class.[45]

CHANGE: The International Women's Congress* held in Mexico City in 1975 did little to change the lot of women. Generally it dealt with matters at a very abstract level and on a world-wide basis, and had little effect on the actual situation of women in Mexico. Pedro Ojeda Paullada, the male attorney general of Mexico, was selected as head of the Mexican delegation to the conference. The conference then followed international protocol and selected the head of the host delegation as head of the conference, leaving the conference presided over by a male.

International Women's Year was also marked by the passage of an equal rights amendment. This amendment gave women full equality before the law and the "right to decide in a free, responsible and informed manner on the number of children they will have and the interval between them." Like legislation passed during the Cárdenas administration, its effect will depend not on its written content, but on the government's will to implement it.

Even in the 1970's there has only been a gradual evolution in the role of women. In a country where innovations ranging from hot pants to Hari Krishna appear within six months of their appearance in the United States, a viable women's movement has been conspicuous in its absence. This failure has been in part due to the deep-rooted machismo of Mexican men. Also the lack of a preceding civil rights movement to give the Mexican woman's movement ideology, tactics and impetus has hurt.[46] Women themselves are hampered by only relating to their nuclear family, and thus feeling that their problems are individual and not susceptible to solution through mass movements.[47] Finally even the progressive movements which exist pay little attention to the role of women within their ranks. The Mexican Workers Party (See Chapter 25) for example published instructions in cartoon form on how to organize local chapters of the party. In the cartoons there were 23 individual characters portrayed. Twenty of these characters were male, and of the three female characters, one was typing in an office and the other two were doing nothing.[48]

Despite the lack of strong government support or an organized woman's movement, the woman's role is clearly changing, especially in large metropolitan areas. Increasingly the traditional middle class model of the

---

*The conference was often called the Wives' Conference, since it was attended by the wives of so many heads of state or other important figures.

sheltered woman is disappearing, and instead international urban culture is becoming the norm for women. Women date, pursue professional careers with or without marriage, and are less concerned about remaining virgins before marriage. This trend is evident at the National University where 30% of the students are women.[49]

If preliminary indications are any guide, future gains will be made despite the López Portillo administration, not because of it. In his pre-election touring López Portillo addressed a national women's meeting and stated, "The struggle for equality, of which women's equality is an exceedingly important part given that she makes up half of humanity, is a battle of our political culture against nature which has made her unequal in capacity, conditions, and function, and equal in her needs."[50]

CHAPTER 20: UNEMPLOYMENT

Cities, especially Mexico City, will continue to fill with millions of people, unemployed and without hope, who are a danger to the established social order and who in the near future could give rise to an uncontainable, fatal attack on the existing order, which by comparison would make the black ghetto rebellions in the United States look like children's games.[1]

Unemployment is one of Mexico's most pressing problems. In 1977 2 million people out of a work force of 17.5 million were reported to be unemployed. In addition since there is no unemployment insurance, people take menial jobs for survival immediately upon losing their previous job. They are not officially unemployed even though their jobs pay little and produce little. Persons working at such jobs are called underemployed and number from five to seven million.[2]

One of the major causes of unemployment is the use of technology developed in advanced countries to eliminate jobs. This technology is imported to Mexico and continues to eliminate jobs—just what the country doesn't need. And as has been noted, this technology tends to concentrate income. As income is concentrated, those with high incomes buy expensive consumer goods (such as color TV's and cars) which require relatively little labor, providing fewer jobs. Were income less concentrated, the poor would have more money to spend on consumer goods such as shirts and shoes which would provide greater employment. As more and more people are without jobs, there is less pressure for employers to raise wages, buying power falls, and more are unemployed.

Proponents of the present high-technology model say that what is needed is to invest in the most productive factories possible, use these facilities to increase the wealth of the country, and then finally provide everyone with a job involving high technology and high output. One rarely finds backers for this argument among those who are forced to live in squalor for a generation while high technology, hopefully, provides the promised good job for all.

A second major factor contributing to unemployment is the tendency for the wealthy to send money out of the country or consume it in lavish living. This uses up resources which otherwise could have been invested in job-creating enterprises.[3]

Population increase is also responsible for the high degree of unemployment and underemployment. Currently 500,000 new jobs are needed each year just to give jobs to people seeking work for the first time. However only 350,000 jobs open up each year. This already bleak picture is further worsened by the fact that with the babies already born the number of jobs which must be created to handle new job seekers will rise to one million by 1985.[4] Even if effective birth control were implemented immediately, it would only affect the job market in the 1990's since children already born will be coming into the job market though the 1980's.

The lack of employment was cited as Mexico's worst problem in Echeverría's 1975 State of the Union Address. If underemployment is taken to mean those making less than the average 1970 minimum wage ($55.70 a month), 45% of workers are underemployed.[5] This figure of underemployment includes an increasing number of professionally trained persons such as engineers. The estimated loss to the economy from not adequately employing the population is equal to some 18% of the national product.[6]

Sixty five percent of all underemployed workers are in agriculture.[7] Continued mechanization has almost eliminated agriculture as a source of new jobs. From 1950 to 1970 agricultural employment only increased from 4.9 million to 5.1 million.[8] The overabundance of agricultural workers is indicated by the fact that two million workers could leave their jobs without affecting production at all.* Other workers would merely begin to work full time, and the same crops would be produced.[9] The 1960 agriculture census showed that less than 15% of agricultural workers worked 200 or more days per year; 57% worked less than 100 days; and 29% worked less than 35.[10] In regions which are predominantly agricultural, such as

---

*This actually happened during World War II as braceros (contract laborers) left Mexican agriculture and went to work in the US. Despite their being fewer farm workers, production increased.

Chiapas, Oaxaca, and Guerrero, underemployment reaches 90%.

Industrial workers make up only 10% of all underemployed workers.[11] Industrialization has traditionally been considered the solution to Latin America's employment problems. However the high technology being used is preventing it from solving this problem. In 1950 23.2% of all workers (903,783 individuals) worked in industry. By 1970 the figure had only risen to 26.9% of workers (2,167,888 individuals).[12] If one considers modern industry those industrial establishments employing over 15 persons per establishment, only 9.6% of workers were in modern industry in 1970.[13] Another way of looking at the effect of high technology is to compare the 1970-75 increase in economic growth, 16.4%, with the increase in employment, which was only 3.1%.[14]

The other major area of employment is in commerce and services. This sector includes a wide variety of jobs such as office workers, sales clerks, bank employees, government bureaucrats, street vendors and domestics. This sector clearly reflects the problems of rural unemployment, since as people see the futility of their situation in the countryside, they come to the city, and failing to get a good job, they go into the service sector. Recent arrivals take a wide variety of jobs such as selling newspapers, watching cars, street vending, and the like.

Employment in this sector, which went from 2.1 million in 1950 to 6.3 million in 1970, is rising faster than any other sector.[15] Many workers in this sector are underemployed, as indicated by the underemployment rate of 39.3% in services and 33.1% in commerce.[16] What this reflects is that the internal migrations of the last thirty years have to a large degree shifted unemployment from rural areas to urban areas.

The overall picture is clearly getting worse. As the population continues to rise, the number of jobs being created has been going down. As a result in the last 25 years while the population increased at 3.5% a year, the number of jobs only increased at 2.9%.[17] Currently it would cost $15 billion to create new jobs for the 722,000 who enter the job market each year. Present state and private investment however only come to about $8.4 billion a year.[18] Nor are there any solutions in sight for the near future since reversing the trend of development of the last 30 years and making massive investments not oriented toward immediate profits would take a change in values of the leaders. The government in fact is still pressing in the opposite direction by offering tax incentives to those using labor saving machinery.[19] Multinationals clearly contribute to the employment problem in that they have 2.5 times as much invested per worker as do domestic companies in the same industry.[20]

Given current technology, it would take $96 billion to create enough jobs for everyone presently needing one. That is ten times the amount invested annually by the public and private sectors together.[21] Since each new industrial job created requires an investment of $20,000, it is unlikely industry will provide a solution to the unemployment problem. However agriculture holds more promise in that jobs only cost from $2800 to $4000 to create.[22] In order to create the millions of jobs needed it will be necessary to use less expensive technology. In addition, waste by Mexico's wealthy and the drain of profits from the country by multinationals must be controlled so necessary capital can be accumulated.

One attempt by the government to shift away from reliance on high-technology has been its hand-built road program. In order to alleviate rural unemployment and provide communication to isolated villages, the government has financed the building of a system of dirt roads largely constructed with hand tools. Some 28,000 miles of these roads have been built.[23] Even this rather limited example shows what low technology can do. The cost of the hand-built roads was $5,200 per kilometer, compared with $8,800 for similar roads built with machinery. Perhaps more significantly, some 60% of the cost of machine-built roads would have been spent abroad for the purchase of machinery, using up valuable foreign exchange. This program though is only a drop in the bucket, due to the relatively small amount invested, $360 million, and the fact that it is seen as a temporary measure. Once the road in a particular area is finished, the program ends and the workers are once again unemployed.

PART V: SOCIAL SERVICES

CHAPTER 21: HEALTH

Health and sickness are collective phenomena which are related to the rest of society.[1]

Traditionally western medicine considers illness in terms of a particular individual with a particular disease which can be cured with a particular treatment. This approach is fostered by the doctor-patient relationship, with the doctor seeking payment for treating the disease. Such an outlook however fails to take into consideration many of the factors which will determine who gets sick and how severe the disease will be. Such factors include diet, housing, working conditions, stress, air pollution, knowledge of hygiene, and the availability of sewage treatment, running water, and medical care.[2]

Only 17-20% of the population has an adequate diet.[3] Malnutrition is so widespread that it has been called the greatest obstacle to development.[4] The malnourished are not only less active mentally, but the physical growth of 25% of rural children and 6% of urban children is actually stunted.[5] Malnutrition frequently begins during the mother's pregnancy, leaving the new-born child weak. This weakness is then accentuated by an inadequate diet as a child. The malnourished children that reach school often do so poorly that their poverty-stricken parents take them out within a year or two to supplement their meager income, thus creating a new generation of poverty-stricken illiterates. An estimated 5.5 million children are malnourished,[6] of which an estimated 100,000 die each year as a result.[7]

As migrants flood into the city and fail to obtain needed nourishment, kwashikore and rickets become common.[8] The increased buying power of the affluent makes food less accessible to the poor, and finally inflation has priced many foods beyond their reach. From 1971 to 1974 caloric consumption of the peasantry, already the worst-fed sector, declined 20%.[9]

Another major problem is the lack of medical facilities. Some 26 million have no access to medical care.[10] President Echeverría promised that by 1984 medical care would be extended to some 90% of the population.[11] Even if this promise is more than wishful thinking it ignores the basic problems of malnutrition, poor housing, and lack of sewage treatment.

Only $5 per person per year is being spent by the government on health care, well below the Latin American average.[12] There are only two hospital beds per 1000 population. This rate is also one of the lowest in Latin America.[13] The problem in health care is not merely one of poor care in rural areas as is often proclaimed by proponents of economic development. In 1969 for example, the infant mortality rate* in Mexico as a whole was 65.8, but was 76.8 for the Federal District, showing that problems have been increasing with urbanization.[14]

In rural Mexico medical care is often simply non-existent. Those with the highest disease rates are agricultural day laborers who have inadequate housing, poor working conditions, and lack a plot for growing their own food.[15] People in rural areas are often ignorant of the availability of free government-provided medical care, and often cannot afford transport to such facilities. When people in rural areas are faced with an acute medical crisis, they must sell their means of support to meet expenses for medical service and transport. Even if patients recover, the sale of the productive cow or land reduces their income further and leaves them even more susceptible to disease.[16]

*Infant mortality refers to the number of deaths before age one for each 1,000 births.

Urban residents suffer from a variety of specifically urban problems. Pollution is a major factor, contributing to respiratory diseases, especially among those too poor to afford housing which is relatively air-tight. The poor are further penalized by not being able to afford housing in areas of low pollution, and by being crowded into housing lacking in sewage and running water. Even those with steady work suffer from not having unions strong enough to vigorously push the issue of industrial safety and work-place contamination, or for that matter, a salary adequate for feeding and housing their family.[17]

The distribution of doctors in Mexico reflects the social structure of the country. The entire country has one doctor per 1420 people, which though far from ideal, is more or less adequate.[18] However rather than being evenly distributed, there is one doctor per 474 persons in the Federal District, while there is only one per 4344 in the state of Zacatecas.[19] Rural areas outside major cities have even fewer doctors. For example there is only one doctor for every 15,000 persons in rural Jalisco.[20]

There are now 70,000 medical students, many of whom are poorly prepared for medical study and who learn little and often drop out.[21] However rather than being the solution to a medical problem, doctors are becoming an employment problem. Cities are oversupplied, and rural populations are too poor to support doctors who in any case are reluctant to leave the city.

Another health problem is produced by the pharmaceutical industry. This industry, which is 90% foreign owned, has investments of $400 million and profits of $160 million a year.[22] (Some estimates of their profits run as high as $400 million a year).[23] These companies grossly inflate prices and promote the indiscriminate use of antibiotics. Such antibiotics are promoted through advertisements and traveling salesmen who palm them off on rural stores like candy. Drugs are then sold without prescriptions and without supervision of anybody with medical knowledge.[24] This results in needless expense and the taking of drugs unrelated to the disease being treated. Such drug consumption builds immunity by disease organisms, so that the drugs are useless when needed. Finally in order to maximize sales, drug companies will claim drugs are useful for treating diseases which, according to Food and Drug Administration Regulations, they cannot claim in the US. Similarly they will fail to provide warnings of harmful side effects they are required to warn people of in US.[25] Finally, as is the case throughout the industrial sector, products were not designed for the Mexican market. Drugs produced by American companies are often too expensive and require sophisticated equipment which is unavailable.[26]

Of the 458,000 Mexicans who die each year, 200,000 are under five. If the mortality rate was the same as Cuba's, the country in Latin America with the lowest mortality, 213,000 of these people would survive each year, including 114,000 children.[27] The three major causes of death, which account for a third of all deaths, could largely be prevented with modern medicine and an adequate standard of living. The major killer is pneumonia which kills people at six times the rate in the US and four times the rate in Cuba. The second major cause is gastrointestinal disease (diarrhea, etc.) which is the major cause of medical consultations and is largely caused by poor food handling, contaminated water, and poor knowledge of hygiene. The third major cause, maternal death, strikes the poor three times as often as the rich.[28]

Due to better living standards and better medicine there was a rapid decline in mortality after the revolution. From 1930 to 1960 mortality went down 60%. Similarly infant mortality rates decreased throughout the century, and reflected the decline of such diseases as small-pox, yellow fever, and malaria. In 1965 though infant mortality began to rise again. "This situation is alarming when one remembers that infant mortality reflects the living standard which apparently has been declining in recent years."[29] The latest figures released (for 1972 and 1973) showed a marked improvement, perhaps reflecting the fact that 18 million children were immunized during the Echeverría administration.*[30] These figures show how infant mortality (deaths before age one per 1000 births) has changed:

1910 323
1930 131
1950 96.2
1960 74.2
1965 60.7
1970 68.5
1972 60.9
1973 52

The diseases which can readily be eliminated, such as small-pox, are no longer a problem, and further reductions in the death rate will require control of flu, pneumonia, and gasrointestinal diseases. These diseases reflect the standard of living, and their elimination would require adequate water supplies, sewage treatment, good housing and diet, changes which can only be brought about by increasing income and providing better access to education for the majority of the population.[33]

There are three medical care systems, each of which reflects social status. The affluent patronize private doctors and hospitals, and increasingly go abroad for treatment. They make up some 15.5% of the population, and have 49.9% of the doctors and 42.5% of the hospital beds at their disposal.[34]

The institutional sector is the second health care system. It provides free care to persons in any of several categories. Included in this sector are employees covered by social security or union health care plans, as well as government employees. One third of the population is covered under this system.[35]

The number of persons included in the institutional sector has been increasing rapidly. From 1960 to 1970 the number of persons covered by social security and the federal employees health program went from 3.8 million to 10.5 million. While this may seem impressive, it is less than the increase in the population during this time.[36] Generally benefits are extended to workers in areas most

---

*Other sources merely report an increase in infant mortality.[31] In any case conclusions as to short term changes are suspect due to the unreliability of statistics.[32]

vital to the economy, such as oil and autos. Social security benefits may be offered to win the loyalty of organized dissidents, as was the case with henequen and sugar cane workers during the Echeverría administration. The social security program is financed in part by the government. In so doing the government takes tax money from the whole population to care for workers in private industry. Furthermore businesses which are supposed to contribute often fall behind in their payments, so that by 1972 the business sector owed the government $160 million in back payments.[37]

Finally there is what can be called the charity sector. Included in this sector are those who cannot afford private medical care and who are not in the institutional system. Many in this sector make up the 26 million who receive no medical care. Facilities available for those in this sector are few and far between. An example of the care provided to charity patients is the General Hospital in Mexico City. There 91.8% of the patients earn less than $80 a month.[38] Only $8 is spent there per patient per day.[39] Nationwide charity patients make up some 63.3% of the population and yet only have 33.1% of the hospital beds.[40] There is one doctor per 4236 persons in this sector, as compared to one per 500 in private medicine and one per 1691 in social security clinics.[41] Often *brujos* (warlocks) or herbalists serve as an alternative source of treatment if Western medicine is inaccessible or not culturally acceptable to the patient.

The diseases being treated at charity hospitals show what is termed the "pathology of poverty." Thirty times as many die from amebiasis (amoebic infection) among charity patients as among private patients.[42] There is a high frequency of infectious disease, gynecological and obstetric problems, compounded with problems of malnutrition and alcoholism. Often the same individual has various diseases in an advanced state making them either impossible or difficult to cure.[43] The average age of those autopsied in the General Hospital is 42, while only 11.9% of the patients in private hospitals who die are under 40.[44] "The principal cause of death in the General Hospital is poverty, although it is not mentioned in the death certificate."[45] The Ministry of Health and Welfare budgets $10.63 per person per year for charity hospitals, compared to $93.57 per person per year for the social security program.[46]

Despite the "pathology of poverty," Mexico's health problems are beginning to reflect Mexico's development. The death rate from causes associated with underdevelopment (infectious disease, parasites, and respiratory diseases in children under five) declined from 1136 per 100,000 in 1930 to 480 in 1950 to 218 in 1969. However cancer deaths, associated with developed countries, increased from 15 per 100,000 population in 1930 to 20 in 1950 and 34 in 1967.[47]

HECTOR GARCIA

CHAPTER 22: HOUSING

Housing shortage results from rapid population increase and the shift of population from rural areas to urban ones. Unequal income distribution gives the majority so little buying power that low income housing is not an attractive investment for private contractors. Finally rampant real estate speculation pushes up the cost of building sites. This real estate speculation further concentrates income. By selling building sites to workers at inflated prices, the propertied classes recoup a share of the already-low wages they pay.[1]

The more affluent live in housing classified as "good" or "luxurious." These two categories correspond roughly to the 9.39% of housing units which have five or more rooms. The average cost of housing categorized as "good" is $16,000, while "luxurious" costs an average of $56,000 per unit.[2]

Persons of more moderate income are often able to obtain housing through government programs. However such programs suffer from a lack of rural housing, produce housing that is too expensive for most families, and provide so few housing units that only a small part of the total need for housing is met.

The largest government housing program is INFONAVIT (National Institute for the Worker Housing Fund). This program requires employers to contribute an amount equal to 5% of the worker's income to a special housing fund. The money in the fund is used to build houses, which the worker then moves into and buys from the government agency which built it. The program, which was begun by Echeverría, had 3.85 million workers from 231,000 workplaces enrolled by 1975. During its first three years only 55,000 housing units were built at a cost of $908 million.[3] By the end of the Echeverría administration only 100,000 units had been built.[4] The average cost of the units in 1975 was $8,000,[5] a price well beyond the means of most workers.

INFONAVIT construction projects are often located so as to maximize profits for real estate speculators who have a hand in deciding where the projects are to be located. In addition much of the money for the fund, rather than building new housing, ends up in politicians' pockets. In Acapulco, of the $2 million allocated for INFONAVIT land purchase, only $100,560 was actually paid to the owners of the land. The rest went to the state governor, the local congressman, and other officials involved.[6] No attempt is made to organize low-cost self-help projects using readily available materials. Rather construction uses expensive, capital-intensive techniques and is carried out by private contractors who often have political contacts. "One would suspect that INFONAVIT's function was to serve capitalists, not workers, and to revitalize construction and related industries."[7]

Several other government programs similar to INFONAVIT exist but on a smaller scale. They focus on housing urban workers with above average incomes. In his 1975 State of the Union Message Echeverría stated that all federal housing programs together had built 60,000 housing units the previous year. (Just to meet the population increase, over 400,000 units are needed each year.)

Finally the majority of the population, too poor even for government programs, must make do with what they can, increasingly the shanty near the big city. Two-thirds of the population lives in one or two room housing units. Furthermore 40% of housing units have dirt floors, 38.9% lack running water, 60% have no bath with running water, and 58.4% have no waste water or sewage.[8] Mexico's housing density of 2.9 persons per room compares poorly with Brazil's 1.3 and Argentina's 1.4.[9]

The housing problem is not just a matter of quality. There is a tremendous shortage of housing of any kind. The number of housing units needed, the housing deficit, is estimated at 4 million. Figuring two people per room in urban areas and three in rural areas, some 2.135 million additional units are needed. A fifth of urban housing and a quarter of rural housing needs replacing, for a total of 1.9056 million more. The total new housing needed is thus 46% of the existing 8.3 million housing units reported in the 1970 census. In addition the population growth from 1969 to 1980 will require another 4.686 million housing units.[10]

The lack of housing and the poor quality of existing housing is due to poor income distribution, not a lack of resources to build housing. If resources currently invested in luxury housing were diverted to public housing projects, adequate residences could be provided for everyone.[11]

The solution to the housing problem is both economic and political. Politically the decision must be made to sacrifice the luxury of the rich to provide adequate housing for the majority. Experimentation is also needed to develop less capital-intensive construction techniques. Currently the cost of each housing unit is $12,000, if the cost of building, sewage, electricity, roads, and other improvements is included.[12] Given the need for over 400,000 units per year just to keep up with population growth, not to mention replacing substandard housing, the cost is over $4.8 billion a year.

∙∙∙∙∙∙∙∙∙∙∙∙∙

The exceptionally tight housing situation has produced numerous conflicts. The most publicized was the Rubén Jaramillo Colony, near Cuernavaca, Morelos. There some 3,000 families took over a subdivision which had been laid out but never built. The land had been seized by the state for tax delinquency and just by chance had ended up in the hands of the governor's son. On March 31, 1973 the 15,000 squatters simply occupied the land and built houses, rent free. Seeing the futility of trying to solve housing problems without dealing with anything else, they pooled their incomes, which ranged from $1 to $3 a day, and founded co-operative stores, bakeries and slaughter houses. Improvements, such as laying sewer pipes and building schools were done with volunteer labor. Realizing that alcohol was not only a major cause of violent conflict, but a heavy financial drain on the community, the consumption and sale of alcohol was banned. Finally residents ran their own affairs without the help of the PRI through town meetings and directly elected officials.

Inevitably this challenge to real estate, commercial and

political interests produced a response. On September 28, 1973, 2000 soldiers and 100 police attacked before dawn, killing three residents. The settlement was occupied militarily, all co-operative institutions were disbanded, and the leadership of the community either fled or was arrested. Some 100 of those arrested were taken to Military Camp No. 1 in Mexico City. The pretext for the attack was that the community was harboring guerrillas.

The town still exists, although the name of the martyred peasant leader was dropped and it is now called the "Flower Colony." The PRI runs the show pretty much like in any other small town and you can get alcoholic beverages now. As of March 1977 it was still occupied by the army.

Another occupation of unused land took place on the outskirts of Oaxaca. This occupation so threatened local businessmen who were holding it for speculation that they said they would close all the businesses in the city if the squatters were not evicted. Governor Manuel Zárate then called the army in to rout the squatters and arrest 1200 of them. The next night Governor Zárate attended a party given by local businessmen to celebrate the victory over the squatters.[13]

Another incident points up the safety hazard presented by urban shanty towns. On January 26, 1976, some 250 shacks on the edge of Mexico City burned, killing three children. Residents of the community accused authorities of setting the fire to get rid of them. Evidence to support the accusation is purely circumstantial, but nonetheless convincing. The settlement, known as Oct. 2 colony to commemorate the date of the 1968 massacre of the student movement, was one of the most politically organized neighborhoods in Mexico City and had long been the target of government officials trying to oust them. The fire started beside the home of the colony's leader, and on the day of the fire police also returned to the site of the 1968 massacre to break up an anti-government concert.[14]

In order to defuse the explosive situation on the edge of cities where speculators hold land idle and the homeless try to find shelter, an urban zoning law was passed at the end of the Echeverría administration. Despite the howls of agony which came up from the private sector (especially from real estate speculators), the law was quite mild. It provided planning for urban growth, water use, and the designation of areas for single and multiple unit housing, parks and industrial areas. It was very similar to urban zoning laws existing in the US, but with the additional provision for national as well as local planning.[15]

CHAPTER 23: EDUCATION

No educational problem can be completely resolved as long as there is not a transformation of society, because, more than is generally realized, it is society that makes the school, and not the school which makes society.[1]

There was relatively little growth in Mexico's educational system during the first century of independence. The dominant idea was that the masses couldn't benefit from education even if they had it, so it was a waste of money to try to educate them. Not surprisingly some 80% of the population was illiterate in 1910.[2] The coming to power of the uneducated during the revolution put an end to this idea forever.

As with many of the reforms of the revolution, change came slowly in education. By 1930 only 34.3% of the 6-14 year-old children were in school, and only 3.4% of the 15 to 19 year-olds were.[3] The educational system began its rapid expansion during the Cárdenas administration. Teachers were sent into rural areas to establish schools. These teachers were not only educators, but agents of social change, organizing peasants and building support for Cárdenas. School work was made less abstract and was linked to factory and farm production. Cárdenas's rural teacher-organizers met with violent resistance from conservative landlords. From 1934 to 1940 an average of 3 rural teachers a month were murdered.[4]

Even as late as 1950 there were as many school-age children out of school as there were in school.[5] Beginning in 1964 major efforts were made to make education accessible to the vast majority of children. The growth of the educational system as a whole is indicated by the fact that in 1910 6% of the total population was attending school, then in 1930 9% was, in 1950 13%, and finally by 1970 21% of the entire population was in school.[6]

PRIMARY SCHOOL: Efforts at achieving universal education have been most successful at the elementary level. The number of children in primary school has increased as follows:

1950	3.0 million
1960	4.1 million
1964	6.6 million
1970	9.4 million
1975	12.7 million

A result of this rapid growth is serious overcrowding; there is an average of 53.6 children per teacher, more than there were in 1910.[7]

Despite the increase in attendance, there are still some 1.3 million children in the 6-14 age group who are not attending school.[8] Only 30% of those who enroll in elementary school ever graduate. The rest fall behind, repeat grades and eventually drop out.[9]

SECONDARY EDUCATION: The increasing number of children who graduate from primary school are now beginning to swell secondary enrollment. Secondary school enrollment has increased as follows:

1958	348,000
1964	751,000
1971	1,463,000
1975	2,800,000

HECTOR GARCIA

This expansion too has led to overcrowding. In some slum areas on the edge of Mexico City one must stand in line for 24 hours just to get permission to take the exam for admittance to junior high school.[10]

In addition to the increase in numbers there has been increased emphasis on technical schools. Their number increased from 240 in 1971 to 1042 in 1976. The number of junior-high-level agricultural technical schools went from 58 to 551 during the Echeverría administration. There were also 58 intermediate and 8 advanced agricultural schools established.[11]

HIGHER EDUCATION: In the 1970-1 school year enrollment in higher education was 200,000; by 1976-7 it had risen to 496,133.[12] The negative side of this increase is that due to poor preparation, inadequate financial aids, and the poor job market awaiting those who do graduate, only 50% of those entering the university ever graduate.[13] In addition, due to the generally low quality of previous schooling, political tumult in the university, and the unwillingness to flunk out large numbers of students, the quality of graduates generally leaves much to be desired.[14] Most professors hold full-time outside jobs and only appear at the university to give classes. Only 6.4% of the faculty at the national unversity are full time.[15]

LEGACY OF PAST: Even though the majority of school-age children are now in school, Mexico will face a long period during which most of its adult population has little schooling. In 1970, of the population over 25, 37.7% had no formal education, 39.4% had 1-5 years, 13.8% had finished elementary school, and only 5% had finished high school.[16] Similarly illiteracy will still remain a problem, with estimates of the number of illiterates running as high as 24% of the population.[17] The absolute number of illiterates, given the population increase, has remained almost constant. Similarly despite the increases in school attendance, the national average of 3.6 years of schooling is increasing slowly. At the present rate it will take 50 years for the average to reach six years.[18]

A tremendous effort is required to keep up with the population growth. In 1960 there were 3.4 million children out of school, while in 1970, despite a higher percentage in school, there were 5.2 million out of school. Only during the Echeverría administration did the number of children not in school begin to decrease. This decrease was brought about by the building of 12,000 classrooms a year. This rate of school building will not be maintained due to budget cuts.[19]

RURAL SCHOOLING: The impressive gains in the number of children attending school has done little to break rural children out of their closed system. Extreme rural poverty makes a supposedly "free" education a luxury. One must still pay for supplies and clothes, and in addition a child in school means losing wages of a child in the fields. Given the poverty in rural areas, immediate survival is more important than getting an education.[20] In addition caciques often oppose schools because they want an ignorant, docile labor force.[21] Few rural schools even have the first six grades, so not surprisingly only 15% of rural children go on to finish the seventh grade.[22] Children entering school in the Federal District are twice as likely to graduate from elementary school as children entering in Oaxaca, three times as likely to enter secondary school, seven times as likely to enter high school, and 25 times as likely to enter a university.[23]

EXPENDITURES: The conventional approach to educational problems has been to throw money at them. This has happened in Mexico where the educational budget went from $636 million in 1970 to $3.12 billion in 1976.[24] This left Mexico spending about $50 per capita on education, one of the highest rates in Latin America.[25] According to liberal thought, this should make education available to all, and open up social mobility for the formerly disadvantaged. In fact those who are able to benefit from increased educational expenditure are already relatively well off. The children of the upper and middle class can *afford* to spend the first twenty years of their lives without incomes, taking advantage of educational spending. Spending for higher education, with 3% of total enrollment, is now 18% of the educational budget.[26] On the other hand, children of peasants and workers are forced to drop out for economic reasons, even if schools are free and located nearby. Thus their taxes go not for their education, but to pay for the education of those who can afford it. This situation is illustrated by the family income of students at the National University. Two thirds of the students come from families in the top 5% of income earners, and 91% come from the top 15%.[27]

SECTION VI: OPPOSITION

CHAPTER 24: RECOGNIZED POLITICAL PARTIES

Despite the PRI's near total control of the political scene, Mexico has significant opposition parties. In general these parties don't provide alternative office-holders for the government. Instead they serve the PRI by providing the illusion, but not the reality, of political democracy, making the current system more palatable. The existance of a tamed electoral opposition serves as a channel for dissidents, and diverts them from more radical and potentially threatening activity.[1] Opposition parties also serve as pressure groups for sophisticated urban voters and the wealthy. None of the officially recognized opposition parties represent workers, peasants or the impoverished urban masses.

Despite the PRI-government's toleration for and even support of opposition parties, it manages to keep tight reins on them. Any new party wanting to register must have at least 65,000 members. The party wanting to register must furnish the name, address and occupation of its members, leaving dissidents open to political reprisals. Finally applications have to be approved by the Federal

ELECTORAL STRUGGLE

"SURE IT'S BORING, BUT IT AVOIDS BLOODSHED."

Electoral Commission, most of whose members are PRI appointees.[2]

The size of the PRI machine is another factor limiting the strength of political opposition. The PRI functions with virtually unlimited government funds, plastering its propaganda far and wide. Also its political machine brings in nearly 100% of the votes in many rural areas. Frequently ejido officials watch while ejidatarios fill out their ballots.[3] Finally all elections are judged by the Federal Electoral Commission which has an automatic majority of PRI-government officials.

In order to breathe a little life into an otherwise impotent opposition, the government set up what is called the party deputy system. This system awards congressional seats to opposition parties if they get over 1.5% of the total vote in a congressional election. If they reach 1.5%, they get five automatic seats, and for each half percent in excess of 1.5% they get additional congressional seats up to a maximum of 25. In this way parties which do not obtain a majority in any single congressional district can still have token representation in congress.

The overall effect of this system is minimal. Opposition parties do not choose who will be the party deputies, rather these seats are automatically awarded to the highest vote-getters. Since the PRI certifies elections, it can eliminate any potential party deputy by simply not accrediting his vote.[4] The power of the party deputies is limited by the absence of such a system in the senate and by the lack of power in the congress as a whole. On the basis of the 1976 elections the PAN was awarded 20 party deputies, the PPS 12, and the PARM 8.[5]

PAN: The major opposition party is the PAN*, or National Action Party. This party was created during the Cárdenas administration from remnants of the defeated Cristero movement. It had the backing of middle class people hurt by Cárdenas's reforms, business and lawyers opposed to labor legislation, and hacendados. They were all united by their conservatism, and the party was heavily influenced by the Catholic Church.[6]

Given the rightward turn of the government by the late forties, the wealthy and clergy shifted to the PRI.[7] The PAN's major strength is now in urban centers with their large concentrations of middle class voters.[8] In addition the PAN also attracts some conservative peasants, and some people who are simply angry with the PRI.[9]

A study of voters in Mexico City showed that the strongest PAN support came from middle income groups:[10]

Income	% supporting PRI	% supporting PAN
0-$272/month	72.0	028.0
$273-$480/month	68.7	031.3
over $480	81.8	018.2

The same study noted that despite the PAN's early association with the church, the more religious people were, the more they tended to favor the PRI.

In general the degree to which the PAN attracts individuals is a measure of dissatisfaction with the PRI. Sometimes workers support the nominally more conservative PAN simply because there is no other alternative to the PRI.[11] Similarly in local elections, dissatisfaction with a particularly bad PRI candidate may benefit the PAN candidate. Sometimes the right uses the PAN to attack the PRI on a particular issue while pretending to be loyal to the PRI.

Ideologically the PAN stands for replacing PRI officials with PAN ones but not for changing the system. Criticism concentrates on corruption, bureaucracy and excessive centralism.[12] There is a conscious effort to make the political line of the PAN so weak that it will not alienate anyone.[13] The PAN's omissions tend to define it more than

*PAN also means "bread" in Spanish.

any of its positive statements. It does not support strikes by labor unions, nor attempts by peasants to get land, nor efforts to limit US economic and cultural intervention in Mexico. In fact given its middle class position, it is quite comfortable with the standard of living the US presence in Mexico has provided its rank and file. This satisfaction with the relationship between the US and Latin American business went to the extent of criticizing the Echeverría administration for so strongly identifying itself with the Allende government in Chile.[14] In any case the PAN is safely to the right of the PRI so that it does not challenge the current system of private ownership and multinational investment.[15]

The PAN is the only party other than the PRI which regularly nominates its own candidate for president. In addition it puts up a slate of candidates for many governorships, congressional and senate seats, and for the mayors of some cities. The PAN's success in attracting votes is indicated by the percentage of the total votes its presidential candidates have gotten:[16]

PAN candidate's share of vote
1952	7.82%
1958	9.42%
1964	10.98%
1970	13.83%

This steady increase in votes ended in 1976 when the party split between two potential nominees, a right wing candidate, Pablo Emilio Madero, and another with views closer to the European Christian Democrats. Despite Madero's getting 74% of the delegate votes at the party convention, he could not persuade the other candidate to withdraw and let him get the 80% majority required by party rules. Amid cries denouncing the "Marxist-Jesuit" influence creeping into the party, the convention ground to a halt and no candidate was nominated. Ironically the PRI was more upset by the deadlocked convention than the PAN. The PRI repeatedly attempted to get the PAN to call a new convention to nominate a candidate, any candidate, so López Portillo wouldn't look like a complete fool on the campaign trail without any opposition.

The PAN candidates for lesser offices have met with limited success. For the first time in 1973 the PAN won congressional seats outright, three in the Federal District and one in Puebla, reflecting its strength in urban areas. In 1973 the PAN received 33% of the votes in the Federal District, up from 27.2% in the previous non-presidential elections in 1967. The places where the PAN got over 30% of the vote in 1973, the Federal District, Puebla, the State of Mexico, and Jalisco, contain major urban centers.[17] In the 1976 elections the PAN failed to win a single congressional seat. However its president later charged the PRI with widespread electoral fraud.[18]

Despite the official encouragement of political opposition, in individual cases local officials may not be quite so charitable to the PAN. For example a PAN assembly in Naucalpan, State of Mexico was attacked April 28, 1974 by plain-clothes policemen carrying pistols and steel bars. Following that uniformed police came in and took down PAN displays, saying that they would offend Echeverría, who was scheduled to visit the area.[19]

POPULAR SOCIALIST PARTY: The Popular Party was founded in the late forties by Vincente Lombardo Toledano, a labor leader, in reaction to the rightward turn of the revolution. Initially it took a strong stand against foreign monopolies and called for regulating foreign investment, although it never said much about regulating Mexican capitalists.[20] In 1955 Lombardo Toledano declared that the party had adopted scientific socialism and changed its name to the Popular Socialist Party (PPS). Despite this declaration the PPS didn't take an active role in on-going struggles, even though Lombardo Toledano's charisma attracted some workers.

During the Echeverría administration the PPS lost the last vestiges of its leftism and became more closely associated with the PRI. This association with the PRI provides the facade of a left opposition, just as the PAN provides the facade of right-wing opposition. The PRI-government even let the PPS register as an official party despite its not having enough members to fulfill the legal requirement.[21] It is commonly thought that the PRI also subsidizes the PPS financially, although there is no hard evidence.[22] It was even suggested that the PRI provided the money to build the new PPS building in Mexico City.[23]

Unlike the PAN, the PPS doesn't nominate its own candidate for president. It simply waits until the PRI appoints the new presidential candidate, and then announces that that individual will also be the PPS's candidate. The PPS does nominate separate candidates for many state and local offices. These nominees rarely get elected, as is indicated by the PPS's only getting 2.61% of the vote in the 1973 congressional elections.

A conspicious exception to the inability of the PPS candidates to seriously contest elections occurred in the State of Nayarit in 1975. As is frequently the case, apparent opposition to the PRI results from the PRI choosing unpopular candidates. In this case the PRI appointee for state governor had been the police chief fired for his role in killing student demonstrators in Mexico City, June 10, 1971. In addition the PPS used the domination of the state by caciques and foreign control of the local tobacco industry as campaign issues. The PPS campaign was taken so seriously by the PRI that police and soldiers in plain clothes were sent out to block people traveling to the state capital for the PPS candidate's rally. Nevertheless 50,000 showed up. The state head of the CTM said in advance of the elections that those not supporting the PRI would be fired from their jobs.[24]

The PPS was credited with 44,152 votes, compared to the PRI's 69,672. However after the election PPS President Cruickshank stated that there were so many cases of fraud that the elections should be annulled. The defeated PPS candidate claimed ballot boxes were stuffed by PRI officials before voting, and some ballot boxes had been stolen by the army. The PRI on the other hand charged that PPS sympathizers were the ones who had been stealing ballot boxes.[25]

This confrontation with the PRI was an exception to the normal pattern, and if anything, relations between the PRI and PPS seem to be getting closer. In 1976 the PRI appointed PPS President Cruickshank as senator from Oaxaca, and announced that he would be a joint PPS-PRI candidate. Charges were made that the PRI had bought him off in exchange for recognizing the defeat of the PPS candidate for governor of Nayarit.[26] Also the PRI announced that there would be joint PPS-PRI candidates for governor in Chiapas and Morelos.

In general the PPS has only won minor local victories. Even when it wins an election there is no guarantee that the results will be respected. For example in the 1972 municipal elections in Jultipán, Morelos, the PPS claimed its candidate won the mayorship. When the PRI also claimed victory, townspeople occupied the city hall in support of the PPS candidate. Police then attempted to dislodge the occupiers. Rioting broke out, and the army was called in to restore order, leaving 23 dead in its wake.[27]

AUTHENTIC PARTY OF THE MEXICAN REVOLUTION (PARM): Another recognized party is the PARM. This party exists to receive handouts the government offers to recognized political parties. It is variously referred to as a club to give legislative scholarships to supposed veterans of the revolution[28] or simply as a political joke in bad taste.[29] Its officials are forced to deny that its party deputy seats are sold on the open market.[30] Generally the PARM is believed to receive a subsidy from the government.[31] Those who attempt to label the PARM call it right of center. Despite having gotten only 1.8% of the votes in the 1973 congressional elections, in 1976 the PARM bounced back to win a congressional seat in Nuevo Laredo, the only seat lost by the PRI.

This winning of a congressional seat illustrates that PRI losses usually occur only if its candidate is unusually unpopular. In this case the PRI candidate was Ruperto Villarreal Montemayor, former mayor of Nuevo Laredo. After serving as the PRI mayor he began using the family newspaper EL DIARIO to support the PARM. He then switched back to the PRI and ran for congress. He was seen as a hopeless opportunist and lost in July 1976. This election though also showed that the PRI wins all the elections except those it chooses to lose. In August the PRI nullified the July elections and called a new election which the PRI won on December 19, 1976. A PARM party deputy serving as poll watcher tried to bring someone to the police station for stuffing ballot boxes. The car was stopped on the way by a plain-clothes policeman and the party deputy ended up in critical condition in the hospital after getting shot by the police. Finally in order to calm tempers the PRI candidate was declared the official "winner" while the "losing" PARM candidate was made a party deputy.[32]

While it is possible that Mexico might evolve into a multiparty system, most likely as a result of splits in the dominant groups, that would not radically change Mexico. Since none of the recognized parties offer any alternatives to the present system, the likely result of a viable second party would be less corrupt, more responsive officials, but no major change in the economic system.

CHAPTER 25: MASS OPPOSITION

1. 1968 STUDENT MOVEMENT

The Mexican government's attempts to organize workers and peasants into national groups enjoyed overwhelming support during the Cárdenas administration. The general feeling was that even though people had received little from the revolution in material terms, at least their present sacrifices would provide a better future for all. However after 1940 it became increasingly obvious that a few were enjoying a magnificent present at the expense of the majority. The resulting discontent was reflected by the workers' movements of the late 1940's and 1950's, various peasant movements, and by strikes of teachers, doctors and students. However it was the 1968 student movement which ended all illusions concerning the role of the PRI-government.[1]

The 1968 student movement started as an insignificant street fight between students from two high schools in Mexico City. When police came on July 23 to break up the fighting, they were too zealous, and chased some of the students into their school building, clubbing everyone in sight, including students and teachers who had nothing to do with the disturbances. This produced a typical response, a march three days later to protest police brutality. When the protest march merged with the annual student demonstration on the anniversary of the Cuban Revolution, police, rather than ignoring the students, again waded in with clubs. Before the day was over, students seized several city buses, and occupied several high schools. When students still hadn't emerged from one

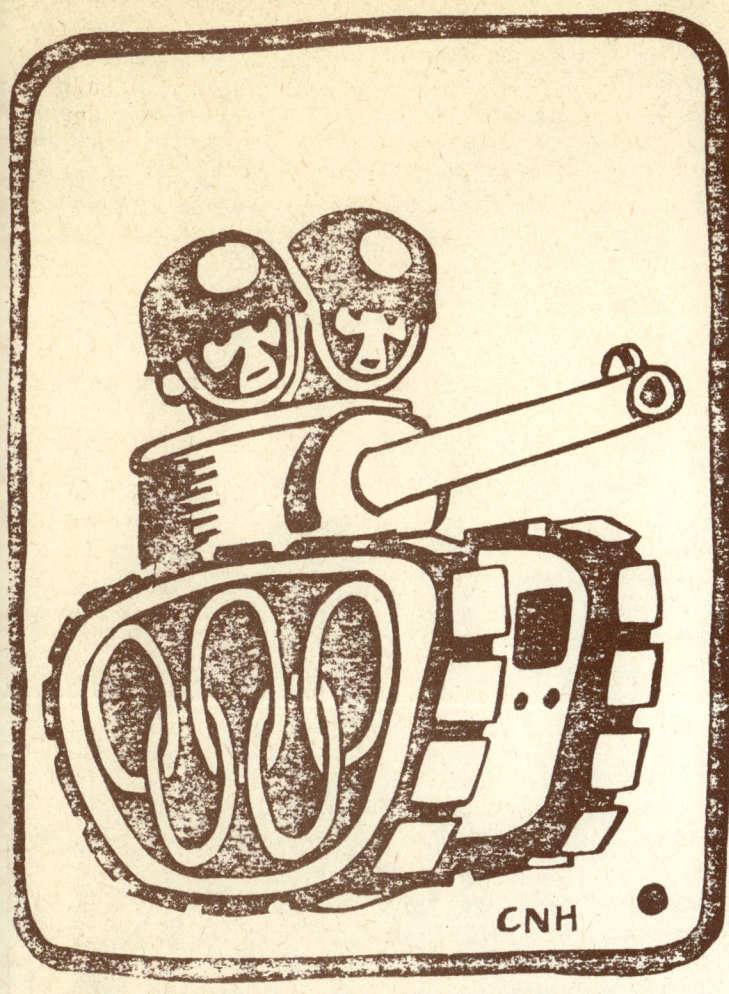

Rather than making minor concessions to end the movement, the government continued its brutality. Store windows were smashed by police during demonstrations to make the movement look irresponsible.[2] Houses were searched without warrants, phones were tapped, and students were arrested without charge. Despite the supposed autonomy of the National University, it was occupied by the army September 18 to prevent it from being used as the focal point of the movement. On September 24 the Politechnic Institute was also occupied. Even before the massive violence of October 2, an estimated 80 to 100 were killed by police.[3]

Not surprisingly the repression and the government's refusal to negotiate changed the political outlook of the strikers. They began to question the basic values of a system they had implicitly believed in only shortly before. At the same time students began to spread out into working class neighborhoods, passing out leaflets, giving quick speeches, and fleeing before the police arrived. The

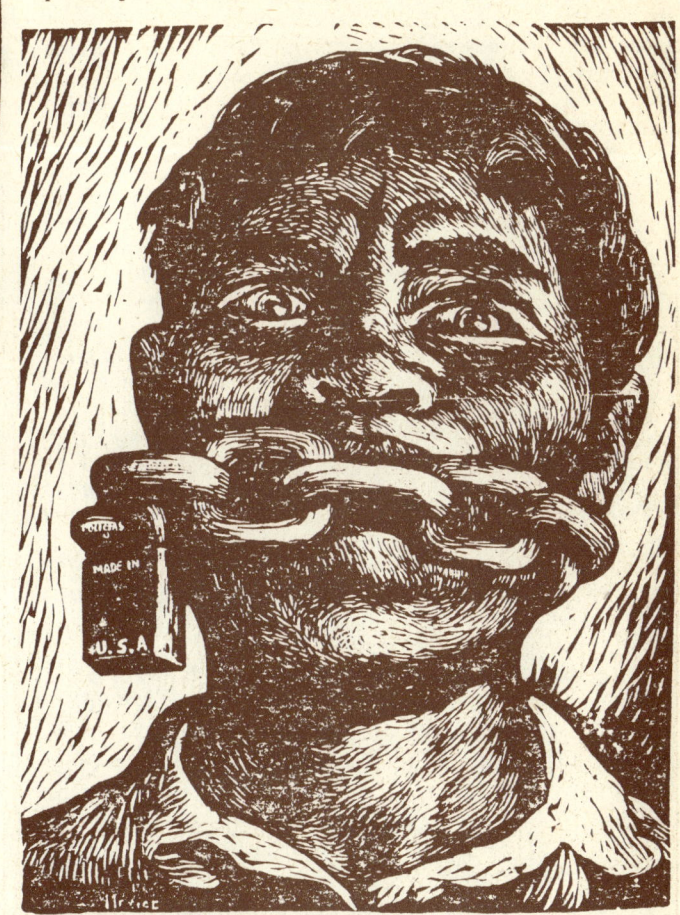

Poster from 1968 Student movement

of the schools by July 31, without warning, police and the army used a bazooka on the school's massive wooden door. The death toll was never revealed. This repression resulted in still more protest; on August 1, 50,000 people marched from the National University and four days later 150,000 protesters marched from the Politechnic Institute.

In addition the National University, the Politechnic Institute, and their affiliated high schools went out on strike. Six demands were issued by the strikers on August 6. These demands reflected a belief that somehow, somewhere, democracy, reform and social justice were still a part of the Revolution. The demands were (1.) freedom for political prisoners, (2.) disbanding the granaderos, the Mexico City tactical police squad, (3.) the dismissal of the police chief, (4.) the repeal of Article 145, which defined the crime of social dissolution, (i.e., trouble makers could be arrested if the government so desired), (5.) compensation for the wounded and the families of the dead, and (6.) the arrest and trial of public officials guilty of atrocities.

More massive demonstrations followed. On the 13th of August 130,000 marched through the streets of Mexico City. For the first time in recent Mexican history an incumbent president was criticized publicly. On August 27 a demonstration was held with 300,000 persons. On September 13 there were 100,000 at a rally, with the loudest cheering coming after speeches attacking the government for having sold out the country to American interests.

LIBERTAD DE EXPRESION MEXICO 68

Poster from 1968 Student movement

same thing happened on city buses. By the end of September most of the students saw the original six demands as only a beginning, and were demanding political rights, economic justice, and an end to dependency on the US.

Attempts to negotiate with the government never got off the ground. Students, realizing that any leader was susceptible to bribes or violence, formed a 150 member National Strike Council, and rotated members to insulate any one individual from government pressure as much as possible. The students' precondition for negotiations was that they be public. This was totally unacceptable to the government. Not only would it make it hard to threaten or bribe, but it would lead others to expect the same treatment.

The inevitable result was violent repression. If the violence couldn't be directed at leaders, it would be directed at the masses. A march scheduled for October 2 had been prohibited by the government, so strikers decided on a rally "to avoid violence." As thousands were peacefully listening to speakers in the Plaza of Three Cultures, in the Tlatelolco housing project, they were surrounded by 5,000 soldiers.[4] What followed is reported by a foreign correspondent who was there:

> *At that moment, a helicopter appeared over the square, coming down, down, down. A few seconds later, it dropped two green flares into the middle of the crowd. I called out: "Boys, something is going to happen, they've got flares," and they said, "Aw, come on, you are not in Vietnam!" But, I said, "In Vietnam, when a helicopter drops flares, it's because they want to locate the place to bomb." Not three seconds later, we heard a great noise as troop carriers arrived and stationed themselves around the side of the square. The soldiers jumped down with their machine guns and immediately started shooting. Not into the air, as you do to scare, but at the PEOPLE. Just then, we noticed that on the roofs there were more soldiers and machine guns and automatic pistols....*
>
> *At that point, there was heavy firing from soldiers on the ground, with rifles, machine guns, automatic pistols: machine guns from the roofs, and guns in the helicopter.*[5]

Estimates of the dead range from the NEW YORK TIMES' 200 to the 325 which the MANCHESTER GUARDIAN published. There was never an accurate account published, and the bodies were burned to avoid a politically embarrassing string of funerals just before the Olympics.[6]

This, and the arrests and police brutality which followed, brought a rapid end to the student movement. The National Strike Council, which had eliminated the role of leader, was too cumbersome to respond, if indeed there were viable responses for students who only weeks before had believed in a democratic Mexico. The suppression of the 1968 student movement was as significant an event in Mexican history as Independence, the Reform, and the Revolution.[7]

> *...at the very moment in which the Mexican government was receiving international recognition for forty years of political stability and economic progress, a swash of blood dispelled the official optimism and caused every citizen to doubt the meaning of that progress.*[8]

2. STUDENT MOVEMENT

The student movement has waxed and waned since 1968, depending on local issues and the degree of repression. In 1973 and early 1974 troops were used against students in Yucatán, Sinaloa, Puebla and the National University.[9] A key ingredient of this unrest is a demand for higher education which the system is not meeting, and the lack of professional jobs available for those who do graduate.[10]

One of the most serious confrontations occurred in Puebla in 1973. Puebla has long been dominated by some of the most reactionary church and political groups in the country. Students there were quite active politically and allied themselves with independent peasant and workers' groups, such as the one at the nearby VW plant. When students demonstrated in the streets of Puebla on May Day 1973, they were fired on by police shooting dum-dum bullets from the roofs of nearby buildings. At the May 3 funeral procession for the four students killed on May Day, 30,000 students, workers and peasants joined the march. The governor, whose publicly-stated position was that his police had orders to "shoot to kill, without warning, anyone who disturbs the peace," was removed for his inability to peacefully handle the situation.[11]

Most recently activities attributed to students have become so bizarre that it becomes extremely difficult for anyone to know what is going on. In April 1976 a group identified as the Popular Student Front took 14 university employees hostage and barricaded themselves in one of the buildings of the University of Puebla. During the take-over of the building, one person was killed and six were wounded. The occupiers threatened to kill the hostages if efforts were made to dislodge them. The demand of those in the building was that the University Rector be fired for having used his position to channel money to the Mexican Communist Party. The Mexican Communist Party, as well as the Mexican Workers' Party, stated that the occupiers were from the Socialist Workers' Party, a group which "suffered from total decomposition and had become an instrument of provocation and repression."[12]

Such occurrences bolster the widely-held belief that much of what claims to be the left is actually the right wing trying to embarrass certain functionaries, discredit the left, and force the government into a more repressive stance. In the early 1970's Echeverría's trips abroad coincided with political conflicts at the National University, presumably promoted by interests using protest as a way to embarrass Echeverría.[13]

Goons known as "porros" are another problem for the student movement. These porros are recruited by police or politicians to break up political activities they deem undesirable. Part of their reward is free rein to terrorize and rob for purely personal reasons.[14] This often makes it impossible to do political organizing in high schools and universities. An example of such interference occurred when eleven persons were wounded by gunfire during contested student government elections at the National University Law School.[15]

3. MEXICAN WORKERS' PARTY

Numerous opposition groups of an infinite variety of political persuasions existed during the Echeverría administration. The Mexican Workers' Party (PMT) was one of the few which had an impact on the national scene. Organization of the party began shortly after Echeverría took office. Two of the organizers were Heberto Castillo, an engineer who became involved with the student movement in 1968, and Demetrio Vallejo, the rail worker jailed for 11 years after the 1959 rail strike. For two years they toured the country in a manner resembling that of Francisco Madero in 1910, holding public meetings and denouncing the injustices of the government. Organizers were subject to constant harassment by local police. One of the many incidents involved Castillo being picked up in August 1973 while walking down a street in Mexico City. He was taken to police headquarters, beaten, told to stop writing and supporting the workers' movement, and released with two broken ribs.[16] In September 1974 a national conference was held and the party was formally established as the Mexican Workers' Party (PMT).

At this meeting, which was attended by 300 delegates from 20 states, Castillo was named party president. The PMT declaration of principles stated that

> *banks, basic private industries, means of communication, transport, and public services should be nationalized.... Inflation affects the needy and benefits the rich. To combat it, the food industry and the production of basic necessities should also be nationalized, and strict price controls and inflation allowances should be instituted.*[17]

A statement in the party magazine also declared:[18]

1. No human being has the right to exploit the work of others.
2. The Mexican people have the firm duty to prevent foreign nations from exploiting Mexican workers or riches, or from intervening in Mexico's internal affairs.

3. Development should be financed internally by taxing the rich.
4. The state should create jobs for the unemployed.

After the party was formally constituted, its leaders continued to travel around the country speaking about conditions in Mexico, and attempting to get local chapters of the party established. In 1976 the party was unable to get registered as an official party, so its activities were directed at organization and dissemination of information. Harassment, mostly minor, was constant, making it almost impossible to function, given the limited resources of the party. At one meeting police stopped and disabled vehicles taking people to a PMT meeting. Peasant leaders threatened those attending.[19] At a meeting in Pachuca, police closed off the plaza to vehicles and turned off the lights. Meanwhile advance men preparing for the next meeting in Tulancingo were arrested, and their money and literature were confiscated.[20] Near La Lagunilla, Puebla, a PMT organizer's car was hit by gunfire as he was driving. He had previously received death threats.[21] At another rally in Ciudad Lázaro Cárdenas, near the new Las Truchas Steel Works, city busses quit running to the plaza where a PMT rally was to be held. (Most workers don't own cars.) Two hours of extra overtime were ordered at the construction site so that workers would be unable to attend, and electricity was cut off so the 2000 who did attend had no PA system.[22]

4. COMMUNIST PARTY

The Communist Party of Mexico was founded in 1919. It cooperated so closely with the Cárdenas administration that party membership was seen as a ticket to a government job.[23] The party continues, sometimes being encouraged as during the Cárdenas administration, sometimes being tolerated, and sometimes being repressed as during the 1968 student movement.

The party publishes a magazine, OPOSICION, which circulates freely but not widely. It organizes students, peasants and workers. Since the party does not publish membership figures, one has to rely on widely varying estimates. Philip Agee, the former CIA agent, estimated membership at 5,000, mainly from rural areas and the urban lower and lower middle classes.[24] Other estimates vary widely and range from 15,000[25] to more than 65,000, the number needed to be legally registered as a political party.[26]

Generally the party was tolerated by the Echeverría administration. There were exceptions though, as when long-time member Hilario Moreno was arrested and charged with possessing subversive literature and a false passport. He was found dead in his cell ten days later.[27] Danzós Palomino, member of the party and long-time peasant organizer, has been in and out of jail for the last decade. Lucío Cabañas, the guerrilla leader in Guerrero, was a member of the party before forming his guerrilla group.[28]

At the 16th Party Congress in 1973 the party stated:

In the opinion of the Communist Party, the authoritarian structure as well as the paternalist nature of the state, the despotic political regime, and the historical tradition of the masses in effecting political change, the closeness of the United States, the existence of an increasingly well-consolidated repressive apparatus, make it impossible to reach socialism by peaceful means. We see the way to revolutionary transformation as the result of a combination of wage struggles, street demonstrations, partial or general strikes, united with peasant land occupations, urban insurrections and guerrilla actions of all kinds.[29]

In 1976 the party chose as its presidential candidate Valentín Campa, a rail worker jailed in 1959. Since the Communist Party is not registered, his campaign was only symbolic. He traveled around Mexico drawing crowds of several thousand. This gave him the opportunity to state the party's current position which is to gain official recognition and participate in politics as the Italian Communist party does. This would enable the party to form an alliance of democrats, progressives, socialists, and communists, and achieve, "unity without hegemony, without imposition or dogmatism," and effect a multi-party peaceful transition to socialism.[30]

5. OBSTACLES TO CHANGE

There is a constant low level of violent repression which makes it unnecessary to resort to more dramatic repression such as occurred in 1968. A study done on acts of violent repression in the month of February 1976 showed that political violence had left 11 dead, 21 wounded, 44 arrested and 2 kidnapped, in 11 attacks by police, 2 by the army, 2 by paramilitary groups, 4 by landlords' private gunmen, 2 by company officials, 2 by union gunmen, 3 by porros, and 4 by unidentified individuals.[31] In addition political activists in many cases simply disappear and are never heard of again.[32]

Torture is another means of maintaining the status quo. Amnesty International

has received allegations of systematic torture carried out by institutions that are responsible to government ministries...

In addition to the use of torture during official interrogations, the Mexican press has published reports of paramilitary groups detaining left-wing sympathizers (recently two priests) and subjecting them to severe tortures, including electric shocks; then releasing them. This is a clear use of torture as intimidation.[33]

An example of such torture occurred after the April 1976 arrest of Salvador Cervantes, a student activist from Querétaro. After his arrest Cervantes was questioned about leaflets publicizing a May Day demonstration. The leaflets called for the ousting of the state governor. Despite his denial of any connection with the leaflets, he "was tortured by police. They applied electric shocks after covering him in water. He was beaten and forced to kneel with his arms outstretched for more than two hours."[34]

Protest groups not violently smashed are frequently so co-opted that there is no possibility of their making radical demands. Demonstrations in Hidalgo in April 1975 to oust the governor were not repressed since the governor was clearly incompetent and probably was already slated for firing. However all those moving into leadership roles in the movement to oust him had a clear stake in the current government. The leaders of the protest included the regional secretary of the CNOP, the secretary of a professional group of the CNOP, the president of the National Organization of Small Farmers, the Organizational Secretary of the CNC, and various congressmen.[35]

The government systematically recruits talented, ambitious members of the opposition, thus depriving it of leadership, talent, and support. Such recruitment is so frequent that it has created cynicism about the real motivations of any opposition leader. One never knows if the leader is really trying to foster change or simply propelling himself into a position of leadership so the government will buy him off with a cushy job. To the extent this makes people distrust opposition leaders, it serves the government admirably.

Finally, given the lack of precedent for peaceful transfer of power from one group to another in Mexican history, there is a fear that the process of change will inevitably lead to widespread violence. Coupled with this fear is an awareness that when people "challenge existing institutions, the poor are usually the ones who suffer most."[36]

CHAPTER 26: ARMED OPPOSITION

The two major rural guerrilla groups in recent years have been in the state of Guerrero, which is one of the least developed in the country. There 82.5% of workers are in agriculture and 85.36% of incomes are below $80.00 a month.[1] Politics are usually corrupt and only three governors in the state's history have completed their terms.

In 1931 Genaro Vázquez Rojas was born into a poor peasant family in Acatlán, Guerrero. He became a school teacher and later began working full time with a group trying to oust a particularly inept governor of Guerrero, Raúl Caballero Aburto. In October 1958 the opposition movement mustered 5,000 persons to demonstrate against him in the state capital. The army moved in to quell the demonstration and break a student strike at the state university, arresting 120 persons in the process. This only inflamed the protest movement, leading merchants to close their shops and denounce the governor. Thirteen people were killed and 36 wounded when a later demonstration was fired upon by troops.[2] This prompted the federal government to fire the governor, a standard practice when governors cannot avoid violent conflict.

The group with which Genaro worked, the Guerrero Civic Action Group put up a slate of candidates for the December 1962 elections. None of the insurgent candidates won, presumably due to electoral fraud. Demonstrations followed again; in Iguala 3,000 people gathered in front of the city hall to protest the imposition of PRI officials. While Genaro was addressing the group, the army surrounded the meeting and began shooting. In the confusion Genaro fled into the hills, leaving six dead and four wounded behind him.[3]

Genaro managed to stay hidden until 1966 when he was arrested in Mexico City and charged with the murder of those killed at the Iguala protest meeting. He was taken back to Guerrero and jailed in Iguala. In April 1968 he was freed by guerrillas when he was being taken from the jail for medical treatment. Two of the guards and one of the guerrillas were killed in the attack.

Genaro rejoined the protest group he had worked with to oust Caballero. The group was renamed the National Civic Revolutionary Association. Given their inability to engage in peaceful protest, they began to engage in gun battles with army patrols and police and to stage kidnappings and robberies. The most notorious action was the November 1971 kidnapping of Jaime Castrejón Diez, rector of the state university and owner of many of the Coca-Cola bottling plants in Guerrero. When government efforts to locate the guerrillas and their kidnap victim failed, the government was forced to fly nine political prisoners to Cuba and pay a $200,000 ransom for the return of the rector.

Genaro's group, despite such dramatic actions as the Castrejón kidnapping, never developed a mass base and never controlled well-defined territory. Its political position was stated in a letter:[4]

1. Overthrow of major capitalists and pro-imperialist landlords.
2. Create a coalition government of workers, peasants, students and progressive intellectuals.
3. Political and economic independence for Mexico.
4. A social order to benefit the working majority.

Just after this was published Genaro was killed in a car wreck. Apparently the accident occurred when the car he was riding in from Mexico City to Morelia hit a bridge abutment. One of the guerrillas in the car later said in an interview that the wreck had been an accident and that the car was not being pursued at the time. The interviewer also noted that the army reported finding $30,000 in the car, while actually there had been over $80,000.[5]

Genaro's body was returned to his home town for burial and despite heavy military security, 2000 attended the funeral.[6] Later that month five other members were arrested, and since then no other activities have been attributed to the group.

The other major guerilla leader of the past decade has a history remarkably similar to that of Genaro Vázquez. Lucio Cabañas was also from Guerrero and became a school teacher in the town of Atoyac. While Genaro was carrying on the fight against Governor Caballero at the state level, Cabañas was doing so at the local level. While teaching in Atoyac a campaign was begun to remove an unpopular school principal supported by the local PRI city government. Lucio's role in the protest movement came to the attention of local authorities who decided to silence him. In May 1967 at one of the protest meetings in Atoyac, police surrounded the meeting. Townspeople, not wanting to leave a small group easy prey for the police, rushed to the meeting to provide protection for those already there. Finally shooting broke out and in the resulting confusion Genaro managed to escape and make his way into the surrounding mountains. However several residents of Atoyac were killed, as were some policemen.[7]

Once in the mountains Lucio organized a group which functioned in much the same way as Genaro's group. They robbed banks and staged kidnappings which netted them both publicity and funds. The Cabañas organization, called the Party of the Poor, issued communiques taking credit for various actions and explaining their political significance. One of these communiques stated that "actions of expropriation should not be considered as isolated events, but as part of the insurrection aimed at the economic system which exploits and oppresses us."[8] The group numbered as many as two hundred, many of whom frequently entered and left the mountainous area where the group fought.[9]

By far the most dramatic action of the group was the kidnapping of state senator and governor-designate of Guerrero, Rubén Figueroa in June 1974. Figueroa had gone to negotiate with Cabañas and then was kidnapped.[10] The kidnappers demanded the federal government pay a $4 million ransom, free certain political prisoners, and make settlements favoring specific strikers and land claimants. The Guerrero state government was directed to, among other things, fire the Acapulco police chief and free all common criminals.[11] When the government failed to meet these demands a standoff resulted.

For the next 63 days Figueroa was held prisoner while thousands of troops scoured the mountains of Guerrero looking for him and arresting many peasants without charge.[12] Finally Figueroa was freed near Atoyac, Guerrero, under circumstances which have never been made clear. According to official sources an army patrol encountered a group holding Figueroa and killed eight of the guerrillas in an exchange of fire. While the guerrillas were engaged in combat, Figueroa managed to slip away and make his way over to the army and identify himself. This version has been received with skepticism, and it has been claimed that a $192,000 ransom was paid. The shooting, according to the skeptics, was merely the army shooting up a peasant village so it could save face and claim to have rescued Figueroa.[13]

In March 1972 the Party of the Poor published a political platform which was reprinted in the paper EXCELSIOR.[14] Included in its platform were plans for (1.) overthrowing the rich, (2.) forming a government of the poor with laws to protect the workers, (3.) expropriation of factories and large estates, which would be turned over to workers, (4.) supplying workers and farmers with tools and credit, (5.) turning over means of communication to workers, (6.) equality for women, (7.) access to all levels of education for the masses, (8.) fighting racial discrimination, and (9.) complete Mexican economic and political independence from the US and other countries.

Another statement by the party called for

A NEW REVOLUTION, a proletarian revolution which will destroy the state apparatus of the bourgeoisie and give political and economic power to the workers; a revolution directed by workers and peasants which will destroy private property and end the exploitation of man by man.[15]

The Party of the Poor received its fatal blow when Cabañas and 19 others were killed in December 1974 in a battle with the army. This group never had significant impact after that. Later eight survivors of the group were captured near Yautepec, Morelos[16] and the last prominent individual of the group was killed in a shootout with the police in Mexico City.[17]

Neither of the groups Genaro Vázquez and Lucio Cabañas headed were able to continue after their leading figures were killed. Both groups suffered not only from military attack, but from massive public spending in the area to win the "hearts and minds" of the peasants. This investment included dams, reforestation, road building, and government coffee purchases.[18]

There have been several urban guerrilla groups in Mexico in the last decade. The group which has received the most publicity has been the 23rd of September League, named for the date of an attack on a military barracks at Ciudad Madero, Chihuahua in 1965. As with most of the urban guerilla groups in Mexico, it is extremely hard to get accurate information about it. The 23rd of September League is so trigger-happy that it appears that its members either have a strange concept of revolution or, as is often claimed, the entire group is now an effort of the right to discredit the left and push the government into a more repressive stance.

On November 2, 1975 in Juchitán, Oaxaca, four persons who claimed to be from the September 23 League arrived at a demonstration organized by the Worker-Student-Peasant Coalition of Oaxaca. They began to harangue the crowd, telling them that they were all hopeless pacifists serving capitalism. After that demonstrators began to jostle the four, and they began to shout at the peasants. When the demonstrators began to close in on them, they began firing pistols into the crowd. Eight demonstrators were killed, and of the 23rd of September League, one was dead, two escaped, and one was arrested.[19]

In 1976 several spectacular actions were attributed to the 23rd of September League. In May they kidnapped the daughter of the Belgian ambassador and received $400,000 ransom for her release. Then in June eight policemen were killed when 23rd of September members machine-gunned them as they were standing in formation in front of a police station in Mexico City. In August David Sarmiento Jiménez, a 26-year-old identified as the head of the league, was killed in an unsuccessful attempt to kidnap López Portillo's sister. The first kidnap of the López Portillo presidency was also attributed to the league. This involved the industrialist Isaac Duek, who was released after a 4.7 million peso ransom was paid.[20]

So little is known of the 23rd of September League that it is hard to distinguish between actions which actually represent the group, and actions performed by others to discredit the League or the left in general. In fact a statement by those claiming to be the original members of the group, now jailed, stated that none of the original members were still a part of the League and that those now using the name had nothing to do with the founders.[21]

The League is just one of several urban guerrilla groups, of which little is known. The groups have had very little success at getting their ideas into the media, in contrast to the two rural guerilla groups already discussed. Aside from the 23rd of September League, the best known group is the Revolutionary Front of Popular Action. This group kidnapped the American counsel in Guadalajara, Joseph Leonhardy. He was released 3 days later after an $80,000 ransom was paid and 30 political prisoners were flown to Cuba. Later they kidnapped Echeverría's father-in-law, José Guadalupe Zuno, held him for nine days, and released him.

In contrast to other countries such as Argentina, American businessmen in Mexico have generally avoided kidnappings. One of the few such instances in Mexico was the kidnap and subsequent ransom for $12,000 of a First National City Bank president.[22] The confusion surrounding urban groups is increased by infiltration and right wing financing of the ultraleft to discredit the left and embarrass the government.[23] The nebulous nature of these groups was indicated when a series of bombs went off in the Federal District, Oaxaca, and San Luis Potosí on the same night. The bombs were attributed to the 23rd of September League by the governor of Oaxaca, to a Marxist-Leninist group called the People's Union by the district attorney of San Luis Potosí, and to right-wingers with international ties by the Ministry of National Patrimony.[24]

Guerrilla violence has become a regular part of the political scene. The level of violence was shown by the listings under the section on "Terrorism" in the TIME MAGAZINE format publication TIEMPO. The section on terrorism listed the following events for the week which preceded its October 7, 1974 publication date:

—23 men and 10 women arrested in Quintana Roo for running guns for the 23rd of September League.

—4 kidnappers of a woman in Guerrero were arrested, 1 was killed, and 5 more were reported at large. The kidnapping was attributed to the Ernesto Che Guevara Feminine Front.

—14 members of the Revolutionary Front for Popular Action were captured in Guadalajara. They were thought to have been involved in the kidnapping of Counsel Leonhardy and of Echeverría's father-in-law.

—in addition other kidnappings and payroll robberies of uncertain political significance were reported.

PART VII:

CHAPTER 27: MEDIA

Advertising "proposes to each of us that we transform our lives, buying something more. This more, it proposes, will make us in some way richer— even though we will be poorer by having spent our money."[1]

One of the basic differences between the early development of the North Atlantic nations and the present development of Mexico is that the former underwent development without mass media. Depending on its context, mass media can spur development, as in Cuba where viewers are taught skills and are encouraged to produce more by the media. There actors on TV have a life style similar to that of the viewer. However media can create values and desires for material goods which are not in keeping with the reality of underdevelopment, encouraging consumption without increasing productivity. Often values and consumption patterns introduced by the media reflect the economy of a foreign country, as is the case with Mexico.

In the developed world media can make individuals consume, and thus utilize the surplus productive capacity of the advanced nations.[2] However in the underdeveloped world no such rationale for media-induced consumption can be found. In countries like Mexico, mass media create tastes and demands which are beyond the ability of the country to satisfy. Both ads and programs, often foreign-produced, expose viewers to conspicuous consumption.[3] Constant exposure to American upper middle class life style conditions the individual to accept such norms.[4] Ads push alcoholic beverages, cigarettes, luxury cars, perfumes, and shopping trips to San Antonio, Texas. In addition tastes for needed goods are radically changed. White bread and soft drinks have become a high priority even in the poorest villages due to mass media.[5] People are led to believe that mere consumption is not enough, and that they need goods made with the latest labor-saving technology in order to achieve happiness and gain status.[6] The ten top products advertised in Mexico reflect the values created in ads:

	Annual expenditure on ads:
Beer	$38.5 million
Drugs	$19.2 "
Soft drinks	$18.6 "
Food products	$11.9 "
Autos	$10.7 "
Wine & liquor	$ 9.8 "
Electrical apparatus	$ 9.2 "
Cosmetics	$ 8.4 "
Tobacco	$ 8.2 "
Soap	$ 5.8 "

Except for alcoholic beverages, the industries manufacturing these products are overwhelmingly foreign controlled.

Advertising, especially on TV, is growing much more rapidly than the economy as a whole. The advertising budget is now $480 million a year, up from only $129.6 million in 1963.[7] Instead of cutting prices, producers are increasingly turning to ads to increase sales.[8] Television absorbs 56.7% of ad revenue, followed by radio with 15.96%, newspapers with 13.75%, magazines with 4.83%, and movies with 2.08%.[9]

US-owned ad agencies handle 70% of the value of all ads.[10] Of the top ten ad agencies, 6 are subsidiaries of American companies and the rest are jointly owned by Mexicans and foreigners.[11] Even the ad agencies not owned by foreigners produce ads largely for products made by foreigners.

The degree to which advertising is dominated by the US is shown by the major advertisers in various fields:[12]

Autos:	GM*, Ford*
Detergent:	Proctor & Gambel*, Colgate*
Food:	General Foods*, Kraft*, Heinz
Tobacco:	Reynolds*, Phillip Morris*, British American Tobacco
Medicines:	Bristol-Meyers*, Picto
Tires:	Goodyear*, Goodrich-Euzkadi*, Firestone*, Uniroyal*
Radio-TV:	General Electric*, Phillips
Cosmetics and Pharmaceuticals:	Warner Lambert*, American Home Products*
Soft drinks:	Coca Cola*, Pepsi*, Seven Up*
Chemicals:	American Cyanimid*, Dupont*, Union Carbide*

*indicates company also leads in US ad sales.

Advertising often forms part of a closed circle. US corporations in Mexico place ads with US ad agencies, increasing the sales of the US corporation, which in turn increases the business for the US ad agency, etc. Since American ad companies spread their costs worldwide, it is hard for Mexicans to compete. Frequently ads and old US programs are sold as a package, making it even harder to break American domination.[13]

Up to 75% of the international news in the press deals with the US,[14] and most of the copy used comes from AP or UPI. EXCELSIOR publishes more about the US than the NEW YORK TIMES does in all its foreign coverage. The effect of so much US-produced media concerning the US is to create the image of the US as a strong, dynamic nation to be imitated. Liberty and humanism are presented as the opposite of socialism.[15] Often the implicit assumptions of US media rub off on the Mexican press. For example, during the Vietnam War, the National Liberation Front was often referred to as the "enemy."

The touchiness of any material which might reflect negatively on an advertiser's product is shown by this letter to a tobacco company by the public relations director of a broadcasting chain. It was written after an announcer merely reported information on cigarette consumption on the air:

The news program which contained the statement about cigarette consumption reflected the lack of judgement of one of the employees who works in Acapulco station XEKJ. Independently of your personal protest, we have established that indeed the broadcast occurred, something we are very sorry for. This is completely contrary to our policy, and we energetically condemn it. Please accept our apologies, which we also extend to Grant Advertising.[16]

As Echeverría noted on his 1975 trip to Cuba, "The newspapers that enjoy full freedom never attack the transnational corporations that advertise in them."[17]

The political content of copy is also influenced by advertisers. In 1972 a group of advertisers in EXCELSIOR organized an ad boycott to protest its liberal, moderately critical editorial position. This boycott drove it from first in the nation in ad copy in August 1972 to fourth by November.[18]

Government ad buying policies are also directly related to the content of a publication. The government supports the press that it favors by placing ads, buying subscriptions and furnishing the raw materials needed for publication.[19] From 20 to 30% of all advertising is placed by the government for such services as the lottery and Aeromexico, the national airlines.[20] The government also exerts pressure by making loans through Nacional Financiera, loans which need not necessarily be paid back unless the paper begins to criticize the government.

The old government tactic of beating reporters and confiscating presses is now largely a thing of the past, although occasionally on local initiative it still happens.[21] Only a few publications have been closed by the government in recent years. One of those closed was the DIARIO DE MEXICO. It was closed after the caption on a photo of a new ape arriving at the Mexico City zoo, was switched with the caption of a photo of then-President Díaz Ordaz, who has a distinctly simian appearance.[22]

TELEVISION: According to law, Mexican television must be owned and controlled by Mexicans. However there is no such provision controlling its content. US corporations make most of the products advertised, as well as the equipment used to broadcast the ads, and so on. During the Echeverría administration the two principal networks merged into one network called TeleVisa, which controls 90% of the TV stations in Mexico. Even the ownership restriction, designed to promote Mexican national interests, is of little consequence. The Azcarraga's and O'Farril's, the major shareholders in TeleVisa, also own large amounts of stock in American Airlines, Marriot and Western International Hotels, and US Spanish language channels for chicano and Puerto Rican audiences.[23]

TV is the most tightly controlled medium as far as political content is concerned since it has the widest distribution and reaches lower class homes. It is "absolutely impermeable to dialogue or criticism."[24] On the major channels 43% of the programming is foreign produced.[25] These programs emphasize murder, robbery, racism, the greatness of the US, and the consumption of alcoholic beverages.[26] As a result of the heavy exposure to US media

> *it is possible for the children of our country to know more about the virtues of the marines, the wonders of Walt Disney, Jefferson's advanced ideas, the acts of Superman, than of the history of Mexico, the life of Juárez, the political significance of Zapata, or the needs of our country.*[27]

In 1974 the government banned 37 TV programs because they were too violent. These programs included Kung Fu, the Untouchables, and FBI. This was largely a public relations gesture since 2/3 of the programs banned were no longer being shown on Mexican TV, and those programs removed were replaced with other violence-prone foreign programs.[28]

NEWSPAPERS: Mexican newspapers have precious little room for maneuvering after trying to appease both advertisers and the government. Despite the widely proclaimed freedom of the press, one can count on the fingers of one hand those papers which act freely.[29] Generally papers engage in self-censorship to avoid problems.

Occasionally there are direct attacks on the press. Two EXCELSIOR reporters in Pachuca investigating local (very dirty) politics were beaten and robbed by policemen working for local strong man and ex-governor Sánchez Vite.[30] The press is sometimes simply banned. For example the governor of Guerrero said that he had never tried to restrict freedom of the press, but that he has asked the mayor of Acapulco to stop the circulation of papers which print pure "....(unprintable)." He went on to say that he was "macho through and through."[31]

Two features of the Mexican press are the "iguala" and the "gacetilla." The iguala is a sum collected by a usually underpaid reporter from government offices and corporations he regularly covers. This payment serves to guarantee consistent, favorable coverage. The gacetilla is an article paid for just as one would pay for an ad. However it is printed as an ordinary news story, and no mention is made of the fact that it was paid for. If the price is right, it can go on the front page accompanied by pictures. Higher quality papers pride themsleves on not putting gacetillas on the editorial page. Gacetillas sell for about three times an ad of the same size.[32] In addition many reporters expect to be paid not only by their employer but by the person they are covering. "Recruits come from provincial dailies with the idea that a press card is a license for extortion. They expect to be paid by anyone who holds a press conference and then do nothing more than pick up the bulletin that is handed to them."[33] In addition government "parallel salaries" for reporters reached as much as $2,000 a month under the Echeverría administration.[34]

In recent years the paper EXCELSIOR was the NEW YORK TIMES of Mexico. It regularly provided good foreign coverage, especially of Chile, and was an invaluable source of information about Mexico, as is indicated by the number of references to it in this book. However on July 7, 1976 the entire editorial staff was fired. The paper is organized as a cooperative and the non-editorial members of the co-op were organized and voted to no longer employ the paper's editor or its regular columnists. Despite the apparent legality of the move, there was near unanimous conviction[35] that the Echeverría administration was behind the ousting of the editorial staff. Reasons cited were that Echeverría was tired of hearing EXCELSIOR's criticism. It was also suggested that since during his presidency Echeverría had become one of the chief shareholders of the Mexican Editorial Organization, a newspaper chain, he simply wanted to minimize competition. In any case the legacy of Echeverría's "democratic opening" was that there was no independent newspaper left.

MAGAZINES: Magazines, with a more select audience than newspapers, enjoy more freedom of expression. For example, HISTORIA Y SOCIEDAD, of the Mexican Communist Party, and PUNTO CRITICO, an independent leftist magazine both circulate freely if not widely. PROCESO, staffed by writers and editors driven away from EXCELSIOR, is a magnificent source of information. The limit even of a magazine's freedom was shown by POR QUE? This magazine was one of the few cases of orange journalism, a combination of red and yellow. It gave sensational coverage of guerrilla attacks and police brutality. POR QUE? openly sided with guerrilla bands and frequently published their communiques. Significantly it has a mass circulation far beyond the intellectual left.

In the summer of 1974 the army closed down POR QUE?, arresting its editors, staff and printers. Its two editors were held for a week in Military Camp No. 1, despite court orders ordering their release. This closing by the army, which is supposedly totally lacking in judicial power, is rumored to have been carried out to stop POR QUE? from reporting that a ransom was paid for governor-designate Figueroa's release from his kidnappers, thus refuting the army's story that it had freed him.[36]

Generally the magazines with the highest circulation are completely devoid of political content. The magazines with the highest circulation are a police magazine, ALARMA, with press runs of 810,000, and a fashion magazine, LIBROS DE CLAUDIA MODA, with a circulation of 1 million. Three of the major magazines covering politics, TIME, VISION, and the Spanish edition of READER'S DIGEST, are produced by US firms. The Spanish version of READER'S DIGEST has a circulation of 408,000.[37]

BOOKS: Due to higher production costs, books are for a relatively elite audience, and there is less control over content. The print runs for many social science works, such as the ones cited in this book, are often only 3,000.

The number of titles published in Mexico is impressive though. In 1972 4513 titles were published, compared with 4578 in Argentina and 8579 in Brazil with almost twice the population.[38] Except for the 35% of books which are published by the government,[39] most books only circulate among urban elites. The government though does print a large number of books at prices ranging from $.50 to $.80 (pre-devaluation), which do circulate widely. The book-buying public is estimated at

1.2 million.[40] Not only are books too expensive for most people, but there is a woefully inadequate library system. All public libraries together have 11.5 million volumes, of which 8.5 million are ancient texts, government bulletins, and professional theses.[41] Expenditures for libraries run $.0016 per person per year. For the country as a whole that comes to $96,000, compared to a national advertising budget of some $320 million.[42]

CHAPTER 28: THE GRINGOS, PAST

To the memory of the Mexican who shot at, and hit, the American soldier who was raising the Stars and Stripes on the flag pole in front of Mexico's National Palace, September 13, 1847. (Dedication to the book LAS INVASIONES NORTEAMERICANAS EN MEXICO, by Gastón García Cantú.

In the 1820's most of Mexico's foreign trade was with Britain, the world's leading commercial power. While Britain was building a commercial empire in Latin America, the United States was concentrating on territorial expansion. Even before Mexican independence American designs on Mexico were evident. In 1812 the Spanish Ambassador in Washington wrote to the viceroy in Mexico stating that the United States "has proposed nothing less than fixing its border along the Rio Grande to the 31st parallel, and from there on a straight line to the Pacific."[1]

Early American attempts to expand at the expense of Mexico were of little consequence. In 1825 the first American ambassador to Mexico, Joel Poinsett, unsuccessfully attempted to buy Texas, California, New Mexico and parts of the Mexican states of Sonora and Coahuila.[2] In 1827 and 1829 he again made offers to buy various parts of Mexico. Finally Poinsett's involvement with Mexico's internal affairs and his persistent attempts to buy Mexican territory resulted in the Mexican government requesting his recall.

Territorial expansion into Mexico began in Texas. Prior to 1820 there was little settlement in Texas north and east of San Antonio. A traveler there wrote that "from Bejar [San Antonio] to Nacogdoches there are only bears, coyotes, deer, and owls, whose song is in keeping with the lugubriousness of the area."[3] As the American frontier pushed closer to Texas, Anglos began to make forays into Texas, just as they had made forays into Florida to pave the way for its acquisition from Spain in 1819.

The basis for permanent Anglo settlement in Texas was laid in 1820 when Moses Austin received permission to colonize Texas with two hundred families. After Moses died, his son, Stephen F. Austin, went to Mexico City in 1822 to renew the permission for colonization from the newly-independent government.

Settlers were required to swear allegiance to the Mexican government. As their numbers increased it became apparent that they had little in common with the distant government in Mexico City. In an attempt to stem the tide of settlers, the Mexican government withdrew the right of the settlers to keep slaves in Texas. When that failed to slow the flow of colonists, all new settlement was banned in 1830. Nevertheless settlers continued to arrive illegally and by 1833 some 3000 colonists had arrived despite the ban.[4] The Mexican government, itself beset with constant internal strife, was having difficulty governing the settlers in Texas. This resulted in friction, especially when the Mexican government tried to collect import duties on goods shipped from the US to Texas.

Several factors led to the rupture of peaceful relations between the Mexican government and the settlers in Texas. The settlers demanded the right to own slaves, for new settlers to be admitted, for the free importation of goods from the US, and for more familiar political institutions such as trial by jury. Finally there was the question of race.

> *At the close of the summer of 1835 the Texans saw themselves in danger of becoming the alien subjects of a people to whom they deliberately believed themselves to be morally, intellectually and politically superior. The racial feeling, indeed, underlay and colored Texas-Mexican relations from the establishment of the first Anglo-American colony in 1821.*[5]

Given this setting, it is hardly surprising that open hostility broke out between Anglo settlers and the Mexican government. On September 19, 1835, Stephen F. Austin declared, "War is our only recourse. There is no other remedy."[6] The colonists soon formed an army and attacked Mexican detachments stationed in Texas. The following March the colonists formally declared themselves to be an independent republic free from Mexico. Their Declaration of Independence stated:

> *The Mexican government, by its colonization laws, invited and induced the Anglo American population of Texas to colonize its wilderness and under pledged faith of a written constitution, that they should continue to enjoy that constitutional liberty and republican government to which they had been habituated in the land of their birth, the United States of America.*
>
> *It hath sacrificed our welfare to the state of Coahuila by which our interests have been continually depressed through a jealous and partial course of legislation, carried on at a far distant seat of government, by a hostile majority, in an unknown tongue, and this too, notwithstanding we have petitioned in the humblest terms for the establishment of a separate state government, and have, in accordance with the provisions of the national constitution, presented to the general congress a republican constitution, which was, without just cause, contemptuously rejected.*

Seeing that Mexico was on the verge of losing Texas,

Santa Anna marched north to Texas to reestablish authority. In San Antonio he found some 1800 Texans barricaded in an old mission called the Alamo. Santa Anna laid siege to the Alamo for thirteen days. After inflicting heavy casualties on the Mexicans, the Texans finally were captured. Santa Anna had the handful of survivors executed. Somewhat tarnishing the Anglo image of dedicated freedom-fighters in the Alamo was the presence of slave traders and murderers fleeing justice in the US.[7] Two-thirds of those defending the Alamo were recent arrivals in Texas who had come spoiling for a fight. Only half a dozen had been in Texas for over six years.[8] Since settlement had been banned from 1830 to 1834, a large portion of the Alamo's defenders were, to use the current term, illegal aliens.

Once the Alamo had been taken, Santa Anna marched eastward. He easily defeated another Texas force at Goliad, and three hundred Texans were shot after their surrender there.[9] Santa Anna pursued the Texas forces to the banks of the San Jacinto River, near the present site of Houston. Assuming that no attack was imminent, Santa Anna permitted his 1100 troops to take a siesta on the afternoon of April 19, 1836. He was so confident that little attention was paid to security.

During the siesta the 1000-man Texas army attacked and routed the Mexicans. Repeating the violence inflicted on the Anglos at the Alamo and Goliad, Mexican prisoners "were clubbed and stabbed, some on their knees. The slaughter became methodical. The Texas riflemen knelt and poured fire into the packed, jostling ranks."[10] When the shooting was over the Mexican force was defeated, Santa Anna was captured, and some 630 Mexicans and 2 Texans had been killed.

The Texans' victory in the war was due to their familiarity with the terrain, a more politically unified population, and the numerical majority of Anglos. In 1834, of the 27,000 population of Texas, 20,000 were estimated to be Anglos and their slaves. The Mexican population in Texas was divided as whether to support independence or continued Mexican rule. Santa Anna had an extremely long supply line, and had marched from Central Mexico, across deserts, arriving in Texas with soldiers weak and sick from the march. Many of his soldiers were Mayan Indian conscripts who spoke no Spanish and had little interest in the struggle which had enveloped them. Another major factor in the Texas victory was the large amount of money, men, and supplies which poured into Texas from the US during the war.[11]

The captured Santa Anna ordered other Mexican forces in Texas to withdraw and signed a treaty granting independence to Texas so that he would be freed. In October 1836 Sam Houston was elected president of the independent Republic of Texas. For the next nine years Texas existed as an independent nation, even though the legality of Santa Anna's giving Texas away was not recognized by the Mexican government. During this period there was strong sentiment in the US not only to annex Texas, but to acquire much if not all of the territory of Mexico. This desire to push US boundaries outward was known as Manifest Destiny, a combination of the feeling of racial, cultural, and religious superiority, and a sense that America was the most civilized country in the world, with the duty to extend its benefits to the rest of the human race.[12] This feeling was by no means unanimous, as this statement by Henry David Thoreau indicates:

> *Those favoring an expansionist war with Mexico are hundreds of thousands of merchants and farmers, more interested in commerce and agriculture, than in humanity. They are prepared to be just neither with their slaves nor Mexico.*[13]

Another dissenter was the head of the US Senate Foreign Relations Committee, who responded to the general feeling that if we wanted northern Mexico and especially the Port of San Francisco, then we should take it.

> *Isn't this the most remarkable thing in the world? We need San Francisco Bay. Why? Because it is the best port in the Pacific. Mr. President, I had the opportunity of being a criminal judge for a long time, but I never have heard a thief, accused of stealing a horse, say in his defense that he stole it because it was the best horse he could find.*[14]

In this jingoistic atmosphere Texas was annexed to the union in December 1845. The Mexican government stated that, regardless of the status of Texas, the border between Texas and the rest of Mexico was the Nueces River, not the Rio Grande some 150 miles to the south.* President Polk, an avowed expansionist, ordered General Taylor to cross into the disputed area between the Nueces and the Rio Grande. Mexican troops then crossed the Rio Grande and captured a small American detachment on what they considered to be Mexican soil. They later fought Taylor's main force and were driven south of the Rio Grande. The first skirmish was used by President Polk as justification for a declaration of war.‡

General Kearny soon began to march down the Santa Fe Trail from Ft. Leavenworth to Santa Fe, which he occupied in August 1846. He was accompanied by 414 wagons belonging to traders who literally couldn't wait to do business in New Mexico.[15] The lack of resistance in New Mexico has led to the suggestion that the Mexican governor was bribed to let the Americans in.[16] Resistance did flare up later and the first American governor of New Mexico was killed. However this didn't stop the American's westward thrust. Kearny continued west and occupied Los Angeles on January 10, 1847. His way was paved by a dispute between the Mexican military commander and governor in California, an Anglo uprising, and landings of marines at various points along the California coast.

---

*Since Texas and the adjacent area to the south were jointly administered as the state of Coahuila, it is hard to say just where the boundary was. In any case the matter was far from clear, and some maps published in the US after 1836 show the boundary to be the Nueces.

‡The declaration of war was signed on May 13, 1846. This followed the main battle between the Mexicans and Taylor's force which occurred on May 7. However Polk did not learn of the battle until after the declaration of war. It was the first skirmish, occurring on April 24, that was used to justify the declaration of war.[17] In any case the first act of war occurred when the US blockaded the Rio Grande, April 12, 1846.[18]

A second campaign was designed, not to take territory, but to force the Mexican government to sign a treaty legitimizing US control over what is now the American Southwest. In order to carry out this campaign General Taylor marched south from Texas. He took Monterrey and Saltillo and on January 23, 1847, he broke the back of Mexican resistance at the Battle of Angostura, near Saltillo. Troops were also landed at Veracruz, which was captured by American forces in February 1847. Then following the route of Cortés, American troops under General Winfield Scott marched to Mexico City, which was taken September 14, 1847.

Even after the declaration of war there was dissent in the US. Congressman Abraham Lincoln challenged Polk on the war saying,[19]

> *Let him answer fully, fairly, and candidly. Let him answer with facts and not with arguments... But if he can not or will not do this— if on any pretence or no pretence he shall refuse or omit it— then I shall be fully convinced of what I more than suspect already— that he is deeply conscious of being in the wrong... How like the half-insane mumblings of a fever dream is the whole war part of his late message!*

Ulysses S. Grant, an infantry lieutenant in the war, stated "even if the annexation [of Texas] could be justified, the manner in which the subsequent war was forced on Mexico cannot."[20]

The causes for the rapid Mexican defeat can be found in both the US and Mexico. The US was relatively united for the war while Mexico was sharply divided by the liberal-conservative struggle. In fact the conservatives often felt more sympathy for the invading Americans than for the liberals whom they felt to be a threat to their privileges in central Mexico. The splits in Mexico were so great that there were rebellions and jockeying for power at the very time American troops were marching from Veracruz to Mexico City. Yucatán even declared itself neutral in the struggle. Mexico had a population of seven million, many of whom were Indians with no stake in the outcome, compared to the US population of 17 million. American arms, especially its artillery, were better, a reflection of America's industrial development.[21] Had there been a government capable of arousing mass support, the results would have been different. As it was, the defense of Mexico was left almost entirely in the hands of the professional army.

As a result of its defeat Mexico was forced to sign the treaty of Guadalupe-Hidalgo, ceding New Mexico, Arizona, Utah, Nevada, California and part of Colorado to the US for $15 million. Thus Mexico lost half its land including the port of San Francisco, the use of Colorado River water, and the rich agricultural lands and gold fields of California. A Mexican writer noted that the principal

FERNANDO CASTRO PACHECO

U.S. Soldier in Veracruz, 1914

difference between the US and Ghengis Kahn was that the US attempted to disguise the spoils of war under the guise of international law.[22]

After the war some 75,000 Mexicans found themselves under US control. Despite the provisions in the Treaty of Guadalupe-Hidalgo providing for Mexicans in areas ceded to the US to keep their lands, ownership soon passed to American hands. Often taxes would be raised beyond the ability of their Mexican owners to pay, so land could be seized for tax delinquency and auctioned off to Americans. Suits challenging legality of land titles were filed in a deliberate attempt to bankrupt owners with legal fees. Crooked judges would consistently rule in favor of Anglos in land matters.[23] Lynching and other acts of violence also served to reduce Mexican holdings.[24]

The 1848 discovery of gold in California led to a rapid influx of Americans and to an increasingly rapid dispossession of Mexicans. As a result in 1849 the population of California was composed of 87,000 Anglos and 13,000 Mexicans.[25] The feelings expressed by Mexicans stranded in the US were remarkably similar to the feelings of the conquered Aztecs quoted in the first chapter:[26]

> *Our inheritance is turned to strangers—*
>   *Our houses to aliens*
> *We have drunken our water for money—*
>   *Our wood is sold to us,*
> *Our necks are under persecution—*
>   *We labor and have no rest.*

Further US expansion at Mexican expense took place with the Gadsden Purchase in 1853. This area, in what today is southern Arizona and New Mexico, was secured for its mineral resources, the building of an east-west railroad, and to pave the way for further expansion toward the Gulf of California.[27] The purchase of the area was facilitated by bribes.[28] The spirit of the negotiations leading up to the sale is indicated by the American negotiator who stated, "If Mexico doesn't sell the area, we shall take it."[29]

From the time of the Gadsden Purchase until the American Civil War there was constant pressure for further expansion into Mexico.[30] In 1857 the American Ambassador to Mexico said, "Give us what we ask for, ... or we'll take it ourselves."[31] In 1858 President Buchanan addressed Congress and stated that parts of Mexican territory should be occupied in order to collect the Mexican debt, and that if the debt wasn't paid, the territory should be annexed.[32]

Given its involvement with a Civil War, the US couldn't play a major role in the struggle between Maximilian and Juárez. Officially the United States embargoed shipment of arms to either party since they were needed for the war effort and there was fear that exported arms might fall into the hands of the Confederacy. Despite the embargo, there was a flow of American arms to both sides of the Mexican conflict.[33]

Generally the US was pro-Juárez since it saw Maximilian as a threat to further US expansion. On April 4, 1864 the US Congress passed a resolution saying "it does not accord with the policy of the United States to acknowledge a monarchial government, erected on the ruins of any republican government in America, under the auspices of any European power."[34] Once the American Civil War was over, US veterans crossed into Mexico and served on both sides. The tendency was for Confederates to fight for Maximilian and for Union veterans to fight with Juárez. At this time the US embargo was lifted and arms began to flow to Juárez's forces. The shipments included modern rifles and artillery used in Juárez's southward march.[35]

After the war there was a major shift in the relations between the US and Mexico. The dominant liberals in Mexico not only welcomed foreign trade, but were in a much better position to resist further American territorial expansion.[36] Americans saw that there was more than one way to profit from Mexico. Secretary of State Seward voiced this opinion when he stated that Americans should "value dollars more, and domination less," and that business expansion into Mexico would lead to its peaceful annexation.[37]

In exchange for recognizing Porfirio Díaz's government, the United States received concessions to build railroads in Mexico.[38] This opened up Mexico to pervasive American influence. The north of Mexico came under especially strong American control. William Randolf Hearst alone had 3 million hectares there.[39] By the end of the Porfiriato, Mexico accounted for two-thirds of all American investment in Latin America.[40] This led to widespread anti-Americanism. Mexicans were excluded from choice jobs with American companies. American conductors and ticket sellers working for US railroads often did not speak Spanish. The degree of American involvement in Mexico is indicated by the fact that the American embassy in Mexico produced more diplomatic correspondence than any other embassy, often a third of all diplomatic correspondence.[41]

Near the end of the Porfiriato the US saw that Díaz was destined to fall, regardless of American policy. The US then began to try to have Díaz replaced and eliminate the possibility of a social revolution.[42] US support shifted from Díaz to other figures in the government, and then to Madero, who was not seen as a threat to US interests. As a result Madero was allowed to openly carry out his efforts to topple Díaz from US soil. In addition, fearing for Mexican sovereignty, Díaz began to favor British over American interests. It was felt that Madero would reverse this trend.[43] Madero was financed by various American businessmen, such as oilman Henry K. Pierce who gave him $685,000 in hopes that he would be repaid with oil concessions once Madero was in power.[44] US Ambassador Wilson said, "The United States hasn't the slightest interest in intervening in Mexico, as long as the present government doesn't fall, or it is not replaced by irresponsible elements."[45]

Once in office Madero began to lose US support. He was never able to effectively control the whole country, and was thus unable to guarantee the safety of American interests. For the first time in Mexican history he applied a tax to oil produced in Mexico.[46] In addition his inability to smash Zapata's rebellion worried the US government.[47] US policies with regard to Madero were not well coordinated, and President Taft, the State Department, and Ambassador Wilson often had conflicting positions.[48]

As was previously noted, Ambassador Wilson conferred

Pershing's Punative Expedition

with Félix Díaz and Huerta during their coup attempt, and helped them draw up the agreement under which they took power. After seizing power Huerta asked Wilson what to do with the deposed president and vice president. Wilson replied, "Do what you think is best for the peace of the country." Huerta correctly took that as an OK to have Madero and Pino Suárez killed.[49] The feeling of the American community in Mexico concerning Madero was that he was a dangerous reformer who couldn't maintain peace or control Zapata. When he was toppled by Huerta the US-owned English language AMERICAN HERALD ran the headline, "Viva Díaz, Viva Huerta!... After years of anarchy a military dictator looks good to Mexico."[50]

Once in power Huerta began to have problems with the US. Initially the US tried to squeeze concessions in exchange for recognition.[51] Failing to get the desired compensation for losses suffered by US citizens and concessions on other points, the US postponed recognizing Huerta until after the inauguration of President Woodrow Wilson. Once Wilson took office he began to apply his moral notions of government to the Mexican situation. He declined to recognize Mexico since the Huerta goverment lacked "constitutional legitimacy."

Furthermore Huerta favored British investment over American investment, further antagonizing US interests.

In February 1914 Wilson lifted the embargo on arms shipped to Mexico. This enabled the Constitutionalists to receive arms shipments by land. Huerta was already receiving arms by sea. Soon afterward American money began to flow to Carranza and oil companies refused to pay taxes to Huerta.[52] As resistance to Huerta strengthened in Mexico, the US began to see getting rid of Huerta as the quickest way to (1.) restore a constitutional government to the liking of President Wilson, (2.) get a Mexican head of state more favorably disposed to the US, and (3.) end the internal strife which was endangering American investments.

To help push Huerta out the United States launched an invasion of Mexico. The pretext chosen for the intervention was the arrest for one and a half hours of eight Americans from the cruiser Dolphin. They had gone into a restricted area at the Port of Tampico. When the port commander only apologized for their arrest, but wouldn't fire a 21-gun salute, President Wilson took this as an excuse to intervene. The invasion force landed at Veracruz, the destination of a load of weapons for Huerta which was arriving on a German ship. On April 21, 1914, American troops landed. There were some 19 Americans killed in the invasion, and at least 200 Mexicans, including cadets at the naval academy, whose resistance was silenced by naval cannons firing on the city.[53] The occupation of Veracruz inflamed anti-Americanism throughout the country and resulted in the stoning of American hotels, newspapers and consulates, and attacks on Americans.[54]

The attack backfired in that Huerta used the invasion to rally people around him in defense of the nation. Carranza, Huerta's foe, even denounced the invasion as an affront to Mexican national sovereignty. For that remark, Wilson ordered that arms once again be embargoed to the Constitutionalists.[55] The US occupation hastened Huerta's downfall, not by depriving him of arms, but by depriving him of custom's receipts. With Huerta gone, the US had no pretext for further occupation of the port, and the US forces withdrew in November 1914.

With Huerta gone the US put its support behind Carranza, seeing him as preferable to the peasant leaders Villa and Zapata. An outstanding example of the support thrown to Carranza was the US permitting Carranza's troops to be carried by rail through US territory to launch an attack on Villa's forces at Agua Prieta, across the border from Douglas, Arizona.

Perhaps in response to this, on March 9, 1916 Villa's forces launched an attack on the town of Columbus, New Mexico, killing 15 US citizens. A week later General John Pershing marched into Mexico on his "punitive" expedition in an attempt to find Villa. Pershing's response to Villa's 500-man raid was a 12,000-man expedition complete with airplanes and mechanized units. Pershing's troops fought a few indecisive skirmishes with both Villista and Carrancista forces, but never achieved their stated aim of "punishing Villa." Had not the US's options been limited by the coming of WW I, perhaps the US would have pressed the attack more vigorously. As it was, Pershing's forces were withdrawn February 5, 1917.

Once Carranza consolidated power he became something of a disappointment to the US. He tripled oil taxes and revised mining legislation to eliminate foreign monopolies. This was followed by the 1917 Constitution which gave the government control over mineral resources. This rather mild assertion of national sovereignty over mineral wealth brought forth cries for US intervention. World War I however blocked any possible action.[56]

Carranza's attitude toward foreign investment was that foreign investments were not only welcome, but they were the key to Mexican prosperity. However he did not want investments to be concentrated in isolated enclaves producing raw materials, but rather to be in industry and commerce. Furthermore he wanted investors to be under Mexican law and not to expect protection by the armed forces of their country of origin.[57] Carranza saw that a complete break with the US would be suicidal and never contemplated it.[58]

The coup in 1920 opened up a whole new ball game. The US had recognized Carranza to strengthen him in his fight against the radical peasant leaders. By 1920 however there were no threats from the left, so the US could afford to pressure Obregón in exchange for recognizing him.

Obregón stalled for three years rather than yielding to US demands to back down on the nationalist provisions in the 1917 Constitution. It was only after the US cut off credit[59] and threatened to support a rival army faction[60] that Obregón backed down. In order to obtain US recognition Obregón signed the Bucareli agreements in August 1923. These agreements limited Mexican government control over foreign interests, especially oil, and established that (1.) expropriated US haciendas could be paid for in bonds, (2.) a size limit would be placed on the amount of land which could be taken from US citizens by the agrarian reform, (3.) oil lands acquired and improved before the 1917 Constitution was ratified were to remain in the hands of oil companies, and (4.) a claims commission was to be set up for handling claims by Americans for war damage or past expropriation.[61] The payoff for these concessions was quick. Not only was the Obregón government recognized, but the US supported Obregón in putting down the 1924 coup attempt by Adolfo de la Huerta, who had the backing of 60% of the army. This support included 17 planes piloted by Americans, 15,000 rifles, and five million cartridges, all on credit.[62]

From the Treaty of Bucareli until the Cárdenas administration there was an era of good feeling between the US and Mexican governments. These good feelings were largely a result of Mexico not threatening US interests. On June 17, 1925 US Secretary of State Kellogg stated:

It must be perfectly clear that this government will continue maintaining the present government in Mexico only so long as it protects American lives and the rights of Americans and lives up to international agreements and obligations.[63]

The constant threat of US intervention during the 1920's led to the de-radicalization of the workers' movement since it was accepted that if workers became radical, the US would intervene.[64]

The US continued to pull Mexico to the right, especially when US Ambassador Dwight Morrow arrived and became a good friend of President Calles. In 1928 Calles said in his State of the Union message that his government was

without any problems with its northern neighbor. Relations with the US have not only changed, but have changed radically and are now on a plane of higher understanding, cooperation and even of sincere cordiality.[65]

Relations deteriorated again during the Cárdenas administration, especially after the 1938 oil nationalization. However they never reached the acrimonious state they did during the 1910-7 period. President Roosevelt's Good Neighbor Policy channeled response into boycotts instead of the open intervention of a generation earlier.[66] The fact that most of the holdings nationalized were British and Dutch also helped pave the way for US acceptance of the nationalization.[67] The oil nationalization fulfilled Carranza's goal of putting foreign investors on equal footing with Mexican industry and commerce, and preventing the uncontrolled exploitation of raw materials by foreigners.[68] Two months after the oil nationalization

Cárdenas stated:
> *Mexico, underpopulated and extensive, has opened its doors to all foreigners who have no humiliating superiority complexes, nor desire anti-social privileges and who come to our soil to further agriculture, industry, science or the arts with their labor, their capital, or their scientific knowledge, which can then enter our way of life and penetrate our collective soul.*[69]

Once the US accepted these ground rules, it found that by competing on an equal footing with Mexicans, it could enter industry and commerce and manage to do better than it had before.[70]

In 1940 Sinclair was the first US oil company to break ranks and accept $8.5 million for its expropriated oil holdings. In 1941, with WW II looming on the horizon, US-Mexican relations were again smoothed over. Mexico agreed to settle outstanding claims by Americans for $40 million, sign a new trade treaty, and in the process obtain credit to purchase machinery. A claims commission was set up to arbitrate the value of the expropriated oil holdings. In 1942 it set compensation for US oil companies at $23,995,991.[71] (Britain settled for $81 million in 1948).

As a result of the boycott which followed the nationalization of the oil industry, Mexico was forced to barter oil to Germany for manufactured goods. However as relations improved with the US, Mexico finally broke relations with the Axis. In May 1942 two Mexican tankers were sunk by German subs in the Gulf of Mexico and Mexico declared war on Germany. Mexico's main contributions to the war effort were raw materials shipped to the US and 200,000 Mexicans who came to the US to work in agriculture and railroad maintenance. Mexico also sent a squadron of pilots to fight the Japanese.

President Alemán set the tone for post-war US-Mexican relations. Truman and Alemán visited each other's capitals, a first for either an American or a Mexican president. Under Alemán US investment in Mexico's economy, the distinctive feature of post-World War II US-Mexican relations, began its rapid rise. This growth of American investment in Mexico is indicated by these figures:[72]

1943	$268 million
1950	$415 million
1960	$795 million
1970	$1797 million
1973	$1993 million

Pershing's Punative Expedition

CHAPTER 29: THE GRINGOS, PRESENT

The United States, smiling or angry, its hand open or clenched, neither sees nor hears us but keeps striding on, and as it does so, enters our land and crushes us.[1]

Relations between the US and Mexico are highly volatile and one day's headline issues are often forgotten nearly as fast as the name of a losing vice-presidential candidate. In the latter part of 1976 there were comments by US congressmen on the raising of a cactus curtain on the Rio Grande and on Mexico going communist, on the rights of American drug prisoners in Mexican jails, as well as other matters which will probably stay in the news longer. Some American labor unions were pressuring for an end to the border industrialization program and the expulsion of illegal Mexican workers in the US. These measures would be a serious blow to Mexico with its already staggering unemployment. There was also a steady decline in revenue from the tourist trade, coupled with the Jewish tourist boycott, which cost Mexico an estimated $300 million.[2] Finally frequent comments about the devaluation of the peso before it actually occurred might have forced the devaluation by scaring people into converting their pesos to dollars.

Most of the important aspects of US-Mexican relations, such as the $3.2 billion US investment,[3] the largely-American foreign debt, and the American influence on the media, have already been discussed. As a result of these factors and its proximity to the US, some 70% of Mexico's foreign trade is with the US.[4] While exports to the US declined from 68.4% of all exports in 1970 to 59.9% in 1975,[5] Mexican dependency on the US increased during this period due to the huge increase in the foreign debt, 70% of which is owed to the US, and the fact that 90% of foreign tourists continue to come from the US.[6]

1. MEXICAN WORKERS IN THE US

The flow of Mexican workers into the US is one of the major immigrant streams of US history. This migration to the US in search of jobs began with the Mexican-American War, when an area the size of modern India was transferred to the US with a population of 75,000 Mexicans and Indians, two-thirds of whom lived in northern New Mexico.[7] For the rest of the 19th century immigration to the US was completely legal; all one had to do was walk across the border. This legal migration was only a trickle and passed 1,000 per year for the first time in 1904.[8]

Immigration increased rapidly after 1910 as people fled the revolution and responded to the labor shortage in the US produced by World War I and the rapid economic expansion in the Southwest.[9] In 1920 the number of Mexican immigrants rose to 51,000.[10]

Despite the formal control over immigration, the flow of Mexican job seekers continued until the depression. At that time the lack of jobs discouraged immigration and many Mexicans were expelled from the US. The flow increased again during World War II as Mexicans came to the US to replace Americans engaged in combat. The US government contracted Mexican workers, called braceros, and then sold labor contracts to growers. This continued throughout the war. In 1943 the Mexican government declared Texas off limits to braceros due to the racial discrimination they experienced there.[11] The program was extended into the post-war period due to pressure from farm interests.

In 1964 as a result of mechanization lowering the demand for farm workers, as well as pressure from US labor, farm worker and church groups,[12] the bracero program was terminated. After that most Mexicans entering the US to seek jobs were illegal aliens without rights, instead of legal and more-or-less protected braceros. These illegal workers were a boon to employers. They not only provided cheap labor but depressed wages for American workers in the areas where the Mexicans were working. They have been especially desirable since they appear at harvest time and then disappear, unlike resident populations which must

[Cartoon: A family watches a TV that says: "THIS SPECIAL PROGRAM ON OUR NATIONAL INDEPENDENCE DAY IS BROUGHT TO YOU BY FORD MOTOR COMPANY, MOBIL OIL, GENERAL FOODS AND THE..."]

be maintained year round. The heavy influx of illegal Mexican workers has displaced many chicano agricultural workers and was instrumental in the rapid urbanization of chicanos since 1960. In many cases chicanos displaced from agricultural jobs were forced into cities where they had few marketable skills.[13]

As agriculture is becoming increasingly mechanized, more illegal workers are taking urban jobs. Only about a third of the illegal workers are now working in agriculture with a third in services and a third in manufacturing.[14] The overwhelming majority of these workers take urban jobs with low wages, few job rights, and high employee turnover. The oversupply of workers drives down the wages of Americans in these sectors. Most frequently the workers with whom the illegal workers compete for jobs are members of racial minority groups. This oversupply of workers also makes unionization difficult. Given the current organization of US society, the worst working conditions occur in areas with an oversupply of labor. The effect of illegal immigrants then is to worsen working conditions for all workers in the areas in which they are employed.[15]

> *The illegal, whatever his motivations and aspirations, probably moves from poverty to greater poverty, and whatever his experiences, the economic and financial benefit for Mexico, for his family and for himself is small. Those who profit are those who employ or smuggle him.*[16]

Employers are provided with a cheap, docile labor force, only 45% of which makes over the minimum wage.[17] Any demands for unionization or wage increases can be met with a threat to report workers to immigration authorities. Employers have turned in workers just before pay day.[18] This avoids having to pay the worker who is deported. Large amounts of money are made from bringing illegal workers into the US, often under dangerous conditions. The Mexican government benefits from this flow of workers in that it is able to postpone major reform in the rural areas from which most illegals come. Illegal workers are highly productive; 77% pay social security, 73% pay income tax, and they rarely use schools or other public services. "Legally or not, the present wave of Latin American immigrants is enriching and benefiting US society."[19] The fact that US laws make coming in without papers a crime, but not hiring of such people, conveniently serves employers who often count on the cooperation of local law enforcement officials to enforce the laws only when it suits them.[20]

In 1976, 750,000 illegal Mexican workers were expelled from the US, and unofficial estimates put the number who entered the US at over one million.[21] Any solution to the problem will be complicated and will involve social, political, diplomatic and racial issues.[22] No one solution, such as deportation, legalization of the workers here, or letting in more workers, can benefit everyone.[23] Echeverría stated what he felt the best long range solution was, "In Mexico, we need to increase the sources of employment. We need to send more resources out into the countryside. We need to organize farmers in a better way. We need to keep them with the land."[24] That however will take some major changes in Mexican priorities. A response not involving major changes in Mexico would be the unionization of the sectors of the US economy where illegal workers are employed. This would remove the economic incentive for employing them, and provide those hired with decent wages and working conditions.[25] In the meantime an "immigration policy that is overwhelmingly dominated by illegal procedures can generate little that is good, for the participants are frequently easy prey for the most exploitative elements in *both* societies."[26]

2. BORDER INDUSTRY

In response to the ending of the bracero program in 1964 and the high rates of unemployment in border areas, the border industrialization program was established. This involved setting up manufacturing plants on the Mexican side of the border where labor-intensive assembly operations could be performed on parts shipped from the US. Once assembled, the product would be shipped back to the US for final processing and sale. These plants are called "maquiladoras," "border plants," "twin plants" ("twin" referring to the other plant in the US which makes the components assembled in Mexico), or simply "runaway plants." This last term emphasizes that often American workers lose jobs when assembly operations are transferred from the US to Mexico. Provisions in the US tariff code make these operations possible by permitting the assembled goods to be brought back into the US with the tariff being charged only on the value of the wages paid to the unskilled assembly workers in Mexico.

The program grew from a dozen plants with three thousand employees in 1965 to one with 84,500 workers employed by 550 firms in 1974. The recession in the US then reduced the demand for maquiladora-produced goods and employment fell to 78,405 in 1975. By the end of 1976, with economic recovery in the US and the devaluation, employment began to climb again, reaching 80,891.[27] The following figures show the value of investment in these plants:[28]

	Amount invested (millions of dollars)	% of total
Electronic/electrical apparatus	$35.1	55
Textiles	4.3	7
Leather and footwear	7.8	13
Food products	1.1	2
Sporting goods and toys	2.1	3
Wood products	1.5	3
Miscellaneous	10.7	17
Total	$63.7	100%

Workers in Mexico have also gotten substantial wage increases. The relation between wages in the US and Mexico was seven to one in 1965, but by 1976 it was down to three to one.[29] Labor costs at border industry plants rose to as much as $9.60 a day before the devaluation. This has made it more attractive to keep the entire assembly operation in the US or move the assembly to some other country.

In 1972 the Mexican government allowed the establishment of maquiladoras in the Mexican interior. In some areas such as San Luis Potosí wages were $4 a day before devaluation.[30] This made it attractive to locate plants there rather than in the relatively high-wage areas along the border. Eighty-three plants were set up in the Mexican interior under this program.[31]

Increasingly assembly operations such as those carried out along the border are being located in countries where receptive governments guarantee no labor organizing or strikes, a problem to management along the increasingly well-organized and politicized Mexican border. Some of the wages reported for areas competing with Mexico for cheap labor have been Korea with 38¢ per hour, plus room and board,[32] the Dominican Republic with $15 a week,[33] Hong Kong with 38¢ an hour, and Taiwan with 42¢ an hour.[34] Economic recovery in the US is increasing the demand for cheap labor. However it is not clear if the jobs will go back to Mexico or to other cheap labor areas. The devaluation of the peso in September 1976 should make Mexico more attractive, although subsequent wage demands by labor may eliminate much of the advantage gained.

Border industries have done little to solve the employment problem. Some 90% of the workers in these industries are women,[35] usually in the 17-24 age range. Often these women were not in the labor force before but left home and took jobs when the maquiladoras opened. This left the previously unemployed still without jobs and provided no jobs for the stream of migrants which continued to come from rural areas to border cities. The maquiladoras have provided employment to only 2.4% of these migrants.[36] To compound the problem, as employment in the maquiladoras declined, the women who had been working in them began to look for other jobs, worsening the unemployment problem.

The presence of the maquiladora has helped to create a unique bicultural, mutually dependent region. The hope for jobs, higher wages and the proximity of the US has led to massive migration, leaving the border area the most highly urbanized region in Mexico, with 75% living in cities with over 100,000 population.[37] Maquiladora workers crossed over the border and spent two thirds of their salaries on the US side before the devaluation,[38] reducing the benefits of the program to the Mexican economy and making US merchants reliant on the program. Since the 1976 devaluation US goods have largely been priced out of the reach of maquiladora workers whose salaries are paid in pesos, and many retail stores on the US side of the border have closed.

The maquiladora has also failed to have the anticipated positive effects on the Mexican economy. The multinational corporations operating the maquiladoras have not changed their production techniques to use Mexican components and raw materials. This has left the maquiladora an isolated enclave highly dependent on factors beyond Mexican control, such as foreign labor costs and recessions in the US, where 75% of the maquiladora output is shipped.[39]

OH, I LOVE ESTOS MEXICANS, SPECIALLY CUANDO HABLAR DE DIGNIDAD, SOBERANITY AND INDEPENDENCIAS!
Sears
Magnavox
Monsanto
CIBA
SUNBEAM
SCOTT
KENT
ADAMS
JOHN DEERE
CYDSA
IBM
ITT
SHERATON
PEPSI
Nordson
77

The maquiladora, despite the fact much of the money paid to its workers has been spent on the US side of the border, has contributed to Mexico's trade balance. In 1974 maquiladoras brought in $443 million, 7% of Mexico's total export of goods and services.[40] The balance of payments however is being helped at the expense of Mexican workers who are not only being paid low wages, but increasingly being deprived of benefits due to all Mexican workers. Workers must put up with charro-led unions, and 28-day "temporary" contracts signed month after month to prevent workers from getting the protection accorded a permanent employee. The government disrupts union activity, as occurred when police attacked workers in Nogales in April 1975.[41] The government is also coming under increased pressure to reduce labor costs and fringe benefits to prevent plants from moving to areas with even cheaper labor.

The question of the effect of the maquiladora on US workers is more complicated than simply deciding if an assembly job will be located in the US or Mexico. Such decisions involve the possibility of locating assembly in a third country. Also if the decision is made to assemble goods in the US, the possibility must be faced that the goods produced will be too expensive to compete with goods made entirely with foreign parts and labor. Attempts to regulate the imports of such foreign-made goods will risk trade barriers being raised against goods made in the US, which in turn could cost more American jobs than are currently lost to border industries.

The AFL-CIO position is that maquiladoras involve slave labor taking jobs away from American workers.[42] An AFL-CIO spokesman noted, "In Mexico, the legacy of the American-based multinational has been misery. American workers have lost their jobs, Mexican workers have a life of slums, disease and delinquency."[43] Alternatives to the maquiladora usually involve shifting unemployment from one part of the world to another. This is a clear example of the effect of relying on multinationals for so much of world development.

3. AMERICAN ORGANIZATIONS IN MEXICO

There is a wide variety of American organizations in Mexico. Some of these organizations are branches of the American government which openly further US interests. The Agency for International Development (AID), for example, does feasibility studies for private US investors, recruits investors, gives them advice, and helps make local contacts.[44] The United States Information Agency (USIA) stated in one of its memos that its task was "helping achieve United States foreign policy objectives by (a.) influencing public attitudes in other nations, and (b.) serving as an advisory and information source to policy-making organizations."[45]

There are also a number of private organizations paving the way for American investors. The Council of the Americas, backed by 100 of the largest corporations in Latin America, puts pressure on governments, international agencies, and politicians to prevent moves which would be damaging to the business climate.[46] Americans do 80% of the research which is done in Mexico.[47] Such research develops techniques which depend on supplies only available from multinational corporations. Even in areas with no immediate economic importance, research is often dominated by Americans. The Summer Institute of Linguistics, an American group doing missionary work among Indians and translating the Bible into Indian languages, has helicopters, airplanes, radio networks, and often more resources in an area than the INI, the National Indian Institute.[48]

Another US agency maintaining the status quo is the CIA. Given its clandestine nature, only limited information is available concerning its operations. CIA agents writing about their work have at least provided an idea how the CIA operates. Philip Agee revealed that the CIA station chief, then Winston Scott, had close ties with President Díaz Ordaz[49] and then-Interior Minister Echeverría.[50] Agee published the names of 37 agents. The NEW YORK TIMES list of heads of state who had received CIA money included Echeverría.[51] Estimates have put the total number of CIA agents in Mexico at 200.[52]

Agee noted that operations in Mexico were rather boring, and largely confined to operating observation posts, postal intercepts, and telephone taps.[53] Absent from Mexico were the constant manipulation and plotting that Agee took part in while stationed in Ecuador and Uruguay. The reason was that "Mexican security forces are so effective in stamping out the extreme left that we don't have to worry."[54] Agee noted that if "the government were less effective we would, of course, get going to promote repression."[55] He estimated that the agency had 50 employees in Mexico with a budget of $5.5 million.[56] Díaz Ordaz's price for cooperation was a car bought for his girl friend with CIA money.[57]

Howard Hunt reported an incident involving a visit to China by a Mexican leftist. Upon the Mexican's return copies of a Chinese newspaper turned up quoting him as saying that the Chinese were doing fine, but that the unsophisticated Mexican population would never reach that level. That of course caused quite a furor, especially after the type in the article was found to match the type used in other articles in the paper. What happened was that as soon as the Mexican left China, the CIA obtained a copy of the paper announcing his departure, cut out the announcement, and wrote its own article saying that Mexicans were unsophisticated, after having made type identical to that in the rest of the paper.[58]

On a more mundane level there are many organizations established by Americans who live in Mexico. These organizations serve the 11,440 Americans who lived in Mexico in 1970. This American colony is the largest in the Western Hemisphere.[59] The directory of American organizations in Mexico gives an idea of the number of these groups and their diversity:

ABC Hospital, American Benevolent Society, American Bible Society, American Chamber of Commerce, American Institute of Mining and Metallurgical Engineers, American School, American Society of Jalisco, American Society of Mexico, Amistad Magazine, Aneqeh Temple, Aztec Bridge Club.[60]

The list goes on for 76 other organizations. Perhaps the most influential of these groups is the American Chamber of Commerce, with 2100 of the largest corporations in

Mexico as members. It has a budget of nearly $1 million a year, and is closely tied to international business groups. The Chamber works with the US government in Mexico, maintains lobbyists in Washington, and publishes information favorable to US investment in Mexico.[61] This is just one of the many official and unofficial organizations which make up the network of lenders, planners, and advisors who pave the way for American investment.[62]

4. DRUGS

About 90% of the marijuana in the US is from Mexico[63] and according to the US Drug Enforcement Agency 80% of the heroin comes from there.[64] Mexican drugs coming into the US market have an estimated street value of $20 billion a year.[65] To supply this market a Mexican and Mexican-American run drug network has sprung up, largely replacing the Mafia. Operating out of Northwestern Mexico, these drug runners have been named the "Nuestra Cosa," the Spanish equivalent of "Cosa Nostra."[66] American and Mexican government cooperation in eradicating the drug trade have received much publicity. However since Mexican businessmen and officials are in the drug traffic, and Drug Enforcement Agency efforts are ineffectual,[67] there has been little success in curtailing drug shipments.[68]

The poor peasant with little other alternative for a cash crop can make a tidy $3200 a year growing poppies.[69] The heroin purchased at 6000 pesos a kilo in Mexico sells for 25 million pesos a kilo on the street in the US.[70] The Mexican peasant growing marijuana gets about $16 a kilo.[71]

Drugs are a major item in the economy of some areas. The mayor of Culiacán, Sinoloa, a major trans-shipment point for drugs, complained that peasants were being priced out of the food market due to inflation caused by massive drug sales. He noted that if you wanted to find out who was dealing, all you had to do was see who had the largest accounts in the local bank. Also teenage drug use in the town was increasing rapidly.[72] The drug traffic is producing an increase in rural violence. In one instance eight soldiers were killed when dope dealers in Michoacán ambushed an army patrol.[73] Much drug-related violence also spills over into the Culiacán area where there were 150 drug-related murders in 1976.[74]

Much publicity has been generated concerning the plight of Americans who have been jailed for drug offenses. While many are guilty of the offenses charged, their experience in Mexican jails has been a shocking exposure to the seamier side of Mexican society. Facilities tend to be greatly overcrowded. Prisoners are often held for years without trial. Many of the trials which occur are pro forma matters facilitated by confessions written in Spanish and signed by persons unable to read them. Those reluctant to sign are coerced into doing so. Large amounts of money are extracted from prisoners and their families in frequently vain attempts to secure their release. The WALL STREET JOURNAL remarked in an editorial that "it is becoming increasingly difficult to brush aside recurrent allegations of beating and extortion of US prisoners in Mexico."[75] It appears that this harshness has produced a backlash that will result in more lenient treatment and perhaps a prisoner exchange.

The US government has supplied 14 helicopters, 3 light planes,[76] and defoliants used in the Mexican anti-drug campaign, as well as $14 million a year to finance it.[77] US drug enforcement agents work closely with their Mexican and other Latin American counterparts. These US drug agents are totally removed from any of the restraints placed on law enforcement officers in the US. They function in much the same way as CIA agents abroad, disregarding both US law and that of the country in which they are operating. In several instances they have arranged kidnappings in Latin America so persons can be flown to the US and taken into custody.[78]

5. CULTURE

One of the casualties of the barrage of multinational advertising has been traditional Mexican culture. Increasingly Mexicans find themselves eating pancakes for breakfast, Burger Boy hamburgers for lunch, and Shakey's Pizza for supper. Their babies get Gerber Baby Food, and on their Philco Radios and TV's they listen to rock and roll. This introduction of American culture sometimes reaches the absurd. I visited an Indian village in Puebla, accessible only by trail. Few there even spoke Spanish, yet their transistor radios were blaring rock and roll, in English, broadcast from Mexico City.

A classical example of the influx of American culture is provided by Coke and Pepsi. In 1960 there were 1000 independent soft drink bottlers in Mexico, overwhelmingly Mexican owned. Since then 698 of them have been absorbed by Coke and Pepsi.[79] The great assets of multinationals and slick media campaigns paved the way for this takeover. In some cases Pepsi simply moved into town, bought all the competitor's bottles from retail stores and then let the independent bottler collapse. In Ciudad Obregón the Pepsi warehouse was found to have 43,200 bottles belonging to competitors.[80]

Soft drinks not only contribute to malnutrition by diverting money from traditional fresh fruits and drinks, but cost so little to produce that much of the purchase cost can be reinvested in ads to make people drink even more Cokes and Pepsis.[81] Soft drink consumption increased 284% from 1960 to 1974; $397 million was spent to purchase them in 1974.[82]

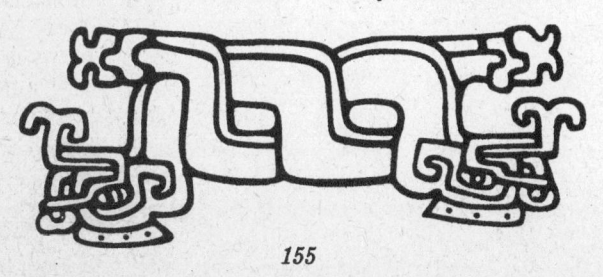

CHAPTER 30: ENVIRONMENT

1. EROSION

One of the oldest environmental problems Mexico faces is erosion. Soil erosion began with overgrazing during the colonial period and has continued to the present. Half of all agricultural land has been damaged by erosion to some degree.[1] Each year some 150,000 hectares of land are rendered useless by erosion, of which only 25,000 are ever restored to production.[2] Currently some 40,000,000 hectares are so badly eroded that restoration is uneconomical.[3]

2. WATER

Water pollution is especially serious in rivers draining the central Mexican plateau. The Pánuco, the most polluted river, receives the untreated sewage of the ten million residents of the Federal District. This comes to some 688,972 tons a year, without even including the industrial wastes dumped in the river.[4] The second most polluted river is the Lerma, which flows west from Mexico City. It passes through Toluca where 9600 kilograms of organic pollutants are dumped into it each day. Later the Lerma passes oil refineries and other industries acquiring more pollutants and so much oil that at times the river can be ignited. It then reaches Lake Chapala, where it discharges 206 cubic meters of solid waste each day.[5]

The 1975 law to Prevent and Control Environmental Pollution set 1977 as the date by which the clean up of water must begin. Some companies began work before this date. Paper companies alone have spent some $20 million, much of which was recovered by recycling wastes.[6]

3. AIR

Air pollution is most severe in Mexico City, although other areas such as Monterrey suffer from it as well. Air in Mexico City is from two to five times as polluted as Los Angeles, depending on which pollutant is being measured. (This is roughly the equivalent to smoking two packs of cigarettes a day.)[7] This degree of pollution results from the concentration of industry in the Mexico City area, the location of Mexico City in a basin surrounded on all sides by mountains, and the number of motor vehicles in the area. It is estimated that vehicles cause up to 70% of the air pollution in Mexico City,[8] with most of the rest coming from industry and wind-blown dust. Each day 400 new vehicles are added to the total of 2 million which operate in the Federal District.[9]

4. CENTRALIZATION

The gigantic agglomeration which is the Federal District, shows signs of deterioration in its population, flora and fauna. New-born children cannot stand the environment we adults have created.[10]

Many of Mexico City's problems result from so many people being concentrated in so small an area. With a population density of 2,787 per square kilometer, the valley has the world's highest population density.[11] The following figures indicate how resources have been concentrated in the Mexico metropolitan area:[12]

	% of national total
Industrial production	50%
Gasoline	33%
Commercial activity	60%
Institutes of Higher Learning	75%
Doctors	50%
Telephones	50%
Automobiles	50%

The concentration of resources in Mexico City has been increasing over the last few decades. In 1940 only 35.5% of industrial production was in this area.[13] US companies have greatly contributed to this process, having located 81% of their manufacturing investments in the Federal District and the adjacent State of Mexico.[14]

5. POPULATION

Does population growth RETARD economic growth? The answer to this first question is seriously confounded by the fact that economic growth AFFECTS population growth as well as vice versa.[15]

Mexico's birth rate has been about the same for the 150 years since its independence. In the first 50 years of independence the population only grew at about 0.6% a year since the death rate was nearly as high as the birth rate. During this time Mexico lost half her area in the Mexican-American War. This territorial loss was attributed to the low population density in the area taken by the US and gave rise to a general pro-natalist mentality in Mexico.[16] Toward the end of the 1800's the death rate began to decrease slightly, and from 1880 to 1906 the population rose at 1.3% a year.[17] After a brief interruption by the revolution the rate of population growth started up again. The growth rate was 1.7% a year in 1930, and then increased to its present 3.4% a year.[18]

The basic reason for the dramatic increase in population growth is the decrease in the death rate since the turn of the century. Around 1900 the death rate (deaths per 1000 population) dropped below 40, then in 1930 it was 26.67, in 1950 16.15, and by 1960 it was 9.15.[19] This change in the death rate resulted from widespread vaccination, antibiotics, insecticides, increased medical care, improved drinking water and sewage treatment, and a generally higher standard of living.

Despite the drop in the death rate there has been no

corresponding drop in the birth rate. In 1930 the birth rate was 49.4 per thousand, and in 1970 it was still 43.[20] Since then it has gone back up to 47.2.[21] The result of this continuing high birth rate is reflected in the population figures for this century.[22]

Year	Population	% increase over previous decade
1910	15,000,000	
1920	14,335,000	-4.4%
1930	16,553,000	15.5%
1940	19,654,000	18.7%
1950	25,791,000	31.2%
1960	34,923,000	35.4%
1970	48,377,000	38.5%

No other country in the world has as many people with as high a rate of population growth as Mexico. The population will double each 17 years with the current 3.5% rate of population increase. In 1976 Mexico's population was 62 million and by the end of the López Portillo administration in 1982 it will be 78 million.[23] More babies are born in Mexico than in the United States and Canada combined.[24] Furthermore there is little sign of a decrease in population growth. The Ministry of Health and Public Assistance stated that from 1970 to 1973 the rate of population growth reached 3.9%.[25] The Inter-American Development Bank estimated it at a whopping 4.2%.[26] The most recent estimate shows a decrease to 3.2% due to the use of family planning techniques by 2.2 million women.[27]

Most observers had expected the Mexican birth rate to begin to decline with increased urbanization and industrialization, as happened in Europe, the US, and Japan. The decline in these areas, starting as early as the late 1700's in Europe, indicates that it is the desire for fewer children, not the number of family planning programs or the availability of sophisticated contraceptives, which produces a decline in birth rate.[28] The continued high birth rate in Mexico can be attributed to a number of causes. Nearly half the population still lives in rural areas where children can be used in agricultural labor. This makes them an economic asset, not a liability. In families whose parents are too poor to send a child to school the earnings of several children are often pooled to put one through school. Once through school this child will hopefully get a relatively well-paying job and then help the others through school. Given the lack of adequate programs for supporting the elderly, parents want to be sure that there are children to support them in old age. The high death rate in poor families means that parents have to have several children to insure that some survive. These same economic arguments apply in urban areas such as Mexico City where much of the population is impoverished. There children not only support elderly parents but can be sent out on the street to sell or do odd jobs and bring in additional income. This indicates that it is poverty which breeds overpopulation, and not the other way around.[29]

The average number of children for rural mothers is 5.7, compared to 4.4 in urban areas.[30] The desire for large families is reinforced by the deeply ingrained macho ethic, the feeling that you aren't really a man unless you have many children. Also there is a time lag between the time when children cease to die in large numbers and the time when birth rates decline in response to this change. Finally the Catholic Church is strongly opposed to birth control. Even a Catholic country though will have a low birth rate if the population so desires, as is evidenced by Italy with its 1.1% population growth.

Echeverría came out against family planning in his inaugural address, but by 1972 he had reversed himself and advocated family planning. Efforts to lower the birth rate were pushed with radio spots such as "Let's be productive, not reproductive." Posters in Mexico City's subway proclaimed, "My daddy and mommy have only a few kids, and therefore they have time to be with us and be happy." The posters followed the advertising norm and portrayed a very light skinned family. The government has produced radio soap operas dealing with the plight of pregnant women and their macho lovers. The approach to birth control has been very low-keyed and has consistently stressed that birth control, or family planning as it is usually called, is voluntary. By the end of 1976, 2757 government-run family planning centers were in operation.[31]

Much of what is defined as overpopulation in Mexico is simply a lack of jobs.

If the root cause of the world population crisis is poverty, then to end it we must abolish poverty. And if the cause of poverty is the grossly unequal distribution of wealth, then to end poverty, and with it the population crisis, we must distribute that wealth, among nations and within them.[32]

Societies that have created jobs and social institutions making children unnecessary for survival must decide what the most appropriate level of population is for them. The Vietnamese[33] and Chinese[34] have decided it is wise to limit population growth. Thanks to institutions such as the commune, the Chinese have been quite successful at limiting family size, in marked contrast to India which has had little success. Cuba on the other hand, even though families there do not need children for survival, would like to see a larger population since it has low population density and large expanses of fertile land.

Population density, soil, and climate are some of the factors to consider in making decisions on desirable population size. If Mexico had the same population density as Great Britain, it would have a population of 650 million. Of course much of Mexico is desert, mountainous, or tropical land unsuitable for agriculture. Another factor to be considered is that a rapidly growing population has a much higher proportion of non-productive children than a stable one. Since these children are not productive, they must be supported by adults who have a lower living standard. Also the living standard of the population as a whole is lowered by the need to make investments such as housing, hospitals, schools, and roads to accommodate the increased population. A rising population will often find itself lacking in a number of vital resources. As populations increase, there is often no new land which can easily be put into production nor cheap water supplies to tap. Large populations also use up non-renewable resources such as oil faster than do small ones.

CHAPTER 31: THE FUTURE

Rodolfo Stavenhagen, a Mexican social scientist, defined three basic courses which Mexico may follow.[1] The first is to continue under increasing influence of the multinational corporation, a process sometimes called Puertoricanization. This refers to the experience of Puerto Rico, the area in Latin America most influenced by the multinational. The results of this course of development are most pronounced in Mexico City. They were described by a writer arriving in Mexico City from Cuba, where such results are conspicuously absent:

A skyline dominated by massive billboards greeted us in Mexico: "Beefeater Gin for a Perfect Martini," "Pepsi," "Enjoy Coca-Cola," "Nescafe Symbol of Friendship," "Holiday Inn Host to the World." The Americanization of Latin America seemed overwhelming after de-Americanized Cuba.

Mexico was building a new Colonel Sanders Kentucky Fried Chicken emporium, the Colonel's "finger lickin' good" slogan translated to read, "It will make your fingers good to lick." I passed up the Colonel's chicken and asked for a taco from a street vendor whose cart was on the Paseo De La Reforma. He had only hotdogs. The store window displays along the Paseo offered Maxwell House instant coffee; Hershey bars; Aunt Jemima hot cakes; V-8 vegetable juice; Del Monte canned tropical fruit; Gordon's distilled dry gin; Ballantine's finest Scotch Wiskey; Toastmaster air conditioners; Hoover vacuum cleaners; Aqua Velva; and Max Factor lipstick.[2]

A second possibility is that Mexico could continue capitalist development, but manage to chart a course independent of the multinationals. This would require a strong government to provide leverage to push the

HECTOR GARCIA

multinationals aside, and more Latin American integration to offset the power of the US. Similarly such changes would require the mass support of the population just as the changes under Cárdenas had mass support. This course is probably the least likely of the three courses since independent capitalist development often tends to come back under the control of the multinationals after a short period. Note the experience in Peru since its attempt for greater economic autonomy in 1968. If such efforts don't fall under foreign control again, they are likely to mobilize the population to such a degree that the society will be carried on to the third alternative.

This third alternative is socialism, the one solution which has provided a Latin American country with the opportunity to eliminate such problems as massive illiteracy, malnutrition, lack of medical care, unemployment, conspicuous consumption by the wealthy few, and lack of national dignity. Before the Cuban Revolution, Cuba shared these problems with Mexico. It no longer does. Presently there is no indication of how such a transformation might take place. However it is worth noting that the major revolutions of the twentieth century have each triumphed by following an uncharted path. The common factor guaranteeing this triumph has been "an incurable optimism and an unbreakable faith in the potential capabilities of humanity."[3]

GLOSSARY

ALCABALA: A tax on the shipment of goods from one area within a colony (or country) to another within the same colony; also a tax on sales.
CACIQUE: A rural strongman.
CAUDILLO: A strong man, often with both political and military power.
CREOLE: A person of European descent born in the New World (in Spanish, *criollo*).
CIENTIFICOS: The economic planners of President Porfirio Díaz.
CNC: The national peasant organization.
CONSTITUTIONALIST: The army or political followers of Venustiano Carranza.
CROM: The national labor organization founded in 1918.
CTM: The national labor organization founded by Cárdenas.
EJIDO: A farm established under the agrarian reform.
ENCOMENDERO: The holder of an encomienda grant.
ENCOMIENDA: A grant entitling its holder to collect tribute from the Indians living in a certain area. Such a grant, in theory, did not give its holder ownership of the land or the right to control Indians living in the area.
HACENDADO: The owner of a hacienda.
HACIENDA: A very large ranch or farm.
HECTARE: The metric unit of land area, equals 2.471 acres.
MERCANTILISM: The economic system preceding modern capitalism, generally involving a relatively small producer, who sold to an independent shipper, who sold to an independent retailer.
MESTIZO: A person of mixed ancestry, especially Indian and European.
PENINSULAR: A person born on the (Iberian) Peninsula, thus, a Spaniard.
PEON: An agricultural worker of low status.
PORFIRIATO: The presidency of Porfirio Díaz, 1876-1911.
PORRO: Goon.
REPARTIMIENTO (or coatequil): An Indian village's requirement to supply a certain number of laborers to Spanish employers. A village would be assigned a quota of workers based on its population. The individuals filling the quota would work for a fixed period, often a week. Then their village would send workers to replace them, thus providing a continual supply of labor to the employer.
VICEROY: An official appointed by the king to administer a colony.

REFERENCES:

Chapter 1: pp. 1-4

1. León-Portilla 1962: 4-14; Prescott 1931: I/195-6.
2. León-Portilla 1962: 13.
3. Benítez 1957: 53.
4. Díaz del Castillo 1956: 86.
5. León-Portilla 1962: 33.
6. Cortés 1971: 66.
7. Díaz del Castillo 1956: 122.
8. Cortés 1971: 69-70.
9. Benítez 1957: 157.
10. Prescott 1931: I/274.
11. Gibson 1966: 39.
12. Benítez 1957: 182.
13. Casas 1965: 67-9.
14. Benítez 1957: 184.
15. Prescott 1931: I/197.
16. León-Portilla 1962: 51.
17. León-Portilla 1962: 66.
18. López Rosado 1968-9: II/112.
19. Cortés 1971: 86.
20. Paz 1961: 93.
21. Teja Zabre 1935: 123.
22. Gibson 1964: 509.
23. León-Portilla 1962: xxvi.
24. McNeill 1976: 202-7.
25. Cortés 1971: 249.
26. Cortés 1971: 188.
27. Prescott 1931: II/258.
28. Calderón de la Barca 1966: 708, note.
29. Prescott 1931: II/286-7.
30. Prescott 1931: I/315.
31. Quoted in Cortés 1962: xxxv.
32. Prescott 1931: I/149.
33. Teja Zabre 1935: 119.
34. Quoted in León-Portilla 1962: 137-8.

Chapter 2: pp. 5-11

1. Sunkel 1970: 278; Semo 1973: 17, 121.
2. Gibson 1964: 78.
3. Cué Cánovas 1946: I/82.
4. *Hispanic American Historical Review* 1971: 435.
5. Borah 1951: 35-6.
6. Wolf 1959: 206.
7. Alperovich 1967: 53.
8. Chevalier 1963: 2.
9. Chevalier 1963: 314.
10. Chevalier 1963: 277.
11. *Historia y Sociedad*, Jan.-March 1969, p. 14.
12. Wolf 1959: 204.
13. Semo 1973: 258.
14. Cumberland 1968: 101.
15. *Hispanic American Historical Review* 1969: 426.
16. Sunkel 1970: 289.
17. Stein & Stein 1970: 100.
18. Semo 1973: 151.
19. Alperovich 1967: 36.
20. López Rosado 1968-9: III/246.
21. Sunkel 1970: 282.
22. Quoted in Aguilar 1974: 40.
23. Liss 1975: 83.
24. Gibson 1966: 85.
25. Cué Cánovas 1946: I/19.
26. Alperovich 1967: 35.
27. Greenleaf 1967: 388.
28. López Gallo 1975: 47.
29. Semo 1973: 133.
30. Gibson 1964: 114.
31. Gibson 1966: 84.
32. Sotelo Inclán 1970: 49.
33. Weckman 1967: 14.
34. *Hispanic American Historical Review* 1973: 399.
35. Quoted in Benítez 1965: 35.
36. Sotelo Inclán 1970: 46.
37. Semo 1973: 83-4.
38. Semo 1973: 90.
39. Gibson 1964: 196.
40. Alperovich 1967: 66-70.
41. Cué Cánovas 1946: I/142.
42. Gibson 1964: 150.
43. Quoted in *Historia y Sociedad*, Jan.-March 1969, p. 34.
44. Cumberland 1968: 50.
45. *Historia Mexicana*, July-Sept. 1962, p. 5.
46. Semo 1973: 199.
47. Semo 1973: 208.
48. Aguirre Beltrán 1976: 125.
49. Aguirre Beltrán 1972: 234.
50. Cué Cánovas 1946: I/143.
51. *Hispanic American Historical Review* 1971: 81.
52. Mariátegui 1971: 4.
53. Alperovich 1967: 50.
54. *Hispanic American Historical Review* 1971: 342.
55. *Latin American Research Review*, Spring 1972, pp. 6-7.
56. Alperovich 1967: 87.
57. Semo 1973: 108.
58. López Gallo 1975: 22.
59. Stein & Stein 1970: 4.
60. Frank 1972: 46-7.
61. Paz 1961: 117.
62. Alperovich 1967: 81.

Chapter 3: pp. 12-15

1. Wolf 1969: 7.
2. Cumberland 1968: 106.
3. Villoro 1953: 25.
4. Aguirre Beltrán 1972: 234.
5. Florescano 1971: 218.
6. Villoro 1953: 17.
7. Alperovich 1967: 104.
8. Chávarri 1960: 37.
9. Chávarri 1960: 43.
10. Chávarri 1960: 55.
11. Chávarri 1960: 71.
12. Cumberland 1968: 113.
13. Cumberland 1968: 116.
14. *Siempre*, March 29, 1972, p. 53.
15. Brandenberg 1964: 32.
16. Quoted in Sotelo Inclán 1970: 200.
17. Cumberland 1968: 133-4.
18. Quoted in Sotelo Inclán 1970: 214.
19. Alperovich 1967: 208.
20. Alperovich 1967: 209.
21. Villoro 1953: 167.
22. Peña 1975: 95.
23. Alperovich 1967: 205.
24. Cué Cánovas 1946: II/46.

Chapter 4: pp. 15-19

1. Cué Cánovas 1946: II/68.
2. Cumberland 1968: 141.
3. Cué Cánovas 1946: II/68.
4. Cumberland 1968: 145.
5. Hale 1968: 117.
6. Hale 1968: 160.
7. Sotelo Inclán 1970: 253.
8. Hansen 1971: 134.
9. Leal 1975: 9.
10. Furtado 1970: 22-3.
11. Tannenbaum 1975: 8.
12. Paz 1961: 124.
13. Borah 1976: 32.
14. Calderón de la Barca 1966: 445.
15. Quoted in Hale 1968: 239.
16. Hale 1968: 237.
17. García Cantú 1969: 55-79.
18. Hale 1968: 241.
19. Alperovich 1967: 221.
20. Morison 1965: 552.
21. Tannenbaum 1975: 10.
22. Keremitsis 1973: 33.
23. Alperovich 1967: 225.
24. Alperovich 1967: 226.
25. Leal 1974: 7.
26. Leal 1975: 8.
27. Moreno Toscano & Florescano 1976: 84.
28. Fernández & May 1972: 9.
29. González 1976: 16-7.
30. Belenki 1966: 45.
31. Alperovich 1967: 259.
32. Brandenberg 1964: 35.
33. Cué Cánovas 1946: II/69.
34. Cué Cánovas 1946: II/192.
35. Cumberland 1968: 183.
36. Connor & Faulk 1971: 119.

Chapter 5: pp. 19-24

1. Paz 1961: 88.
2. Leal 1975: 13.
3. Belenki 1966: 23.
4. Bazant 1976: 159.
5. Belenki 1966: 29.
6. Cockcroft 1968: 28.
7. Frank 1972: 63-4.
8. Quoted in Bazant 1976: 163.
9. Quoted in González 1976: 50.

10. Cockcroft 1968: 28.
11. Belenki 1966: 51.
12. Sotelo Inclán 1970: 318.
13. Keremitsis 1973: 44.
14. Belenki 1966: 83.
15. Belenki 1966: 81.
16. Belenki 1966: 97.
17. Quoted in Belenki 1966: 103.
18. Belenki 1966: 148.
19. Quoted in Belenki 1966: 148.
20. Belenki 1966: 149.
21. González 1976: 11-2.
22. *Revista de la UNAM*, July 1972, p. 52.
23. Calderón 1972: 19.
24. Calderón 1972: 28.
25. Vernon 1963: 37.
26. Paz 1961: 128.
27. Alperovich & Rudenko 1969: 17.
28. Alperovich & Rudenko 1969: 18.
29. Cockcroft 1968: 56.
30. Cumberland 1968: 191.
31. *Problemas del Desarrollo*, Oct.-Dec. 1969, pp. 79-80.
32. Córdova 1973: 18-19.
33. Córdova 1973: 64.
34. Cockcroft 1972: 47.
35. Cockcroft 1968: 29.
36. López Gallo 1975: 267.
37. US Senate 1920: II/2326.
38. Brandenberg 1964: 39.
39. Sotelo Inclán 1970: 508.
40. Galeano 1973: 60.
41. Castaneda 1971: 167.
42. Alperovich & Rudenko 1969: 49.
43. Keremitsis 1973: 199.
44. Keremitsis 1973: 210.
45. Quoted in Turner 1969: xiii.
46. Córdova 1973: 18.
47. Coatsworth 1976: II/43.
48. Hansen 1971: 23.
49. Cumberland 1968: 192.
50. Cumberland 1968: 204.

Chapter 6: pp. 24-35

1. Córdova 1973: 114.
2. Gilly 1971: 45.
3. *Latin American Perspectives*, Summer 1975, pp. 46-7.
4. Cockcroft 1968: 36.
5. Silva Herzog 1972: I/57.
6. Wolf 1969: 24.
7. Córdova 1973: 22.
8. Larov 1960: 95.
9. Gilly 1971: 295.
10. Womack 1969: 51.
11. Sotelo Inclán 1970: 534.
12. Lieuwen 1968: 12.
13. Silva Herzog 1972: I/226.
14. Gilly 1971: 59.
15. Córdova 1973: 188.
16. Larov 1960: 106.
17. Silva Herzog 1972: I/232.
18. Quoted in Córdova 1973: 190.
19. Córdova 1973: 151.
20. Córdova 1973: 153.
21. Gilly 1971: 71.
22. Gilly 1971: 75.
23. Gilly 1971: 77-8.
24. Cumberland 1952: 234.
25. Cumberland 1972: 12.
26. Córdova 1973: 33.
27. Calderón 1972: 43.
28. Millon 1969: 19.
29. Silva Herzog 1972: II/40-1.
30. Gómez 1972: 14.
31. Silva Herzog 1972: II/22.
32. Córdova 1973: 23.
33. Gilly 1971: 88.
34. *Hispanic American Historical Review* 1973: 521.
35. *Siempre*, Jan. 12, 1977, p. ix; Katz 1976: 261.
36. Katz 1976: 265.
37. Katz 1976: 269.
38. Quoted in Katz 1976: 269.
39. Katz 1976: 269.
40. Katz 1976: 270.
41. Katz 1976: 272.
42. Reed 1914: 127.
43. Gilly 1971: 94-5. (For a more complete description of the social background of Villa's army, see: *Siempre*, Jan. 12, 1977, p. ix.)
44. Gilly 1971: 100.
45. Gilly 1971: 112.
46. Gilly 1971: 115-6.
47. Córdova 1973: 165.
48. Gilly 1971: 135.
49. Gilly 1971: 142.
50. Gilly 1971: 144.
51. Gilly 1971: 154.
52. Millon 1969: 28.
53. Cockcroft 1968: 228.
54. *Latin American Perspectives*, Spring 1974, p. 138.
55. Gilly 1971: 188.
56. Womack 1969: 168.
57. Womack 1969: 219.
58. Gilly 1971: 235.
59. Gilly 1971: 235.
60. Womack 1969: 241.
61. Millon 1969: 53.
62. Quoted in Womack 1969: 247.
63. Womack 1969: 247.
64. Gilly 1971: 249.
65. Womack 1969: 253.
66. Gilly 1971: 256.
67. Gilly 1971: 258.
68. Gilly 1971: 261.
69. Gilly 1971: 237.
70. Womack 1969: 275-7.
71. Womack 1969: 277-8.
72. Córdova 1973: 195.
73. Córdova 1973: 193.
74. Córdova 1973: 136.
75. Leal 1974: 175.
76. Córdova 1973: 24-5.
77. Córdova 1973: 25.
78. Millon 1969: 103.
79. Reed 1914: 37.
80. Pozas 1962: 38-9.
81. Córdova 1973: 144.
82. Quoted in Silva Herzog 1972: I/271.
83. Córdova 1973: 245.

Chapter 7: pp. 36-45

1. Cockcroft 1968: 235.
2. Quoted in Córdova 1973: 175.
3. Leal 1974: 12.
4. Michaels & Bernstein 1976: 695.
5. Brandenberg 1964: 57.
6. Córdova 1973: 230.
7. Córdova 1973: 234.
8. Tannenbaum 1966: 179.
9. Quoted in Whetten 1948: 122-3.
10. Lewis 1964: 135.
11. Hansen 1971: 33.
12. Cumberland 1968: 272.
13. Huizer 1970: 31.
14. Vernon 1963: 67.
15. Medin 1972: 13.
16. Córdova 1973: 218.
17. Gilly 1971: 329.
18. Hansen 1971: 33.
19. Medin 1972: 8.
20. Huizer 1970: 43.
21. Huizer 1970: 50.
22. Huizer 1970: 42.
23. *Siempre*, Dec. 31, 1969, p. 44.
24. Fuentes Díaz 1972: 201.
25. Quoted in Gilly 1971: 323.
26. Meyer 1973: 130.
27. Gilly 1971: 337.
28. Hansen 1971: 30.
29. Cumberland 1968: 242, 257.
30. Córdova 1973: 33.
31. Córdova 1973: 29.
32. Shulgovsky 1972: 56.
33. *The Americas*, Jan. 1977, p. 558; Meyer 1974: 260.
34. Córdova 1973: 320.
35. Fuentes Díaz 1972: 202.
36. Shulgovsky 1972: 76.
37. Cumberland 1968: 275.
38. Fuentes Díaz 1972: 233.
39. Medin 1972: 46.
40. Frank 1972: 75-6.
41. Gilly 1971: 355.
42. Huizer 1970: 71.
43. Medin 1972: 125.
44. López Gallo 1975: 448.
45. Cumberland 1968: 249.
46. Shulgovsky 1972: 328.
47. Zevada 1971: 30.
48. Gilly 1971: 353.
49. *Revista de Revistas*, Oct. 31, 1973, p. 12.
50. Ribeiro 1971: 121.
51. Michaels & Bernstein 1976: 702.
52. *Historia Mexicana*, Oct.-Dec. 1960, pp. 333-4.
53. *Historia Mexicana*, July-Sept. 1971, p. 90.
54. Needler 1971: 16.
55. *Siempre*, Aug. 6, 1969, p. 23.
56. Hansen 1971: 115; Huizer 1970: 92.

57. Huizer 1970: 90.
58. *Siempre,* Aug. 20, 1969, p. 20.
59. *Siempre,* Aug. 27, 1969, p. 20.

Chapter 8: pp. 45-47

1. Córdova 1972: 9.
2. Córdova 1972: 19.
3. Córdova 1972: 31.
4. Córdova 1972: 27.
5. Aguilar 1972: 165.
6. Aguilar 1972: 166.
7. González Casanova 1968: 471.
8. Córdova 1972: 30.
9. Córdova 1972: 30.
10. *Revista Mexicana de Ciencia Política,* Oct.-Dec. 1972, p. 62.
11. *Latin American Perspectives,* Summer 1975, p. 141.
12. Córdova 1972: 34.
13. Córdova 1972: 36.
14. Córdova 1972: 42.
15. Córdova 1972: 43.
16. Córdova 1972: 62.
17. Córdova 1972: 63.
18. *Revista Mexicana de Ciencias Políticas y Sociales,* Oct.-Dec. 1975, p. 154.

Chapter 9: pp. 48-55

1. Paz 1961: 122.
2. Cosío Villegas 1972: 37.
3. Fuentes Díaz 1972: 203.
4. Fuentes Díaz 1972: 221-2.
5. Anderson & Cockcroft 1972: 233.
6. *Siempre,* Oct. 11, 1972, p. iii.
7. Furtak 1969: 17.
8. Córdova 1976: 225.
9. Córdova 1976: 223.
10. *Historia Mexicana,* July-Sept. 1971, p. 81.
11. Needler 1971: 16.
12. Shulgovsky 1972: 433.
13. García Cantú 1974: 250-1.
14. Cosío Villegas 1972: 17.
15. Furtak 1969: 26.
16. Victoria 1974: 115.
17. *Estudios Políticos,* Sept.-Dec. 1975, p. 121.
18. Victoria 1974: 137.
19. *Siempre,* Oct. 11, 1972, pp. vi-viii.
20. González Casanova 1970: 20.
21. *Revista Mexicana de Ciencia Política,* April-June 1975, p. 73.
22. Rivanuva 1974: 89.
23. *Proceso,* Nov. 13, 1976, p. 47.
24. Quoted in Fagen & Thouy 1972: 22.
25. *Excélsior,* Jan. 25, 1975, p. 4a.
26. *Nueva Política,* April-June 1976, p. 105.
27. Fagen & Thouy 1972: 31.
28. Anderson & Cockcroft 1972: 229.
29. Fagen & Thouy 1972: 20.
30. *Siempre,* Oct. 9, 1974, p. xii.
31. Cosío Villegas 1975: 21.
32. Carrión 1973: 220.
33. Hansen 1971: 165-6.
34. Carrión 1973: 166.
35. *Excélsior,* March 5, 1976, p. 20a.
36. Córdova 1972: 66.
37. Fagen & Thouy 1972: 43.
38. *URLA Newsletter,* June 1974, p. 19.
39. Carrión 1973: 229.
40. Cosío Villegas 1972: 25.
41. Hansen 1971: 153.
42. *Latin America,* July 6, 1973, p. 209.
43. Carrión 1973: 232.
44. *Excélsior,* Jan. 18, 1973, p. 6a.
45. *Excélsior,* Dec. 12, 1973, p. 10a.
46. *Excélsior,* Feb. 16, 1975, p. 1a.
47. Anderson & Cockcroft 1972: 221-3.
48. Fagen & Thouy 1972: 22-3.
49. Brandenberg 1964: 161-2.

Chapter 10: pp. 55-58

1. Cosío Villegas 1974: 17.
2. Quoted in Cosío Villegas 1974: 27.
3. *Tiempo,* April 23, 1956, p. 8.
4. Quoted in *Revista Mexicana de Ciencia Política,* Oct.-Dec. 1972, p. 74.
5. *Punto Crítico,* Jan. 74, p. 6.
6. *Punto Crítico,* Jan. 74, p. 6.
7. Fuentes 1972: 170-1.
8. *Punto Crítico,* Oct. 1974, p. 5.
9. *Punto Crítico,* Jan. 1974, p. 9.
10. *Punto Crítico,* Jan. 1974, p. 10.
11. *Punto Crítico,* Oct. 1974, p. 5.
12. *Punto Crítico,* Oct. 1974, p. 5.
13. *Excélsior,* April 6, 1976, p. 15a.
14. *Excélsior,* July 14, 1976, p. 1a.
15. *Manchester Guardian Weekly,* May 1, 1977, p. 9.
16. Quoted in *New York Times,* Dec. 3, 1976, p. 14a.
17. *Proceso,* Dec. 4, 1976, p. 24.
18. *Tiempo,* Dec. 27, 1976, p. 13.
19. *Latin American Economic Report Special Supplement on Mexico,* March 1977, p. 12.

Chapter 11: pp. 59-64

1. Palerm 1972: 34.
2. Galbraith 1975: 12.
3. Aguilar 1974: 109.
4. Peña 1975: 95.
5. Aguilar 1974: 60.
6. Ceceña 1970: 30.
7. Quoted in Galeano 1973: 191.
8. Frank 1972: 24-5.
9. Keremitsis 1973: 11.
10. *Latin American Perspectives,* Spring 1974, p. 38.
11. Ribeiro 1971: 449.
12. Aguilar 1974: 158.
13. *Trimestre Económico,* July 1965, p. 406.
14. Sierra 1969: 214-5.
15. Cumberland 1968: 177.
16. Flores Caballero 1976: 107.
17. Fernández & May 1971: 10.
18. Reynolds 1970: 6.
19. Fernández & May 1971: 11.
20. O'Connor 1974: 62.
21. Calderón 1972: 135-6.
22. *Planeación y Desarrollo,* July-Aug. 1973, p. 23.
23. Gilly 1971: 16.
24. Gilly 1971: 16.
25. *Foro Internacional,* Oct.-Dec. 1975, p. 218.
26. Coatsworth 1976: I/64.
27. Coatsworth 1976: II/7.
28. Coatsworth 1976: II/13.
29. Cumberland 1968: 217.
30. *Hispanic American Historical Review* 1974: 49.
31. *Hispanic American Historical Review* 1974: 55.
32. Moreno Toscano & Florescano 1976: 96.
33. Reynolds 1970: 20.
34. Keremitsis 1973: 199.
35. Stavenhagen 1972: 146.
36. *Hispanic American Historical Review* 1974: 23.
37. *Demografía y Economía,* 1972, No. 6, p. 2.
38. Meyer 1973: 10.
39. *Trimestre Económico,* July 1965, p. 405.
40. Gilly 1971: 24.
41. Gilly 1971: 23.
42. Cumberland 1968: 310.
43. Meyer 1973: 113.
44. *Revista Mexicana de Ciencia Política,* Oct.-Dec. 1972, p. 61.
45. *Nueva Política,* April-June 1976, p. 212.
46. Reyna 1972: 510.
47. Córdova 1973: 315.
48. Córdova 1974: 17.
49. Fernández & May 1971: 27.
50. CDIA 1974: 35.
51. Frank 1969: 386.
52. Córdova 1974: 178.
53. Medin 1972: 129.
54. *U.N. Statistical Yearbook 1948,* p. 118.
55. Medina 1974: 20.
56. Cárdenas 1972: 233.
57. Fernández & May 1971: 28.
58. *U.N. Statistical Yearbook 1952,* p. 87.
59. Rivera Marín 1955: 144.
60. Semionov 1973: 144.
61. *Nueva Política,* April-June 1976, p. 90.
62. *Nueva Política,* April-June 1976, p. 102.

Chapter 12: pp. 65-73

1. *Proceso,* March 5, 1977, p. 39.
2. *Mexican-American Review,* July 1976, p. 75.
3. *Fortune,* Sept. 1975, p. 113.
4. *Revista Mexicana de Ciencia Política,* Oct.-Dec. 1972, p. 66.
5. Hansen 1971: 2.
6. Hansen 1971: 3.
7. Fernández Hurtado 1967: 68.
8. *Planeación y Desarrollo,* July-Aug. 1973, p. 23.
9. Beteta 1976: 4.
10. *Cuadernos Políticos,* July-Sept. 1974, p. 53.
11. Cosío Villegas 1972: 67.
12. *Siempre,* Dec. 24, 1975, p. vii.
13. *Mexican Newsletter,* Sept. 30, 1975, p. 9.
14. *Fortune,* Sept. 1975, p. 120.
15. Córdova 1972: 63.
16. *Cuadernos Políticos,* April-June 1976, pp. 57-8.
17. *Seimpre,* Dec. 24, 1975, p. vii.
18. *Punto Crítico,* Nov. 1973, p. 4.
19. *Planeación y Desarrollo,* July-Aug. 1973, p. 29.
20. *Excélsior,* July 21, 1975, p. 22a.
21. Hansen 1971: 87.
22. *Proceso,* Dec. 25, 1976, p. 32. (Much of this apparent growth is due to inflation. Mexican private investment grew 17.2% and foreign investment grew 16.4% during the same period, all in current pesos.)
23. *New York Times,* Sept. 12, 1976, Sec. 3, p. 3.
24. *Planeación y Desarrollo,* July-Aug. 1973, p. 74.
25. *Review of the Economic Situation in Mexico,* Dec. 1976, p. 377.
26. Hansen 1971: 215.
27. Beteta 1976: 4.
28. *Economic Panorama,* May 1, 1976, p. 1.
29. Sepúlveda & Chumacero 1973: 121.
30. *Proceso,* Feb. 26, 1977, p. 23. (Different accounting methods, as well as new investment, probably account for the difference between this figure and the figure for 1970.)
31. Stanford Research Institute 1976: 73.
32. Sepúlveda & Chumacero 1973: 56-7.
33. Padilla Aragón 1975: 15.
34. Newfarmer & Mueller 1975: 36.
35. Newfarmer & Mueller 1975: 37.
36. Padilla Aragón 1975: 20.
37. Zapata 1974: 28.
38. Shelton 1964: 145-6.
39. *Proceso,* Dec. 4, 1976, p. 23.
40. Blair 1964: 200.
41. Ramirez Racaño 1974: 32.
42. *Planeación y Desarrollo,* July-Aug. 1973, p. 28.
43. *Comercio Exterior* 1975: 644.
44. *Excélsior,* Sept. 17, 1974, p. 6a.
45. Newfarmer & Mueller 1975: 19.
46. *New York Times,* Feb. 15, 1976, Sec. 3, p. 7; *Wall Street Journal,* Jan. 28, 1977, p. 2.
47. NACLA 1971: 29.
48. *New York Times,* Sept. 19, 1971, Sec. 3, p. 10.
49. *Trimestre Económico* 1975: 912.
50. Ramírez Racaño 1974: 194.
51. Barnet & Müller 1974: 167.
52. Wionczek 1971.
53. *El Día,* Aug. 20, 1974, p. 4.
54. Barnet & Müller 1974: 278.
55. Barnet & Müller 1974: 282.
56. *Planeación y Desarrollo,* July-Aug. 1973, p. 26.
57. *Latin American Economic Report* 1975: 2.
58. Sunkel 1972: 69.
59. *Lateinamerika,* Spring 1975, p. 29.
60. *Business Week,* Oct. 27, 1973, p. 77.
61. Sepúlveda & Chumacero 1973: 40.
62. *Business Latin America,* April 30, 1975, p. 141.
63. Newfarmer & Mueller 1975: 68.
64. *Siempre,* Jan. 9, 1974, p. 30.
65. *Wall Street Journal,* July 12, 1976, p. 28.
66. Turner 1973: 102.
67. Sepúlveda & Chumacero 1973: 90.
68. Newfarmer & Mueller 1975: 91.
69. Quoted in Newfarmer & Mueller 1975: 17.
70. Aguilar 1970: 122.
71. *Excélsior,* Aug. 7, 1975, p. 1a; *Latin American Economic Report,* April 8, 1977, p. 54.
72. *El Día,* April 21, 1976, p. 4.
73. *Economía Informa,* Feb. 1975, p. 2.
74. *Cuadernos Políticos,* Jan.-March 1977, p. 36.
75. *Comercio Exterior* 1974: 594.
76. *Latin America Economic Report Special Supplement on Mexico,* March 1977, p. 3.
77. *International Financial Statistics,* April 1977, p. 252; *Review of the Economic Situation of Mexico,* Feb. 1977, p. 75.
78. *Proceso,* Nov. 13, 1976, p. 22; *Punto Crítico,* March 15, 1977, p. 9.
79. *Business Week,* Nov. 9, 1974, p. 72.
80. *Business International* 1975: 410.
81. Barnet & Müller 1974: 206.
82. *Business Latin America,* March 9, 1977, p. 77.
83. Pazos 1976: 35.
84. *Wall Street Journal,* Nov. 23, 1976, p. 24.
85. *The Economist,* March 26, 1977, p. 93. (This same source notes *possible* reserves are much higher.)
86. *Proceso,* Dec. 4, 1976, p. 6; March 26, 1977, p. 32.
87. Barnet & Müller 1974: 82.
88. Barnet & Müller 1974: 195.
89. *Foreign Affairs,* Jan. 1977, p. 246.
90. Barnet & Müller 1974: 201.

Chapter 13: pp. 73-82

1. Leyva 1973: 110-1.
2. Huizer 1970: 12.
3. Semo 1973: 14.
4. Bartra 1974: 123.
5. Bartra 1974: 128.
6. Hansen 1971: 33.
7. Vernon 1963: 73.
8. Huizer 1970: 71.
9. Calderón 1972: 71.
10. CDIA 1974: 28.
11. CDIA 1974: 31.
12. CDIA 1974: 17.
13. Huizer 1970: 72.
14. Huizer 1970: 71.
15. Hansen 1971: 33.
16. CDIA 1974: 40.
17. Carmona 1973: 62.
18. Bartra 1974: 125.
19. CDIA 1974: 40.
20. Córdova 1973: 33.
21. *Planeación y Desarrollo,* July-Aug. 1973, p. 24.
22. CDIA 1974: 42.
23. Aguilar 1971: 237.
24. *Revista del México Agrario,* May-June 1976, p. 19.
25. CDIA 1974: 52.
26. *Revista de Revistas,* Jan. 2, 1974, p. 8.
27. Bartra 1975: 6.
28. Paz Sánchez 1973a: 79.
29. *Punto Crítico,* Nov. 1973, p. 26.
30. *Planeación y Desarrollo,* July-Aug. 1973, p. 24.
31. Gómez-Jara 1970: 159.
32. Bartra 1974: 106.
33. CDIA 1974: 1036.
34. CDIA 1974: 458.
35. Bartra 1974: 41.
36. Bartra 1974: 44.
37. CDIA 1974: 230.
38. CDIA 1974: 213.
39. Aguilar 1970: 34.
40. CDIA 1974: 67.
41. CDIA 1974: 73.
42. CDIA 1974: 685.
43. *Excélsior,* April 13, 1975, p. 1a.
44. CDIA 1974: 439-40.
45. CDIA 1974: 203.

46. Leyva 1973: 105.
47. *FAO Production Yearbook 1970*: 466.
48. *Comercio Exterior* 1969: 870.
49. Hansen 1971: 78.
50. *Economía Informa*, July 1974, p. 5.
51. *Economía Informa*, Feb. 1975, p. 7.
52. CDIA 1974: 205.
53. *Excélsior*, May 7, 1976, p. 15a.
54. Stavenhagen 1972: 165.
55. *Comercio Exterior* 1976: 1423-4.
56. García Cantú 1974: 291.
57. *Insurgencia Popular*, Dec. 1976, p. 16.
58. Ledogar 1975: 2.
59. Galeano 1973: 110.
60. Sánchez Zarza 1976: 187.
61. *Saturday Review*, Feb. 7, 1976, p. 5.
62. *Trimestre Económico* 1976: 74.
63. *El Día*, Feb. 1, 1976, p. 1.
64. Zapata 1972: 8.
65. *Cuadernos Políticos*, Oct.-Dec. 1974, p. 73.
66. *Cuadernos Políticos*, July-Sept. 1974, p. 53.
67. Paz Sánchez 1973a: 94.
68. *Proceso*, Dec. 11, 1976, p. 10.
69. *Economía Informa*, Feb. 1975, p. 4.
70. *Revista del México Agrario*, Oct.-Dec. 1975, p. 9.
71. *Revista del México Agrario*, Oct.-Dec. 1975, p. 41.
72. *Foreign Agriculture*, May 3, 1976, p. 6.
73. Paz Sánchez 1973a: 79.
74. Paz Sánchez 1973b: 188.
75. *Comercio Exterior* 1975: 544.
76. CDIA 1974: 144.
77. Cumberland 1968: 11.
78. *Siempre*, April 18, 1973, p. 44.
79. *Revista del México Agrario*, May-June 1976, pp. 111-2.
80. *Excélsior*, April 3, 1975, p. 7a.
81. *Comercio Exterior* 1975: 579.
82. *Siempre*, July 16, 1975, p. 38.
83. *Siempre*, Jan. 22, 1975, p. x.
84. *Mexican Newsletter*, Dec. 31, 1974, p. 7.
85. *Cuadernos Políticos*, Oct.-Dec. 1974, p. 54.
86. *Solidaridad*, June 15-30, 1974, p. 20.
87. *Cauderons Políticos*, Jan.-Mar. 1975, p. 50.
88. *Siempre*, Jan. 15, 1976, p. 28.
89. *Excélsior*, July 28, 1975, p. 1a.
90. *Proceso*, March 19, 1977, p. 37.
91. *Current History*, March 1977, p. 114.
92. *Review of the Economic Situation of Mexico*, Feb. 1977, pp. 62-3.
93. *Business Latin America*, March 9, 1977, p. 76.
94. *Proceso*, Jan. 29, 1977, p. 19.
95. *Punto Crítico*, March 15, 1977, p. 24.

Chapter 14: pp. 82-88

1. Quoted in *Punto Crítico*, Jan. 31, 1977, p. 47.
2. *El Día*, May 9, 1976, p. 7.
3. *Excélsior*, March 2, 1974, p. 10a.
4. *Mexican American Review*, May 1975, p. 35.
5. *Wall Street Journal*, Nov. 30, 1976, p. 31.
6. Sánchez Aguilar 1973: 70.
7. *Proceso*, Dec. 25, 1976, p. 26.
8. *Wall Street Journal*, May 19, 1976, p. 28.
9. *Wall Street Journal*, June 7, 1977, p. 22.
10. *New York Times*, Feb. 7, 1975, p. 49.
11. Aguilar 1970: 125.
12. *Proceso*, Feb. 12, 1977, p. 33.
13. *Current History*, May 1974, p. 222.
14. Carmona 1973: 72.
15. *Proceso*, Nov. 13, 1976, p. 23.
16. *Business Latin America* 1975: 210. (This understates the rate of debt growth during the Echeverría administration since the most rapid growth occurred in 1976.)
17. Aguilar 1970: 125; *Proceso*, Dec. 25, 1976, p. 26.
18. *Proceso*, Feb. 12, 1977, p. 33.
19. Sánchez Aguilar 1973: 206.
20. Padilla Aragón 1975: 8.
21. *New York Times*, June 5, 1977, Sec. 4, p. 1.
22. *Estrategia*, Sept. 20, 1975, p. 44.
23. O'Connor 1974: 189.
24. *Mexican American Review*, May 1975, p. 39.
25. *El Día*, Nov. 27, 1975, p. 1a.
26. *Excélsior*, Nov. 27, 1975, p. 1a.
27. *Business Week*, Dec. 6, 1976, p. 34.
28. *Wall Street Journal*, April 13, 1976, p. 20.
29. *Proceso*, Dec. 4, 1976, p. 7.
30. *Siempre*, Dec. 24, 1975, p. viii.
31. *Siempre*, Sept. 3, 1975, pp. 26-7.
32. Johnson 1972: p. 95.
33. Hayter 1971: 29; *Siempre*, Dec. 29, 1976, p. ix; *Proceso*, May 16, 1977, p. 30.
34. NACLA 1971: 55.
35. Payer 1975: 211.
36. Hudson 1972: 95.
37. Hudson 1972: 124.
38. Bazant 1968: 95.
39. *Excélsior*, June 7, 1975, p. 1a.
40. *Cuadernos Políticos*, April-June 1976, p. 63.
41. Pazos 1976: 46.
42. *Cuadernos Políticos*, April-June 1976, p. 62.
43. *Proceso*, Feb. 12, 1977, p. 33.
44. Sánchez Aguilar 1973: 233.
45. *International Financial Statistics*, April 1977, p. 252.
46. *Review of the Economic Situation of Mexico*, Feb. 1977, p. 47; *Foreign Affairs*, July 1977, p. 696; *Proceso*, Feb. 12, 1977, p. 33.
47. Sánchez Aguilar 1973: 229.
48. *Mexican American Review*, June 1976, pp. 23-4.
49. *Indicadores Económicos*, Feb. 1976, pp. 38-54.
50. *Review of the Economic Situation of Mexico*, Feb. 1977, p. 77.
51. *Hanson's Latin American Letter*, April 30, 1977, p. 1.
52. Sánchez Aguilar 1973: 233.
53. *Excélsior*, Jan. 23, 1976, p. 1a.
54. Quoted in Payer 1975: 201-2.
55. Green 1976: 122.
56. *Forbes*, Dec. 1, 1975, p. 19; *Euromoney*, Dec. 1976, pp. 114-6.
57. Quoted in *New York Times*, Jan. 15, 1976, p. 1.
58. *New York Times*, Jan. 15, 1976, p. 56.
59. *Jeune Afrique*, April 22, 1977, p. 46.
60. *Comercio Exterior*, Supplement to October 1971, p. 6.
61. *Excélsior*, May 15, 1976, p. 1a.
62. *New York Review of Books*, May 27, 1976, p. 16.

Chapter 15: pp. 89-94

1. Folbre 1974: 5.
2. Barnet & Müller 1974: 190.
3. *American Journal of Sociology*, July 1976, p. 57.
4. van Ginneken 1976: 26.
5. *Comercio Exterior* 1974: 695.
6. *Cuadernos Políticos*, Jan.-March 1976, p. 56.
7. Mesa-Lago 1976: 241.
8. *Comercio Exterior* 1975: 574.
9. *Foro Internacional*, July-Sept. 1975, p. 6.
10. *People's Almanac*, p. 1229. (*US News & World Report*, March 28, 1977, p. 55, lists Mexico City as the world's third largest city with a population of 8.6 million.)
11. *Washington Post*, Feb. 6, 1977, p. A15.
12. *El Día*, April 19, 1976, p. 5.
13. *Atlas de México*, p. 131.
14. *Current History*, March 1977, p. 112.
15. *Cuadernos Políticos*, Oct.-Dec. 1974, p. 43.

16. *Latin American Perspectives,* Summer 1975, p. 110.
17. Ramírez Racaño 1974: 149.
18. Ramírez Racaño 1974: 149.
19. Furtado 1970: 61.
20. *Statistical Abstract of the United States 1976,* p. 406.
21. *Statistical Abstract of the United States 1976,* p. 406.
22. *Cuadernos Políticos,* Oct.-Dec. 1974, p. 54.
23. *Interamerican Economic Affairs,* Autumn 1970, p. 56.
24. Rivera Marín 1955: 144.
25. Córdova 1972: 95.
26. Leal 1975: 54.
27. *Latin American Perspectives,* Summer 1975, p. 124.
28. *Latin American Perspectives,* Summer 1975, p. 122.
29. Huacuja & Woldenberg 1976: 33.
30. Pellicer de Brody 1974: 98.
31. Pellicer de Brody 1974: 96.
32. *Comercio Exterior* 1953: 293.
33. Pellicer de Brody 1974: 96.
34. Pellicer de Brody 1974: 101.
35. Barnet & Müller 1974: 92.
36. García Cantú 1974: 313.
37. *Excélsior,* Dec. 12, 1975, p. 1a.
38. *Economía Informa,* Jan. 1975, p. 8.
39. *Comercio Exterior de México,* Feb. 1977, p. 43.
40. *Proceso,* May 16, 1977, p. 31.
41. *Latin America Economic Report Special Supplement on Mexico,* March 1977, p. 1.
42. *Business Week,* Dec. 27, 1976, p. 46.
43. Navarrete 1970: 37.
44. Petras 1970: 52.
45. Paz 1972: 52.
46. Bonilla Sánchez 1973: 162.
47. *UN Demographic Yearbook 1972,* p. 392.
48. *Comercio Exterior* 1975: 578.
49. *America,* Nov. 22, 1975, p. 351-2.
50. *Excélsior,* Nov. 4, 1975, p. 1a.
51. *Land Economics,* Aug. 1976, p. 330.

Chapter 16: pp. 94-100

1. Córdova 1974: 15.
2. Anguiano 1975: 23.
3. Basurto 1972: 49.
4. Alonso 1972: 27.
5. *Problemas Agrarios e Industriales de México,* Jan. 1955, p. 81.
6. Anguiano 1975: 23.
7. Basurto 1975: 259.
8. Basurto 1975: 246.
9. Basurto 1975: 267.
10. *Ciencias Políticas y Sociales* 1959: 328.
11. *Ciencias Políticas y Sociales* 1959: 333.

12. Alonso 1972: 42.
13. Anguiano 1975: 50-1.
14. Anguiano 1975: 76-8.
15. Medin 1972: 83.
16. Córdova 1974: 171.
17. Anguiano 1975: 65.
18. Córdova 1974: 178.
19. Meyer 1973: 270.
20. Cabral & Arroio 1974: II.5.
21. Rivera Marín 1955: 141.
22. *Nueva Política,* April-June 1976, p. 90.
23. *Revista Mexicana de Ciencia Política,* Oct.-Dec. 1972, p. 73.
24. Cabral & Arroio 1974: III.42.
25. Victoria 1974: 110.
26. Alonso 1972: 84.
27. *Proceso,* April 30, 1977, p. 8.
28. Cabral & Arroio 1974: III.38.
29. Cabral & Arroio 1974: IV.1.
30. Alonso 1972: 98.
31. Alonso 1972: 115-6.
32. Alonso 1972: 129.
33. Montes 1972: 44-5.
34. Basurto 1972: 55-6.
35. *Excélsior,* Aug. 31, 1974, p. 8a.
36. *Revista Mexicana de Ciencia Política,* Oct.-Dec. 1972, p. 91-2.
37. García Cantú 1974: 117.
38. *Cuadernos Políticos,* Jan.-March 1976, p. 42.
39. *El Día,* March 11, 1976, p. 7.
40. *Cuadernos Políticos,* Jan.-March 1975, p. 42.
41. Montes 1972: 47.
42. Montes 1972: 49.
43. *Excélsior,* July 4, 1975, pp. 1a, 5a.
44. Montes 1972: 52.
45. Leal 1975: 46.
46. *Excélsior,* May 9, 1975, p. 1a.
47. *Excélsior,* March 24, 1975, p. 16a.
48. *Estrategia,* Sept. 20, 1975, p. 50.
49. *Economía Informa,* Oct. 1975, p. 15.
50. Basurto 1972: 54.
51. *Cuadernos Políticos,* Oct.-Dec. 1975, p. 13, 19.
52. Folbre 1974: 104.
53. *Estrategia,* Sept. 20, 1975, p. 60.
54. *Ultimas Noticias,* March 4, 1973, 1st ed., p. 1.
55. *Estrategia,* Sept. 20, 1975, p. 60.
56. *Proceso,* Dec. 25, 1976, p. 34; *Cristianismo y Sociedad,* 1973, No. 38, p. 29.
57. *Excélsior,* Sept. 17, 1974, p. 7a.
58. *El Día,* Jan. 24, 1976, p. 8. (The minimum salary varies by geographical area. In areas where the cost of living is high, such as Baja California, it reaches as much as 133.90 pesos a day. In certain parts of Oaxaca it is as low as 40.70 pesos a day.)
59. *Siempre,* Dec. 10, 1975, p. 14.
60. United Nations 1971: 143.

61. *Siempre,* May 29, 1974, pp. vi-viii.
62. *Siempre,* April 17, 1974, p. ix; *Excélsior,* Aug. 9, 1975, p. 22a.
63. *Excélsior,* Sept. 17, 1974, p. 7a.
64. *Siempre,* Aug. 13, 1975, p. x.
65. *Insurgencia Popular,* Oct. 1975, p. 18.
66. *Excélsior,* Feb. 8, 1975, p. 6a.
67. *El Día,* Feb. 1, 1976, p. 2.
68. *Excélsior,* March 21, 1976, p. 1a.
69. *Excélsior,* July 22, 1976, p. 4a.
70. *Insurgencia Popular,* Sept. 1, 1976, p. 9.

Chapter 17: pp. 101-108

1. Quoted in Gómez-Jara 1970: 48.
2. Gómez-Jara 1970: 54.
3. Gómez-Jara 1970: 69.
4. *Demografía y Economía,* 1972, No. 18, p. 294.
5. Originally published in *El Machete.* Quoted in Gómez-Jara 1970: 136.
6. Quoted in Gómez-Jara 1970: 145.
7. CDIA 1974: 602.
8. CDIA 1974: 604.
9. CDIA 1974: 42.
10. *Punto Crítico,* Nov. 1973, p. 32.
11. Fuentes 1972: 113.
12. *Revista de Revistas,* Jan. 2, 1974, p. 8.
13. Paré 1975: 40.
14. *Siempre,* Feb. 2, 1972, pp. 18-9.
15. CDIA 1974: 720.
16. Bartra 1974: 77.
17. CDIA 1974: 195.
18. Durán 1972: 154.
19. Gutelman 1974: 254.
20. *The Elements,* June 1975, p. 16.
21. Hansen 1971: 119.
22. Boege & Calvo 1975: 135.
23. Warman 1972: 24.
24. Warman 1972: 72.
25. Bartra 1974: 166.
26. Hansen 1971: 119.
27. Montaño 1973: 152.
28. Calvo & Bartra 1975: 127.
29. Paré 1975: 50.
30. Martínez Vázquez 1975: 156.
31. CDIA 1974: 477.
32. Martínez-Vazquez 1975: 162-3.
33. CDIA 1974: 417-8.
34. *Cuadernos Agrarios,* Jan.-March 1976, pp. 17, 28.
35. *Proceso,* Dec. 4, 1976, p. 44.
36. *Comercio Exterior* 1976: 11.
37. Stavenhagen 1972: 175.
38. *Cuadernos Agrarios,* Jan.-March 1976, p. 25; *New Yorker,* Jan. 24, 1977, p. 41.
39. CDIA 1974: 417.
40. CDIA 1974: 193.
41. CDIA 1974: 193.
42. Bartra 1974: 150.

43. *Monthly Review*, May 1976, p. 14.
44. *Foro Internacional*, July-Sept. 1975, p. 6.
45. CDIA 1974: 471.
46. CDIA 1974: 1974: 631.
47. *The Elements*, June 1975, p. 15.
48. Agee 1975: 516.
49. Gómez-Jara 1970: 168.
50. Agee 1975: 520.
51. Danzós 1974: 132.
52. *Punto Crítico*, Jan. 1974, p. 26.
53. *Punto Crítico*, Nov. 1972, p. 38; June-July 1973, p. 25.
54. *Oposición*, Nov. 1, 1975, p. 1.
55. *Excélsior*, Oct. 31, 1975, p. 7a; Nov. 1, p. 1a.
56. *Wall Street Journal*, April 5, 1976, p. 12.
57. *Excélsior*, June 19, 1976, p. 1a.
58. *Excélsior*, Aug. 28, 1974, p. 6a.
59. *Excélsior*, Dec. 18, 1972, p. 13a.
60. *NACLA's Latin America & Empire Report*, July-Aug. 1976, p. 26.
61. *Excélsior*, June 10, 1977, p. 31a.
62. *Siempre*, Jan. 22, 1975, p. x.
63. *New York Times*, Nov. 23, 1976, p. 54.
64. *Punto Crítico*, Dec. 10, 1976, p. 4.
65. *Latin America Political Report* 1977: 143.

Chapter 18: pp. 108-112

1. *Current History*, May 1974, p. 204.
2. *Hispanic American Historical Review* 1968: 29.
3. Aguirre Beltrán 1973: 241.
4. *Revista Mexicana de Sociología* 1974: 478.
5. Lagarde 1974: 86.
6. Instituto Nacional Indigenista 1971: 164.
7. *Excélsior*, Nov. 10, 1975, p. 5a.
8. *El Día*, March 31, 1976, p. 1.
9. Arizpe 1976: 113.
10. Lagarde 1974: 79.
11. Lagarde 1974: 76.
12. Lagarde 1974: 42.
13. Fuente 1965: 70.
14. Fuente 1965: 71.
15. *Archives Européennes de Sociologie*, 1973, No. 1, p. 6.
16. *Archives Européenes de Sociologie*, 1973, No. 1, p. 15.
17. Aguirre Beltrán 1973: 13.
18. Díaz Hernández 1972: 25.
19. Díaz Hernández 1972: 101.
20. Díaz Hernández 1972: 33.
21. *Revista Mexicana de Sociología* 1974: 474. (The use of Indian fiestas for promoting business is nothing new. See for example, Traven 1970: 94.)
22. Fuente 1965: 168.
23. Fuente 1965: 168.
24. Pozas & Pozas 1971: 95.
25. Castaneda 1972: 80.
26. Morión 1970: 121.
27. Aguirre Beltrán 1973: 147.
28. *Excélsior*, Sept. 15, 1974, p. 7a.
29. *Siempre*, Sept. 17, 1972, p. vi.
30. *Excélsior*, Aug. 4, 1975, p. 9a.
31. *El Día*, Oct. 7, 1976, p. 1.
32. Medina 1973: 12.
33. *Excélsior*, Jan. 20, 1976, p. 21a.
34. Instituto Nacional Indigenista 1971: 208.
35. *Excélsior*, July 15, 1975, p. 7a.
36. *Excélsior*, July 15, 1975, p. 8a.
37. *Excélsior*, Jan. 27, 1975, p. 7a.
38. *Excélsior*, Jan. 27, 1975, p. 7a.
39. *Excélsior*, June 9, 1976, p. 7a.
40. *Excélsior*, Oct. 14, 1975, p. 8a.
41. *Revista del México Agrario*, Oct.-Dec. 1975, p. 210.

Chapter 19: pp. 113-119

1. Carreras Maldonado & Montero Duhalt 1975: 125.
2. *Punto Crítico*, Aug. 1972, p. 26.
3. Womack 1969: 170.
4. *Punto Crítico*, Aug. 1972, p. 27.
5. *Siempre*, Jan. 3, 1973, p. xii.
6. CDIA 1974: 461.
7. Elu de Leñero 1975: 80.
8. Elu de Leñero 1975: 102.
9. *Mensaje*, Sept. 1972, p. 514.
10. *Western Political Quarterly*, Dec. 1965, pp. 348-50.
11. Vernon 1963: 159.
12. *Siempre*, Oct. 18, 1972, p. viii.
13. Paz 1961: 79-80.
14. *Excélsior*, Oct. 4, 1975, p. 6a.
15. *Gaceta Médica de México*, Jan. 1974, p. 21.
16. *Tiempo*, May 13, 1974, pp. 9-10.
17. Acevedo 1971: 41.
18. *Excélsior*, Feb. 1, 1976, p. 14a.
19. *Punto Crítico*, Dec. 1972, pp. 37-9.
20. Acevedo 1971: 53.
21. Fernández Bazavilvazo 1975: 167.
22. Elu de Leñero 1975: 133.
23. Elu de Leñero 1975: 38.
24. Elu de Leñero 1975: 36.
25. Elu de Leñero 1975: 37.
26. Elu de Leñero 1975: 47.
27. Elu de Leñero 1975: 50.
28. Elu de Leñero 1975: 52.
29. Elu de Leñero 1975: 55-7.
30. *Punto Crítico*, Aug. 1972, p. 30.
31. Elu de Leñero 1975: 169.
32. Elu de Leñero 1975: 68.
33. Elu de Leñero 1975: 71.
34. Elu de Leñero 1975: 14.
35. Elu de Leñero 1975: 108.
36. Elu de Leñero 1975: 174.
37. Elu de Leñero 1975: 175.
38. *American Anthropologist* 1949: 609.
39. Elu de Leñero 1975: 92.
40. Wolf 1959: 239.
41. Chiñas 1975: 84.
42. *América Indígena*, Jan.-March 1975, p. 118.
43. *Punto Crítico*, Dec. 1972, p. 36.
44. *Revista Mexicana de Ciencia Política*, July-Aug. 1971, p. 102.
45. *Diálogos*, Nov.-Dec. 1973, p. 31.
46. *Latin American Research Review*, Summer 1972, p. 125.
47. *Punto Crítico*, Jan. 1973, p. 20.
48. *Insurgencia Popular*, May 1975.
49. *Current History*, March 1977, p. 131.
50. *El Día*, June 7, 1976, p. 6.

Chapter 20: pp. 119-121

1. *Excélsior*, Aug. 30, 1975, p. 7a.
2. *Latin America Economic Report* 1977: 70.
3. *Solidaridad*, Oct. 1-15, 1975, p. 25.
4. *La Nación*, Oct. 10, 1973, p. 12.
5. *Comercio Exterior* 1974: 734.
6. Carmona Amorós 1974: 12.
7. *Revista Mexicana de Trabajo*, Jan.-March 1975, p. 89.
8. *Comercio Exterior* 1974: 731.
9. *Trimestre Económico* 1975: 677.
10. *El Día*, Aug. 20, 1974, p. 2.
11. *Comercio Exterior* 1974: 733.
12. *El Día*, July 8, 1975, p. 7.
13. *Trimestre Económico* 1976: 39.
14. *Latin America Economic Report* 1977: 70.
15. Bonilla Sánchez 1973: 162.
16. *El Día*, Jan. 19, 1976, p. 2.
17. *Excélsior*, Nov. 7, 1976, p. 20a.
18. *Latin American Economic Report* 1976: 88.
19. *Trimestre Económico* 1975: 840.
20. *Trimestre Económico* 1975: 912.
21. Elu de Leñero 1971: 28.
22. *Estrategia*, March-April 1975, p. 91.
23. *Engineering News Record*, March 13, 1975, pp. 18-9.

Chapter 21: pp. 121-123

1. *Cuadernos Políticos*, July-Sept. 1975, p. 82.
2. *Cuadernos Políticos*, July-Sept. 1975, p. 86.
3. *Salud Pública de México*, May 1973, p. 38.
4. *Gaceta Médica de México* 1969: 1091.
5. Zubirán 1974: 7.
6. *Excélsior*, Dec. 20, 1975, p. 1a.
7. *Excélsior*, July 26, 1975, p. 15a.

8. Zubirán 1974: 34; *Gaceta Médica de México*, Dec. 1974, p. 377.
9. *Latin American Perspectives*, Summer 1975, p. 118.
10. Ulloa 1972: 77.
11. *El Día*, Aug. 19, 1974, p. 4.
12. *New York Times*, March 7, 1976, Sec. 4, p. 4.
13. *Gaceta Médica de México*, Oct. 1971, p. 428.
14. *Gaceta Médica de México*, Jan. 1972, p. 46.
15. *Cuadernos Políticos*, July-Sept. 1975, p. 86.
16. *Cuadernos Políticos*, July-Sept. 1975, p. 89.
17. *Cuadernos Políticos*, July-Sept. 1975, p. 87.
18. *Cuadernos Políticos*, July-Sept. 1975, p. 89.
19. *El Día*, Sept. 20, 1975, p. 6.
20. *Excélsior*, Sept. 10, 1975, p. 21a.
21. *Proceso*, Jan. 8, 1977, p. 21.
22. *Cuadernos Políticos*, July-Sept. 1975, p. 92.
23. *El Día*, Aug. 20, 1974, p. 4.
24. *Cuadernos Políticos*, July-Sept. 1975, p. 92.
25. Ledogar 1975: 26, 40.
26. *Le Monde Diplomatique*, July 1976, p. 6.
27. *Cuadernos Políticos*, July-Sept. 1975, p. 85.
28. *Revista Médica del Hospital General*, 1970: 372.
29. *Revista Médica del IMSS* 1972, p. 134.
30. *Excélsior*, June 19, 1976, p. 5a.
31. Elu de Leñero 1975: 174-5.
32. *Gaceta Médica de México*, Jan. 1972, p. 46.
33. *Gaceta Médica de México* 1971: 427.
34. *Salud Pública de México*, Nov. 1973, p. 869.
35. *Cuadernos Políticos*, July-Sept. 1975, p. 89.
36. Bonilla Sánchez 1973: 202.
37. *Cuadernos Políticos*, July-Sept. 1975, p. 90.
38. *Revista Médica del Hospital General* 1970: 375.
39. Montaño 1973: 128.
40. *Salud Pública de México*, Nov. 1973, p. 869.
41. *Cuadernos Políticos*, July-Sept. 1975, p. 89.
42. *Cuadernos Políticos*, July-Sept. 1975, p. 88.
43. *Revista Médica del Hospital General* 1970: 382.
44. *Revista Médica del Hospital General* 1970: 380.
45. *Revista Médica del Hospital General* 1970: 382.
46. *Cuadernos Políticos*, July-Sept. 1975, p. 89.
47. *Demografía y Economía* 1971: 150.

Chapter 22: pp. 124-126

1. Puente Leyva 1970: 261.
2. García Zuno 1975: 32.
3. *Excélsior*, Dec. 13, 1975, p. 4a.
4. *El Sol de México*, March 4, 1977, p. 5a.
5. *Mercado de Valores* 1975: 20.
6. *Excélsior*, Jan. 31, 1973, p. 1a.
7. *Siempre*, Dec. 4, 1974, p. 11.
8. *Economía Informa*, May 1974, p. 13.
9. Puente Leyva 1970: 271.
10. Puente Leyva 1970: 272.
11. Puente Leyva 1970: 259.
12. Elu de Leñero 1971: 31.
13. *Excélsior*, July 30, 1975, p. 25a; July 31, p. 20a.
14. *Excélsior*, Jan. 26, 1976, p. 1a; *Revista de Revistas*, Jan. 6, 1974, p. 4.
15. *Mercado de Valores* 1976: 128.

Chapter 23: pp. 126-128

1. Bassols 1964: 436.
2. Cumberland 1972: 273.
3. *Demografía y Economía*, 1967, No. 1, p. 65.
4. *Latin American Perspectives*, Summer 1975, p. 90.
5. *Excélsior*, July 25, 1976, p. 1a.
6. *Foro Internacional*, July-Sept. 1975, p. 7.
7. Latapí 1974: 335; *El Economista Mexicano*, Sept. 1976, p. 149.
8. *Excélsior*, Aug. 7, 1975, p. 14a.
9. *Review of the Economic Situation of Mexico*, Jan. 1977, p. 9.
10. *El Día*, Aug. 23, 1974, p. 9.
11. *Excélsior*, May 16, 1976, p. 7a.
12. *Insurgencia Popular*, Oct. 1976, p. 2.
13. *Excélsior*, June 11, 1977, p. 4a.
14. *Excélsior*, Aug. 28, 1974, p. 7a.
15. *Economía Informa*, Aug. 1976, p. 6.
16. González Salazar 1972: 118.
17. *Wall Street Journal*, March 28, 1977, p. 1.
18. *Excélsior*, June 26, 1975, p. 5a.
19. *Excélsior*, Jan. 13, 1975, p. 17a.
20. *Current History*, May 1974, p. 226.
21. *Excélsior*, March 22, 1974, p. 1a.
22. *El Día*, July 8, 1975, p. 6.
23. *Siempre*, Dec. 17, 1975, p. ii.
24. *Excélsior*, May 16, 1976, p. 5a.
25. *New York Times*, March 7, 1976, Sec. 4, p. 4.
26. *Proceso*, Nov. 20, 1976, p. 33.
27. Latapí 1974: 340.

Chapter 24: pp. 128-132

1. Agee 1975: 518.
2. Carrión 1973: 206.
3. Cosío Villegas 1974: 75.
4. Fuentes Díaz 1972: 386.
5. *El Día*, Aug. 27, 1976, p. 1.
6. Fuentes Díaz 1972: 283.
7. Cosío Villegas 1972: 70.
8. *Excélsior*, Sept. 18, 1975, p. 7a.
9. Anderson & Cockcroft 1972: 235.
10. *Social Science Quarterly*, Dec. 1975, p. 506.
11. *Punto Crítico*, June-July 1973, p. 18.
12. Vernon 1963: 132-3.
13. Segovia 1974: 57.
14. *Excélsior*, Sept. 18, 1975, p. 7a.
15. Cosío Villegas 1972: 69.
16. Segovia 1974: 60.
17. Segovia 1974: 65.
18. *Excélsior*, July 14, 1976, p. 1a.
19. *Revista de Revistas*, May 15, 1974, p. 38.
20. Fuentes Díaz 1972: 346.
21. Agee 1975: 518.
22. Agee 1975: 518.
23. *Excélsior*, April 6, 1976, p. 15a.
24. *Excélsior*, Nov. 3, 1975, p. 9a.
25. *Excélsior*, Nov. 12, 1975, pp. 19a, 21a.
26. *Excélsior*, April 6, 1976, p. 9a.
27. *Por Qué?*, Jan. 3, 1973, p. 12.
28. Carrión 1973: 206.
29. *Excélsior*, Feb. 5, 1976, p. 7a.
30. *Siempre*, April 29, 1972, p. 9.
31. Loaeza 1974: 108.
32. *Proceso*, Jan. 1, 1977, p. 27-8; Jan. 8, p. 24.

Chapter 25: pp. 132-137

1. *Siempre*, Nov. 14, 1973, p. viii.
2. Fuentes 1972: 152.
3. Mora 1973: 58.
4. Hernández 1971: 13.
5. *Look*, Nov. 12, 1968, p. 20.
6. Fuentes 1972: 156.
7. Fuentes 1972: 150.
8. Paz 1972: 12-3.
9. *Current History*, May 1974, p. 230.
10. Huacuja & Woldenberg 1976: 91.
11. *Siempre*, May 23, 1973, p. iii.
12. *Excélsior*, April 28, 1976, p. 15a.
13. *Revista Mexicana de Ciencia Política*, July-Sept. 1973, p. 7.
14. García Cantú 1976: 2.
15. *Excélsior*, April 10, 1976, p. 1a.
16. *Excélsior*, March 25, 1976, p. 7a.
17. *Excélsior*, Sept. 20, 1974, p. 12a.
18. *Insurgencia Popular*, Nov. 1974, p. 19.
19. *Excélsior*, March 21, 1974, p. 7a.
20. *Excélsior*, March 21, 1974, p. 7a.
21. *Excélsior*, April 17, 1975, p. 7a.

22. *Insurgencia Popular,* Oct. 1975, p. 34-5.
23. *Fuentes Díaz* 1972: 368.
24. Agee 1975: 519.
25. *Visión,* Feb. 1, 1976, p. 11.
26. *Excélsior,* July 14, 1976, p. 7a.
27. *Latin America* 1975: 45.
28. Rosales 1975: 82.
29. *Oposición,* Dec. 1-15, 1973, p. v.
30. *El Día,* March 12, 1976, p. 15.
31. *Excélsior,* April 12, 1976, p. 18a.
32. *Proceso,* Feb. 12, 1977, p. 21.
33. Amnesty International 1975: 213-4.
34. *Amnesty Action,* July-Aug. 1976, p. 3.
35. *Excélsior,* April 19, 1975, p. 12a.
36. Fagen & Thouy 1972: 137.

Chapter 26: pp. 137-139

1. Huajuca & Woldenberg 1976: 137.
2. López 1974: 44.
3. López 1974: 49.
4. *Siempre,* Jan. 26, 1972, p. 4.
5. Mora 1972: 180.
6. Mora 1972: 211.
7. Rosales 1974: 76.
8. *Por Qué?,* Feb. 8, 1973, p. 3.
9. Rosales 1974: 89.
10. *Siempre,* June 12, 1974, p. 8.
11. López 1974: 138-9.
12. Rosales 1975: 88.
13. Rosales 1975: 39.
14. López 1974: 87.
15. *Punto Crítico,* Sept. 1972, p. 16.
16. *Excélsior,* Aug. 10, 1975, p. 32a.
17. *Excélsior,* Sept. 1, 1975, p. 1a.
18. Huajuca & Woldenberg 1976: 76.
19. *Siempre,* Dec. 17, 1975, p. 15.
20. *Proceso,* Dec. 18, 1976, p. 29.
21. *Excélsior,* June 24, 1976, p. 20a.
22. *Fortune,* Sept. 1975, p. 177.
23. *NACLA's Latin America & Empire Report,* March 1972, p. 7.
24. *Excélsior,* June 27, 1975, p. 22a.

Chapter 27: pp. 139-143

1. Berger 1972: 132.
2. Licona 1974: 118.
3. Wells 1972: 119.
4. Licona 1974: 123; *Le Monde Diplomatique,* Aug. 1976, p. 5.
5. Barnet & Müller 1974: 183.
6. Johnson 1972: 89.
7. Bernal Sahagún 1974: 124.
8. Wells 1972: 35.
9. Nuerta Ramírez 1975: 21.
10. *Latin America* 1976: 59.
11. Licona 1974: 73.
12. Hernández Gutiérrez 1973: 198; Bernal Sahagún 1973: 112-3.
13. Barnet & Müller 1974: 145.
14. González Casanova 1970: 63.
15. *Latinskaya Amerika,* March-April 1975, p. 10.
16. Bernal Sahagún 1974: 136-7.
17. *Granma Weekly Review,* Aug. 31, 1975, p. 8.
18. Bernal Sahagún 1974: 137.
19. Cosío Villegas 1972: 76.
20. Cole 1972: 79.
21. *Revista de Revistas,* Feb. 26, 1976, p. 11.
22. *Revista Mexicana de Ciencia Política,* July-Sept. 1972, p. 49.
23. *LAWG Letter,* Vol. II, No. 3, p. 5.
24. Cosío Villegas 1972: 125.
25. Bernal Sahagún 1974: 119.
26. García Cantú 1974: 218.
27. Quoted in *Revista Mexicana de Ciencia Política,* July-Sept. 1972, p. 42.
28. Bernal Sahagún 1974: 189-90.
29. Cosío Villegas 1974: 125.
30. *Excélsior,* April 22, 1975, p. 1a.
31. *Excélsior,* June 5, 1975, p. 1a.
32. *Editor & Publisher,* July 8, 1972, p. 14.
33. *Editor & Publisher,* July 8, 1972, p. 29.
34. *New York Times,* Jan. 2, 1977, Sec. 1, p. 13.
35. *New York Times,* July 9, 1976, p. 5; *Washington Post,* July 10, 1976, p. 12.
36. Rosales 1975: 39.
37. *Medios Publicitarios Mexicanos,* Nov. 1976.
38. *UNESCO Statistical Yearbook 1973,* p. 14.
39. *Comercio Exterior de México,* Dec. 1973, p. 34.
40. *Excélsior,* July 22, 1975, p. 1b.
41. *Excélsior,* April 23, 1975, p. 6a.
42. *Plural,* March, 1973, p. 31-3.

Chapter 28: pp. 143-149

1. Quoted in García Cantú 1971: 17.
2. Alperovich 1960: 139.
3. Quoted in García Cantú 1971: 12.
4. Garcia Cantú 1971: 142.
5. Quoted in Acuña 1972: 15.
6. Acuña 1972: 16.
7. Acuña 1972: 17.
8. Acuña 1972: 16-7.
9. Medina Castro 1971: 33.
10. Quoted in Acuña: 18.
11. Acuña 1972: 18.
12. Velasco Márquez 1975: 72.
13. Quoted in García Cantú 1971: 59.
14. García Cantú 1971: 90.
15. Connor & Faulk 1971: 61.
16. Acuña 1972: 58.
17. Connor & Faulk 1971: 31.
18. Price 1967: 153.
19. Quoted in Price 1967: 91-2.
20. Quoted in Price 1967: 95.
21. Belenki 1966: 16.
22. Medina Castro 1971: 87.
23. Acuña 1972: 105.
24. García Cantú 1971: 181.
25. Acuña 1972: 104.
26. Quoted in Acuña 1972: 101.
27. Acuña 1972: 82.
28. Belenki 1966: 20.
29. García Cantú 1971: 176.
30. Belenki 1966: 18.
31. Belenki 1966: 174.
32. Belenki 1966: 174.
33. Miller 1973: 11; García Cantú 1971: 201.
34. Quoted in Miller 1973: 10.
35. Miller 1973: 7.
36. *Pacific Historical Review,* Feb. 1976, p. 24.
37. *Pacific Historical Review,* Feb. 1976, p. 26.
38. Rudenko 1960: 35.
39. Alperovich & Rudenko 1969: 27.
40. Alperovich & Rudenko 1969: 10.
41. Alperovich & Rudenko 1969: 78.
42. Alperovich & Rudenko 1969: 74.
43. Alperovich & Rudenko 1969: 81.
44. Alperovich & Rudenko 1969: 81.
45. Alperovich & Rudenko 1969: 86.
46. Fuentes 1972: 132.
47. Gilly 1971: 79.
48. Cline 1963: 133.
49. Cumberland 1952: 242.
50. Cumberland 1952: 249.
51. Alperovich & Rudenko 1969: 154.
52. Alperovich & Rudenko 1969: 164.
53. Ulloa 1971: 179.
54. Ulloa 1971: 181.
55. Ulloa 1971: 182.
56. Alperovich & Rudenko 1969: 211.
57. Córdova 1973: 32.
58. Córdova 1973: 253
59. *Business History Review,* Autumn 1973, p. 337.
60. Bassols 1967: 70.
61. Cline 1963: 207-8.
62. Meyer 1973: 135.
63. Quoted in *Historia Mexicana,* July-Sept. 1968, p. 91.
64. Basurto 1975: 281.
65. Quoted in Basurto 1975: 262.
66. *Vuelta,* March 1977, p. 22.
67. Pazos 1976: 72.
68. Córdova 1973: 31.
69. Quoted in *Punto Crítico,* June 1972, p. 23.
70. Córdova 1973: 32.
71. Cline 1963: 249.
72. Newfarmer and Mueller 1975: 36.

Chapter 29: pp. 150-155

1. Paz 1972: ix.
2. *Tiempo,* Feb. 28, 1977, p. 16.
3. *Wall Street Journal,* Dec. 24, 1976, p. 1.
4. *Proceso,* Jan. 29, 1977, p. 39.
5. *Proceso,* Nov. 20, 1976, p. 11.
6. *Proceso,* Jan. 29, 1977, p. 39.

7. *International Labour Review*, Nov. 1975, p. 352.
8. *International Labour Review*, Nov. 1975, p. 353.
9. *Aztlán*, Summer 1975, p. 181.
10. *International Labour Review*, Nov. 1975, p. 353.
11. Levenstein 1974: 204.
12. *Southwest Economy and Society*, Oct.-Nov. 1976, p. 11.
13. *International Labour Review*, Nov. 1975, p. 359.
14. *International Labour Review*, Nov. 1975, p. 357.
15. *International Labour Review*, Nov. 1975, p. 359.
16. Quoted in *International Labour Review*, Nov. 1975, p. 362.
17. *Hanson's Latin American Letter*, July 31, 1976, p. 1.
18. *International Labour Review*, Nov. 1975, p. 362.
19. *Excélsior*, June 19, 1976, p. 3a.
20. Bustamante 1975: 33.
21. *New York Times*, June 19, 1977, Sec. 1, p. 12.
22. *International Labour Review*, Nov. 1975, p. 368.
23. *International Labour Review*, Nov. 1975, p. 368.
24. *Department of State Bulletin* 1974: 665. (López Portillo also noted that US import restrictions reduce the number of manufacturing jobs in Mexico. *Forbes*, April 1, 1977, p. 28.)
25. Bustamante 1975: 42.
26. *International Labour Review*, Nov. 1975, p. 316.
27. *Wall Street Journal*, Nov. 21, 1975, p. 36; *Comercio Exterior* 1977: 41.
28. *Mexican-American Review*, March, 1975. p. 65.
29. *Business Latin America* 1976: 62.
30. *Excélsior*, March 8, 1975, p. 13a.
31. Dillman 1976: 6.
32. *Forbes*, April 1, 1977, p. 28.
33. Ledogar 1975: 83.
34. *New York Times*, May 15, 1977, Sec. 1, p. 20.
35. Bustamante 1976: 10.
36. Bustamante 1976: 20.
37. *Latinskaya Amerika*, Sept.-Oct. 1974, p. 40.
38. Bustamante 1976: 18.
39. Dillman 1976: 1.
40. *Excélsior*, Jan. 26, 1976, p. 19a.
41. *New York Times*, May 26, 1975, p. 22.
42. *Wall Street Journal*, Nov. 21, 1975, p. 36.
43. AFL-CIO 1973: 74.
44. NACLA 1971: 45.
45. Quoted in Wells 1972: 96.
46. Ramirez Racaño 1974: 69.
47. *Excélsior*, June 19, 1976, p. 1a.
48. *Excélsior*, June 19, 1976, p. 14a.
49. Agee 1975: 499.
50. Agee 1975: 525.
51. *New York Times*, Feb. 19, 1977, p. 9.
52. *Excélsior*, Sept. 15, 1974, p. 1a.
53. Agee 1975: 499.
54. Agee 1975: 499.
55. Agee 1975: 499.
56. Agee 1975: 535.
57. Agee 1975: 275.
58. Hunt 1974: 78.
59. *1970 Census of Population. Subject Reports: Americans Living Abroad*, p. 1.
60. *Amistad*, April 1976, pp. 36-46.
61. *NACLA's Latin America & Empire Report*, VIII, No. 1, p. 16.
62. Scheer 1974: 99.
63. *Washington Monthly*, Jan. 1977, p. 46.
64. *Excélsior*, March 13, 1976, p. 30a.
65. *Excélsior*, Jan. 21, 1976, p. 11a.
66. *Penthouse*, Feb. 1977, p. 48.
67. *Foreign Affairs*, July 1977, p. 687.
68. *Excélsior*, July 18, 1976, p. 2a.
69. *Penthouse*, Feb. 1977, p. 122.
70. *Proceso*, Nov. 13, 1976, p. 11.
71. *Excélsior*, July 10, 1976, p. 23a.
72. *Excélsior*, May 16, 1976, p. 30a.
73. *Excélsior*, July 23, 1976, p. 27a.
74. *Los Angeles Times*, Jan. 30, 1977, p. 1.
75. *Wall Street Journal*, Sept. 13, 1976, p. 14.
76. *Proceso*, Nov. 13, 1976, p. 11; *Harper's*, June 1977, p. 51.
77. *Texas Monthly*, Sept. 1976, p. 86.
78. *Playboy*, Feb. 1976, p. 82.
79. *Excélsior*, Jan. 5, 1976, p. 7a.
80. *Siempre*, April 26, 1972, p. 60.
81. Ledogar 1975: 111.
82. Stanford Research Institute 1975: 53.

Chapter 30: pp. 156-158

1. CDIA 1974: 110.
2. *Tiempo*, Feb. 28, 1977, p. 16.
3. *Excélsior*, Feb. 12, 1975, p. 15a.
4. *Excélsior*, Feb. 20, 1976, p. 32a.
5. *Excélsior*, Aug. 19, 1975, p. 15a.
6. *Business Latin America* 1976: 19, 36.
7. *Newsweek*, Aug. 27, 1973, p. 88.
8. *Excélsior*, March 5, 1976, p. 13a.
9. *Latin America* 1976: 59.
10. *Gaceta Médica de México*, Jan. 1972, p. 47.
11. *El Día*, March 24, 1975, p. 13.
12. *Proceso*, Jan. 15, 1977, p. 8.
13. Medina 1972: 70.
14. Sepúlveda 1974: 52.
15. Conroy & Folbre 1976: 37.
16. *Comercio Exterior* 1974: 694.
17. *Comercio Exterior* 1974: 695.
18. *Comercio Exterior* 1974: 695.
19. *Demografía y Economía* 1971: 151.
20. Elu de Leñero 1975: 119.
21. *Excélsior*, June 19, 1976, p. 4a.
22. CDIA 1974: 372.
23. *New York Times*, July 1, 1976, p. 2.
24. *New York Times*, July 1, 1976, p. 2.
25. *Excélsior*, June 19, 1976, p. 4a.
26. Inter-American Development Bank 1976: 373.
27. *Proceso*, Jan. 8, 1977, p. 30.
28. Conroy & Folbre 1976: 24.
29. *Ramparts*, Aug. 1975, p. 59.
30. *Comercio Exterior* 1974: 396.
31. *Current History*, March 1977, p. 108.
32. *Ramparts*, Aug. 1975, p. 59.
33. *Proceso*, Dec. 18, 1976, p. 57.
34. *Feminist Studies*, Vol. II, No. 2-3.

Chapter 31: pp. 158-60

1. *Latin American Perspectives*, Spring 1974, p. 144.
2. *Harper's*, April 1973, p. 68.
3. *Latin American Perspectives*, Spring 1974, p. 146.

170

BIBLIOGRAPHY

Abbreviations:

CDIA: Centro de Investigaciones Agrarias
INAH: Instituto Nacional de Antropología e Historia
INI: Instituto Nacional Indigenista
NACLA: North American Congress on Latin America
SEP: Secretaría de Educación Pública
UNAM: Universidad Nacional Autónoma de México

Acevedo, Marta. *Ni Diosa Ni Mártir*. Mexico City: Extemporáneos, 1971.

Acuña, Rodolfo. *Occupied America*. San Francisco: Canfield, 1972.

AFL-CIO. *U.S. Multinationals: The Diming of America*. A Report Prepared for the AFL-CIO Maritime Trades Department Executive Board Meeting, February 1973.

Agee, Philip. *Inside the Company: CIA Diary*. Harmondsworth, Middlesex: Penguin, 1975.

Aguilar, Alonso. "El Proceso de Acumulación de Capital," pp. 11-171 in: *México: Riqueza y Miseria* (4th ed.). Mexico City: Nuestro Tiempo, 1970.

Aguilar, Alonso. *Problemas Estructurales del Subdesarrollo*. Mexico City: UNAM, 1971.

Aguilar, Alonso. "La Oligarquía," pp. 77-231 in: *La Burguesía, La Oligarquía, y El Estado*. Mexico City: Nuestro Tiempo, 1972.

Aguilar, Alonso. *Dialéctica de la Economía Mexicana* (5th ed.). Mexico City: Nuestro Tiempo, 1974.

Aguirre Beltrán, Gonzalo. *La Población Negra De México* (2nd ed.). Mexico City: Fondo de Cultura Económica, 1972.

Aguirre Beltrán, Gonzalo. *Regiones de Refugio*. Mexico City: SEP/INI, 1973.

Aguirre Beltrán, Gonzalo. *Obra Polémica*. Mexico City: SEP/INAH, 1976.

Alonso, Antonio. *El Movimiento Ferrocarrilero en México: 1958-1959*. Mexico City: Era, 1972.

Alperovich, M. S. "La Historia de las Relaciones entre México y Estados Unidos en la Historiografía Mexicana de Postguerra," pp. 127-156 in: *La Revolución Mexicana: Cuatro Estudios Soviéticos*. Mexico City: Insurgentes, 1960.

Alperovich, M. S. *Historia de la Independencia de México*. Mexico City: Grijalbo, 1967.

Alpervich, M.S. & B.T. Rudenko. *La Revolución Mexicana de 1910-1917 y la Política de los Estados Unidos* (3rd ed.). Mexico City: Fondo de Cultura Popular, 1969.

Amnesty International. *Amnesty International Report on Torture*. New York: Farrar, Straus and Giroux, 1975.

Anderson, Bo & James D. Cockcroft. "Control and Co-optation in Mexican Politics," pp. 219-244 in: *Dependence and Underdevelopment*. Garden City: Anchor/Doubleday, 1972.

Anguiano, Arturo. *El Estado y la Política Obrera del Cardenismo*. Mexico City: Era, 1975.

Arizpe, Lourdes. "La Ideología del Indio y la Economía Campesina," pp. 99-132 in: *Capitalismo y Campesinado en México*. Mexico City: SEP/INAH, 1976.

Barnet, Richard J. & Ronald E. Müller. *Global Reach*. New York: Simon & Schuster, 1974.

Bartra, Roger. *Estructura Agraria y Clases Sociales en México*. Mexico City: Era, 1974.

Bartra, Roger. "Campesinado y Poder Político en México," pp. 5-30 in: *Caciquismo y Poder Político en el México Rural*. Mexico City: Siglo XXI, 1975.

Bassols, Narisco. *Obras*. Mexico City: Fondo de Cultura Económica, 1964.

Bassols Batalla, Narisco. *El Pensamiento Político de Alvaro Obregón*. Mexico City: Nuestro Tiempo, 1967.

Basurto, Jorge. "Obstáculos al Cambio en el Movimiento Obrero," pp. 47-70 in: *El Perfil de México en 1980*, Vol. 3. Mexico City: Siglo XXI, 1972.

Basurto, Jorge. *El Proletariado Industrial en México (1850-1930)*. Mexico City: UNAM, 1975.

Bazant, Jan. *Historia de la Deuda Exterior de México (1823-1946)*. Mexico City: Colegio de México, 1968.

Bazant, Jan. "Desamortización y Nacionalización de los Bienes de la Iglesia," pp. 155-190 in: *La Economía Mexicana en la Epoca de Juárez*. Mexico City: SEP/Setentas, 1976.

Belenki, A. B. *La Intervención Extranjera de 1861-1867 en México*. Mexico City: Ediciones de Cultura Popular, 1966.

Benítez, Fernando. *In the Footsteps of Cortes*. London: Peter Owen, 1957.

Benítez, Fernando. *The Century After Cortes*. Chicago: University of Chicago Press, 1965.

Berger, John. *Ways of Seeing*. Harmondsworth, Middlesex: Penguin, 1972.

Bernal Sahagún, Víctor M. *Anatomía de la Publicidad en México*. Mexico City: Nuestro Tiempo, 1974.

Beteta, Mario Ramón. *Prospectus* [issued Feb. 19, 1976 for 9 ½% external bonds due March 1, 1981]. Mexico City: Secretary of Finance and Public Credit, 1976.

Blair, Calvin, "Nacional Financiera," pp. 191-240 in: *Public Policy and Private Enterprise in Mexico*. Cambridge: Harvard University Press, 1964.

Boege, Eckart & Pilar Calvo. "Estructura Política y Clases Sociales en una Comunidad del Valle del Mezquital," pp. 131-147 in: *Caciquismo y Poder Político en el México Rural*. Mexico City: Siglo XXI, 1975.

Bonilla Sánchez, Arturo. "Un Problema que se Agrava," pp. 125-173 in: *Neolatifundismo y Explotación* (3rd ed.). Mexico City: Nuestro Tiempo, 1973.

Borah, Woodrow, *New Spain's Century of Depression*. Los Angeles and Berkeley: University of California Press, 1951.

Borah, Woodrow. "Legacies of the Past: Colonial," pp. 29-37 in: *Contemporary Mexico*. Berkeley: University of California Press, 1976.

Brandenberg, Frank. *The Making of Modern Mexico*. Englewood Cliffs, N.J.: Prentice-Hall, 1964.

Bustamante, Jorge. *Espaldas Mojadas: Materia Prima para la Expansión del Capital Norteamericano*. Mexico City: El Colegio de México, 1975.

Bustamante, Jorge. *Maquiladoras: A New Face of International Capitalism in Mexico's Northern Frontier*. Paper presented at the Sixth National Meeting of the Latin American Studies Association, Atlanta, Georgia, March 1976.

Cabral, Roberto & Raimundo Arroio, Jr. *El Proceso de Industrialización en México, 1940-50*. Thesis, Escuela Nacional de Economía, 1974.

Calderón, José María. *Génesis del Presidencialismo en México*. Mexico City: El Caballito, 1972.

Calderón de la Barca, Fanny. *Life in Mexico*. Garden City, N.Y.: Doubleday, 1966.

Calvo, Pilar & Roger Bartra. "Estructura de Poder, Clases Dominantes y Lucha Ideológica en el México Rural," pp. 88-130 in: *Caciquismo y Poder Político en el México Rural*. Mexico City: Siglo XXI, 1975.

Cárdenas, Lázaro. *Obras I: Apuntes 1913/1940*. Mexico City: UNAM, 1972.

Carmona, Fernando. "La Situación Económica," pp. 13-102 in: *El Milagro Mexicano* (3rd. ed.). Mexico City: Nuestro Tiempo, 1973.

Carmona Amorós, Salvador. *La Economía Mexicana y el Nacionalismo Revolucionario*. Mexico City: El Caballito, 1974.

Carreras Maldonado, María & Sara Montero Duhalt. "La Condición de la Mujer en el Derecho Civil Mexicano," pp. 71-125 in: *Condición Jurídica de la Mujer en México*. Mexico City: UNAM, 1975.

Carrión, Jorge. "Retablo de la Política 'a la Mexicana'," pp. 164-246 in: *El Milagro Mexicano* (3rd. ed.). Mexico City: Nuestro Tiempo, 1973.

Casas, Bartolomé de las. *Tratados de Fray Bartolomé de las Casas*. Mexico City: Fondo de Cultura Económica, 1965.

Castaneda, Carlos. *A Separate Reality*. New York: Simon & Schuster, 1971.

Castaneda, Carlos. *Journey to Ixtlan*. New York: Simon & Schuster, 1972.

Ceceña, José Luis. *México en la Orbita Imperial*. Mexico City: El Caballito, 1970.

Centro de Investigaciones Agrarias. *Estructura Agraria y Desarrollo Agrícola en México*. Mexico City: Fondo de Cultura Económica, 1974.

Chávarri, Juan N. *Historia de la Guerra de Independencia*. Mexico City: Editora Latino Americana, 1960.

Chevalier, Francois. *Land and Society in Colonial Mexico*. Berkeley: University of California Press, 1963.

Chiñas, Beverly. *Mujeres de San Juan*. Mexico City: SEP/Setentas, 1975.

Cline, Howard F. *The United States and Mexico* (revised). Cambridge: Harvard University Press, 1963.

Coatsworth, John H. *El Impacto Económico de los Ferrocarriles en el Porfiriato* (2 vols.). Mexico City: SEP/Setentas, 1976.

Cockcroft, James. *Intellectual Precursors of the Mexican Revolution, 1900-1913*. Austin: University of Texas Press, 1968.

Cockcroft, James. "Social and Economic Structure of the Porfiriato: Mexico, 1877-1911," pp. 47-70 in: *Dependence and Underdevelopment*. Garden City: Doubleday/Anchor, 1972.

Cole, Richard Ray. *The Mass Media of Mexico: Ownership and Control*. Ph.D. Dissertation, University of Minnesota, 1972.

Connor, Seymour V. & Odie B. Faulk. *North America Divided*. New York: Oxford University Press, 1971.

Conroy, Michael & Nancy Folbre. *Population Growth as a Deterrent to Economic Growth: A Reappraisal of the Evidence*. Hastings-on-Hudson: Institute of Society, Ethics, and the Life Sciences, 1976.

Córdova, Arnaldo. *La Formación del Poder Político en México*. Mexico City: Era, 1972.

Córdova, Arnaldo. *La Ideología de la Revolución Mexicana*. Mexico City: Era, 1973.

Córdova, Arnaldo. *La Política de Masas del Cardenismo*. Mexico City: Era, 1974.

Córdova, Arnaldo. "La Transformación del PNR en PRM: El Triunfo del Corporativismo en México," pp. 204-227 in: *Contemporary Mexico*. Berkeley: University of California Press, 1976.

Cortés, Hernán: *5 Letters of Cortes to the Emperor*. New York: Norton, 1962.

Cortés, Hernán. *Letters from Mexico*. New York: Grossman, 1971.

Cosío Villegas, Daniel. *El Sistema Político Mexicano*. Mexico City: Joaquín Mortiz, 1972.

Cosío Villegas, Daniel. *El Estilo Personal de Gobernar*. Mexico City: Joaquín Mortiz, 1972.

Cosío Villegas, Daniel. *La Sucesión Presidencial*. Mexico City: Joaquín Mortiz, 1975.

Cué Cánovas, Agustín. *Historia Social y Económica de México*. Mexico City: Editorial América, 1946.

Cumberland, Charles C. *Mexican Revolution: Genesis Under Madero*. Austin: University of Texas Press, 1952.

Cumberland, Charles C. *Mexico: The Struggle for Modernity*. New York: Oxford University Press, 1968.

Cumberland, Charles C. *Mexican Revolution: The Constitutionalist Years*. Austin: University of Texas Press, 1972.

Danzós, Ramón. *Desde la Cárcel de Atlixco*. Mexico City: Ediciones de Cultura Popular, 1974.

Díaz del Castillo, Bernal. *The Discovery and Conquest of Mexico*. New York: Farrar, Straus and Cudahy, 1956.

Díaz Hernández, Jorge. *El Indigenismo en México como Problema Económico*. Thesis, Escuela Nacional de Economía, 1972.

Dillman, C. Daniel. *Mexico's Border Industrialization Program (BIP): Current Patterns and Alternative Futures*. Paper presented at the Sixth National Meeting of the Latin American Studies Association, Atlanta, Georgia, March 1976.

Durán, Marco Antonio. *El Agrarismo Mexicano* (2nd ed.). Mexico City: Siglo XXI, 1972.

Elu de Leñero, María del Carmen (ed.). *Mujeres Que Hablan*. Mexico City: Instituto Mexicano de Estudios Sociales, 1971.

Elu de Leñero, María del Carmen. *El Trabajo de la Mujer en México*. Mexico City: Instituto Mexicano de Estudios Sociales, 1975.

Fagen, Richard R. & William S. Tuohy. *Politics and Privilege in a Mexican City*. Stanford: Stanford University Press, 1972.

Fernández, José Antonio & Herbert May. *El Impacto Económico de la Inversión Extranjera en México*. Mexico City: Editorial Tabasco, 1971.

Fernández Bazavilvazo, Mercedes. "Condición de la Mujer en el Derecho Laboral Mexicano," pp. 173-196 in: *Condición Jurídica de la Mujer en México*. Mexico City: UNAM, 1975.

Fernández Hurtado, Ernesto. "Private Enterprise and Government in Mexican Development," pp. 45-68 in: *Mexico's Recent Economic Growth*. Austin: University of Texas Press, 1967.

Flores Caballero, Romeo. "Etapas del Desarrollo Industrial," pp. 107-128 in: *La Economía Mexicana en la Epoca de Juárez*. Mexico City: SEP/Setentas, 1976.

Florescano, Enrique. *Estructuras y Problemas Agrarios de México* (1500-1821). Mexico City: SEP/Setentas, 1971.

Folbre, Nancy. *Economic Growth and Income Distribution in Latin America*. Masters Thesis in Economics, University of Texas at Austin, 1974.

Frank, Andre Gunder. *Latin America: Underdevelopment or Revolution*. New York: Monthly Review, 1969.

Frank, Andre Gunder. *Lumpenbourgeoisie: Lumpendevelopment*. New York: Monthly Review, 1972.

Fuente, Julio de la. *Relaciones Interétnicas*. Mexico City: Instituto Nacional Indigenista, 1965.

Fuentes, Carlos. *Tiempo Mexicano*. Mexico City: Joaquín Mortiz, 1972.

Fuentes Díaz, Vicente. *Los Partidos Políticos en México*. Mexico City: Editorial Altiplano, 1972.

Furtado, Celso. *The Economic Development of Latin America*. Cambridge: Cambridge University Press, 1970.

Furtak, Robert. *Revolutionspartei und Politische Stabilität in Mexico*. Hamburg: Ubersee-Verlag, 1969.

Galbraith, John Kenneth. *Money*. Boston: Houghton, Mifflin, 1975.

Galeano, Eduardo. *Open Veins of Latin America*. New York: Monthly Review, 1973.

García Cantú, Gastón. *El Socialismo en México, Siglo XIX.* Mexico City: Era, 1969.

García Cantú, Gastón. *Las Invasiones Norteamericanas en México.* Mexico City: Era, 1971.

García Cantú, Gastón. *Política Mexicana.* Mexico City: UNAM, 1974.

García Cantú, Gastón. *La Hora de los Halcones.* Puebla: Universidad Autónoma de Puebla, 1976.

García Zuno, José Pablo. *El Problema Habitacional en México.* Thesis, Escuela Nacional de Economía, 1975.

Gibson, Charles. *The Aztecs Under Spanish Rule.* Stanford: Stanford University Press, 1964.

Gibson, Charles. *Spain in America.* New York: Harper & Row, 1966.

Gilly, Adolfo. *La Revolución Interrumpida.* Mexico City: El Caballito, 1971.

Gómez, Marte R. *Pancho Villa: Un Intento de Semblanza.* Mexico City: Fondo de Cultura Económica, 1972.

Gómez-Jara, Francisco A. *El Movimiento Campesino en México.* Mexico City: Editorial Campesina, 1970.

González, Luis. "La Era de Juárez," pp. 11-55 in: *La Economía de México en la Epoca de Juárez.* Mexico City: SEP/Setentas, 1976.

González Casanova, Pablo. "Mexico: The Dynamics of an Agrarian and Semicapitalist Revolution," pp. 467-85 in: James Petras & Maurice Zeitlin (eds.), *Latin America: Reform or Revolution?* New York: Fawcett, 1968.

González Casanova, Pablo. *Democracy in Mexico.* New York: Oxford University Press, 1970.

González Salazar, Gloria. *Subocupación y Estructura de Clases Sociales en México.* Mexico City: UNAM, 1972.

Green, Rosario. *El Endeudamiento Público Externo de México 1940-1973.* Mexico City: Colegio de México, 1976.

Greenleaf, Richard E. "The Mexican Inquisition and the Enlightenment," pp. 388-97 in: *History of Latin American Civilization, Vol. I.* Boston: Little, Brown & Co., 1967.

Gutelman, Michel. *Capitalismo y Reforma Agraria en México.* Mexico City: Era, 1974.

Hale, Charles A. *Mexican Liberalism in the Age of Mora, 1821-1853.* New Haven: Yale University Press, 1968.

Hansen, Roger D. *The Politics of Mexican Development.* Baltimore: Johns Hopkins, 1971.

Hayter, Teresa. *Aid as Imperialism.* Harmondsworth, Middlesex: Penguin, 1971.

Hernández, Salvador. *El PRI y el Movimiento Estudiantil de 1968.* Mexico City: El Caballito, 1971.

Hernández Gutiérrez, Ignacio. "La Burguesía Nativa y el Capital Extranjero," pp. 150-203 in: *La Burguesía Mexicana.* Mexico City: Nuestro Tiempo, 1973.

Huacuja R., Mario & José Woldenberg. *Estado y Lucha Política en el México Actual.* Mexico City: El Caballito, 1976.

Huizer, Gerrit. *La Lucha Campesina en México.* Mexico City: Centro de Investigaciones Agrarias, 1970.

Hunt, E. Howard. *Undercover: Memoirs of an American Secret Agent.* New York: Putnam, 1974.

Instituto Nacional Indigenista. *¿Ha Fracasado el Indigenismo?* Mexico City: SEP/Setentas, 1971.

Inter-American Development Bank: *Economic and Social Progress in Latin America: Annual Report 1975.* Washington, D.C.: Inter-American Development Bank, 1976.

Johnson, Dale L. "Dependence and the International System," pp. 71-111 in: *Development and Underdevelopment.* Garden City: Anchor/Doubleday, 1972.

Katz, Friedrich. "Agrarian Changes in Northern Mexico in the Period of Villista Rule, 1913-1915," pp. 259-273, in: *Contemporary Mexico.* Berkeley, University of California Press, 1976.

Keremitsis, Dawn. *La Industria Textil Mexicana en el Siglo XIX.* Mexico City: SEP/Setentas, 1973.

Lagarde, Marcela. *El Indigenismo, un Proceso Ideológico.* Thesis, Escuela Nacional de Antropología e Historia, 1974.

Larov, N. M. "La Revolución Mexicana de 1910-1917," pp. 87-125 in: *La Revolución Mexicana: Cuatro Estudios Soviéticos.* Mexico City: Insurgentes, 1960.

Latapí, Pablo. "Las Necesidades del Sistema Educativo Nacional," pp. 330-358 in: *La Sociedad Mexicana.* Mexico City: Fondo de Cultura Económica, 1974.

Leal, Juan Felipe. *La Burguesía y el Estado Mexicano* (2nd ed.). Mexico City: El Caballito, 1974.

Leal, Juan Felipe. *México: Estado, Burocracia y Sindicatos.* Mexico City: El Caballito, 1975.

Ledogar, Robert J. *Hungry for Profits.* New York: IDOC/North America, 1975.

León-Portilla, Miguel. *The Broken Spears.* Boston: Beacon, 1962.

Levenstein, Harvey A. *Labor Organizations in the United States and Mexico.* Westpoint, Conn.: Greenwood, 1971.

Lewis, Oscar. *Pedro Martínez.* New York: Random House, 1964.

Leyva, Emilio. "Burguesía Agrícola y Dependencia," pp. 101-139 in: *La Burguesía Mexicana.* Mexico City: Nuestro Tiempo, 1973.

Licona, Hugo de Jesús. *La Publicidad y Sus Implicaciones Económicas y Sociales en México.* Thesis, Escuela Nacional de Economía, 1974.

Lieuwen, Edwin. *Mexican Militarism.* Albuquerque: University of New Mexico Press, 1968.

Liss, Peggy K. *Mexico Under Spain 1521-1556.* Chicago: University of Chicago Press, 1975.

Loaeza, Soledad. "El Partido Acción Nacional: La Oposición Leal en México," pp. 101-125 in: *La Vida Política en México 1970-1973.* Mexico City: Colegio de México, 1974.

López, Jaime. *10 Años de Guerrillas en México: 1946-74.* Mexico City: Posada, 1974.

López Gallo, Manuel. *Economía y Política en la Historia de México* (11th ed.). Mexico City: El Caballito, 1975.

López Rosado, Diego G. *Historia y Pensamiento Económico de México* (3 vols.). Mexico City: UNAM, 1968-9.

Mariátegui, José Carlos. *Seven Interpretive Essays on Peruvian Reality.* Austin: University of Texas Press, 1971.

Martínez Vázquez, Víctor Raúl. "Despojo y Manipulación Campesina," pp. 148-194 in: *Caciquismo y Poder Político en el México Rural.* Mexico City: Siglo XXI, 1975.

McNeill, William H. *Plagues and People.* Garden City: Anchor/Doubleday, 1976.

Medin, Tzvi. *Ideología y Praxis Política de Lázaro Cárdenas.* Mexico City: Siglo XXI, 1972.

Medina, Andrés. *Tres Puntos de Referencia en el Indigenismo Mexicano Contemporáneo.* Mexico City: Sección de Antropología, Instituto de Investigación Histórica, UNAM, 1973.

Medina, Lino. *Oligarquía Mexicana: Crisis y Revolución.* Mexico City: S.P.I., 1972.

Medina, Luis. "Origen y Circunstancia de la Idea de Unidad Nacional," pp. 7-32 in: *La Vida Política en México 1970-1973.* Mexico City: Colegio de México, 1974.

Medina Castro, Manuel. *El Gran Despojo.* Mexico City: Diógenes, 1971.

Mesa-Lago, Carmelo. "Social Security Stratification and Inequality in Mexico," pp. 228-255 in: *Contemporary Mexico.* Berkeley: University of California Press, 1976.

Meyer, Jean. *La Révolution Mexicaine.* Paris: Calmann-Lévy, 1973.

Meyer, Jean. *La Cristiada: Los Cristeros.* Mexico City, Siglo XXI, 1974.

Michaels, Albert L. & Marvin Bernstein, "The Modernization of the Old Order: Organization and Periodization of Twentieth-Century Mexican History," pp. 687-710 in: *Contemporary Mexico*. Berkeley: University of California Press, 1976.

Miller, Robert R. *Arms Across the Border*. Transactions of the American Philosophical Society, Vol. 63, 1973.

Millon, Robert P. *Zapata: The Ideology of a Peasant Revolutionary*. New York: International, 1969.

Moirón, Sara. *En el Nombre del Indio*. Mexico City: Editorial Económica Escolar, 1970.

Montaño, Guillermo. "Los Problemas Sociales," pp. 103-163 in: *El Milagro Mexicano* (3rd ed.). Mexico City: Nuestro Tiempo, 1973.

Montes, Eduardo. *¿Cómo Combatir al Charrismo?* Mexico City: Ediciones de Cultura Popular, 1972.

Mora, Juan Miguel de. *Las Guerrillas en México y Jenaro Vázquez Rojas*. Mexico City: Editora Latino Americano, 1972.

Mora, Juan Miguel de. *T-68 (Tlatelolco 1968)*. Mexico City: Editores Asociados, 1973.

Moreno Toscano, Alejandra & Enrique Florescano. "El Sector Externo y la Organización Espacial y Regional de México (1521-1910)," pp. 62-96 in: *Contemporary Mexico*. Berkeley: University of California Press, 1976.

Morison, Samuel Eliot. *The Oxford History of the American People*. New York: Oxford University Press, 1965.

Navarrete, Ifigenia M. de. "La Distribución del Ingreso en México," pp. 15-71 in: *El Perfil De México en 1980*. Mexico City: Siglo XXI, 1970.

Needler, Martin C. *Politics and Society in Mexico*. Albuquerque: University of New Mexico Press, 1971.

Newfarmer, Richard S. & Williard F. Mueller. *Multinational Corporations in Brasil and Mexico: Structural Sources of Economic and Non-economic Power*. Report to the Subcommittee on Multinational Corporations of the Committee of Foreign Relations, United States Senate, 94th Congress, 1st Session.

North American Congress on Latin America. *Yanqui Dollar*. New York: NACLA, 1971.

Nuerta Ramírez, Octavio. *La Televisión en México*. Thesis, Escuela Nacional de Economía, 1975.

O'Connor, James. *The Corporation and the State*. New York: Harper & Row, 1974.

Padilla Aragón, Enrique. "Los Problemas de la Economía Nacional," Supplement to *El Día*, June 30, 1975.

Palerm, Angel. "Ensayo de Crítica al Desarrollo Regional en México, pp. 13-62 in: *Los Beneficiarios del Desarrollo Regional*. Mexico City: SEP/Setentas, 1972.

Paré, Luisa. "Caciquismo y Estructura de Poder en la Sierra Norte de Puebla," pp. 31-61 in: *Caciquismo y Poder Político en el México Rural*. Mexico City: Siglo XXI, 1975.

Payer, Cheryl. *The Debt Trap*. New York: Monthly Review, 1975.

Paz, Octavio. *The Labyrinth of Solitude*. New York: Grove, 1961.

Paz, Octavio. *The Other Mexico*. Mexico City: Grove, 1972.

Paz Sánchez, Fernando. "Problemas y Perspectivas del Desarrollo Agrícola," pp. 56-104 in: *Neolatifundismo y Explotación* (3rd Ed.). Mexico City: Nuestro Tiempo, 1973a.

Paz Sánchez, Fernando. "Problemas y Perspectivas del Desarrollo Agrícola," pp. 188-197 in: *Neolatifundismo y Explotación* (3rd ed.). Mexico City: Nuestro Tiempo, 1973b.

Pazos, Luis. *Devaluación en México*. Mexico City: Diana, 1976.

Pellicer de Brody, Olga. "El Llamado a las Inversiones Extranjeras 1953-1958," pp. 75-104 in: *Las Empresas Transnacionales en México*. Mexico City: Colegio de México, 1974.

Peña, Sergio de la. *La Formación del Capitalismo en México*. Mexico City: Siglo XXI, 1975.

Petras, James. *Politics and Social Structure in Latin America*. New York: Monthly Review, 1970.

Pozas, Ricardo. *Juan the Chamula*. Berkeley & Los Angeles: University of California Press, 1962.

Pozas, Ricardo, & Isabel H. de Pozas. *Los Indios en las Clases Sociales de México*. Mexico City: Siglo XXI, 1971.

Prescott, W. H. *The Conquest of Mexico* (2 vols.). New York: Dutton, 1931.

Price, Glen W. *Origins of the War with Mexico*. Austin: University of Texas Press, 1967.

Puente Leyva, Jesús. "El Problema Habitacional," pp. 253-303 in: *El Perfil de México en 1980, Vol. II*. Mexico City: Siglo XXI, 1970.

Ramírez Racaño, Mario. *La Burguesía Industrial*. Mexico City: Nuestro Tiempo, 1974.

Reed, John. *Insurgent Mexico*. New York: D. Appleton, 1914.

Reyna, José Luis. "Movilización y Participación Políticas," pp. 503-35 in: *El Perfil de México en 1980*, Vol. III. Mexico City: Siglo XXI, 1972.

Reynolds, Clark. *The Mexican Economy*. New Haven: Yale University Press, 1970.

Ribeiro, Darcy. *The Americas and Civilization*. New York: Dutton, 1971.

Rivanuva, Gastón. *El PRI: El Gran Mito Mexicano*. Editorial Tradición, 1974.

Rivera Marín, Guadalupe. *El Mercado de Trabajo*. Mexico City: Fondo de Cultura Económico, 1955.

Rosales, José Natividad. *¿Quién es Lucio Cabañas?* Mexico City: Posada, 1974.

Rosales, José Natividad. *La Muerte (?) de Lucio Cabañas*. Mexico City: Posada, 1975.

Rudenko, B. T. "México en Vísperas de la Revolución Democrático-Burguesa de 1910-1917," pp. 9-86 in: *La Revolución Mexicana: Cuatro Estudios Soviéticos*. Mexico City: Insurgentes, 1960.

Sánchez Aguilar, Edmundo. *The International Activities of U.S. Commercial Banks, a Case Study: Mexico*. Ph.D. Dissertation, Harvard University, 1973.

Sánchez Zarza, Arturo, et. al. *La Estructura Monopólica Mexicana en el Período 1965-73*. Thesis, Escuela Nacional de Economía, 1976.

Scheer, Robert. *America After Nixon*. New York: McGraw-Hill, 1975.

Segovia, Rafael. "La Reforma Política," pp. 49-76 in: *La Vida Política en México 1970-1973*. Mexico City: El Colegio de México, 1974.

Semionov, S. I. "México durante el Período de Avila Camacho," pp. 117-47 in: *Ensayos de Historia de México*. Mexico City: Ediciones de Cultura Popular, 1973.

Semo, Enrique. *Historia del Capitalismo en México*. Mexico City: Era, 1973.

Sepúlveda, Bernardo. "Política Industrial y Empresas Transnacionales en México," pp. 3-71 in: *Las Empresas Transnacionales en México*. Mexico City: Colegio de México, 1974.

Sepúlveda, Bernardo & Antonio Chumacero. *La Inversión Extranjera en México*. Mexico City: Fondo de Cultura Económico, 1973.

Shelton, David. "The Banking System," pp. 111-189 in: *Public Policy and Private Enterprise in Mexico*. Cambridge: Harvard University Press, 1964.

Shulgovski, Anatol. *México en la Encrucijada de su Historia* (2nd ed.). Mexico City: Ediciones de Cultura Popular, 1972.

Sierra, Justo. *The Political Evolution of the Mexican People*. Austin: University of Texas Press, 1969.

Silva Herzog, Jesús. *Breve Historia de la Revolución Mexicana* (2 vols./2nd ed.). Mexico City: Fondo de Cultura Económica, 1972.

Sotelo Inclán, Jesús. *Raíz y Razón de Zapata.* Mexico City: Editorial CFE, 1970.

Stanford Research Institute. *The Impact of Foreign Private Investment on the Mexican Economy.* Menlo Park: Stanford Research Institute, 1976.

Stavenhagen, Rodolfo. *Sociología y Subdesarrollo.* Mexico City: Nuestro Tiempo, 1972.

Stavenhagen, Rodolfo. "Aspectos Sociales de la Estructura Agraria en México," pp. 11-55 in: *Neolatifundismo y Explotación* (3rd ed.). Mexico City: Nuestro Tiempo, 1973.

Stein, Stanley J. & Barbara H. Stein. *The Colonial Heritage of Latin America.* New York: Oxford University Press, 1970.

Sunkel, Osvaldo. *El Subdesarrollo Latinoamericano y la Teoría del Desarrollo.* Mexico City: Siglo XXI, 1970.

Sunkel, Osvaldo. *Capitalismo Transnacional y Desintegración Nacional en América Latina.* Buenos Aires: Ediciones Nueva Visión, 1972.

Tannenbaum, Frank. *Peace by Revolution.* New York: Columbia University Press, 1966.

Teja Zabre, Alfonso. *Guide to the History of Mexico.* Mexico City: Press of the Ministry of Foreign Affairs, 1935.

Tenebaum, Barbara. "Straightening Out Some of the *Lumpen* in the Development," pp. 3-16 in: *Latin American Perspectives,* Summer 1975.

Traven, B. *The Carreta.* New York: Hill & Wang, 1970.

Turner, John Kenneth. *Barbarous Mexico.* Austin: University of Texas Press, 1969.

Turner, Louis, *Multinational Corporations and the Third World.* New York: Hill & Wang, 1973.

Ulloa, Berta. *La Revolución Intervenida.* Mexico City: Colegio de México, 1971.

Ulloa, Manuel I. "Imperialismo y Reforma Educativa," pp. 56-80 in: *Reforma Educativa.* Mexico City: Nuestro Tiempo, 1972.

United Nations. *Income Distribution in Latin America.* New York: United Nations, 1971.

United States Senate Committee on Foreign Affairs. *Investigation of Mexican Affairs* (2 vols.). Washington: Government Printing Office, 1920.

van Ginneken, Wouter. *Rural and Urban Income Inequalities in Indonesia, Mexico, Pakistan, Tanzania, and Tunisia.* Geneva: International Labour Organization, 1976.

Velasco Márquez, Jesús. *La Guerra del 47 y la Opinión Pública (1845-1848).* Mexico City: SEP/Setentas, 1975.

Vernon, Raymond. *The Dilemma of Mexico's Development.* Cambridge: Harvard University Press, 1963.

Victoria, José Luis, et al. *Industrialización y Lucha de Clases en México.* Thesis, Escuela nacional de Economía, 1974.

Villoro, Luis. *La Revolución de Independencia.* Mexico City: UNAM, 1953.

Warman, Arturo. *Los Campesinos.* Mexico City: Nuestro Tiempo, 1972.

Weckman, Luis. "The Middle Ages in the Conquest of America," pp. 10-22 in: *History of Latin American Civilization,* Vol. I. Boston: Little, Brown & Co., 1967.

Whetten, Nathan L. *Rural Mexico.* Chicago: University of Chicago Press, 1948.

Wells, Alan. *Picture-Tube Imperialism?* Maryknoll, N.Y.: Orbis, 1972.

Wionczek, Miguel S., et al. *Multinational Control of the Mexican Pharmaceutical Industry.* New York: United Nations, 1971 (mimeo).

Wolf, Eric. *Sons of the Shaking Earth.* Chicago: University of Chicago Press, 1959.

Wolf, Eric R. *Peasant Wars of the Twentieth Century.* New York: Harper & Row, 1969.

Womack, John Jr. *Zapata and the Mexican Revolution.* New York: Knopf, 1969.

Zapata, Fausto. "Development in Freedom." Text of a speech given Nov. 6, 1972 at Mexican Association of Sales and Marketing Executives, Mexico City.

Zapata, Fausto. *Notes on the Political System and Foreign Investment.* Mexico City: Publicidad y Offset, 1974.

Zevada, Ricardo J. *Calles, el Presidente.* Mexico City: Nuestro Tiempo, 1971.

Zubirán, Salvador et al. *La Desnutrición del Mexicano.* Mexico City: Fondo de Cultura Económica, 1974.

MEXICO

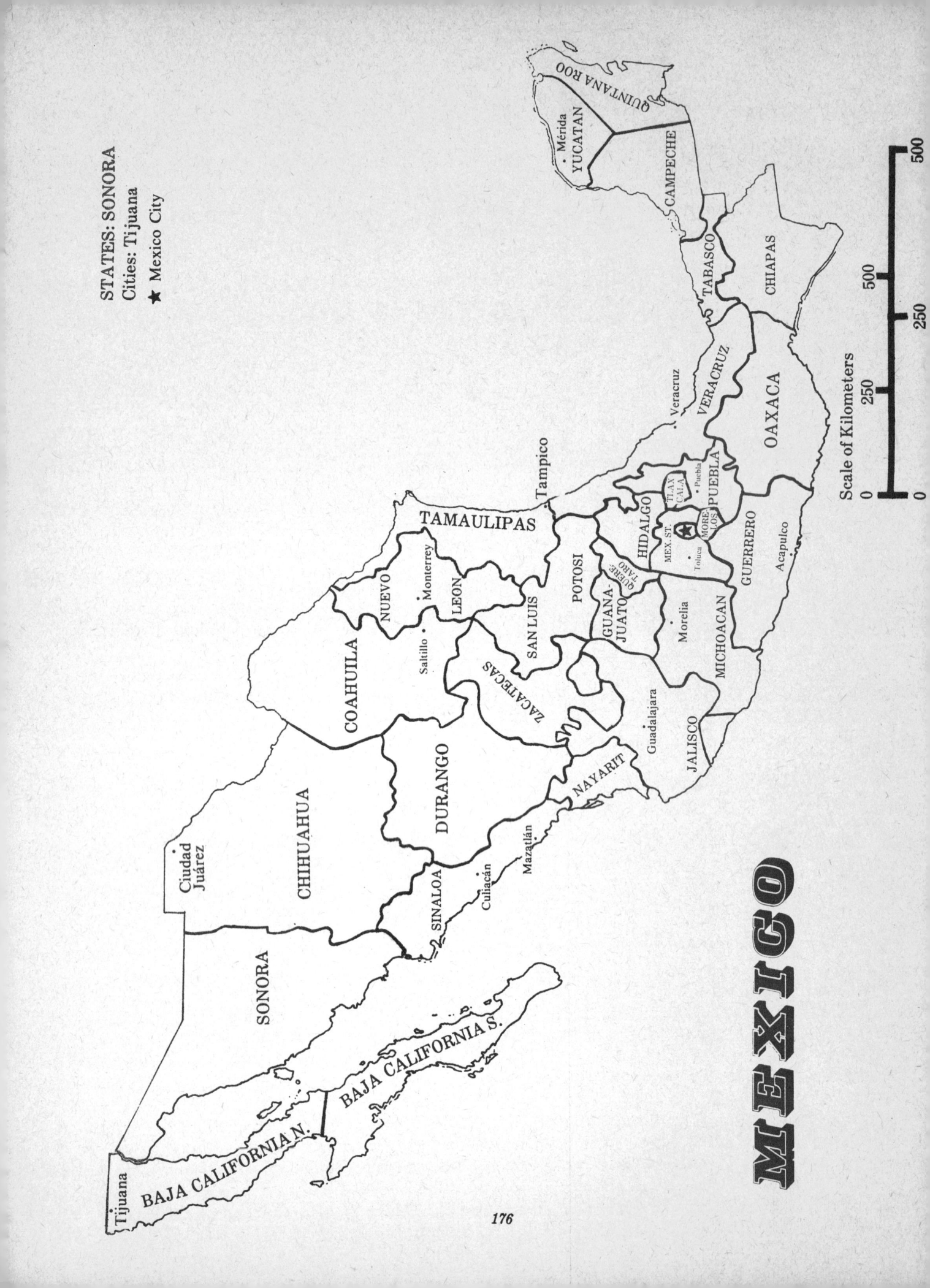

STATES: SONORA
Cities: Tijuana
★ Mexico City

Scale of Kilometers
0 250 500

176